THE FOREIGN POLICY SYSTEMS

OF NORTH AND SOUTH KOREA

BYUNG CHUL KOH

THE FOREIGN POLICY SYSTEMS
OF NORTH AND SOUTH KOREA

UNIVERSITY OF CALIFORNIA PRESS
BERKELEY · LOS ANGELES · LONDON

University of California Press
Berkeley and Los Angeles, California

University of California Press, Ltd.
London, England

© 1984 by
The Regents of the University of California

Printed in the United States of America
1 2 3 4 5 6 7 8 9

Library of Congress Cataloging in Publication Data

Koh, Byung Chul.
  The foreign policy systems of North and South Korea.

  Bibliography: p.
  Includes Index.
  1. Korea (South)—Foreign relations. 2. Korea (North)—Foreign relations. I. Title.
DS917.82.K64 1984   327.519   82-23807
ISBN 0-520-04805-9

TO MICHELLE AND CHRISTOPHER

CONTENTS

Illustrations   ix
Preface   xi
Abbreviations   xv

1 · INTRODUCTION   1

2 · PATTERNS OF FOREIGN POLICY: AN OVERVIEW   8
Triple Strategic Goals: Legitimacy, Security, and Development   8
Emphasis on Self-reliance   14
Blending of Rigidity and Flexibility   18

3 · OPERATIONAL ENVIRONMENT: EXTERNAL SETTING   21
The Global System   21
The Regional System of Northeast Asia   27
Bilateral Systems   28

4 · OPERATIONAL ENVIRONMENT: INTERNAL SETTING   33
Economic Power   33
Military Power   53
Political Dynamics   61

5 · PSYCHOLOGICAL ENVIRONMENT: ATTITUDINAL PRISM   70
Ideology   70
Historical Legacy   79
Personality Predispositions   80

6 · PSYCHOLOGICAL ENVIRONMENT: ELITE IMAGES   86
   North Korea   87
   South Korea   98

7 · DECISION MAKING: STRUCTURES AND ROUTINES   108
   North Korea   109
   South Korea   114

8 · FOREIGN POLICY OUTPUTS: STRATEGIC AND OPERATIONAL DECISIONS   122
   Strategic Decisions   122
   Operational Decisions   130

9 · FOREIGN POLICY OUTPUTS: TACTICAL DECISIONS, SYMBOLIC AND SUBSTANTIVE ACTIONS   166
   North Korea's Tactical Decisions   166
   South Korea's Tactical Decisions   172
   Conduct of the Dialogue   174
   Symbolic and Substantive Actions   193

10 · IMPACT OF FOREIGN POLICY   199
   Pyongyang's Reunification Policy   199
   Seoul's Reunification Policy   202
   Pyongyang's Policy Toward Moscow and Beijing   204
   Seoul's Policy Toward the United States   210
   Seoul's Policy Toward Japan   214
   Pyongyang's Policy Toward the Nonaligned Nations   219
   Seoul's Policy Toward the Third World   225

11 · CONCLUSIONS   229
   Patterns of Foreign Policy   229
   Sources of Foreign Policy   232
   Outputs of Foreign Policy   237
   Foreign Policy in Comparative Perspective   241
   Policy Implications   248

   Bibliography   253
   Index   265

ILLUSTRATIONS

FIGURES

1. A Framework for Comparative Analysis of Foreign
   Policy Systems   5
2. North Korean Party and Government Organs with
   Possible Inputs into Foreign Policy   112
3. South Korean Government Organs with Possible Inputs
   into Foreign Policy   116

TABLES

1. Chronological List of Countries with Which North
   Korea Has Established Ambassadorial-Level
   Diplomatic Relations   11
2. Chronological List of Countries with Which South
   Korea Has Established Ambassadorial-Level
   Diplomatic Relations   12
3. South Korea's Foreign Trade   36
4. Major Targets of South Korea's Fifth Five-Year Plan
   and Beyond   39
5. North Korea's Foreign Trade Estimates   43
6. Selected Indicators of the North Korean Economy   52
7. Comparison of Military Strength Between North and
   South Korea, 1981–82   55

8. North Korea's Military Expenditures	59
9. South Korea's Military Expenditures	60
10. Diplomatic Relations and U.N. Vote on Korea, 1975	196
11. Diplomatic Relations and U.N. Vote on Korea, 1975 (Percentages)	197

PREFACE

The impetus for this study was provided by a research grant from the Joint Committee on Korean Studies of the Social Science Research Council (SSRC) and the American Council of Learned Societies (ACLS). The grant made it possible for me to spend the summer of 1974 in Seoul, Tokyo, and Washington, D.C., collecting materials on the key dimensions of the two Korean states that might help illuminate their respective foreign policy behaviors. An invitation to present my preliminary findings to a workshop on comparative study of North and South Korea held in San Juan, Puerto Rico, in January 1976, under the auspices of the SSRC and the ACLS led to the preparation of an 85-page paper, which has become the skeleton of this book.

Because commitments to numerous other projects proved to be extremely time consuming, I was unable to complete the first draft of the book until the summer of 1981. However, given the nature of this study—which examines not only foreign policy per se but, more importantly, its multiple sources, no matter how elusive they may be—my efforts devoted to other projects were not in vain. For they dealt, for the most part, with various aspects of the Korean equation; many of the publications that resulted from them were utilized in the preparation of this manuscript. In short, this book is the culmination of eight years of research, reflection, and writing.

Aimed at scholars, students, journalists, policymakers, and other persons interested in learning about the patterns, and implications, of competition and conflict between North and South Korea, the study tries to do several things: first, to present a reasonably comprehensive discussion of the contexts and sources of the foreign policies of Seoul and Pyongyang, with the aim of helping the reader to place contemporary issues and developments in proper perspective; second, to provide an explicit comparison of the key dimensions of the two Korean states; third, to offer plausible explanations of their principal strategic, operational, and tactical decisions, with special emphasis on those relating to the all-important issue of reunification; and, finally, to provide an analysis that is informed by disciplined speculation and geared to generating conceptual understanding.

A native son of Korea who dares to write about the problems of his troubled fatherland inevitably runs the risk of offending the sensibilities of his compatriots. Although I was born, raised, and educated in Seoul, I have spent as much time in my adopted country, the United States, as I have in my mother country. If two decades of immersion in American academia have taught me anything, it is the value of scholarly objectivity—of seeking the truth with as much detachment as is humanly possible and with all the energy and enthusiasm one can muster. I hope that my unrelenting effort to live up to that exacting standard in the course of preparing this study has not been in vain. In the last section of the concluding chapter I attempt to spell out some of my normative commitments; suffice it here to point out that my emotional identification as a Korean is not with any particular regime but with the Korean nation (*minjok*) as a whole. If, in interpreting and evaluating the policies, decisions, and actions of North and South Korea, I inadvertently inject my own values, I must plead that they emanate from my wholehearted commitment to the well-being of my *minjok* and, ultimately, of my fellow human beings everywhere.

During all those long years of struggling to keep this project alive, I have incurred tons of debt, both intellectual and other. First and foremost, I am grateful to the Joint Committee on Korean Studies of the SSRC and the ACLS for providing me with the seed money to start the project. I am particularly indebted to Prof. Chong-Sik Lee of the University of Pennsylvania, then chairman of the joint committee, for prodding me to put together my initial ideas and for offering constructive criticisms on them. Next, I must acknowledge my debt to the Campus Research Board of the University of Illinois at Chicago for awarding me a foreign travel grant in the summer of 1981, which helped to defray a substantial portion of my travel expenses to North Korea. Frank Tachau, then chairman of my department, was an enthusiastic supporter of my North Korean trip and was instrumental in my obtaining the much-needed travel subsidy.

For kindly inviting me to spend a productive summer, in 1979, as a visiting professor at the Institute of Foreign Affairs and National Security of the Ministry of Foreign Affairs, the Republic of Korea, I express my sincere thanks to Dr. Young Hoon Kang, then chancellor of the Institute and corrently ROK ambassador to the Court of St. James, and to Dr. Se-Jin Kim, then director-general of the institute's Office of Research and currently ROK consul-general in New York. They went far beyond the call of duty to make my sojourn both rewarding and comfortable.

As the following pages show, I have learned a great deal from my trip to the Democratic People's Republic of Korea in July and August 1981. I extend my hearty thanks to Prof. C. I. Eugene Kim of Western Michigan University for organizing the trip, to Prof. Chae-Jin Lee of the University of Kansas for his stimulating companionship throughout the nineteen-day journey, and to the remaining three colleagues, Professors Young Whan Kihl (Iowa State University), Sung Chul Yang (University of Kentucky Center at Fort Knox), and Han Shik Park (University of Georgia) for helping to make our trip a rewarding learning experience for all of us. The scores of North Korean scholars, officials, cadres, and other persons who welcomed us as compatriots and tried very hard to make our stay in their country as memorable as possible have earned my lasting gratitude. Since they undoubtedly prefer to remain anonymous, I shall only mention the official hostess of our group, Secretary Ho Jong Suk of the Central Committee of the Workers' Party of Korea and chairman of the DPRK Committee for Aiding Overseas Nationals. She and her comrades have helped us to realize that blood is indeed thicker than ideology.

Over the years I have benefited immensely from the diligent labors of numerous scholars working in the Korean field. My notes and bibliography will help identify some of those whose ideas have enriched this study. The two anonymous readers of the first draft of the study merit my special praise and gratitude. Their incisive comments and helpful suggestions have enabled me to improve the manuscript markedly. For all the errors of fact and judgment that still remain, however, I am solely responsible.

For his indefatigable help in obtaining Japanese-language materials for nearly a decade, I am deeply grateful to Mr. Tetsuro Tsutsui. For her love, understanding, and encouragement, which have sustained me all these years, I owe an inestimable debt to my wife, Hae Chung. Finally, I dedicate this book to my two children, Michelle and Christopher, who have put up with a father who is perpetually busy with his interminable work for so long. It is, I feel, as much their book as mine.

Although the romanization of Korean words in this book is

based on the McCune-Reischauer system, exceptions have been made for the names of prominent leaders whose idiosyncratic spellings are known. For North Korean names I have followed the spellings used in the *Pyongyang Times*.

January 1983
Glencoe, Illinois

ABBREVIATIONS

ANSP	Agency for National Security Planning
ASEAN	Association of Southeast Asian Nations
CPC	Central People's Committee
CPRF	Committee for the Peaceful Reunification of the Fatherland
DCRK	Democratic Confederal Republic of *Koryŏ*
DFRF	Democratic Front for the Reunification of the Fatherland
DMZ	Demilitarized Zone
DPRK	Democratic People's Republic of Korea
FBIS	Foreign Broadcast Information Service
KCIA	South Korean Central Intelligence Agency
KCNA	Korean Central News Agency
KPA	Korean People's Army
NSCC	North-South Coordinating Committee
ROK	Republic of Korea
RPR	Revolutionary Party for Reunification
SAC	State Administration Council
SPA	Supreme People's Assembly
WPK	Workers' Party of Korea

1   INTRODUCTION

Since the end of World War II, two bloody and prolonged conflicts of international dimensions have been waged in the peninsulas of Korea and Indochina. A striking lesson of these traumatic events is that relatively small nations can have profound and lasting impact on their larger neighbors. Another important lesson is that in a world marked by a clash of ideologies and perceived self-interests, there are serious limits to the ability of major powers to influence, let alone dictate, events in smaller nations. The Korean case is particularly instructive, for after nearly three decades of intermittent turmoil since the armistice, the peninsula still remains a potential tinderbox, from which major powers have yet to extricate themselves.

The key to the seeming anomaly—of tiny North and South Korea demanding an inordinate amount of attention and resources from their formidable neighbors—may be found in the strategic geopolitical location of the Korean peninsula. It is surrounded and dwarfed by three of the world's great powers—China, Russia, and Japan. In terms of size, China is 44 times larger than Korea, Russia 102 times, and Japan 1.7 times. Not only did Korea serve as the invasion route between China and Japan in the late thirteenth and sixteenth centuries, but it became the object, cause, or arena of international conflict several times thereafter. The Sino-Japanese War of 1894–1895 was precipitated by the Tonghak Rebellion in Korea and by the rivalry of the two powers to gain hegemony in the peninsula. Similarly, the Russo-Japanese War of 1904–1905 was sparked by the adversaries' competition over Korea and ravaged the already weakened country. Russian and Japanese troops were to clash again, albeit briefly, in the final days of World War II in the northern part of Korea. Finally, the Korean War of 1950–1953 saw intervention by major powers on a gigantic scale. Nineteen nations, including the two Koreas, participated in the conflict as belligerents, although the brunt of the war was born by the American and South Korean forces on the United Nations' side and the Chinese and North Korean forces on the Communist side.

Although the United States is neither contiguous nor adjacent to Korea, it is nonetheless a Pacific power and hence Korea's neighbor in a functional sense. Indeed, the magnitude of American involvement in Korean affairs has equaled or surpassed that of the three geographic neighbors. In short, notwithstanding its small size, Korea has historically served as an object or arena of rivalry and conflict among its geographic or functional neighbors, all of which happen to be the world's great powers. None of them wants to see the entire peninsula fall into the exclusive sphere of influence of any other power.

If, despite all this, the strategic value of the Korean peninsula per se is debatable, there can be no doubt whatever that any renewal of armed conflict there will have immediate international repercussions. For three of the four Pacific powers have mutual defense pacts with either North or South Korea, and the fourth power, Japan, is heavily committed, albeit in nonmilitary terms, to the security of South Korea. In the case of the United States, its mutual defense treaty with Seoul is bolstered by a substantial military presence on the scene.[1] Most important, the danger of war in Korea has by no means receded. Not only do North and South Korea remain two of the most heavily armed countries in Asia, their mutual antagonism remains unabated, fueled by the memories and scars of a fratricidal conflict. Nor has there been any perceptible change in the single-minded determination of North Korea's aging leader, President Kim Il Sung, to reunify the peninsula on his terms. While this does not mean that he will be so reckless as to launch an unprovoked invasion, it does suggest that he is not likely to shy away from favorable opportunities when and if they present themselves. Given the frequency with which crises have erupted in the recent past—the Pueblo incident of February 1968; the EC-121 incident of April 1969, the Pan-

---

1. In 1977 President Jimmy Carter began the process of reducing the American military presence in South Korea but suspended it two years later pending a reappraisal of the military balance in the Korean peninsula in 1981. In February 1981, President Ronald Reagan "assured President Chun [Doo Hwan of South Korea] that the United States has no plans to withdraw US ground combat forces from the Korean peninsula." The assurance was given during Chun's "official visit" to Washington, DC from February 1 to 3, 1981. See the text of the Reagan-Chun joint communiqué in the *Korea Herald* (Seoul), February 4, 1981.

munjom incident of August 1976, the helicopter incident of July 1977, and the SR-71 incident of August 1981[2]—one cannot rule out the possibility of a sudden armed confrontation or even conflict in the days ahead.

It is therefore plain that what is likely to happen in Korea will not concern the Korean people alone but will have a regional and even global significance. In other words, the four Pacific powers, whose interests both intersect and clash in Korea, have a vital stake in the future of the peninsula. An understanding of how the two halves of Korea behave both vis-à-vis each other and with respect to the outside world, therefore, takes on practical significance.

On an intellectual level, Korea is a particularly challenging case. It is unique in having experienced domination by all of the four Pacific powers—centuries of Chinese suzerainty, four decades of Japanese colonial rule, and several years of military occupation by both the United States and the Soviet Union. Out of this experience has emerged not only a burning sense of national identity on the part of the Korean people but also their remarkable capacity for survival under adversity and for adaptation to a hostile environment. An examination of how the two Korean states, embroiled in relentless mutual animosity, have adapted to the singularly fluid international environment is likely to be an intellectually stimulating task.

Nor is this all. From a scholarly point of view, Korea is an ideal setting, or case material, for comparative analysis. The two halves of Korea share many things in common—their ancestry, language, historical legacy, and cultural heritage. Yet, over the past three decades, they have evolved into two mutually hostile and ideologically polarized states, bent on undermining each other at every available opportunity. A comparative study of their respective patterns of response to external stimuli may well make a contribution to an understanding of foreign policy behavior in general.

No matter how important the subject matter may be, the value of a scholarly study will hinge, to a considerable degree, on the rigor

---

2. On August 26, 1981, the crew of an SR-71 US Air Force reconnaissance plane reported being fired at by the North Korean surface-to-air missile while "flying in South Korean and international air space." The US government expressed "serious concern" over the alleged North Korean action and warned that it would take "whatever steps are necessary to assure the future safety of our pilots and planes." North Korea, while accusing the US of violating its territorial air space, denied that it had fired an antiaircraft missile at the plane. Although the incident did not escalate any further, it had the potential of igniting a serious confrontation between the US and North Korea. See *New York Times*, August 28, 1981; *Han'guk ilbo* (Seoul), August 29, August 31, and September 1, 1981; *Korean Central News Agency*, Pyongyang, August 28, 1981, as monitored by the Foreign Broadcast Information Service (FBIS), the US Department of Commerce. See *FBIS Daily Report*, vol. 4: Asia and Pacific.

of its methodology and the caliber of its data. It is frequently the latter, however, that determines the former, and herein lies the major stumbling block confronting this study. For the caliber of available data bearing on the capabilities and behavior patterns of the two Korean states is dismally low. In the case of North Korea, one must rely largely on evidence emanating from the regime itself—notably its own publications, which are completely controlled by the government and the ruling political party. Serving as they do the multiple functions of indoctrination, internal and external propaganda, and esoteric communication, these publications leave a great deal to be desired from the standpoint of objectivity, reliability, and information. The situation in South Korea is only slightly better. Although markedly more accessible to the outside world than its northern counterpart, South Korea has thus far fallen appreciably short of being an open society. Not only has there typically been censorship of varying rigor throughout its brief history, the successive South Korean regimes have also manipulated the contents of their own publications for propaganda and other purposes with considerable skill. Hence one needs to be extremely cautious about interpreting the true meaning of published information emanating from both North and South Korea.

If the nature and quality of the available data impose severe constraints on the kinds of intellectual operations that can be performed, they by no means preclude a scholarly inquiry that aims at a reasonable degree of objectivity and insight—one that steers the middle ground between the Scylla of hyperfactual description and the Charybdis of free-wheeling armchair speculation. As a rough guide in my venture, I propose to employ a conceptual map consisting of several discrete analytic categories. The function as well as the underlying theme of the map is to direct one's attention to the obvious but important fact that foreign policy, defined as the totality of a nation's acts, both symbolic and substantive, aimed at influencing the attitude and behavior of other nations, has both complex sources and diverse consequences. An outline of the map is presented in figure 1. It borrows freely from the works of a number of scholars, most notably, Michael Brecher.[3] Briefly, the analytic scheme shown in figure 1 postulates three broad categories: (1) inputs, (2) conversion pro-

---

3. Michael Brecher, *The Foreign Policy System of Israel: Setting, Images, Process* (New Haven: Yale University Press, 1972). See also: David Easton, "An Approach to the Analysis of Political System," *World Politics* 9, 3 (April 1957): 383–400; idem, *A Framework for Political Analysis* (Englewood Cliffs, N.J.: Prentice-Hall, 1965); Patrick J. McGowan and Howard B. Shapiro, *The Comparative Study of Foreign Policy: A Survey of Scientific Findings* (Beverly Hills, CA: Sage Publications, 1973); Harold and Margaret Sprout, *Man-Milieu Relationship Hypotheses in the Context of International Politics* (Princeton: Center of International Studies, Princeton University, 1956); idem, "En-

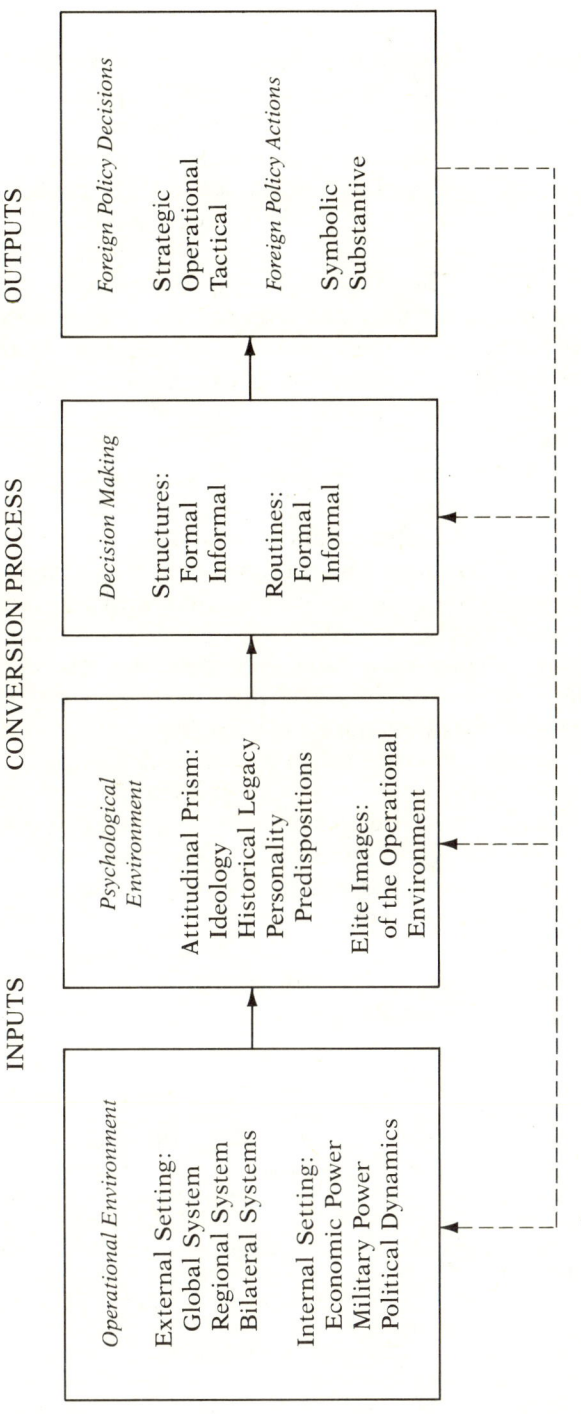

FIGURE 1 · A Framework for Comparative Analysis of Foreign Policy Systems

cess, and (3) outputs. The inputs in turn consist of the operational environment and the psychological environment. The operational environment is divided into external and internal settings, with the former encompassing the global system, the regional system, and bilateral systems. The internal setting subsumes economic power, military power, and political dynamics. All of these concepts will be defined and further delineated in the relevant parts of the book.

The psychological environment is the operational environment as perceived by members of the foreign policy elite. It consists of the twin categories of attitudinal prism and elite images. The former includes both a set of societal influences that condition the manner in which the reality of the operational environment is perceived by decision makers in a given culture—such as ideology and historical legacy—and a set of personality factors that help to provide a perceptual screen. Elite image is the substantive picture of the reality in the head of a decision maker filtered through his attitudinal prism.[4]

The inputs enumerated above are converted into foreign policy outputs by a decision-making process. Hence the conversion process subsumes under its rubric the structures and routines of decision making, both formal and informal. The outputs of a foreign policy system may broadly be divided into decisions and actions, each of which may in turn be subdivided into a number of categories depending upon the time frame, duration of impact, and level of abstraction. Finally, it is postulated that, given a modicum of rationality on the part of a political system, a learning process is likely to occur. That is to say, the outputs of foreign policy will be fed back into the various components of the system in such a way as to modify or change the external and internal settings of the operational environment, the psychological environment, or even the structures and routines of decision making.

As noted already, the nature of available data will not allow a rigorous application of the preceding analytic framework.[5] Nonethe-

---

vironmental Factors in the Study of International Politics," *Journal of Conflict Resolution* 1, 4 (December 1957): 309–328; Graham T. Allison, *Essence of Decision: Explaining the Cuban Missile Crisis* (Boston: Little, Brown, 1971); Maurice A. East, Stephen A. Salmore, and Charles F. Hermann (eds.), *Why Nations Act: Theoretical Perspectives for Comparative Foreign Policy Studies* (Beverly Hills, CA: Sage Publications, 1978).

4. While the conceptualization of the operational environment represents a modification of Brecher's analytic framework, that of the psychological environment is taken directly from it. The distinction between the operational and psychological environments with specific reference to foreign policy was first proposed by Harold and Margaret Sprout (see note 3 above).

5. In addition to the usual array of published sources—newspapers, ideological journals, yearbooks, pamphlets, collections of speeches by political leaders, books written by the latter, scholarly books and articles—I have drawn freely from numerous

less, I hope that the framework will at least serve the dual purpose of facilitating the organization and presentation of the available data, no matter how fragmentary and incomplete, and of constraining us to search for plausible explanations of the diverse dimensions of foreign policy that may otherwise be overlooked. The book begins by surveying the overall patterns of the foreign policies of the two Koreas without any explicit reference to the analytic scheme. It then embarks on a detailed examination of the principal components of the framework as applied to the two Koreas: the external and internal settings of the operational environment, the two dimensions of the psychological environment (attitudinal prism and elite images), the structures and routines of decision making, and the outputs and consequences of foreign policy. The book concludes by recapitulating the salient findings and exploring their implications.

I wish to stress at the outset that in this study the reunification policies of the two Korean states are treated as part of their foreign policies for the following two reasons. First, no matter what the rhetoric and sentiments of Seoul and Pyongyang, the undeniable reality is that North and South Korea are two separate states in every sense of the term. In fact, as measured by the yardstick of interstate relations, they are more apart from each other than they are from most of the strictly "foreign" states. Second, the strategic objective of reunification occupies such a pivotal position in the foreign policies of Seoul and Pyongyang alike that the latter cannot be understood apart from the former. Stripped of the overall context of and implications of reunification policy, the foreign policies of North and South Korea become hollow shells.

It is precisely for the latter reason that the bulk of the study deals with the various aspects of reunification policy. Inasmuch as the focus of the study is on the key dimensions of "foreign policy systems" of the two Korean states, their respective foreign policy outputs are treated as only one, albeit a major, component of the overall picture. Hence the study does not purport to provide detailed chronological analysis of the policies of Seoul and Pyongyang toward the major powers and the Third World.

---

conversations and talks with scholars and officials from both North and South Korea. My three-month sojourn in Seoul as a visiting professor at the Institute of Foreign Affairs and National Security, the Ministry of Foreign Affairs, the Republic of Korea in the summer of 1979 has enriched my understanding of that country's foreign policy system. I have also benefited immensely from a nineteen-day visit to the Democratic People's Republic of Korea in the summer of 1981, during which I had discussions with scholars, cadres, and officials including Vice Premier Chong Jun Gi.

2 PATTERNS OF FOREIGN POLICY: AN OVERVIEW

An overview by necessity entails the danger of oversimplification. With this caveat in mind, I venture to suggest that three themes stand out from the record of the foreign policies of the two Koreas over the past three decades: first, the triple strategic goals of (1) legitimacy, (2) national security, and (3) economic development; second, the growing emphasis on self-reliance; and, finally, a blending of rigidity and flexibility in the patterns of response to changing external stimuli.

TRIPLE STRATEGIC GOALS: LEGITIMACY, SECURITY, AND DEVELOPMENT

The major goals that the two Koreas have pursued in the world arena, when examined from the perspective of actual behavior patterns rather than rhetoric, turn out to be remarkably similar; both have pursued the interrelated goals of legitimacy, national security, and economic development. This, I hasten to add, does not mean that their goals have converged. On the contrary, the goals both presuppose and necessitate a competitive, even conflictive, relationship between Seoul and Pyongyang. An increase in the perceived legitimacy of Seoul, for example, signifies a corresponding decrease in that of Pyongyang, and vice versa. Since both sides perceive each other as potential enemies, moreover, a conspicuous buildup in the military capability of one side, which bolsters its sense of security, is most likely to undercut the security, perceived or real, of the other. The only goal that can logically be pursued simultaneously by both sides without necessarily undercutting each other is the third one—economic development—although it too has enormous potential for generating mutual competition. More important, given its direct implications for the other two goals, it cannot be divorced from them. That is to say, inasmuch as legitimacy is intertwined with prestige, it needs to be underpinned by both economic and military power. The latter two are also interrelated: not only can economic power bolster and sustain military power, the two can also make competing demands on a nation's finite resources. For, while guns and butter may be equally necessary, more guns frequently mean less butter, and vice versa.

That legitimacy should emerge as an overarching objective of foreign policy for both North and South Korea is attributable to the circumstances under which the "temporary" division of the peninsula hardened into a permanent partition. The birth of two divergent regimes in Korea under the de facto aegis of the two rival superpowers—the United States and the Soviet Union—meant that each client state would claim exclusive legitimacy for itself. In the case of the Republic of Korea (ROK), a major boost for its legitimacy was provided by two developments: first, it was a creature, in a sense, of the United Nations, under whose auspices elections for the constituent National Assembly were held in May 1948. Second, the UN General Assembly in December 1948 passed a resolution declaring the ROK government to be a "lawful government" that "is based on elections which were a valid expression of the free will of the electorate of that part of Korea [i.e., south of the 38th parallel] and that this is the only such Government in Korea."[1]

Citing this UN resolution, the ROK government has consistently maintained that it is the only lawful government in the entire Korean peninsula. For its part, the Democratic People's Republic of Korea (DPRK), an offshoot of elections held in the Soviet occupation zone in August 1948, has categorically rejected both Seoul's claims to legitimacy and the validity of UN resolutions favoring South Korea. Efforts to bolster their respective claims in the diplomatic arena have since constituted a significant part of the foreign policies of both countries, with the annual debates on the Korean question in the UN General Assembly becoming the focal point of diplomatic competition.

The DPRK's strenuous diplomatic campaigns in the Third World

1. US Department of State, *The Record on Korean Unification, 1943–1960: Narrative Summary with Principal Documents*. Department of State Publication No. 7084, Far Eastern Series No. 101 (Washington, DC: Government Printing Office, 1960), p. 76.

over the years thus reflect the priority that Pyongyang has placed on the legitimacy issue. The results of North Korean efforts are impressive. As table 1 shows, there has been a spectacular increase in the number of countries with which North Korea has ambassadorial-level diplomatic relations. Whereas in December 1962 North Korea had full diplomatic ties with only 15 countries as compared to South Korea's total of 56 (See table 2), by mid 1976 the gap between Seoul and Pyongyang had all but evaporated, with North Korea counting 93 full diplomatic partners as compared to South Korea's total of 96. More important, whereas in 1962 not a single country simultaneously recognized both Seoul and Pyongyang, in 1976 a total of 49 countries did so. Finally, in the thirtieth session of the UN General Assembly held in the fall of 1975, a resolution favorable to North Korea was passed for the first time in the history of that organization. The same session also adopted a resolution favorable to South Korea, thus creating the anomaly that the UN officially embraced two contradictory resolutions on Korea.[2]

The second major foreign policy goal of the two Koreas, national security, is intimately linked to the first goal. Indeed, it can be argued that the Soviet-backed invasion of the South by North Korea in 1950 represented an effort forcibly to settle the legitimacy issue once and for all. The marked growth in North Korea's economic and military capabilities, coupled with increasing bellicosity in both its rhetoric and behavior in the period following the armistice of July 1953, has posed a palpable threat to South Korea's national security. Hence Seoul's campaign to buttress its legitimacy in the world arena has been paralleled by an all-out effort to strengthen its defense capability vis-à-vis Pyongyang. This has, in effect, entailed a two-pronged effort: on the one hand, the maintenance of American deterrent power both in terms of its treaty commitments to Seoul and military presence in Korea and, on the other, the modernization of South Korea's own military arsenal with the assistance of the United States. In the 1970s, Washington's moves to scale down and even phase out its military presence in Korea spurred Seoul to build up its own defense industry with a view to attaining a self-reliant defense capability.

Given the mutual enmity between the two halves of Korea, Seoul's efforts to bolster its security are closely monitored by Pyongyang. Because of its previous record of aggression, the North Korean regime is widely viewed as a potential aggressor, leading observers to overlook the possibility that as far as its own perceptions are concerned, Pyongyang's security problem is no less pressing than Seoul's.

2. B. C. Koh, "The Battle Without Victors: The Korean Question in the 30th Session of the UN General Assembly," *Journal of Korean Affairs* 5: 4 (January 1976): 43–63.

TABLE 1 · Chronological List of Countries with Which North Korea Has Established Ambassadorial-level Diplomatic Relations

1948 U.S.S.R.	1971 Yugoslavia	1974 Niger
Poland	Sierra Leone	Jamaica
Mongolia	Malta	Venezuela
Czechoslovakia	1972 Cameroon	Botswana
Romania	Rwanda	Austria
Hungary	Chile[d]	Switzerland
Bulgaria	Uganda	1975 Fiji
1949 Albania	Senegal	Portugal
China (PRC)	Upper Volta	Thailand
East Germany	Pakistan	Kenya
1950 Vietnam	Madagascar	Burma
1958 Algeria	Zaire	Ethiopia
Guinea	1973 Togo	Mozambique
1960 Cuba	Benin	Tunisia
Mali	Gambia	Sao Tome &
1963 Yemen	Mauritius	Principe
Egypt	Sweden	Cape Verde
1964 Indonesia	Iran	Singapore
Mauritania[a]	Argentina[e]	Comoro
Cambodia	Finland	Angola
Congo	Norway	1976 Nigeria
(Brazzaville)	Malaysia	Papua New Guinea
Ghana	Denmark	Seychelles
1965 Tanzania	Iceland	1977 Barbados
1966 Syria	Bangladesh	1978 Western Samoa
1967 Burundi	India	Tuvalu
Somalia	Liberia	1979 Grenada
1968 Iraq[b]	Afghanistan	Nicaragua
Southern Yemen	1974 Libya	St. Lucia
1969 Equatorial	Gabon	Dominica[g]
Guinea	Costa Rica	1980 Zimbabwe
Zambia	Guinea-Bissau	Lesotho
Chad	Nepal	Mexico
Sudan	Guyana	1981 Lebanon
Central African	Laos	St. Vincent
Republic	Australia[f]	Vanuatu
1970 Maldives	Jordan	1982 Nauru
Sri Lanka[c]		Malawi
		Surinam

SOURCES: *Chosŏn chung'ang yŏn'gam*, 1980 (Pyongyang: Chosŏn Chung'ang T'ongsin-sa, 1980); *Kita Chōsen kenkyū*, November, 1980; *Nodong sinmun*, passim.
[a] Relations were suspended from June 1977 to March 1980.
[b] Relations were broken off in October 1980.
[c] Relations were suspended from March 1971 to March 1975.
[d] Broken off in September 1973. [e] Broken off in June 1977.
[f] Broken off in November 1975. [g] Agreement not implemented.

TABLE 2 · **Chronological List of Countries with Which South Korea Has Established Ambassadorial-level Diplomatic Relations**

1948 U.S.A.	1962 Mexico	Iceland
China (ROC)	Nicaragua	Jamaica
1949 United Kingdom	Argentina	Saudi Arabia
France	Colombia	Senegal
Philippines	Spain	Iran
1956 South Vietnam[a]	New Zealand	Guatemala
Italy	Honduras	Switzerland
1957 West Germany	Israel	1963 Canada
Turkey	Upper Volta	Rwanda[d]
1958 Thailand	Chile	Uganda
1959 Norway	Paraguay	Peru
Sweden	Dominican	Zaire
Denmark	Republic	Austria
Brazil	Madagascar	Togo[e]
1960 Malaysia	Sierra Leone	Central African
1961 Netherlands	Morocco	Republic
Greece	Jordan	Vatican
Portugal	Gabon	Ethiopia
Belgium	Costa Rica	1964 Kenya
Ivory Coast	El Salvador	Liberia
Niger	Congo	Uruguay
Benin[b]	(Brazzaville)[c]	1965 Malawi
Chad	Haiti	Malta
Cameroon	Panama	Luxembourg
Australia	Ecuador	Gambia

That is to say, in the eyes of North Korea's political elite, South Korea and particularly its ally and patron state, the United States, pose a palpable threat to Pyongyang's security.[3] A significant factor in North Korea's relations with Moscow and Beijing is its continuing need to shore up its defense capability by maintaining the military alliances with both of its neighbors and patron states and by insuring the inflow of military hardware and economic and technical assistance.

Both legitimacy and national security are inseparably bound up with economic development. For an impressive record of economic growth would not only enhance a nation's prestige both at home and

---

3. A legitimate question may be raised regarding the truthfulness of Pyongyang's statements about the danger of attack by the US and South Korea. See, for example, the statements issued by the DPRK Foreign Ministry on February 14 and April 7, 1982 in *Nodong sinmun*, February 15 and April 8, 1982. Based on my extensive discussions with North Korean academics, cadres, and officials in the summer of 1981, I am convinced that their sense of insecurity and fear of another war sparked by the US are genuine; more on this in chapter 6.

TABLE 2 · (continued)

	Bolivia		Afghanistan[g]		Sri Lanka
	Venezuela	1974	Oman		Djibouti
	Japan		Qatar	1978	Guinea
1966	Lesotho		Nepal		Solomon Islands
1967	Maldives		Laos[h]		Tuvalu
1968	Botswana		Grenada[i]		Dominica
	Guyana	1975	Burma	1979	St. Lucia
	Swaziland		Singapore		Kuwait
1969	Tunisia		Surinam		St. Vincent
1970	Cambodia[f]	1976	Bahrain	1980	Nigeria
	Tonga		Papau New		Kiribati
1971	Fiji		Guinea		Vanuatu
	Mauritius		Seychelles[j]		Libya
1972	Western Samoa	1977	Sudan	1981	Lebanon
1973	Finland		Mauritania		Antigua and
	Indonesia		Ghana		Barbuda
	India		Barbados		
	Bangladesh				

SOURCES: Republic of Korea, Ministry of Foreign Affairs, *Han'guk oegyo samsimnyŏn*, 1948–1978 (Seoul, 1979); *Kita Chōsen kenkyū*, November 1980; *Han'guk ilbo*, passim; and *Korea Herald*, passim.

[a] Broken off in April 1975.
[b] Broken off in May 1975.
[c] Broken off in May 1965.
[d] Broken off in March 1980.
[e] Broken off in September 1974.
[f] Broken off in April 1975.
[g] Broken off in September 1978.
[h] Broken off in July 1975.
[i] Broken off in July 1980.
[j] Broken off in May 1980.

abroad but also facilitate its diplomatic endeavors in a most tangible way. That military capability, to be self-reliant, must be undergirded by substantial economic power is obvious. Economic modernization, therefore, has received a high priority in Seoul and Pyongyang alike, and the foreign policy behaviors of both have clearly reflected their respective preoccupation with this goal. Pyongyang's relations with Moscow and Beijing can also be understood from this perspective. So, too, can one explain Seoul's pursuit of strong ties with Washington and Tokyo in terms of the former's security and economic needs.

Although analysts in Seoul and Washington argue that Pyongyang's top priority has been military preparedness, to which economic development has been a necessary handmaiden, the visitor to North Korea is struck by the extent of economic construction and by the degree to which the goal of economic modernization pervades North Korean society. If economic development has always loomed large in the policy calculus, both domestic and foreign, of North Korea in the postwar period, its relative salience in South Korea has varied with successive regimes. Syngman Rhee, for example, failed to launch any vigorous program of comprehensive economic development during his long tenure (1948–1960), and the regime of Premier John M. Chang was too short-lived to have any impact on the economic front. It was not until Park Chung Hee came on the scene that economic development became the national preoccupation of South Korea.

EMPHASIS ON SELF-RELIANCE

At the heart of the two Koreas' multifaceted policy of economic development lies their common desire to attain self-reliance. In North Korea, self-reliance or its Korean equivalent, *chuch'e*, has been elevated to the lofty status of national ideology.[4] That the quest for self-reliance has implications for both domestic and foreign policies is not hard to understand, given the linkage between the two. Kim Il Sung's conviction that political independence will be a hollow slogan unless and until it is buttressed by economic independence has not only inspired and helped to sustain the frenetic pace of economic construction at home but also guided Pyongyang's external relations to a marked degree. But the quest for self-reliance has been Janus-faced. On the one hand, it has meant efforts to generate maximum economic aid from all possible sources, particularly Moscow and Beijing. On the other hand, it has led to the assertion of independence vis-à-vis patron states. Thanks to the fortuitous dynamics of the Sino-Soviet dispute, North Korea has managed the feat of receiving substantial aid from both of the Communist powers while jealously guarding its independence—of coupling economic dependence with political autonomy.

Inasmuch as the quest for self-reliance bespeaks the apotheosis of nationalism, it strikes a responsive chord in the hearts and minds of the people; it can even be viewed as a sine qua non of successful political leadership, especially in a country recently liberated from the yoke of colonialism. It is not surprising, therefore, to find that virtually all Korean political leaders, regardless of ideological predelictions, have extolled its virtues. The degree and vigor with which self-reliance has been pursued, however, have varied from leader to

4. For a comparison of the *chuch'e* ideology in North and South Korea, see B. C. Koh, "*Chuch'esong* in Korean Politics," *Studies in Comparative Communism* 7, 1 and 2 (Spring/Summer 1974): 83–97. A more detailed discussion of *chuch'e* is presented in chapter 5 of this book.

leader. Despite his heavy dependence on the United States for the conduct of the Korean War, President Syngman Rhee was remarkably independent of Washington. His most celebrated act of defiance vis-à-vis Washington was the release of 27,000 anti-Communist North Korean prisoners of war in June 1953, which seriously jeopardized the armistice negotiations then under way. In fact, it required a considerable amount of persuasion and pressure by Washington to allay Rhee's fear that a cease-fire would not prevent renewal of North Korean aggression against the South. Paradoxically, it was Rhee's fierce independence that was largely instrumental in institutionalizing Seoul's heavy military dependence on the United States. For he succeeded in securing Washington's commitment to a mutual defense treaty with Seoul on the heels of the Korean armistice.[5]

In the case of Premier Chang Myon (1960–1961), two things made it extremely difficult for him to practice self-reliance: his short tenure in office, and the pressing need for economic aid from the United States. The foremost task confronting the Second Republic was to stabilize the economy, which in turn necessitated a maximization of US assistance. After much diplomatic effort, it succeeded in obtaining Washington's commitment to provide $180 million in aid. On the other hand, it can be argued that the Chang regime's pursuit of new diplomatic goals—such as an explicit renunciation of force as means of reunification, the adoption of a "UN formula" for the same purpose, and an active pursuit of diplomatic normalization with Japan—reflected its earnest desire to attain self-reliance in the long run.[6]

Throughout his long tenure as the ruler of South Korea (1961–1979), Park Chung Hee, too, was a proponent and a practitioner of *chuch'e*. In terms of domestic policy, Park's concern with *chuch'e* was translated into vigorous pursuit of economic modernization with spectacular results. In terms of foreign policy, it was best illustrated in his successful quest for the normalization of diplomatic relations with Japan. Although there was considerable US involvement in the negotiation process, with Washington exerting pressure on both Seoul and Tokyo, a major variable in the equation was Park's determination to achieve his goal, coupled with his willingness to make substantial concessions to Japan amid fierce domestic opposition.

    5. For an insider's account of Rhee's stormy relations with the US, see Robert T. Oliver, *Syngman Rhee and American Involvement in Korea, 1942–1960* (Seoul: Panmun Book Co., 1978), especially chapters 18–20.
    6. Republic of Korea, Ministry of Foreign Affairs, *Han'guk oegyo ŭi isimnyŏn* [Twenty Years of South Korean Diplomacy] (Seoul: Oemu-bu, Oegyo Yŏn'gu-won, 1967), pp. 126–133.

Underlying all this was his perception that Japanese capital and technology would be indispensable to the success of his modernization program at home.[7] Just as Pyongyang's policy of self-reliance entailed substantial economic and military dependence on Moscow and Beijing, so Seoul's quest for autonomy necessitated increasing reliance on external economic resources.

Choi Kyu Hah, who served first as acting president (October 26–December 6, 1979) and then as president (December 6, 1979–August 16, 1980), did not depart appreciably from the foreign policy line of his assassinated predecessor. Nor could he do so, for he was a ceremonial head of state devoid of any real power. To make the matter worse, he was burdened with the onerous task of dealing with the strains that had been created by the December 12 incident—a coup engineered by Maj. Gen. Chun Doo Hwan and his colleagues in which they defied the established chain of command—the authority of the commander of the US armed forces in Korea—and seized control over the ROK armed forces. Although the manner in which Chun seized power suggested the possibility that he might be less susceptible to American influence than any of his predecessors, his actual policy direction has not been notably independent. His nationalistic leanings are clearly counterbalanced by the need to sustain the security commitments of Washington as well as economic ties with the United States and Japan. The coincidence of Chun's seizure of power and the advent of the conservative administration of President Ronald Reagan in Washington has enabled the new South Korean leader to achieve a major diplomatic coup: in February 1981, he became one of the first foreign heads of state to be received by President Reagan and secured from the president personal assurances of the sanctity of US security commitments and of increased military and economic cooperation.

There were other aspects of the behaviors of both North and South Korea that tended to contradict or undercut their respective quests for self-reliance. North Korea's strategy of economic development, for example, was less an adaptation than an adoption of the Stalinist strategy. Similarly, given their timing and content, the celebrated *Ch'ŏllima* movement and the consolidation of agricultural cooperatives were obvious attempts to emulate China's Great Leap Forward and the commune movement. Nor can one overlook the colossal contradiction between the idea of *chuch'e*—that one ought to be one's own master and use one's own brain and brawn to solve one's prob-

---

7. Yung-Hwan Jo, "Japanese-Korean Relations and Asian Diplomacy," *Orbis* 11: 2 (Summer 1967): 582–593; Kwan Bong Kim, *The Korea-Japan Treaty Crisis and the Instability of the Korean Political System* (New York: Praeger, 1971).

lems—and the frenzied cult of Kim Il Sung's personality, which exhorts the North Korean masses not simply to revere their "great leader" but to think his thoughts, emulate his behavior, and implement his instructions.[8]

In the case of South Korea, Park Chung Hee's invocation of *chuch'e* as the ideological justification for the so-called October Revitalizing Reforms (*Siwol Yusin*)—which, in effect, institutionalized his one-man rule for an indefinite period—greatly undermined its true meaning. Among other things, the term *Siwol Yusin* was clearly reminiscent of the Japanese term *Meiji Ishin* (Meiji Restoration), for which Park had previously expressed an open admiration.[9] More substantively, the resemblance between the constitutional order proclaimed by the *Siwol Yusin* and the political system of the Republic of China in Taiwan was so striking as to buttress the widely held view that there was a deliberate emulation—that a team of scholars had been secretly dispatched to Taiwan to study the political system for possible borrowing by Park Chung Hee. Finally, if an integral attribute or corollary of *chuch'e* is the ability of the people to determine their own destiny, it is plain that a drastic curtailment of political liberties—particularly the right to articulate dissenting political views and the right to participate in the political process in a meaningful, as distinct from a ceremonial, fashion—seriously cripples the concept.[10]

In terms of both rhetoric and practice, North Korea has clearly outperformed South Korea in the quest for self-reliance. Seoul's strategy of economic development has underscored both international capital and foreign trade; hence international interdependence has been a major facet of South Korean policies, both domestic and foreign. On the other hand, Pyongyang's apotheosis of self-reliance has not precluded the use of either foreign trade or aid, and there has been a growing emphasis on the expansion of foreign trade in recent years.

---

8. Koh, "*Chuch'esong* in Korean Politics," pp. 92–93. During my 1981 visit to the DPRK I received the strong impression that almost nothing happened in that country without the "guidance of the great leader." His teachings and instructions were invoked by the leading cadres of all the institutions I visited—which ranged the whole gamut from an amusement park to a university—as the key to their operations. The unmistakable message was: "The Great Leader shows us the way, and we follow him with loyalty and enthusiasm." More on the implications of this phenomenon later in the book.

9. Park Chung Hee, *The Country, the Revolution, and I* (Seoul: Hollym Corp. Publishers, 1963), pp. 117–120.

10. Koh, "*Chuch'esong* in Korean Politics," pp. 93–94.

BLENDING OF RIGIDITY AND FLEXIBILITY

Both North and South Korea have manifested rigidity and flexibility in their responses to changes in their overall environments. The three basic goals of legitimacy, security, and development have of course endured with notable resilience. Closely related to this is the rigidity of the reunification strategies pursued by the two sides. Briefly, North Korea has pursued the strategy of building a strong revolutionary base in the North, fostering a revolutionary movement in the South, and consolidating antiimperialist (that is, anti-US) forces throughout the world. Its ultimate aim is to "complete the Korean revolution in all parts of Korea." Meanwhile, South Korea has pursued the strategy of "prevailing over communism" by strengthening its "national power," of which economic capability is the pivotal component. While this strategy is quite similar to the first part of North Korea's strategy, it is plain that the two are fundamentally incompatible: whereas Pyongyang seeks a unified Korea where communism a la Kim Il Sung (*Kim il-sŏng chuŭi*) is either the exclusive or dominant ideology, Seoul strives for the total elimination of Communist influence from a unified Korea.

Equally resilient has been the mutual distrust between the two Koreas. Fueled by the bitter memories of the fratricidal civil war, the Korean people in the two halves of the peninsula are profoundly distrustful of each other, a situation that is aggravated by intense ideological indoctrination and harsh penalties for deviations from the official lines in both Koreas. Symptomatic of the depth of animosity—and of the importance of the legitimacy issue discussed earlier—is the pointed refusal of both sides to refer to each other by their official names.[11] What is worse, they routinely refer to each other as "puppets," conveniently overlooking the reality of decreasing external influence in the two Koreas and increasing independence.

Such rigidity, however, has been tempered by tactical flexibility on the part of both sides. In the face of significant change in the international environment of East Asia, signaled by the Sino-American rapprochement, the two Koreas momentarily jettisoned their hostile postures and initiated a dialogue. Nevertheless, this turned out to be a half-hearted accommodation to the winds of change, because it was accompanied not by any change in their basic reunification strategies but by the desire to manipulate the opportunity to advance their di-

---

11. A notable deviation from this practice occurred in January 1980, when DPRK Premier Li Jong Ok addressed a letter to the "Prime Minister of the Republic of Korea" and the latter reciprocated. It is nonetheless striking that this has occurred only once in the 32-year period since the establishment of the two Korean states in 1948.

vergent goals, both manifest and latent. The fact remains, however, that the erstwhile policy of completely ignoring each other's existence was irrevocably changed.

South Korea has formally embraced what amounts to a two-Koreas policy—witness its June 1973 proposal for the simultaneous entry of the two Koreas into the United Nations. Although North Korea has categorically rejected and vehemently denounced Seoul's proposal, its actual behavior belies its strident rhetoric: not only has Pyongyang lost no time in exercising the customary right of setting up an observer mission at the UN headquarters after being admitted into the World Health Organization in May 1973, but it has also established full diplomatic relations with 60 countries (as of June 1982) that also recognize South Korea. Pyongyang also belongs to more than a dozen international organizations to which Seoul belongs.[12]

The pattern of tempering rigidity with flexibility was repeated in early 1979 when diplomatic relations were normalized between the US and the PRC. Against the backdrop of an impending visit of PRC Vice-Premier Deng Xiaoping to the United States, President Park made a dramatic proposal to North Korea urging the resumption of dialogue "at any time, at any place, and at any level" and "without any preconditions." Following North Korea's counterproposal a few days later, preliminary negotiations got under way between the two sides, raising the hope for a breakthrough in the deadlocked North-South talks. A clash of basic strategic goals and tactical aims between the two sides, however, led to the rerun of a familiar scenario. Pyongyang's first official reference to the "Republic of Korea," in January 1980, led to the resumption of contacts between "working-level" representatives of the two Koreas in Panmunjom. The persistence of divergent objectives and mutual mistrust, coupled with turbulent political change in South Korea, helped to turn the periodic contacts into rituals. After ten such contacts spanning seven months, the two sides broke off negotiations in September 1980.

In summary, despite the persistence and even exacerbation of mutual animosity, the overall foreign policy patterns of the two Koreas over the past three decades have been marked more by similarities than by differences. They have both pursued the interrelated goals of legitimacy, security, and development. They have both apotheosized self-reliance and made herculean efforts to attain it. Finally, they have both manifested strategic conservatism and tactical opportunism: while tenaciously clinging to their respective preconceived goals and attitudes, they have nonetheless managed to adapt, how-

12. Oemu-bu, *Hyŏnhwang* [Current Situation], a report submitted to the Committee on Foreign Affairs, the National Assembly, the Republic of Korea, the 101st extraordinary session, March 1979 (Seoul), p. 8.

ever grudgingly, to the shifting currents of big-power relations in the periphery of the Korean peninsula.

In the remainder of the book, we turn to a detailed examination of the sources and consequences of the foreign policies of the two Koreas, using the conceptual map outlined in chapter 1 as our guide. Most of the salient patterns of foreign policy sketched above will be reexamined and scrutinized with a view to generating plausible explanations.

3   OPERATIONAL ENVIRONMENT: EXTERNAL SETTING

A towering feature of the operational environment of the two Koreas is the presence of four of the world's great powers, including the two superpowers. This striking fact contributes appreciably to the blurring of conceptual distinctions between the global system and the regional system, two of the three components of the external setting of the operational environment. For, by virtue of their global influence, the four powers also play the dominant role in the Northeast Asian regional system. Hence, to sketch the contours of the global system is to delineate the most salient features of the regional system as well.

THE GLOBAL SYSTEM

Our purpose in this section is not to provide a comprehensive review of major changes in the global system during the past three decades but to note those aspects of change which appear to have special relevance for Korea. They are (1) the emergence of multiple centers of power, (2) the "alignment of the nonaligned," (3) détente among great powers in the decade of 1970s, and (4) the growing recognition of the interdependence of nation states, large and small. It is plain that these are overlapping and interconnected themes.

From Bipolarity to Multipolarity

The first decade after the end of World War II was marked by the polarization of the global system into two ideological camps led by the United States and the Soviet Union, respectively. Backed by their military and economic might, the two states became superpowers, with each drawing a coterie of lesser powers. Loosely labeled the "free world" and the "Communist world," the two power blocs retained a semblance of inner cohesion and ideological solidarity. The hegemonial positions of the two superpowers, however, were soon beset by the process of erosion.

First to be challenged was Moscow's claim to dominate the Communist world. For the Sino-Soviet dispute, which began to surface in 1956 and became openly acrimonious by the early 1960s, shattered the facade of unity in the international Communist movement once and for all. Rooted in historical and racial enmity and fueled by a clash of political goals, national pride, and the personality of top leaders, the quarrel between the two Communist giants escalated to a schism of major proportions. Paralleling this development was the increasing assertiveness of other Communist nations, including North Korea, which began to extol the virtues of independence and equality of all Communist parties. Most recently, nonruling Communist parties in Western Europe have all but broken ties, ideological or otherwise, with Moscow, spawning what is known as "Euro-communism." In a word, the international Communist movement has become truly polycentric.

The gradual erosion of the Soviet hegemony in the East was matched by the emergence of rival centers of power in the free world, brought about by the spectacular economic recovery of Western Europe—particularly the states comprising the European Economic Community—and Japan. While the United States continues to play a leading role in the North Atlantic Treaty Organization as well as in the scores of bilateral alliances, including the Washington-Tokyo alliance, its position is no longer as predominant as it once was. That is to say, there is a growing emphasis on mutual consultations and cooperation—on equal partnership. The new stress on "trilateral diplomacy," which underscores the importance of collaboration between industrial democracies in Western Europe, North America, and Japan, is symptomatic of this situation.

The "Alignment of the Nonaligned"

Equally noteworthy is the growing influence of the Third World, which further symbolizes the fragmentation of power in the contemporary international setting. If we subsume under this rubric those nations that have shed their colonial yoke and become independent since 1945 and that are struggling to rid themselves of the stigma and pain of economic backwardness, then we find that they constitute the overwhelming majority of the world states and world population alike. Although they initially embraced the policy of nonalignment in order "to preserve their sovereign independence from powerful military alliances," these nations have coalesced into what former US Secretary of State Henry A. Kissinger has called the "most solid bloc in the world today . . . , the alignment of the nonaligned."[1]

The emergence of this bloc, which, in the words of Kissinger, "divides the world into categories of North and South, developing and developed, imperial and colonial, at the very moment in history when such categories have become irrelevant and misleading,"[2] has drastically altered the complexion of the United Nations. The world organization, particularly the General Assembly, has been transformed from a diplomatic forum where the United States had a major voice and influence into an arena of ideological confrontation where the United States is the perennial object of condemnation. Sharing "a deep dissatisfaction over the cards they were dealt when they became independent," desirous of "a weightier political role in the international state system," impatient "to narrow the great gulf of economic inequality," and "eager to dramatize their causes even if this involves a disregard for traditional niceties of diplomacy," Third World countries vehemently attack and "repeatedly outvote" the United States and its allies.[3] A rare example of unanimous support for the United States by fifteen members of the UN Security Council, which included both Third World and Communist nations, was provided in December 1979, when the council adopted a resolution demanding, inter alia, the immediate release of US diplomatic personnel being held hostage in the US Embassy in Tehran, Iran. The changing power configuration in the UN has special implications for Korea due to the close bonds between South Korea and the world organization that have been forged over the last three decades.

It should be noted that the gap between rich and poor nations

1. US Department of State, "The Global Challenge and International Cooperation," speech by Secretary Henry A. Kissinger before the Institute of World Affairs of the University of Wisconsin, Milwaukee, Wisconsin, July 14, 1975 (Washington: Department of State, Bureau of Public Affairs, Office of Media Services, 1975), p. 4.
2. Ibid.
3. The quotes are from US Department of State, "The US Role in the United Nations," *Current Policy*, no. 11, March 1976 (Washington: Department of State, Bureau of Public Affairs, Office of Media Services, 1976), p. 1. For criticisms of the UN by US Ambassador Jeane Kirkpatrick, see Bernard D. Nossiter, "Questioning the Value of the United Nations," *New York Times Magazine*, April 11, 1982, pp. 16–20.

that the Third World countries uniformly decry is by no means absent in the "nonaligned" bloc itself. The disparity in wealth between a handful of petroleum exporting countries on the one hand and the vast majority of the bloc on the other is as wide as that separating the industrialized nations of the West and Japan from the developing countries of the Third World. The power of the elite among the nonaligned bloc was graphically demonstrated in the Arab oil embargo of 1973. Indeed, with the quadrupling of oil prices, the configuration of economic power in the world has begun to change; a spectacular increase in revenues for the oil exporting countries has been paralleled by spiraling inflation and recession in the rest of the world, including the industrialized nations. However, declining demand for oil and the consequent glut of oil in the world market in the early 1980s have dimmed the prospects for any dramatic increase in the wealth and power of oil-exporting nations.

From Confrontation to Détente

Amid all the turmoil and growing assertiveness of the Third World, the world's great powers have noticeably improved their mutual relations. Confrontation, interspersed with an outright military conflict, has been replaced by détente, a measurable reduction of tensions. A notable exception to this general trend is the continuation of the Sino-Soviet dispute. Another significant development is the strain in Washington-Moscow relations following the Soviet invasion and occupation of Afghanistan in December 1979.

The most noteworthy development in big-power relations has been the opening of relations between the United States and the People's Republic of China. Following the historic visit of President Nixon to the People's Republic in February 1972, the two erstwhile enemies patched up their differences to a marked degree, forging a unique relationship in the annals of world diplomacy. Liaison offices were set up in their respective capitals, becoming de facto embassies. When President Ford visited the PRC in December 1975, he helped to set a diplomatic precedent in which two successive US presidents made state visits to a country that the United States did not officially recognize. Finally, the two countries established full diplomatic relations in January 1979.

Meanwhile, the relationship between Washington and Moscow was transformed from intermittent confrontation to "détente." A major factor underlying this development was the change in the military balance triggered by the dazzling growth of the Soviet nuclear arsenal and weapons technology. Not only did there emerge a rough "parity" in the nuclear arsenals of the two superpowers, but the staggering destructiveness of the modern weapons made it imperative that they avoid the course of confrontation. The change in Washington-Moscow relations was signaled by summit diplomacy, the signing of SALT (Strategic Arms Limitation Treaty) I and other agreements on bilateral cooperation. The advent of the Carter Administration in Washington in 1977, with its emphasis on human rights, temporarily strained American-Soviet relations.

The signing of SALT II in June 1979 nonetheless symbolized the continued vitality of the Soviet-American détente. What significantly altered the picture, however, was the Soviet invasion of Afghanistan in December 1979. When 50,000 Soviet troops invaded and forcibly occupied the strategic Asian country, assassinated its president and several of his family members, and installed a puppet regime, the United States roundly condemned the moves. President Carter called the Soviet action "an extremely serious threat to peace," "a callous violation of international law and the United Nations Charter," and "a deliberate effort of a powerful atheistic government to subjugate an independent Islamic people."[4] He imposed a series of economic sanctions, including a grain embargo, and led the movement to boycott the Moscow Olympic Games in the summer of 1980. All this led to a notable cooling of relations between the two superpowers.

The situation deteriorated further with the inauguration of Ronald Reagan as US president in 1981. He, along with his secretary of state, Alexander M. Haig, took a staunchly anti-Soviet posture. Reagan publicly attacked not only Soviet policies and actions around the world but the Soviet system of communism as well, describing it as an "aberration." Furthermore, his decision to sell arms to the PRC and the revelation, made in June 1981, that the US and the PRC had been jointly operating an electronic intelligence-gathering station in China since 1980 to monitor Soviet missile tests served to strengthen the impression that Washington and Beijing were moving toward the formation of a de facto anti-Soviet alliance.[5] In sum, "détente" appeared to be dead insofar as the two superpowers were concerned.

A major byproduct of the Sino-American opening in the early 1970s has been the normalization of relations between the PRC and Japan. If anything, the animosity between the two countries was much more deep-rooted than that between the PRC and the United States. Yet, ironically, Tokyo went Washington one better by establishing full diplomatic relations with Beijing in September 1972—six years ahead of Washington. This could be accomplished primarily be-

    4. US Department of State, "President Carter: Soviet Invasion of Afghanistan," *Current Policy*, no. 123, January 4, 1980 (Washington: Department of State, Bureau of Public Affairs, Office of Media Services, 1980), p. 1.
    5. *New York Times*, June 17 and 18, 1981.

cause of the absence of a major stumbling block—the Taiwan issue. For the absence of an alliance relationship made it possible for Japan to "separate politics from economics" and sever all but economic ties with the Republic of China on Taiwan. These dramatic changes in the relationships among the four Pacific powers have huge implications for the two Koreas.

Growing Interdependence

If any one word can sum up the dimensions of the change that has occurred in the global system over the past three decades, it is "interdependence." The transition from a bipolar to a multipolar world where the newly independent countries of the Third World aggressively pursue a fair share of political and economic power and where the great powers have markedly improved their relations, albeit with some notable exceptions, reflects the growing recognition on the part of the 160 or so sovereign nation states of the world of the inextricably interdependent nature of their destiny on this ever-shrinking and ever-crowded planet.

As former Secretary of State Kissinger put it:

> When weapons span continents in minutes, our security is bound up with world peace. When our factories, farms, and financial strength are deeply affected by decisions taken in foreign lands, our prosperity is linked to world prosperity. The peace of the world and our own security, the world's progress and our own prosperity, are indivisible.[6]

The same logic applies to other nations of the world. The Arab oil embargo of 1973 and its worldwide impact demonstrated not only the vulnerability of the industrial nations of the West and Japan to conditions beyond their control but also the precariously interwoven nature of the fabric of the world economy. For the serious economic crisis precipitated by the embargo had adverse effects on virtually all countries, rich and poor, large and small. The only short-term beneficiaries of the action turned out to be a handful of oil-exporting countries.

Equally noteworthy is the potential for a catastrophe that is inherent in the nuclear arms race. Given the awesome powers of destruction at the disposal of the superpowers, one shudders at the probable consequences of another world conflagration. The growing realization of this danger helped to precipitate a worldwide campaign against nuclear weapons in late 1981 and early 1982. This also

6. US Department of State, "Global Challenge," p. 1.

underscores the importance of preventing putatively regional conflicts, for they may escalate into a wider international war involving the superpowers. As noted, such a danger is ever present in the Korean peninsula because of the crisscrossing alliance relationships between the two potential belligerents on one hand and the four Pacific powers on the other.

THE REGIONAL SYSTEM OF NORTHEAST ASIA

In terms of geographic contiguity, the Northeast Asian regional system consists of the People's Republic of China, Japan, North Korea, South Korea, and Taiwan. Although not a strictly Asian power, the Soviet Union is not only contiguous to China, Korea, and Japan, but also has important strategic interests in the region; it is therefore a legitimate member of the Northeast Asia regional system. The same is true of the United States, which former President Gerald R. Ford emphatically declared in December 1975 to be "a nation of the Pacific basin, [having] a very vital stake in Asia and a responsibility to take a leading part in lessening tensions, preventing hostilities, and preserving peace."[7] Secretary of State Cyrus Vance reaffirmed Ford's statement in June 1977, when he said: "We are and will remain a Pacific nation, by virtue of our geography, our history, our commerce, and our interests."[8] Finally, President Reagan, in February 1981, "affirmed that the United States, as a Pacific power, will seek to ensure the peace and security of the region."[9] That these statements are not empty rhetoric is amply shown by the striking fact that until 1979 the United States maintained treaty commitments to, and military presence in, all of the non-Communist states in the region. The situation changed somewhat with the termination of the Washington-Taipei mutual defense treaty on January 1, 1980. Economically, however, the United States continues to maintain strong ties with all the nations of the region.

As already noted, the most striking change in the Northeast Asian regional system is the significant reduction of tensions among

    7. US Department of State, "President Ford's Pacific Doctrine," *News Release*, December 7, 1975, Honolulu, Hawaii (Washington: Department of State, Bureau of Public Affairs, Office of Media Services, 1975), p. 1.
    8. US Department of State, "United States and Asia," speech by Secretary Cyrus Vance before the Asia Society, June 29, 1977, New York (Washington: Department of State, Bureau of Public Affairs, Office of Media Services, 1977), p. 1.
    9. See the Reagan-Chun joint communiqué in the *Korea Herald*, February 4, 1981.

the four Pacific powers, particularly between Beijing on one side and Tokyo and Washington on the other. The Sino-Soviet relationship remains one of implacable adversaries, with all the outward signs of mutual animosity. It is generally agreed that the deterioration of the Beijing-Moscow relations may have been the key factor in Beijing's decision to improve ties with Washington and Tokyo. Faced with an encirclement by three potential enemies with growing economic and military capabilities—namely, the Soviet Union, the United States, and Japan—the People's Republic may have decided to neutralize what it perceived to be the less menacing of the trio.[10] One consequence of Beijing's improved ties with Washington and Tokyo has been to spur Moscow to shore up its own relations with the latter two, although the results have been rather meager.

Another consequence or concomitant of the Sino-American opening and the Sino-Japanese normalization has been a perceptible increase in the international stature of the PRC. Not only did Beijing win its long-contested right to represent China in the United Nations, but it has obtained diplomatic recognition from all but a handful of the world's nations. Since its installation in the China seat in the UN, the PRC has clearly emerged as a leader of the Third World. Beijing's diplomatic upsurge has been accompanied by a corresponding decline in the relative international standing of Taiwan, although the latter's impressive record in economic development remains intact. In short, most of the features of the global system sketched earlier are found in the regional system of Northeast Asia as well, with the most salient ones being the reduction of tensions among major powers and the crystallization of multipolarity.

BILATERAL SYSTEMS

The relations of the two Koreas with each other and with the four major powers constitute the final component of their external setting. These relations also comprise the outputs of their respective foreign policies. For South Korea, the most crucial bilateral relationships have thus far been those with the United States and Japan. Seoul's ties with Washington, which not only provide a military shield but also serve as a significant trading partner, have been extremely close. Seoul's dependence on Washington, however, has been steadily declining, thus transforming the bilateral relationship from one of patron-client states to one of full-fledged allies.

10. For Beijing's perception of "encirclement," see Ross Terrill, *800,000,000: The Real China* (New York: Delta Books, 1971), pp. 131–140.

Two closely related events of the past decade have underscored both the depth of the Seoul-Washington ties and Seoul's determination to preserve them at all costs. They are the widely publicized Park Tong Sun affair—dubbed the "Koreagate"—and the controversial policy of the Carter Administration to withdraw American ground troops from South Korea. The two are related in that, according to information obtained by the US government, South Korea's alleged influence-buying operations vis-à-vis the US Congress were precipitated by Washington's decision to withdraw 20,000 US troops from South Korea in 1971. However, Seoul's concerted efforts to safeguard the level of the American military presence on the peninsula suffered a significant setback in 1977, when President Carter initiated steps to carry out his campaign pledge to withdraw US ground troops over "a four- or five-year time period."[11]

The stated rationale for this policy was that, thanks to "South Korea's growth and strength," a "carefully phased withdrawal of American ground troops [would] not endanger the security of South Korea." Carter stated that Washington would proceed very cautiously in full consultation with both Seoul and Tokyo, that the United States would maintain the American air, naval, and other supporting elements in Korea, and that it would help in the fortification of Seoul's defense capabilities.[12] Following his state visit to South Korea in the summer of 1979, and in light of a revised, upward estimate by the US intelligence community of North Korea's military capability, Carter announced that withdrawal of US ground troops from South Korea would be held in abeyance until 1981. Then, in February 1981, President Reagan told ROK President Chun Doo Hwan during their summit meeting in Washington that there would be no reduction in the number of US ground troops in South Korea.

Meanwhile, South Korea's dependence on and penetration by Japanese capital and technology have grown so rapidly since the conclusion of their normalization treaty in 1965 that Japan has become almost as vital to Seoul's survival as the United States. In fact, Japan has emerged as South Korea's number one source of imported goods, surpassing the United States. In 1981, Japan accounted for 24.4 percent of South Korea's total merchandise imports and 16.4 percent of exports, while the United States accounted for 23.2 percent of South Korea's total merchandise imports and 26.5 percent of exports.[13]

Although Seoul's recent policy of improving relations with "non-

11. *New York Times*, March 10, 1977.
12. "America's Role in Consolidating a Peaceful Balance and Promoting Economic Growth in Asia," Address by Secretary Vance," *Department of State Bulletin* 77: 1988 (Aug. 1, 1977): 143.
13. *Korea Herald*, February 3, 1982.

hostile" Communist nations has produced limited but tangible results vis-à-vis Moscow (as well as several Eastern European countries), it appears to have had little effect on Seoul-Beijing relations thus far. The PRC remains unswerving in its support for North Korea and its hostility toward South Korea—hostility that borders on the denial of South Korea's very existence.[14] There has, nonetheless, been some change since Mao Zedong's death in September 1976. In November 1980, for example, the Japan External Trade Organization (JETRO) reported that South Korea had imported $13,330,000 worth of goods from the PRC in the first seven months of that year, while exporting to China $4,250,000 worth of South Korean goods. The trade was said to have been conducted through Japanese and Hong Kong firms.[15] In 1981, the volume of indirect trade between Seoul and Beijing reportedly reached $120 million.[16]

In July 1981, a Chinese scholar—Yuan Chuangjing—who is a member of the law institute of the PRC Academy of Social Sciences attended an international workshop on the Law of the Seas in Seoul. The scholar, holding a PRC passport, reportedly came to South Korea not directly from China but from the United States where he was serving as a visiting scholar.[17] Despite such examples, Beijing has remained staunch in support of Pyongyang and its refusal to endorse a "two-Koreas" policy. This position may be related to two principal considerations: (1) Beijing's desire not to alienate North Korea for fear that the latter may drift into the Soviet camp; and (2) Beijing's unresolved Taiwan problem, which makes it difficult not to support Pyongyang's insistence that there is and can be only one Korea.[18]

Just as Beijing strives to keep Pyongyang out of the Soviet orbit, so is Moscow anxious not to let Pyongyang drift into Beijing's sphere of influence. Since the mid 1960s, Moscow has maintained cordial, albeit by no means warm, relations with Pyongyang, serving as the primary supplier of military hardware as well as economic and technical aid for the latter. In short, the Sino-Soviet rivalry has enabled

14. For example, a map of the world published in a Chinese magazine ignores even the division of Korea, designating the entire peninsula as the Democratic People's Republic of Korea. Neither the 38th parallel nor the Demilitarized Zone is shown. See *Jinmin Chūgoku* (Beijing), October, 1975, pp. 76–77. This magazine is published in Japanese. Beijing's practice is consistent with that of North Korea. See *Chosŏn haengjŏng kuyŏkto* [Map of Administrative Districts of Korea] (Pyongyang: Kwahak Paekkwa Sajŏn Ch'ulp'an-sa, 1978).

15. *Agence France Presse*, Tokyo, November 4, 1980, as monitored by *FBIS Daily Report*.

16. *Han'guk ilbo*, Chicago Edition, June 1, 1982.

17. *Kyōdō News Agency*, Tokyo, July 7, 1981, as monitored by *FBIS Daily Report*.

18. For a perceptive analysis of Beijing's policy toward the two Koreas, see Hong Yung Lee, "Korea's Future: Peking's Perspective," *Asian Survey* 17, 11 (November 1977): 1088–1102.

North Korea to count both of the Communist giants as its patron states while safeguarding its independence.[19]

Although—and perhaps because—Pyongyang perceives the United States as the principal stumbling block to its strategy of reunification and hence as its number one enemy, it has made numerous attempts to improve its relations with Washington. However, such attempts have been invariably coupled with maneuvers aimed at downgrading Seoul and driving a wedge between the latter and Washington. Pyongyang's repeated proposals for direct bilateral talks with Washington is a case in point. The United States, however, has flatly refused to engage in any dialogue with North Korea unless South Korea is included as a party. The Carter Administration temporarily changed the picture somewhat. First, the long-standing ban on travel to North Korea by US citizens was lifted, along with similar restrictions regarding Vietnam and Cuba. Second, President Carter's plan to withdraw US ground troops from South Korea over a four- or five-year period signaled the possibility that North Korea's long sought after goal of removing the American military presence might be a step closer to realization. Third, perhaps because of the foregoing, North Korea appreciably toned down its anti-American propaganda in the first few months of the Carter Administration.

One of the first signals emanating from the Reagan Administration concerning Pyongyang was a jolting one: in March 1981, the US Department of State turned down the request of DPRK observers at the United Nations for permission to travel to Washington, D.C., to attend an international trade conference jointly sponsored by the UN and the World Bank. A State Department spokesman noted that North Korea was not a member of the World Bank and that "we are not indifferent to the extraordinary level of crude invective being hurled at the US administration and President Reagan personally by the North Korean government."[20]

Pyongyang's relations with Japan have grown substantially in recent years, primarily in terms of trade and unofficial contacts. The volume of trade between the two countries, for example, increased 33 times between 1961 and 1974, although it decreased substantially in 1975 and 1976 due to North Korea's payment problems.[21] By 1979, however, the 1974 record was surpassed, and 1980 saw further increase in two-way trade.[22] Meanwhile, the number of visitors be-

---

19. More on Pyongyang's relations with Moscow and Beijing in chapter 10.
20. *Korea Herald*, March 17, 1981.
21. *Kita Chōsen kenkyū* 3, 35 (April 1977): 31.
22. The value of two-way trade was $361 million in 1974, $436 million in 1979, and about $570 million in 1980. Ibid. 3, 70 (May 1980): 28; and *Korea Herald*, January 8, 1981.

tween the two countries rose 82 times between 1970 and 1974.[23] From Pyongyang's perspective, the value of Japan lies not only in its assets as a trading partner but also in the presence of some 600,000 Koreans with divided loyalties in that country. The latter factor has turned Japan into an arena of competition between Pyongyang and Seoul as well as a base of subversive operations directed against South Korea. North Korea's expressed desire to normalize relations with Japan, however, has thus far failed to generate any enthusiasm in Tokyo.

Finally, bilateral relations between the two Koreas remain essentially unchanged, for the appearance of détente on the Korean peninsula, generated by the initiation of a dialogue between Seoul and Pyongyang, has proved to be totally illusory. The level of mutual distrust and animosity between the two Koreas is so dangerously high that one begins to wonder if their political reintegration is even remotely possible, the putatively strong bonds of common language and cultural heritage notwithstanding.

23. Seung K. Ko, "North Korea's Relations wtih Japan since Detente," *Pacific Affairs* 50, 1 (Spring 1977): 32. In the summer of 1981 I saw large numbers of Japanese visitors in North Korea. I got the impression that they were the largest group of foreigners in that country.

4 OPERATIONAL ENVIRONMENT: INTERNAL SETTING

ECONOMIC POWER

Just as important as the external setting of the operational environment is its internal setting, of which three dimensions are particularly noteworthy: economic power, military power, and political dynamics. We begin, therefore, by delineating the respective economic capabilities of the two Koreas. It must be stressed at the outset that our goal here is not to present a comprehensive comparative analysis but simply to highlight the salient aspects of the two economies. A major impediment to even a cursory comparison of the North and South Korean economic systems is the paucity of data concerning the North Korean economy. Since the early 1960s, North Korea has not published any comprehensive statistics on its economic performance; most of its published data are in the form of ratios and percentages, rather than in absolute figures. Moreover, there are significant differences in the concepts and methods used by Seoul and Pyongyang in measuring their respective economic activities, further compounding the task of comparison.

Despite these difficulties, one thing clearly stands out in the economic landscape of both halves of Korea: during the three decades since the Korean armistice, both have succeeded in turning their war-shattered economies into sizable industrial complexes; in so doing, they have both registered impressive rates of growth. In the last few years, however, North Korea appears to have encountered growing difficulties. South Korea, after maintaining its momentum of growth for a while, has also entered into a recession, a situation that has been exacerbated by political and social turmoil following the assassination of President Park Chung Hee in October 1979.

Seoul's Economic Growth

The Korean War of 1950–1953 left the entire peninsula in a shambles. It was primarily with the massive inflow of external assistance, mainly from the United States, that South Korea succeeded in restoring its production facilities to the prewar level by the end of 1956. However, this was accompanied by a skyrocketing inflation: the average annual rate of inflation was 47 percent in the 1954–1956 period. Although South Korea's economic situation improved moderately during the 1957–1961 period, it was not until 1963 that real progress began to be registered.[1]

After first seizing power in a military coup in May 1961 and then consolidating his political control as the elected head of a civilian government, President Park Chung Hee set out to modernize the South Korean economy with all deliberate speed. His determination was translated into a series of five-year economic plans, the successful implementation of which, in the words of a World Bank report published in early 1977, "has tranformed [South] Korea from one of the poorest developing countries, with heavy dependence on agriculture and a weak balance of payments financed almost entirely by foreign grants, to a semi-industrialized, middle-income nation with an increasingly strong external payments position and the prospect of eliminating the current account deficit in the next 5–10 years."[2]

Statistical indicators of South Korea's economic growth since 1962 are quite striking: The average annual growth rate in real Gross National Product (GNP) for the first Five-Year Plan period (1962–1966) was 7.8 percent; the rate for the second Five-Year Plan period (1967–1971) was 8.6 percent; and that for the third Five-Year Plan period (1972–1976) was 9.8 percent.[3] The real GNP growth rate for 1976 was a stunning 15.5 percent—the second highest in South Korea's history, and those for 1977 and 1978 were 10.5 and 12.5 percent, respectively.[4] The rate for 1979 was 6.4 percent. In 1980, however, South

---

1. Seung Hee Kim, "Economic Development of South Korea," in Se-Jin Kim and Chang-Hyon Cho (eds.), *Korea: A Divided Nation* (Silver Spring, MD: Research Institute on Korean Affairs, 1976), pp. 116–117.

2. *Korea Newsreview*, April 2, 1977, pp. 18–19.

3. *1979 nyŏndo chung'ang sanghwang-p'an (an)* [Central Status Charts for 1979 (draft)] (Seoul: Prime Minister's Office, 1979), p. 3.

4. Republic of Korea, Economic Planning Board, *Major Statistics of the Korean Economy* (Seoul: EPB, 1979), p. 3.

Korea suffered a setback for the first time since the early 1960s: its GNP declined 6.2 percent in real terms. In 1981 Seoul's GNP registered a net growth of 7.1 percent.[5]

"Per capita income, which in current prices stood at less than $100 in 1961, had risen to about $700 in 1976 and, in real terms, the rise was nearly threefold over the period."[6] By the end of 1978, per capita GNP had surpassed the $1,000 mark, rising to $1,279. In 1979, it reached $1,624.[7] More impressive is the phenomenal leap in South Korea's merchandise exports: they rose from a mere $33 million in 1960 to $20,993 million in 1981—a 636-fold increase over the period.[8]

According to the World Bank, the key factors that have contributed to South Korea's "outstanding economic gains" included the following: (1) political stability, (2) strong leadership, (3) a firm commitment to development, (4) a favorable social environment, (5) a "well educated, disciplined and industrious" labor force, (6) "large inflows of foreign grants and loans," and (7) finally, "an early recognition of the potential contribution of trade in manufactured goods in compensating for Korea's paucity of natural resources, leading to the adoption of a development strategy concentrating on the expansion of labor-intensive manufacturing."[9]

Whether South Korea can sustain the momentum of growth will hinge on the success with which it deals with a number of problem areas, which include the following: One is the vulnerability of the South Korean economy to changes and fluctuations in the world economy. Given such a heavy reliance on international trade, a serious recession or a rash of protective measures on the part of its major trading partners would have immediate and crippling effects on Seoul's economic situation. On the other hand, Seoul's vulnerability on this score is being steadily lessened by "some progress in diversifying the commodity structure of exports and moving in the direction of more sophisticated skill-intensive products" as well as by a diversification of trading partners. Whereas the United States and Japan together accounted for about 70 percent of South Korean exports until 1973, their combined share dropped to 56 percent in 1975 and to 43 percent in 1981.[10] Seoul has made an impressive headway in penetrat-

5. *Korea Newsreview*, January 9, 1982, p. 9; *Korean Newsletter Supplement* (Washington, DC: Korean Information Office, Embassy of Korea), March 3, 1982, p. 5.

6. Quoted from the World Bank report, as summarized in *Korea Newsreview*, April 2, 1977, p. 18.

7. *Hapdong News Agency*, Seoul, April 7, 1980, as monitored by FBIS.

8. *1979 nyŏndo chung'ang sanghwang-p'an (an)*, p. 3; *Korea Herald*, February 3, 1982.

9. *Korea Newsreview*, April 2, 1977, p. 18.

10. *Korea Herald*, February 1, 1981 and February 3, 1982. The quotation is from the February 1, 1981 issue.

TABLE 3 · **South Korea's Foreign Trade (in Million US Dollars)**

Year	Exports (X)	Imports (M)	Trade Balance (X − M)	Total Value (X + M)
1962	55	422	−367	477
1963	87	560	−473	647
1964	119	404	−285	523
1965	175	464	−288	638
1966	250	716	−466	966
1967	320	996	−676	1,316
1968	455	1,463	−1,008	1,918
1969	623	1,824	−1,201	2,447
1970	835	1,984	−1,149	2,819
1971	1,068	2,394	−1,326	3,462
1972	1,624	2,522	−898	4,146
1973	3,225	4,240	−1,015	7,465
1974	4,460	6,852	−2,392	11,312
1975	5,081	7,274	−2,193	12,355
1976	7,715	8,774	−1,059	16,489
1977	10,047	10,811	−764	20,858
1978	12,711	14,524	−1,813	27,235
1979	15,055	20,339	−5,284	35,394
1980	17,505	22,292	−4,787	39,797
1981	20,993	26,132	−5,139	47,125

SOURCES: Republic of Korea, Economic Planning Board, *Major Statistics of Korean Economy*, 1979 (Seoul, 1979), p. 7; and *Korea Herald*, February 1 and 3, 1981 and February 3, 1982.

ing the market in Europe and, particularly, in the Middle East. In 1980 South Korea traded with 163 countries in the world, and its export dependency on ten major importing countries declined from 76.5 percent in 1979 to 69.8 percent in 1980.[11] In 1976 construction service exports, primarily to the Middle East, totaled $2.5 billion, generating foreign exchange earnings of $497 million.[12] In 1979 overseas construction contracts won by South Korean firms amounted to $6.4 billion.[13] Revenues generated by construction service exports in the same year surpassed $2 billion. In 1981 the total value of construction contracts awarded to South Korean firms reached $12.5 billion, surpassing the target of $7 billion by nearly 80 percent.[14] These earnings helped to offset Seoul's chronic deficit in balance of trade (see table 3).

Another closely related source of potential difficulty is the mas-

11. Ibid., March 28, 1981.
12. *Korea Newsreview*, April 2, 1977, p. 18; ibid., February 5, 1977, p. 13.
13. *Korea Herald*, January 9, 1980.
14. Ibid., February 17, 1980 and January 1, 1982.

sive influx of foreign capital. As noted, South Korea has opted for a strategy of economic development that relies heavily on "foreign financing of investment outlays and balance of payments deficits."[15] As of January 1982, South Korea's total external debt was approximately $32,500 million.[16]

In the late 1970s, South Korea's ability to bear the mounting debt-servicing burden increased steadily. Equally noteworthy is a sharp increase in its foreign exchange reserve, which rose 75 percent in 1976 over the previous year (to $2,961 million) and 46 percent in 1977 over the previous year (to $4,322 million). In 1978, however, it registered a modest increase of 15 percent over the previous year (to $4,937 million) and appeared to be on a downslope due to the combined effects of constantly rising crude oil prices and the sluggish exports of South Korean commodities. In early 1980, Seoul's foreign exchange reserve stood at $5,700 million.[17] Also noteworthy is an appreciable decline in Seoul's debt-servicing ratio—the ratio of debt service payments to exports of goods and nonfactor services: it declined from an average of about 21 percent in the early 1970s to about 11 percent in 1976. By the early 1980s, the ratio hovered around 13 percent, a respectable figure.[18]

Still another possible problem area is the urban-rural gap. Notwithstanding the remarkable pace of industrialization in South Korea, 33 percent of its population—nearly 13 million—lived on farms in 1976.[19] Their per capita income lagged behind that of urban residents, due primarily to "the slow growth of nonagricultural incomes in the rural sector," which "have remained at around 20 percent of farm household incomes for the last five years."[20] Here again, however, the picture has begun to change. The vigorous implementation of the *Saemaŭl* (New Village) Movement, accompanied by substantial government subsidies, has closed the income gap between cities and the countryside. In fact, "rural household, as opposed to per capita, income has exceeded that of urban workers since 1974, although the highest income groups are excluded from the urban statistics."[21] Indicative of the dramatic improvement in the standard of living of the rural people is the finding of a 1980 government-sponsored survey

---

15. Ibid., January 31, 1982.
16. Ibid., February 3, 1982.
17. *Korea Newsreview*, January 19, 1980, p. 7.
18. Ibid., April 2, 1977, p. 19 and March 21, 1981, p. 21; *Korea Herald*, January 31, 1982.
19. *Korea Newsreview*, March 12, 1977, p. 16. By the end of 1981 the proportion of rural residents had dropped to 26 percent. Ibid., March 27, 1982, p. 24.
20. Ibid., April 2, 1977, p. 19.
21. Susumu Awanohara, "Letter from Seoul," *Far Eastern Economic Review*, November 12, 1976, p. 78.

that 86 percent of agricultural households had television sets and 99 percent had electricity.[22]

The problem of rural-urban income disparities is a part of the larger problem of income distribution. Significantly, the World Bank study cited above found that the "distribution of income in [South] Korea compares favorably with that in most developing countries." It added:

> A survey in 1970 showed that the bottom 40 percent of people in [South] Korea got 18 percent of total income while the top 20 percent got 45 percent. These shares are more egalitarian than in most other developing countries. This is partly due to the spread of education and to the elimination of big disparities in asset ownership in the period before rapid industrialization took place.[23]

On the other hand, statistics released by the Korea Development Institute (KDI) in August 1979 suggest that income inequality still remains a serious problem. The KDI survey found that 14.8 percent of the South Korean population (5,198,000 persons or 1 million households) were below the "absolute poverty" line, which was set at an income of 9,432 won (about $19) per month for an urban family of five and at 7,890 won (about $16) per month for a rural family of five.[24] Even more disturbing is the revelation that, as of November 1979, 68.1 percent of South Korea's wage earners enjoyed total exemption from income taxes because their household income (for a family of five) fell short of 130,000 won (about $268) per month.[25]

According to data released by the ROK Economic Planning Board (EPB) in February 1982, the trend toward a slow deterioration of income distribution in the latter half of the 1970s was arrested in 1980. For example, the share in the total income of the bottom 40 percent of South Korean citizens rose from 15.5 percent in 1978 to 16.1 percent in 1980, while the share of the upper 20 percent group decreased from 46.7 percent to 45.4 percent in the same period. The EPB report also showed that the "monthly income of households belonging to the lowest 10 percent of the income ladder was 38,000 won" (about $57) in 1980, while "that of those belonging to the highest 10 percent was 709,000 won" (about $1,070). The average monthly income per household in the same year was 241,000 won (about $364).[26]

22. *Han'guk ilbo*, May 21, 1981.
23. *Korea Newsreview*, April 2, 1977, p. 19.
24. *Tong'a ilbo*, August 4, 1979.
25. *Han'guk ilbo*, November 26, 1979.
26. *Korea Herald*, February 14, 1982. The exchange rate of 662.60 won to US $1.00 that prevailed in December 1980 was used to arrive at the dollar figures.

TABLE 4 · **Major Targets of South Korea's Fifth Five-Year Plan and Beyond**

Item	Unit	1980	1986	1988	1991	Annual Rate of Growth (%) 82–86	87–91
GNP							
1980 dollars	100 million	574	900	1,008	1,234	7.6	7.0
1980 won	1,000 billion	35.0	53.7	61.5	75.3	7.6	7.0
Population	million	38.1	41.8	43.1	44.9	1.6	1.4
Per capita GNP							
1980 dollars	—	1,506	2,170	2,340	2,751	5.9	5.5
1980 won	1,000	919	1,283	1,427	1,678	5.9	5.5
Rise in GNP deflation	percentage	27.7	9.5	9.0	9.0	10.8	9.0
Merchandise exports current dollars	100 million	172	530	745	1,250	11.4	10.0
Merchandise imports current dollars	100 million	216	555	755	1,200	8.4	8.0
Current account balance current dollars	100 million	−53	−36	−17	50	—	—

SOURCE: *Korea Newsreview*, August 29, 1981, p. 11.

As Table 4 shows, the Fifth Five-Year Plan (1982–1986) envisages an average annual growth in real GNP of 7 to 8 percent. It aims to bring down the rate of inflation to a single digit by 1986, a feat that has never been accomplished in all of the previous plans. It further projects a significant increase in the rate of domestic savings to GNP—from 21.2 percent in 1980 to 29.6 percent in 1986—and a corresponding decrease in reliance upon overseas savings for funds—from 9.8 percent of GNP in 1980 to 2.9 percent in 1986. The plan has five priority tasks: (1) to enhance both stability and efficiency in the economy; (2) to strengthen international payment position and attain economic security; (3) to shift the industrial structure on the basis of comparative advantage; (4) to encourage a balanced development of national land and conserve natural environment; and (5) to accelerate social development. A key emphasis will be placed on the leading role of free market forces, with government taking a low posture. In fact, the plan is described for the first time as an "indicative" plan; it is designed merely to indicate the general framework and direction in which investment choices will be made by the private sector.[27]

Whether the targets of the Fifth Five-Year Plan can be attained

27. *Korea Newsreview*, August 29, 1981, pp. 10–11; *Korea Herald*, Janaury 1, 1982, supplement, p. 6.

will hinge on many variables. Internally, political stability will be a pivotal variable. For it is directly linked with South Korea's ability to increase its productivity, to maintain the competitiveness of its products in the world market, and to attract a continuous stream of foreign capital in the form of loans and direct investments. Externally, the state of the world economy, the stability of the prices of crude oil and other raw materials, the trade policies of South Korea's principal trading partners, and, most important, the preservation of peace in the Korean peninsula will prove to be crucial. In sum, the international dimensions of the South Korean economy place a special burden on Seoul's diplomacy.

Pyongyang's Economic Growth

North Korea, too, has performed the arduous feat of transforming a backward economy ravaged by war into a predominantly industrial economy capable of producing an impressive array of machinery and other products at home. As a thoroughgoing "Stalinistic command economy," North Korea, after socializing all means of production and collectivizing its farms, proceeded to carry out a series of multiyear economic development plans with primary emphasis on the development of heavy industry.[28] Its initial goal of restoring the pre-1945 productive capacity was hampered by the Korean War. After the signing of the armistice in July 1953, Pyongyang concentrated on reconstructing its war-torn economy, a goal it claims to have attained by 1956.

In the Five-Year Plan (1957–1961), which turned out to be a de facto four-year plan, thanks to an early attainment of its targets, North Korea sought to lay a solid foundation for industrialization. According to Joseph S. Chung, however, the bulk of the North Korean efforts during this period was directed in reality at restoring the pre-Korean War capacity in principal industrial products; it was not until the advent of the Seven-Year Plan (1961–1967), which was later extended for three years, that Pyongyang began to make significant headway in industrialization.[29] Chung estimates that North Korea's national income multiplied 12.5 times between 1946 and 1967 and 8.6 times between 1953 and 1967, "registering an annual growth rate of 12.7 percent and 16.6 percent, respectively, during 1947–67 and

28. For a comprehensive analysis of the North Korean economy, see Joseph S. Chung, *The North Korean Economy: Structure and Development* (Stanford, CA: Hoover Institution Press, 1974). See also idem, "North Korea's Development Strategy and Economic Performance," in Kim and Cho (eds.), *Korea: A Divided Nation*, pp. 182–199.

29. Chung, "North Korea's Development Strategy," pp. 186–187.

1954–67." Its per capita income grew 11.0 and 13.1 percent, respectively, during the two periods.[30]

North Korea began to encounter slowdowns and difficulties in mid 1960 at a time when South Korea was beginning to make an impressive headway in its developmental program. The average annual growth rate in industrial output declined from 36.6 percent during the Five-Year Plan period (1957–1960) to 12.8 percent during the Seven-Year Plan period (1961–1970). This was substantially lower than the target growth rate of 18 percent.[31] In fact, two developments could be viewed as North Korea's tacit admission of economic stagnation: First, it suddenly discontinued the practice of publishing annual comprehensive economic statistics in 1967. Second, it announced in October 1966 that the Seven-Year Plan would be extended for three years, citing the need to divert funds to defense construction as the main reason for the move.

There were not only slowdowns but also production reverses; the latter occurred in "such important products as pig iron, iron ore, steel, metal-cutting machines, tractors, chemical fertilizers and textiles." Significantly, even with the three-year extension, North Korea apparently failed to fulfill many of its industrial output targets. Its published figures indicate that only in the production of coal did Pyongyang attain its original goal, falling short of targets in such strategic items as electric power, steel, chemical fertilizers, cement, and textiles. Nonetheless, it must be borne in mind that the original output targets were overly ambitious and that, targets aside, North Korea's productive capacity in the preceding items is quite impressive. The per capita output level of key industrial outputs—such as "1,184 kilowatt hours of electricity, 1,975 kilograms of coal, 158 kilograms of steel"—in 1970 was an achievement of no mean proportions.[32]

Although North Korea announced in September 1975 that it had fulfilled its Six-Year Plan (1971–1976) sixteen months ahead of schedule—in commemoration of the thirtieth anniversary of the founding of the Workers' Party of Korea (WPK) on October 10, 1975— its failure to publish specific output figures suggested the persistence of bottlenecks. Even in terms of its published ratios and percentages, the targets for such items as steel, cement, pig iron, and granulated iron still remained to be fulfilled.[33] In fact, Pyongyang designated 1976 as the "year of readjustment" during which "the central task for socialist economic construction" would be the fulfillment of the un-

30. Chung, *The North Korean Economy*, p. 145.
31. Chung, "North Korea's Development Strategy," p. 189.
32. Ibid., pp. 189–190.
33. *Pyongyang Times*, September 27, 1975.

fulfilled targets of the Six-Year Plan. Kim Il Sung declared in January 1977 that all the targets of the Six-Year Plan had been "completely fulfilled."[34] But, once again, the new year was designated as the "year of readjustment" (*wanch'ung ŭi hae*) during which North Korea would try to "ease the strains created in certain economic sectors in the course of implementing the Six-Year Plan and to make preparations for launching a new long-term plan."[35]

The most telling sign of North Korea's economic problems was its widely publicized inability to repay its trade debts. As table 5 shows, North Korea had incurred trade deficits for ten consecutive years since 1968; its total debts to trading partners were estimated in late 1976 at about $1,800 million, of which about $1,000 million was owed to Western European nations and Japan. About $300 million was believed to be overdue as of 1977.[36]

The genesis of Pyongyang's payment problem may be traced to its decision in 1972 to go on "its first international buying spree," accumulating between 1972 and 1975 "a trade deficit of about US$1,300 million with non-Communist countries and US$700 million with communist nations."[37] Pyongyang's purchases included "a complete French petrochemical complex, one of the world's largest cement plants, a large fertilizer plant, Japanese textile factories and steelmaking equipment."[38] According to Japanese analysts, the decision stemmed from a wholesale revision of the Six-Year Plan (1971–1976), which in turn was stimulated by the North Koreans' opportunity during their dialogue with South Koreans in mid 1972 to observe firsthand the vigor and scale of South Korea's economic growth. Determined not to be outdone by Seoul in the field of economic competition, Pyongyang apparently decided to step up the scale and pace of its industrialization program and began to import large quantities of plants and heavy machinery from the West and Japan on credit.[39]

The first blow to North Korea's balance of payment position came on the heels of the Arab oil embargo and the subsequent quadrupling of crude oil prices. However, the impact of the oil crisis on Pyongyang appears to have been substantially cushioned by the

34. *Kŭlloja* (Pyongyang), January 1977, p. 1.
35. Ibid., p. 4.
36. "North Korea," *Asia 1977 Yearbook* (Hong Kong: Far Eastern Economic Review, 1977), p. 15.
37. Ibid. Note that this estimate is inconsistent with the data in table 5, which show that the total deficit in North Korea's balance of trade in the 1972–1975 period is $1,467 million. There is no way of knowing which of the two conflicting sets of estimates is closer to the truth.
38. *New York Times*, August 8, 1975, a dispatch from Hong Kong by Fox Butterfield.
39. *Shūkan Asahi* (Tokyo), October 15, 1976, pp. 24–26.

TABLE 5 · North Korea's Foreign Trade Estimates[a] (in Million US Dollars)

Year	Exports (X)	Imports (M)	Trade Balance (X − M)	Total Value (X + M)
1949	76.3	106.0	−29.7	182.3
1953	31.0	42.0	−11.0	73.0
1956	65.8	74.5	−8.7	140.3
1959	113.0	235.0	−122.0	348.0
1960	154.0	166.0	−12.0	320.0
1961	160.0	166.4	−6.4	326.4
1962	224.0	128.5	+95.5	352.5
1963	190.7	230.1	−39.4	420.8
1964	193.4	222.2	−28.8	415.6
1965	208.3	232.8	−24.5	441.1
1966	244.2	219.2	+25.0	463.4
1967	260.2	239.8	+30.4	500.0
1968	255.5	308.5	−53.0	564.0
1969	278.0	394.0	−116.0	672.0
1970	310.4	385.7	−75.3	696.1
1971	315.2 (68.4)	574.3 (64.3)	−259.1 (+4.1)	889.5 (132.7)
1972	401.6 (85.1)	651.4 (161.0)	−249.8 (−75.9)	1,053.0 (246.1)
1973	528.6 (139.9)	842.3 (328.7)	−313.7 (−188.8)	1,370.9 (468.6)
1974	683.9 (266.5)	1,312.1 (783.6)	−628.2 (−517.1)	1,996.0 (1,050.1)
1975	806.8 (325.6)	1,082.2 (545.6)	−275.4 (−220.0)	1,889.0 (871.2)
1976	627.3 (222.7)	1,004.8 (475.6)	−377.5 (−252.9)	1,632.1 (698.3)
1977	803.5 (339.3)	840.2 (378.1)	−36.7 (−38.8)	1,643.7 (717.4)
1978	1,246.2 (575.8)	1,047.8 (461.6)	+198.4 (+114.2)	2,294.0 (1,037.4)
1979	1,552.9 (775.8)	1,336.9 (624.9)	+216.0 (+150.9)	2,889.8 (1,400.7)

SOURCES: The data for 1949–1956 and 1960–1967 are from Joseph S. Chung, *The North Korean Economy: Structure and Development* (Stanford: Hoover Institution Press, 1973), p. 105. The data for 1959 and 1968–1970 are adapted from Pong S. Lee, "Patterns of Economic Development: A Comparative Study of North and South Korea," paper presented to the workshop on comparative study of North and South Korea, January 16–17, 1976, San Juan, Puerto Rico. The data for 1971–1979 are based on Lee Hong-youn, "Structure and Prospect of North Korean Trade," *Vantage Point* (Seoul) 4, 9 (September 1981): 1–13. Lee Hong-youn's sources are International Monetary Fund, *Direction of Trade*, Annual 1980; Naeoe Press, August 20, 1980; and U.N. Commodity Trade Statistics.

[a] Figures in parentheses refer to non-Communist trade.

friendly gesture of Beijing, which reportedly charged its neighbor the "friendship price" of $4.50 per barrel for its oil from 1975 to 1979.[40] The energy crisis and the worldwide inflation have also raised the prices of the other items that North Korea imports from the rest of

40. China reportedly sold the following quantities of oil to North Korea in the 1975–1979 period. 1975: 18,000 barrels per day (bpd), 1976: 18,000 bpd, 1977: 8,000 bpd, 1978: 20,000 bpd, 1979: 20,000 bpd. The price charged was US $4.50 per barrel

the world, while the prices of North Korea's major export items have continued to decline.[41] In an apparent effort to alleviate its balance of payment problem, North Korea "reportedly began to renege on deliveries of [its] metal exports—zinc, magnesium, gold, copper and tungsten—in hopes that world prices would rise. But the market fell instead, and Pyongyang was left with large stockpiles."[42]

North Korea's failure to pay its trade bills resulted in a sharp downgrading of its international credit rating. Japan, Sweden, and West Germany "suspended the issuing of export insurance on deals with Pyongyang."[43] North Korea acknowledged the existence of its payment problem in July 1975, but called it a "temporary phenomenon" caused by bottlenecks in international maritime shipping: North Korea's difficulty in chartering freighters allegedly led to delays in its delivery of export commodities, which in turn led to temporary decline in export revenues.[44] In June 1977 President Kim Il Sung repeated the preceding explanation of the causes of Pyongyang's international payment problems but added an additional factor—"the economic difficulties of the advanced capitalist countries of the West caused by the fuel crisis." In his words, "they are unable to purchase our goods.... So we are taking economic measures to produce ... goods [that] the Western countries can purchase even under the present conditions."[45]

In December 1976 North Korea and the Japan-[North] Korea Trade Association reached an agreement whereby North Korea "pledged to pay 2.6 billion yen in interest on overdue settlements every three months" beginning in 1977 and to begin repayment of debts per se (principal) in 1978. However, North Korea reportedly "paid only about 600 million yen in interest in all of 1977" and requested a three-year extension of the starting date for repayment of the principal debts.[46]

As if to underscore the seriousness of Pyongyang's foreign exchange problems, North Korean diplomats—in fact, all the diplo-

---

throughout this period. *Petroleum Economist*, July, 1980, p. 293. I am grateful to Professor Chae-Jin Lee of the University of Kansas for sharing the preceding information with me.

41. Susumu Awanohara, "North Korea: Deeper in Debt," *Far Eastern Economic Review*, June 6, 1975, p. 52.

42. *New York Times*, August 8, 1975.

43. Ibid.

44. This explanation was offered by Kim Yong Nam, the WPK's secretary in charge of international affairs, to a Japanese Liberal-Democratic party delegation visiting North Korea. *Kita Chōsen kenkyū* 2, 14 (July 1975): 24–26.

45. *Pyongyang Times*, July 23, 1977. Kim made these remarks in an interview with Andre Fontaine of *Le Monde* in Pyongyang on June 20, 1977.

46. *Hapdong News Agency*, Tokyo, January 11, 1978, as monitored by FBIS; *Kita Chōsen kenkyū* 4, 44 (February 1978): 53.

matic staffs of the DPRK embassies—were expelled from Denmark, Norway, and Finland in October 1976 on charges of having abused their diplomatic privileges by engaging in illegal imports and black market sales of narcotics, liquor, and cigarettes. Additionally, five North Korean diplomats, including an ambassador, left Sweden voluntarily amid their host government's investigation of their suspected involvement in similar activities. Given the nature of North Korean society, it seems highly improbable that the alleged acts were perpetrated to enrich the pockets of the individual diplomats. That they were apparently committed on a massive scale simultaneously in all of the Scandinavian countries strongly suggests that they either had originated from, or had been cleared by, the higher authorities in Pyongyang.[47]

In June 1981 it was reported in the Western press that North Korea has "quietly sounded out several companies believed to be French and West German, to see if they would be interested in establishing mineral-processing plants in North Korea in return for a portion of the output." If such joint ventures should materialize, that would signal a major departure from Pyongyang's vaunted policy of *chuch'e* in economic construction. The move was interpreted by Western observers as "an attempt by Pyongyang to resume the inflow of foreign plant it began in the early 1970s and which led directly to its still-unresolved debt problems. . . ." Pyongyang's debts to "45 Japanese banks and traders totalling around Y120 billion (US$534 million) were rescheduled—over 10 years—in 1979," but in July 1980, "the Japan-North Korean Trade Association reported that Pyongyang had been unable to make an Y8 billion payment on time." In June 1981 banking sources in London reported that "North Korea has failed for the past eight or nine months to make payments on some Deutschemarks 650 million (US$272 million) of refinanced debt."[48]

Aside from the fact that North Korea has been incurring deficits in its balance of trade for all but two of the past ten years or so, only about 40 percent of its export earnings are believed to be in hard currency. For the "major portion [of its exports] goes to communist countries with which it deals on a barter basis." "Based on the latest trade figures, and assuming its exports to noncommunist countries grow by the 17.5% a year average it forecasts for total trade during the 1980s, North Korea faces a debt-service ratio on its hard-currency export earnings of 30–35% for the next four years."[49]

47. For AP, UPI, AFP, and Reuter dispatches on the incidents, see *Korea Herald*, October 17–27, 1976.
48. Ron Richardson, "Breaking the Shell," *Far Eastern Economic Review*, June 26, 1981, p. 72.
49. Ibid. It should be noted that the trade data Richardson presents, which are estimates by the US Central Intelligence Agency, do not agree with those given in

North Korea's abundant mineral resources are one bright spot on the horizon: "It is the world's largest producer of magnesite, the main ore of magnesium, and accounts for 57% of world tungsten output. Both metals are keenly sought after for high-technology alloys. In addition, North Korea is a significant producer of lead, zinc and graphite and is one of the leading miners of anthracite or hard coal."[50]

Against this background, North Korea has stepped up its efforts to expand foreign trade. President Kim Il Sung stressed in his main report to the Sixth Congress of the WPK in October 1980 that foreign trade must be developed quickly, setting the specific target of a 4.2-fold increase in export volume by 1989. He underlined the importance of diversification and credibility (*sin'yong che'il chuŭi wonch'ik*): North Korea, he said, should expand trade with socialist countries, Third World countries, nonaligned countries, and other countries; in all sectors of the North Korean economy priority should be given to the production of export goods, to the upgrading of their quality, and to the keeping of their delivery dates without fail.[51]

While the precise details of North Korea's trade are elusive (see table 5 for rough estimates), it appears that the Soviet Union has thus far been Pyongyang's most important trading partner, although its relative importance has been gradually declining. In 1960, for example, the Soviet Union accounted for 82 percent of North Korean exports to foreign countries and 72 percent of its total imports. By 1970 Moscow's share of North Korea's foreign trade (exports and imports combined) had dropped to 52 percent. In the same year Beijing's

---

table 5. The US CIA estimates, for example, that North Korea incurred a deficit of $30 million in 1979, whereas table 5 shows a surplus of $216 million.

50. Ibid., p. 73.

51. Kim Il Sung, *Chosŏn Nodong-dang che yukch'a taehoe esŏ han chung'ang wiwonhoe saŏp ch'onghwa pogo* [Report to the Sixth Congress of the Workers' Party of Korea on the Work of the Central Committee] (Pyongyang: Samhak-sa, 1980), pp. 62–63. It is important to point out that this was by no means the first time that Kim Il Sung emphasized the importance of foreign trade for North Korea. In February 1970 Kim urged workers in local industry to increase the production of exportable consumer goods at the rate of 10 percent per annum for the next five years; he even proposed the establishment of an import-export agency in *each province*. In August 1973, he stressed the importance of earning foreign currency, which he said North Korea urgently needed to purchase modern equipment from abroad; he suggested a stepped-up breeding of silk worms as a source of foreign exchange earnings. In March 1975 he underscored the need to expand trade again, saying that North Korea should diversify its trading partners. He urged the upgrading of the quality of North Korean products sold abroad, strict adherence to contracts (*sinyong cheil chuŭi*), and effective use of ships hired by the DPRK Ministry of Trade. Finally, Kim mentioned the importance of expanding foreign trade again in his new year messages in 1979 and 1980. See Kim Il Sung, *Selected Works*, vol. 5 (Pyongyang: Foreign Languages Publishing House, 1972), pp. 378–379; *Kim Il-sŏng chŏjak sŏnjip* [Selected Works of Kim Il Sung], vol. 6 (Pyongyang: Inmin Ch'ulp'ansa, 1974), p. 266; ibid., vol. 7 (Pyongyang: Han'yang Ch'ulp'ansa, 1979), pp. 214–215; *Nodong sinmun*, January 1, 1979 and January 1, 1980.

share of North Korea's trade was 14 percent, Eastern European countries' 13 percent, Japan's 8 percent, and Western European countries' 6 percent. By 1974 the picture had changed dramatically, with non-Communist countries accounting for more than half of North Korea's foreign trade volume. Insofar as individual countries were concerned, the Soviet Union still led the list of Pyongyang's trading partners with a 22 percent share in the latter's worldwide trade volume, followed by Japan (18 percent) and the PRC (14 percent). As of 1975, the ranking of Pyongyang's major trading partners was as follows: the Soviet Union (25 percent), the PRC (18 percent), and Japan (13 percent).[52] Although complete data are not available, it appears that the Soviet Union continued to be Pyongyang's number one trading partner, with Japan trailing behind it, at the end of 1979. The total trade volume between North Korea and the Soviet Union in 1979 appeared to be around $771 million, while that between North Korea and Japan in the same year was $436 million.[53]

In 1980 the Soviet exports to North Korea reportedly reached $436.2 million, while its imports from North Korea were valued at $430.6 million.[54] A Soviet expert on the North Korean economy, who was interviewed by Chae-Jin Lee in Moscow in October 1981, estimated that the Soviet share of the total North Korean trade in 1980 was about 30 percent, as compared with China's share of 21 percent and Japan's share of 18 percent. He estimated that the corresponding figures for 1981 were about 32 percent for the Soviet Union, 17 percent for China, and 19 percent for Japan. He also told Lee that in 1981 the Soviet Union agreed to reschedule loan repayments due (400 million rubles or about $560 million) and provided new credits of 170 million rubles ($236 million) to North Korea.[55]

---

52. The 1960 figures are based on Pong S. Lee, "Patterns of Economic Development: A Comparative Study of North and South Korea," paper presented to the workshop on comparative study of North and South Korea, Janaury 16–17, 1976, San Juan, Puerto Rico; the remainder were obtained by the author from the US Department of State during his week-long visit there as a "Scholar-Diplomat" in June 1977.

53. The former figure was arrived at in the following manner: According to a Soviet Foreign Trade Ministry publication (*Vnecinaya Torgovlya*, January 1980), the value of commodities traded between Moscow and Pyongyang in the first nine months of 1979 was 352.5 million rubles. Multiplying this figure by twelve-ninths, we get 470 million rubles—the estimated total for the entire year. Converting this into dollars, using the official exchange rate of $1=0.661 rubles, we get $711 million. The figure for Japan-North Korea trade was provided by the Finance Ministry of the Japanese Government. *Kita Chōsen kenkyū* 6, 68 (February 1980): 53–54 and ibid. 70 (May 1980): 28.

54. *Far Eastern Economic Review*, June 19, 1981, p. 60. In the first eleven months of 1980, Japan exported to North Korea $340 million worth of goods, while importing from North Korea $171 million worth of merchandise. *Korea Herald*, January 8, 1981.

55. Chae-Jin Lee, "Economic Policy and Living Conditions in North Korea," a chapter in a book on North Korea being edited jointly by C. I. Eugene Kim and B. C. Koh.

In a study published in January 1978, the National Assessment Center of the US Central Intelligence Agency noted that "while North Korea's real GNP was doubling between 1965 and 1976, real GNP in the South more than tripled" and projected "the economic gap in South Korea's favor" to "widen substantially over the next five years."[56] The study cited three principal reasons for "the South's overall edge in economic performance during the past decade": (1) "the faster growth in labor productivity stemming in large part from the differences in education and training"; (2) "P'yongyang's heavy defense burden"; and (3) "a higher return on industrial investment" in the South. With respect to the first factor, the study suggested that a heavy emphasis on political indoctrination in North Korean schools may have adversely affected the level of technical expertise. With respect to the second factor, the study pointed to North Korea's annual allocation of "an estimated 15 to 20 percent of its GNP" to defense; the estimate that "about 12 percent of North Korea's males of military age (17 to 49) are in the regular armed service, a level exceeded only by Israel"; and "a high-cost underground construction program designed to protect important industrial and military installations." Finally, the study pointed out that while both Koreas have managed to generate large sums for productive investments in industry, "Pyongyang has not allocated these funds efficiently." By contrast, Seoul "has used these funds productively. Its incremental capital-to-output ratio of 2.2 has been among the lowest in the world."[57]

Some clues to the principal bottlenecks in the North Korean economy could be gleaned from Kim Il Sung's own analysis of the economic problems faced by his country. In his New Year's message in January 1977, Kim underlined the importance of easing "temporary strains" in the economy, which were found in five interrelated areas—transportation, mining, electric power, agriculture, and guidance and management. The "year of readjustment" would deal with these problems with the aim of paving the way for a new long-term economic plan.[58]

The crux of the transportation problem lay in the failure of North Korea's transportation capacity to keep pace with the growing demands of industrialization. Since raw materials and other factors of production could not be transported in timely fashion from their places of origin to factories, the latter could not be run at full capacity. To make the matter worse, mining industries lagged behind pro-

56. US Central Intelligence Agency, National Foreign Assessment Center, *Korea: The Economic Race Between the North and the South* (January 1978), p. i.
57. Ibid., pp. i–ii.
58. The following three paragraphs are adapted from B. C. Koh, "North Korea in 1977: Year of 'Readjustment,'" *Asian Survey* 18, 1 (January 1978): 36–37.

cessing industries. In short, not only did the supply of coal, iron, and nonferrous ores fall short of the demands of North Korea's processing industries, but what was available was not being distributed promptly due to serious bottlenecks in North Korea's transportation network.

There was also a serious shortage of electric power. The available supply of electric power failed to keep pace with the rapidly increasing demands of industrialization. A major contributing factor was a severe drought, which hampered the operation of hydroelectric power stations—believed to account for two-thirds of electricity generated in the country. Additionally, the problems in mining and transportation adversely affected the operation of thermal power (steam power) stations as well.

Another problem had to do with agricultural production. The drought meant a sharp decline in the supply of water, a vital ingredient of agricultural production, while the limited supply as well as topography of cultivable land impeded North Korea's efforts to "scale the height of ten million tons of grain production in the near future." Finally, there were signs that the North Korean economy was plagued by poor guidance and management by cadres, that machinery and equipment were poorly maintained, and that measures to economize on fuel, raw materials, and other materials were inadequate.

Although Kim Il Sung reported in January 1978 that the "temporary strains" in the economy had been "completely eased" thanks to the heroic efforts of the workers in the various branches of the economy, he continued to lay emphasis on mining, transportation, agriculture, and guidance work. He noted in particular that the main target of the second Seven-Year Plan (1978–1984) would be the mining industry. In his words, "only when this industry is kept definitely ahead of other branches, will it be possible to successfully solve the question of fuel and power, feed the processing industries with enough raw materials, and largely expand the sources of foreign currency."[59]

The same set of priorities was enunciated in Kim's New Year's message in 1979. One noteworthy feature was his special emphasis on foreign trade. Noting that both North Korea's expanded foreign relations and the enlarged scale of its economy called for the development of foreign trade, Kim said that North Korea "should give priority to the production of export goods in all sectors of the people's economy, should improve their quality, and [should] deliver them as scheduled without fail." He also stressed the triple goals of *"chuch'e-orientation, modernization, and science-orientation"* (*chuch'e-hwa*,

59. See the text of Kim's new year address in *Kŭlloja*, January 1978, pp. 2–6.

hyŏndae-hwa, kwahak-hwa) in economic construction. By *chuch'e*-orientation is meant the emphasis on self-reliance, for example, making full use of domestic raw materials in all branches of the economy. By "modernization" is meant the "struggle to turn backward technology into modern technology." Finally, "science-orientation" entails an all-out effort to develop science and technology in all sectors of the economy, strengthen scientific research, and encourage innovations in technology.[60]

In January 1980, Kim Il Sung reported that great progress had been made in North Korea's mining industry, transportation sector, foreign trade, and agriculture. The steps taken included expansion and modernization of coal and other mines, further electrification of railways, expansion of ports, and improving the organization and efficiency of transport facilities. The volume of North Korean exports increased by 30 percent over the previous year, and the goal of producing nine million tons of grain was attained, according to Kim. Overall, the total value of industrial output was said to have increased by 15 percent over the previous year. He also reported that North Korea's "per capita national income" in 1979 was $1,920.[61]

Hints of continuing difficulties, however, were contained in Kim's report:

> The central task of socialist economic construction this year [1980] is to bring about a radical progress by *normalizing production* and carrying out the technical revolution briskly in all its spheres.
> We must work hard to normalize production in all branches of the national economy.
> At present our country has vast productive potentials. *If* we operate all our factories and enterprises at full capacity and normalize production on a high level, we will be able to increase

---

60. *Nodong sinmun*, January 1, 1979.

61. Ibid., January 1, 1980. This figure, it should be noted, is higher than the official figure for South Korea's per capita GNP in 1979—$1,624. The ROK National Unification Board in July 1980 estimated North Korea's per capita GNP in 1979 at $719. North Korea's GNP in the same year was given as $12,510 million, as opposed to South Korea's GNP of $61,060 million. The grain output figure given by the board was also markedly lower than the official North Korean figure: 4,797,000 tons. *Hapdong News Agency*, Seoul, July 31, 1980, as monitored by FBIS. Some of the discrepancy between the South Korean estimate of North Korea's grain output and North Korea's own figure may be attributable to North Korea's practice of reporting the figure for unhulled grains. When hulled and dried, the weight of grain drops by 25 percent or more. With respect to North Korea's per capita GNP, the impression I obtained during my 1981 trip is that Kim's figure is greatly exaggerated. There is simply too wide a gap between $1,920 and the average annual income of North Korean workers—about $540 in 1981.

production considerably and make our people still better off with the existing economic foundation.

In order to carry on production rhythmically, we must thoroughly implement the party's policy of keeping the mining industries ahead of the manufacturing industries. Only when the mining industries keep definitely ahead is it possible to solve fuel and power problems successfully, supply the manufacturing industries with sufficient raw materials and greatly expand the sources of foreign currency.[62]

From the above, one can safely infer that production was not normal, that factories and enterprises were operating at below capacity, that the mining industries still lagged behind the manufacturing industries, and that the fuel and power problems had yet to be solved. Finally, Kim called it "imperative to strengthen the ideological struggle against conservatism, passiveness, and fear of technology, enhance the role of scientists and technicians and carry on a vigorous technical innovation drive among the producer masses."[63] This is a thinly veiled admission that the problems of bureaucratism, apathy, and lethargy continued to plague the North Korean economy.

Later in the year, however, Kim Il Sung sounded a more optimistic note. In his report to the Sixth Congress of the WPK on October 10, Kim gave a glowing account of North Korea's accomplishments in all domains and then unveiled the goals of the North Korean economy during the decade of the 1980s. The last column of table 6 presents all but one of the targets Kim Il Sung set for 1989: "100,000 million kwh of electricity, 120 million tons of coal, 15 million tons of steel, 1.5 million tons of nonferrous metals, 20 million tons of cement, 7 million tons of chemical fertilizers, 1,500 million metres of fabrics, 5 million tons of sea foods, and 15 million tons of grain." Additionally, Kim enunciated the goal of reclaiming 300,000 *chŏngbo* (hectares) of tideland and acquiring 200,000 *chŏngbo* of new land. When all of these objectives are attained, Kim said, "the total annual industrial output value at the end of the 1980s will be 3.1 times greater than the present figure or 1,000 times as much as in 1946." North Korea, in Kim's words, "will proudly take its place among the nations leading the world in economic progress." He expressed confidence that the goals would be attained, citing North Korea's already solid economic foundations, "abundant natural wealth," "unlimited scientific and technological resources," "millions of working people reared and tempered

---

62. *Korean Central News Agency* (KCNA), Pyongyang, January 1, 1980, as monitored by FBIS. Emphasis added.

63. Ibid.

TABLE 6 · Selected Indicators of the North Korean Economy

Item	Unit	1970	1976	1984[a]	1989[b]
National income	1946=100	1,414	2,545[c]	4,836	
Gross value of industrial output	1946=100	7,130	17,634	38,795	100,000
Electric power	billion kwh	16.5	29.7	60.0	100
Coal	million ton	27.5	55.0	80.0	120
Pig and granulated iron	1,000 ton	1,900	3,200	7,000	
Steel	1,000 ton	2,200	4,000	8,000	15,000
Metal cutting machines	—	12,500	30,000	50,000	
Tractors (15 hp)	—	17,100	21,210	45,000	
Chemical fertilizers	1,000 ton	1,500	3,000	4,800	7,000
Cement	1,000 ton	4,000	8,000	13,000	20,000
Nonferrous metals	1,000 ton				1,500
Textiles	million meters	400	580	800	1,500
Marine products	1,000 ton	1,140	1,600	3,500	5,000
Grains	1,000 ton	5,000	8,000	10,000	15,000

SOURCES: Joseph S. Chung, "Economic Planning in North Korea: Shifting Goals, Management, and Performance," paper presented to the Conference on North Korea, cosponsored by the Korean Association of Communist Studies and the Institute of East Asian Studies, University of California, Berkeley, February 23–28, 1981. Kim Il Sung, *Report to the Sixth Congress of the Workers' Party of Korea on the Work of the Central Committee* (Pyongyang: Foreign Languages Publishing House, 1980), pp. 49–59.

[a] Figures in this column represent the targets of North Korea's Second Seven-Year Plan (1978–1984). Although both low and high targets were indicated for electric power, coal, iron, steel, and cement, only high targets are presented here.

[b] Figures in this column represent the targets unveiled by President Kim Il Sung at the Sixth Congress of the Workers' Party of Korea in October 1980.

[c] Estimate based on the target of the Six-Year Plan (1971–1976).

in practical work to build socialism," "a big contingent of talented scientists and technicians," and "the economic leadership personnel equipped with rich experience and good executive ability."[64]

A recurrent emphasis on the need to normalize production in

64. Kim Il Sung, *Report to the Sixth Congress of the Workers' Party of Korea on the Work of the Central Committee* (Pyongyang: Foreign Languages Publishing House, 1980), pp. 50–51 and 54.

Kim's New Year's messages in 1981 and in 1982 suggested the persistence of bottlenecks. In the 1981 message Kim also reiterated the need to "implement thoroughly the party's policy of keeping extractive industries ahead of manufacturing industries." He also underscored (1) the need to expand power-generating capacity; (2) the importance of improving organization and guidance in transportation, of firmly establishing discipline and order in transportation work, and of transporting equipment and materials in factories and enterprises on time; and (3) the problem of "regularizing and standardizing enterprise management" and enforcing responsibility in economic guidance work.[65]

In the 1982 message, Kim said: "in all fields and all units of the national economy we should put production on a high, normal basis through a powerful mass technical innovation movement and a meticulous organization of economic work, and fulfil the State plans without fail daily, monthly, quarterly, and in all indices." He laid a particular emphasis on the implementation of "four nature-remaking tasks—tideland reclamation, cultivation of new land and construction of the Nampo lock gate and the Taechon power station."[66] In sum, while North Korea's achievements in economic construction are considerable, it has yet to overcome a number of hurdles.

MILITARY POWER

Although, from a logical point of view, a nation's economic capability constitutes the essential underpinnings of its military capability, in reality the relationship between a nation's economic and military power is seldom linear. Perceived threats to its security, availability of external aid, willingness and ability to pay the opportunity costs of military buildup, and other factors may lead a nation to maintain a military arsenal that is in marked disproportion to its economic capability. Both Koreas appear to exemplify such an anomalous situation. It must quickly be added, however, that a steady growth in economic power has enabled both Seoul and Pyongyang to go a long way toward the realization of their common goal of military self-sufficiency.

A narrow peninsula (600 miles long and 100-150 miles wide) not

---

65. Kim Il Sung, *Sinnyŏn-sa* [New Year Address], 1981 (Pyongyang: Samhaksa, 1981), pp. 7–10.

66. "New Year Address by the Great Leader Kim Il Sung, General Secretary of the Central Committee of the Workers' Party of Korea, President of the Democratic Peo-

much larger than the state of Minnesota, Korea has one of the largest concentrations of combat-ready soldiers in the world. As table 7 shows, nearly 1.4 million soldiers on active duty, nearly 3,400 medium tanks, over a thousand combat aircraft, and over 600 naval vessels confront each other across the Demilitarized Zone. What is more, there are a sizable number of tactical nuclear weapons in the hands of 38,000 US troops who are stationed in the South. To describe the peninsula as a powder keg, then, would not be an overstatement.

According to the International Institute for Strategic Studies of London, North Korea's military capability as of 1981 included 782,000 persons on active duty in armed forces; 2,500 medium tanks; 4,100 artillery pieces (up to 152 mm); four surface-to-surface missile (SSM) battalions with 39 FROG-5/-7 SSMs; four surface-to-air missile (SAM) brigades with 250 SA-2s in 45 sites; 700 combat aircraft (including 120 MiG-21s and 20 Su-7s); and 516 naval vessels (including 19 submarines). The same institute described South Korea's military capability in 1981 as encompassing 601,600 persons on active duty in armed forces; 860 medium tanks; 2,104 artillery pieces (up to 203 mm); two SSM battalions with 12 *Honest John* SSMs; two SAM brigades with 80 HAWKs and 45 *Nike Herculus* SAMs; 378 combat aircraft (including 54 F-4D/Es and 228 F-5A/B/Es); and 98 naval vessels (including 10 destroyers and 7 frigates).[67]

An assessment of the military balance in the Korean peninsula, however, requires not simply a quantitative comparison of the respective military arsenals of the two Koreas but also a consideration of their qualitative dimensions and, particularly, of the constraints of basic geographical factors. As Ralph N. Clough notes, Korea's rugged terrain sharply limits the mobility of mechanized forces and tanks. It puts a premium on defense, since the would-be aggressor is forced "to concentrate his forces in confined areas where they are highly vulnerable to air attack." Nor is the terrain hospitable to air defense, "for the hills limit the range of radar, making it possible for enemy aircraft in many places to slip in down a valley below and undetected by the radar screens of defensive units." Moreover, Seoul is only 30 miles south of the DMZ, while Pyongyang is 90 miles north of it. This means that the warning time is extremely short, making it "difficult to scramble interceptors in time; thus both sides are vulnerable to preemptive air attacks." Since logistical support will depend heavily on ground transportation, especially the railroad, it can easily be disrupted. All this suggests that in a conventional war, the pivotal

---

ple's Republic of Korea," *Press Release*, DPRK Permanent Observer Mission to the United Nations, New York, January 1, 1982.

67. International Institute for Strategic Studies, *The Military Balance, 1981–1982* (London: IISS, 1981), pp. 82–84.

TABLE 7 · Comparison of Military Strength Between North and South Korea, 1981–1982

Item	North Korea	South Korea	Total	N.K. ÷ S.K.
Population	18,450,000[a]	38,755,000[b]	57,205,000	.48
Total armed forces	782,000	601,600	1,383,600	1.30
Gross National Product (in million US $)	?[c]	61,650[d]		
Defense expenditures (in million US $)	1,505[e]	3,885[f]	5,390	.39
Medium tanks	2,500	860	3,360	2.91
Light tanks	150	—	150	
Armored personnel carriers	1,000	696	1,696	1.44
Guns & howitzers	4,100	2,104	6,204	1.95
Mortars	11,000	5,300	16,300	2.08
Antitank guns & guided weapons	?[g]	180 plus		
Multiple rocket launchers	1,900	?[h]		
Recoilless launchers	1,500	?[i]		
Antiaircraft guns	8,000	66	8,066	121.21
Missiles: SSM	39	12	51	3.25
SAM	250	125	375	2.00
Combat aircraft	700[j]	378[k]	1,078	1.85
Naval vessels	516[l]	98[m]	614	5.27

SOURCES: International Institute for Strategic Studies, *The Military Balance, 1981–1982* (London: IISS, 1981), pp. 82–84; *Korea Newsreview*, Jan. 9, 1982, p. 9 and March 27, 1982, p. 24; *Vantage Point* (Seoul) 5, 3 (March 1982), p. 16.

[a] An estimate based on the number of electoral districts announced in the election for the Seventh Supreme People's Assembly in February 1982. Each of the 615 districts by law represents 30,000 people.

[b] *Korea Newsreview*, March 27, 1982, p. 24. Calculated from the size of the rural population.

[c] The International Institute for Strategic Studies estimated North Korea's 1979 GNP at $14.1 billion. See the citation below.

[d] *Korea Newsreview*, January 9, 1982, p. 9. Based on the exchange rate of 700 won to US $1.00.

[e] See table 8. The exchange rate of 2 won to US $1.00 was used.

[f] See table 9. Based on the exchange rate of 700 won to US $1.00.

[g] An undetermined number of 45mm, 57mm, Type 52 75mm antitank guns and AT-3 *Sagger* antitank guided weapons are in the North Korean inventory.

[h] An undetermined number of M-10 126mm multiple rocket launchers are in the South Korean inventory.

[i] An undetermined number of LAW recoilless launchers are in the South Korean inventory.

[j] Of which 120 are MIG 21s and 20 are SU-7s.

[k] Of which 54 are F4D/Es and 228 are F-5A/B/Es.

[l] Of which 19 are submarines and 94 are landing craft.

[m] Of which 10 are destroyers and 24 are landing craft. There are no submarines in the South Korean navy.

component will be the infantry, provided that "it is adequately backed by mortar and artillery fire and close air support."[68]

Due to its proximity to the DMZ and accessibility from the latter through two North-South corridors, Clough further notes, Seoul is peculiarly vulnerable to "a mass onslaught by North Korean forces"—"a blitzkrieg." An important deterrent is the American military presence, that is, the deployment of the US Second Infantry Division on one of the corridors and the presence of US Air Force and naval units on or near the Korean peninsula.[69] Should the Second Division be withdrawn from South Korea, therefore, it would most probably lead to a significant reduction in America's deterrent power in Korea. In a prolonged war, however, South Korea is likely to enjoy an edge because its population outnumbers that of North Korea by two to one.

Pyongyang's nearly two-to-one advantage over Seoul in the number of combat aircraft must be balanced against qualitative considerations. For example, over 40 percent of North Korea's combat aircraft consists of the outmoded MiG-15s and -17s. As for its more modern aircraft, MiG-19s and Su-7s are believed to be "inferior in air combat" to either F-4Ds or F-5s, both of which are in South Korea's arsenal. Only MiG-21s "are considered roughly equal" to F-5s.[70] When one adds to the above the presence of two US Air Force tactical air wings in South Korea, with F-4Ds, F-4Es, F-16s, and Ov-10s,[71] and the availability of other ground- and carrier-based US combat aircraft in the periphery of Korea,[72] North Korea's advantage in air power is significantly reduced, if it does not evaporate altogether.

Similarly, Pyongyang's five-to-one advantage over Seoul in the number of naval vessels turns out to be illusory. For 318, or 62 per-

68. Ralph N. Clough, *Deterrence and Defense in Korea: The Role of U.S. Forces* (Washington, DC: Brookings Institution, 1976), p. 7.

69. Ibid., pp. 7–8.

70. Ibid., pp. 12–13. In 1982 South Korea was awaiting the delivery of 36 F-16, 36 F-5E, and 32 F-5F fighters purchased from the US. International Institute of Strategic Studies, *The Military Balance, 1981–1982*, p. 84.

71. Lawrence E. Grinter, "South Korea, Military Aid, and US Policy Options," *The National Security Affairs Forum* (Washington, DC: National War College), Spring/Summer, 1975, p. 42. The number of US-owned combat aircraft deployed in South Korea in 1976 was put at sixty. Clough, *Deterrence and Defense in Korea*, p. 18. Seven F-16s were deployed in South Korea in September 1981. By April 1982, a total of 48 F-16s were scheduled to be deployed in lieu of F-4 phantoms. *Korea Herald*, September 15, 1981.

72. The rapidity with which the American air power can be bolstered in South Korea was demonstrated in the wake of the killing of two US Army officers in Panmunjom by North Korean guards in August 1976, when F-4 phantom and F-11 fighter-bombers were deployed from Okinawa and Idaho to Korea, and the aircraft carrier *Midway* was dispatched to Korean waters. In addition, B-52 strategic bombers made daily flights from Guam to Korea. *New York Times*, August 20–23, 1976.

cent, of the ships are fast-attack craft equipped with guns or torpedoes, 94, or 18 percent, are landing craft, and 30 are coastal patrol craft. In tonnage, the ROK Navy has an edge over its adversary to the north. The former has also strengthened its arsenal of antisubmarine patrol aircraft and patrol boats.[73]

Both Korean states have been working toward the goal of self-sufficiency in military matériel and have made notable progress in recent years. Whereas South Korea lacked the facilities and technology for producing even rifles until the early 1970s, by 1978 it had acquired the capability to produce "highly sophisticated long-range missiles and multi-firing rockets." In the same year it also began to produce "M-48A3 and M-48A5 tanks identical in performance to the latest M-60A1 tanks of the US Army." Seoul has begun to "mass-produce such crew-served weapons as mortars of various calibers, recoilless guns, Vulcan anti-aircraft guns and grenade launchers, and various ammunition including mines and grenades." Further, it is "prepared to produce 105 mm and 155 mm caliber guns, 3.5-inch rocket guns and TOW missiles en masse." Additionally, South Korea can and does turn out heavy hardware such as armored equipment, armored personnel carriers, amphibious vehicles, helicopters, and destroyers. In April 1982, ROK President Chun Doo Hwan announced that South Korea's "Air Force will mark an epoch this year by flying the first combat aircraft manufactured by our own hands." The aircraft he referred to is a F-5M fighter-bomber.[74]

Until the mid 1970s North Korea had been considerably ahead of South Korea in the production of weapons. It acquired the capability to produce small arms such as AK automatic rifles and ammunition in the 1950s, and by the 1960s it was mass-producing RPD light machine guns (7.62 mm), KPV heavy machine guns (14.5 mm), 82 mm B-10 recoilless guns, 40 mm grenade launchers, 107 mm rocket launchers, and 14.5 mm antiaircraft machine guns. In the 1970s North Korea began to produce destroyers, submarines, high-speed landing vessels, gunboats, and T-54 and T-55 tanks. It is believed to be capable of producing T-62 tanks and to have even manufactured a few MiG-19 fighter planes "on an experimental basis."[75]

Notwithstanding all this, the importance of military aid and purchases from patron states and allies will most likely be undiminished for both Seoul and Pyongyang. From 1974 to 1978, North

---

73. International Institute for Strategic Studies, *The Military Balance, 1981–1982*, p. 83; *A Handbook of Korea*, 4th edition (Seoul: Korean Overseas Information Service, 1982), pp. 466–467.

74. *A Handbook of Korea*, 4th edition, p. 460; *Korea Herald*, April 9, 1982, international edition.

75. Paek Hwan-gi, "Armament Industry of North Korea (I)," *Vantage Point* 5, 3 (March 1982): 3–6.

Korea imported arms valued at $490 million, of which 45 percent ($220 million) came from the Soviet Union and 39 percent ($190 million) came from the PRC. South Korean arms purchases in the same period amounted to $1,400 million, of which 93 percent ($1,300 million) was supplied by the United States.[76] Given the continuing need for military assistance and purchases, the two Korean states have an added incentive to conduct their diplomacy vis-à-vis the major powers with caution and skill.

Although published statistics on military expenditures are notoriously unreliable, we may nonetheless take note of trends in the defense spending of the two Koreas. Tables 8 and 9 present the relevant figures as revealed in the official budgets of both countries. North Korea's military expenditures began to increase sharply in 1964, surpassing 30 percent of total government spending in 1967. They remained at that level until 1971. During these years North Korea not only stepped up its "defense construction" but also increased its belligerency toward South Korea and the United States. The abortive commando raid on South Korea's presidential mansion in January 1968, the forcible seizure of the US spy ship *Pueblo* in the same month, and the shooting down of the US naval reconnaissance plane EC-121 in April 1969 were among the more dramatic manifestations of Pyongyang's posture and policy in the period. The sharp decline in Pyongyang's defense spending as a proportion of its total government expenditures since 1972 coincided with the advent of the short-lived détente between the two Koreas. The rupture of the North-South dialogue, however, did not result in any appreciable increase in the ratio of North Korea's defense spending to its total budget: it remained at about 16 percent in the 1972–1978 period and began to decline slightly in subsequent years. In absolute terms, however, North Korea's military spending has continued to increase steadily, reaching an estimated one billion dollars in 1976. By 1981 it had reached the $1.5 billion level, and it was expected to surpass $1.6 billion in 1982. Both in per capita terms and in proportion to its Gross National Product, North Korea's military spending appears to be exceedingly high (see table 7).

Meanwhile, the average ratio of South Korea's annual military expenditures to its total government expenditures from 1960 to 1975 was about 28 percent. The ratio increased to 33 percent in 1976 and has been slowly rising ever since. Significantly, however, it was not until 1975 that the absolute amount of Seoul's publicly acknowledged military spending began to rival that of Pyongyang. In 1976, when the

76. US Arms Control and Disarmament Agency, *World Military Expenditures and Arms Transfers, 1969–1978* (Washington, 1980), p. 160.

**TABLE 8 · North Korea's Military Expenditures
(in 10,000 North Korean Won[a])**

Year	Total Government Expenditures (A)	Military Expenditures (B)	B as % of A (C)
1960	196,787	6,100	3.1
1961	233,800	5,917	2.5
1962	272,876	6,163	2.2
1963	302,821	6,359	2.1
1964	341,824	25,637	7.5
1965	347,613	35,109	10.1
1966	357,140	44,643	12.5
1967	394,823	120,026	30.4
1968	481,289	155,938	32.4
1969	504,857	156,506	31.0
1970	508,200	149,412	29.4
1971	630,168	195,982	31.1
1972	738,861	125,606	17.0
1973	831,391	128,034	15.4
1974	967,219	155,722	16.1
1975	1,136,748	186,426	16.4
1976	1,232,550	205,835	16.7
1977	1,334,920	209,582	15.7
1978	1,474,360	234,423	15.9
1979	1,697,260	(256,287)[b]	15.1
1980	1,883,691	(275,019)[b]	14.6
1981	2,033,300	(300,928)[b]	14.8
1982	2,254,600[c]	(326,917)[c]	14.5[c]

SOURCES: *Tong'a yŏn'gam*, 1975 (Seoul: Tong'a Ilbo-sa, 1975), p. 508; *Kita Chōsen kenkyū*, April 1975, p. 23, 26; May 1976, p. 7; May 1977, pp. 8–9; May 1978, pp. 47–48; June 1979, pp. 24–25; May 1980, pp. 5–6; *Vantage Point*, May 1981, p. 14 and April 1982, p. 15. All of these sources use North Korea's official budget reports.

[a] The exchange rate for the North Korean currency in 1972 was estimated by Pong S. Lee to be between 2.26 and 2.57 won to US $1.00 in terms of "purchasing power parity." See his article, "An Estimate of North Korea's National Income," *Asian Survey* 12, 6 (June 1972): 521–525. In August 1981, the official exchange rate quoted in Pyongyang was 2 won to US $1.00.

[b] Since North Korea stopped publishing absolute figures for defense spending in 1979, the numbers in the parentheses were derived from percentages.

[c] Projected, not actual, expenditures.

TABLE 9 · South Korea's Military Expenditures (in Million South Korean Won[a])

Year	Total Government Expenditures (A)	Military Expenditures (B)	B as % of A (C)
1960	41,995	14,707	35.0
1961	57,153	16,599	29.0
1962	88,393	20,474	23.2
1963	72,839	20,479	28.1
1964	75,180	24,926	33.2
1965	93,534	29,874	31.9
1966	140,942	40,542	28.8
1967	180,932	49,553	27.4
1968	262,064	64,708	24.7
1969	370,532	84,382	22.8
1970	441,329	102,335	23.2
1971	546,278	134,738	24.7
1972	701,143	173,909	24.8
1973	651,586	183,468	28.2
1974	1,041,600	294,300	28.3
1975	1,586,931	462,794	29.2
1976	2,258,500	738,100	32.7
1977	2,870,000	984,000	34.3
1978	3,550,046	1,257,813	35.4
1979	4,533,800	1,559,300	34.4
1980	6,466,756	2,315,043	35.8
1981	8,042,086	2,719,352	33.9
1982	9,578,124[b]	3,298,574[b]	34.4

SOURCES: Republic of Korea, Secretariat, Office of the President, *Han'guk kyŏngje ŭi ŏjewa onŭl* (Seoul, 1975), p. 347; *Korea Annual*, 1977 (Seoul: Hapdong News Agency, 1977), p. 110; *Korea Newsreview*, September 24, 1977; December 10, 1977; September 23, 1978; and September 22, 1979; *Korea Herald*, November 30, 1980; *Han'guk ilbo*, December 4, 1981.

[a] The exchange rate for the South Korean currency as quoted by the Bank of Korea fluctuated widely during the 1960–1982 period. For example, the rate between won and US $1.00 was 65.00 in February 1960, 271.50 at the end of 1965, 316.65 at the end of 1970, 398.90 in January 1973, 480.00 in December 1974, 483.93 in December 1979, 662.60 in December 1980, 702.80 in December 1981, and 735.00 in June 1982. See Republic of Korea, Economic Planning Board, *Korea Statistical Yearbook*, 1973 (Seoul, 1973), p. 405; *Tong'a yon'gam*, 1975 (Seoul: Tong'a Ilbo-sa, 1975), p. 363; *Korea Herald*, Dec. 9, 1976; Dec. 30, 1980; Dec. 31, 1981; and June 2, 1982.

[b] Projected, not actual, expenditures.

latter surpassed the billion dollar mark, the former nearly reached one and a half billion dollars. Seoul's defense spending jumped to $2.7 billion in 1978, surpassed $3 billion in 1979, reached $3.7 billion in 1980, and climbed to $3.9 billion in 1981. It is expected to hover around $4.5 billion in 1982.[77] Since South Korea has twice as many people as North Korea and its GNP is probably three or four times that of North Korea, its military spending is slightly greater than that of North Korea in per capita terms but substantially lower in proportion to GNP[78] (see Table 7).

Since both sides probably understate their actual military expenditures in published budget documents, it is possible that the changes revealed in tables 8 and 9 may reflect nothing more than manipulation of official statistics aimed at external consumption. On the other hand, it is most likely that the official figures do not overstate actual expenditures. In sum, the general picture that emerges from a comparison of selected public indicators of military strength in the two Koreas is that neither side possesses any overwhelming superiority over the other: in other words, a rough military balance seems to prevail in the Korean peninsula, a condition that may help explain the fact that, notwithstanding the deep-seated antagonism between the two Korean regimes, a precarious state of relative peace, interspersed with periodic outbursts of violence, has been maintained in the area over the past three decades.

POLITICAL DYNAMICS

The overriding aspect of the political dynamics of the two Koreas is that both have highly centralized political systems in which power is concentrated in the hands of their respective top leaders. Until the death of ROK President Park Chung Hee in October 1979, both could be characterized, at the highest level of abstraction, as essentially one-man dictatorships: Presidents Kim Il Sung and Park Chung Hee alike enjoyed virtually unlimited power as well as indefinite tenure. Kim Il Sung, in power since the founding of the DPRK in September 1948, was unanimously reelected president (*chusŏk*) of the DPRK by

---

77. US Department of State, *Report on Korea, 1980*, March 30, 1981, p. 3; *Han'guk ilbo*, December 4, 1981.

78. In 1981 North Korea's per capita military spending was about $82, while South Korea's was about $100. The proportion of defense spending to GNP was about 6.3 percent for South Korea in the same year. Depending on what kind of estimate of Pyongyang's GNP one uses (e.g., one-third or one-quarter of Seoul's), the corresponding proportion for North Korea ranged from 7.3 percent to 10 percent.

the Sixth Supreme People's Assembly (SPA) in December 1977. He had previously been elected to the newly created post by the Fifth SPA in December 1972. His pre-1972 title had been premier. Kim was unanimously reelected to his third term as president by the Seventh SPA in April 1982.[79]

Meanwhile, Park Chung Hee, who had first seized power in a coup in May 1961, was reelected to his second six-year term as president of the ROK by a near unanimous vote (2,577 in favor, and one invalid vote) of the Second National Council for Unification in July 1978.[80] Neither Kim nor Park had faced any opponent in their respective elections. Park had previously served two four-year terms and a half of his third four-year term as president before drastically changing, under martial law, the rules and structure of South Korea's political system in October 1972, thus paving the way for his continuation in office for an indefinite number of six-year terms.[81]

The assassination of Park on October 26, 1979 by Kim Jae Kyu, director of the ROK Central Intelligence Agency (KCIA), abruptly changed the political landscape in South Korea. Park's immediate successor, Choi Kyu Hah, who was elected president on December 6 by the rubber-stamp electoral college Park had created in October 1972, pledged to work toward the establishment of a new political order, explicitly renouncing any political ambitions on his own part. He pledged to resign from office as soon as the groundwork for transition to democracy had been laid. Before Choi could officially announce the composition of his cabinet, however, Major General Chun Doo Hwan, commander of the Army Security Command, executed what has subsequently proved to be an effective coup d'etat. On December 12, Chun and his associates seized control of the ROK armed forces by arresting General Chung Seung Hwa, Army Chief of Staff and Martial Law Commander, four other generals, and their top aides. A total of 23 persons were officially reported as having been either killed or wounded in the December 12 incident. The official version of the incident implicated the arrested generals in the assassination of Park, but none of them was ever tried. All of them are believed to have been released after Chun's political control was consolidated beyond challenge.

After exercising his power from behind the scenes as the military strongman, Chun gradually took over the formal reins of power from President Choi's government. His first significant step was to

79. *Kita Chōsen kenkyū* 4, 43 (January 1978): 5–6; *Nodong sinmun*, April 6, 1982.
80. *Han'guk ilbo*, July 8, 1978.
81. For a critical analysis of Park's October 1972 "reforms," see B. C. Koh, "*Chuch'esong* in Korean Politics," *Studies in Comparative Communism* 7, 1 and 2 (Spring/Summer 1974): 83–97.

have the government proclaim an expanded emergency martial law on May 17, 1980, invoking the need to bring under control the turmoil that had been created by widespread protest demonstrations by college students throughout the country. The May 17 proclamation not only extended the emergency martial law, which had been in effect since December 27, 1979, to the entire country, including the Cheju Island, but also banned all political activities and tightened up press censorship which had been in effect since December 1979. Finally, the Marital Law Command announced the arrest of twenty-six leading politicians and former government officials on charges of either having amassed wealth through corrupt practices or having abetted and aided student demonstrators. Among those arrested were Kim Jong Pil, who had succeeded Park Chung Hee as president of the ruling Democratic-Republican party and had been widely viewed as a leading contender for the presidency, and Kim Dae Jung, South Korea's most celebrated dissident as well as a potential candidate for the presidency. Whereas Kim Jong Pil, together with others who were accused of illicit financial gains, was later released in exchange for the return of his wealth to the state treasury, Kim Dae Jung was indicted, tried, and convicted by a military court on charges of plotting rebellion and violating the National Security Law, the Anti-Communist Law, the Foreign Exchange Control Law, and Martial Law decrees. He was sentenced to death in September 1980, but the sentence was commuted to life imprisonment in January 1981. It was further reduced to twenty years of imprisonment in March 1982.[82]

The proclamation of the expanded Emergency Martial Law and, particularly, the arrest of Kim Dae Jung helped to touch off massive protest demonstrations in Kwangju, the capital city of Kim Dae Jung's native province in the southwestern part of Korea. Fueled by the brutality of the paratroopers who had been dispatched by the military authorities to suppress them, the demonstrations quickly escalated to an armed insurrection, in which the rebels held complete control of the city for a week. The Martial Law Command reported after the recapture of the city by government troops that a total of 170 persons, including 144 civilians, had been killed during the insurrection. In addition, 380 persons had been wounded, according to the official report. Unofficial estimates of the casualties were much higher.[83]

    82. For an official explanation of Kim Dae Jung's alleged offenses, see *Report on the Investigation of Kim Dae-jung* (Seoul: Korean Overseas Information Service [KOIS], July 1980) and *The Truth About the Attempted Insurrection by Kim Dae-jung and His Followers* (Seoul: KOIS, August 1980). For a critical view of the charges, see *Monthly Review of Korean Affairs* (Arlington, VA: Friends of the Korean People) 2, 8 (August 1980): 1–4. See also *Korea Herald*, March 3, 1982, for the disposition of the case.
    83. The brutality of the South Korean troops in handling Kwangju demonstrators was documented by extensive foreign news coverage of the uprising, including

On May 31, four days after the bloody suppression of the Kwangju uprising, the military strongman of South Korea took another step toward the formal assumption of power. A parallel military government named "Special Committee for National Security Measures" consisting predominantly of generals in the ROK armed forces was set up, and Chun became the chairman of its standing committee. In that capacity, Chun all but replaced President Choi Kyu Hah in running the government. On August 5, Chun had himself promoted to the rank of general, thus adding two stars in the eight months since his December 12, 1979 coup. Within a few days the rigidly controlled press in South Korea began to print numerous articles regarding Chun's qualifications as the leader of a "new era" and, especially, the support Chun allegedly enjoyed among South Korea's principal allies, particularly the United States. On August 13, Kim Yong Sam, president of the opposition New Democratic party, announced his permanent retirement from politics. This meant that all of Chun's principal rivals—the three Kims (Kim Jong Pil, Kim Dae Jung, and Kim Yong Sam)—had been eliminated from the political arena.

On August 16, President Choi Kyu Hah resigned from his office. On August 22, Chun retired from active duty in the ROK Army in preparation for the assumption of the presidency. Five days later, he was elected president by the rubber-stamp electoral college, the National Council for Unification, by a vote of 2,524 to zero, with one invalid vote. It had taken Chun exactly eight and a half months since his coup d'etat to take over complete control of the government both in form and substance. In October, a new constitution was approved by 91.6 percent of voters in a national referendum. Among other

---

vivid scenes shown on major TV network news in the US. The *New York Times* carried gruesome pictures of military brutality on its front pages almost daily; see its May 20–28, 1980 issues. An *Agence France Presse* (AFP) dispatch from Kwangju dated May 29, 1980 had the following description: "Paratroopers attacked the crowd at random, a French missionary told this correspondent [Marie-France Rouze]: 'From the archbishop's offices on the sixth floor of a building I saw them grab seven people including a man in his 30s wearing a light gray suit. I can still see him. They kicked him all over as hard as they could, including twice in the face. Then they abandoned him in a puddle of blood. Ten minutes later, he started to budge. I saw a paratrooper strike him three more times. By the time I went downstairs, they all had been taken away. I also saw them hit a woman of 35 or 40 with a club several times.' The missionary said sobbing nuns telephoned him to say they saw paratroopers strip girl students naked before taking them away by truck. A doctor said the wounded people admitted to Chonnam University hospital had been clubbed, bayonetted, or shot. A man about 39 said he lost his left eye as the result of a blow. A young American woman working for the U.S. Peace Corps (of teachers) said her Korean friends related that the youngest person killed was only four years old, and the oldest, 70." *FBIS Daily Report*, vol. 4, no. 105, May 29, 1980, E2.

things, it provided for indirect election of the president, who would serve a single seven-year term. On February 25, 1981, Chun was reelected president in accordance with the new basic charter. He had received 4,755, or 90.23 percent, of 5,271 electoral votes.[84]

Differences Between the North and the South

Notwithstanding the striking similarity in the structure of power between the two Koreas, there are important differences between their respective political systems, of which a few need to be underscored.

First, unlike the DPRK, which has seen only one ruler throughout three decades of its history, the ROK has experienced four transfers of power in the same period, although two of them were extraconstitutional and violent, and the third was occasioned by the violent death of Park Chung Hee. The fourth, while ostensibly peaceful, was actually based on a military coup. Whether Chun Doo Hwan will honor his pledge to help attain the first peaceful transfer of power in South Korea's political history remains to be seen.

Second, the South Korean people have been exposed to democratic ideals and practice during the past three decades. They have learned and practiced the right of political dissent even at the price of torture and death. Indeed, the resilience of political opposition in South Korea was such that even the harsh oppressive measures that the Park regime had imposed on its populace since October 1972 in the name of "revitalizing reforms" (*yusin*) and national security had failed to quench it.

A third and related difference is that South Korea under Park tolerated token political opposition. Opposition political parties continued to exist, albeit precariously, and feeble voices of dissent were permitted in South Korea's emasculated National Assembly. The chain of events that led to the demise of Park was set off by his attempt to muzzle the leader of the principal opposition party, which in turn touched off violent protest demonstrations in major cities. Park's successor, Chun Doo Hwan, has allowed the formation of political parties. In the 276-seat National Assembly, which came into being in March 1981, Chun's ruling Democratic Justice party controls 151 seats, with the remaining seats divided among five opposition parties and independents.[85]

Symptomatic of the cautious posture of opposition politicians and of their apparent self-censorship are the remarks made by Yu Chi

---

84. *Korea Herald*, February 26, 1981.   85. Ibid., March 27, 1981.

Song, president of the Democratic Korea party, the largest opposition party in the National Assembly. After stating, in talks with the faculty and students of the University of Hawaii in Honolulu on June 23, 1981, that his party was waiting to see whether the Chun Doo Hwan government would implement its pledge to democratize South Korea politics, Yu said:

> Enough legitimacy can be found in the government, in that political parties have been founded, the president has been elected and lawmakers have been chosen under the Constitution adopted in a national referendum.

He noted that the role of the opposition parties in South Korea "is to check and monitor the incumbent government rather than to flaunt differences in ideology and thought, since Korea is a divided country." Asked to comment on the causes of the Kwangju Uprising of May 1980, Yu simply made an oblique comment: "We should realize that confusion will lead to an irrevocable national tragedy, since ours is a divided nation."[86]

As he gained more experience, power, and self-confidence, President Chun began to take a number of measures, many of them largely symbolic, designed to ameliorate the political climate: He met with leaders of all political parties represented in the National Assembly in February and June 1981; exhorted his cabinet ministers to appear before the Assembly to answer questions; went there himself to deliver speeches (something his predecessor Park Chung Hee had not done since 1968); frequently made on-the-spot inspections, both announced and unannounced, of facilities and projects; held "dialogue" with, and even slept in the homes of, "ordinary citizens"; eliminated mandatory uniforms and hair styles for middle and high school students; lifted the midnight-to-4 A.M. curfew which had been in effect throughout South Korea for 36 years; and awarded amnesty or reduced sentences to 2,863 convicts, including 297 political prisoners (not one of the prominent dissidents, however, was released). In reviewing and praising Chun's first year in office as president of the Fifth Republic, South Korea's controlled press nonetheless managed to voice a few muted criticisms. Among the problems that remained to be addressed, according to *Han'guk ilbo*, were the imbalance between rhetoric and concrete action, the climate of distrust (as reflected in the proliferation of "vicious" rumors), and the imbalance between the ruling and opposition parties (a veiled reference to the impotence and ornamental character of opposition parties).[87]

86. Ibid., June 25, 1981.
87. For a series of articles on Chun Doo Hwan's first year in office, see *Han'guk ilbo*, March 3–6, 1982.

The New York Times was more blunt in its appraisal of Chun's first year:

> South Korea remains essentially a one-party state and Mr. Chun has made only modest progress toward his own avowed goal of "democracy." And there is much residual bitterness among those on whom he cracked down hard during his rise to power, particularly in the universities, the press and rival political factions.

It added that Chun's version of democracy calls for "'judicious nurturing of the national strength through dialogue and compromise,' with 'major efforts to insure clean government.' Politicians could interpret this Confucian sentiment as meaning, in essence, 'Follow me.'" The paper also pinpointed Chun's dilemma: "if he eases up he might be forced from power or lose the confidence of the armed forces leaders, his ultimate prop, but if he does not liberalize, resistance may grow underground."[88]

The "climate of distrust" of which *Han'guk ilbo* spoke was further fanned by the eruption of the so-called "curb loan scandal" in May 1982. The scandal involved manipulation of commerical papers, influence peddling, and illegal profiteering by a well-connected couple, Lee Chol Hi and Chang Yong Ja. Lee is former deputy director of the KCIA and former member of the National Assembly, while his wife, Chang, is a sister-in-law of the uncle of Mrs. Chun Doo Hwan. The face value of the commercial papers involved was nearly $1 billion, and the couple was reported to have netted $180 million. A total of 18 persons, including Mrs. Chun's uncle, Lee Kyu Kwang, were arrested, and 11 cabinet members were replaced in connection with the scandal. Given President Chun's repeated emphasis on building a new society free of corruption, this scandal was a particularly embarrassing one. It gravely undermined his credibility and may even have implications for the stability of his regime. It also exposed the vulnerability of South Korea's financial institutions to influence peddling and the fragility of its money markets, both legitimate and underground.[89]

The fourth and final difference between the polities of the North and the South is particularly noteworthy: a personality cult of monumental dimensions towers over the North Korean landscape, before which the exaltation of the late Park Chung Hee on the part of the South Korean people paled into insignificance. The magnitude of the

---

88. Henry Scott Stokes, "South Korea Under Chun: New Vigor But Little Shift Toward Democracy," *New York Times*, March 4, 1982, p. 6.

89. For details on the scandal and its aftermath, see *Han'guk ilbo*, May 10–June 8, 1982; see especially the government report submitted to the National Assembly on May 28, 1982 in ibid., May 31, 1982.

Kim cult and its pervasive influence in North Korean life are truly striking to the visitor to the DPRK. They help make it a unique specimen among the political systems of the contemporary world.[90]

It should be noted that the differences between the internal political dynamics of the two Koreas may be due in part to the different attitudes and behaviors of their respective patron states. That is to say, the resilience of democratic aspirations, the frequency and vigor with which they have surfaced on the South Korean landscape, and the toleration of token opposition by the successive regimes—all of these symptoms are clearly related to the twin facts that Washington has played a major role in indoctrinating the South Korean populace to the virtues of democracy and freedom and that it continues to exert some, albeit diminishing, influence on Seoul's governing elite. President Carter's emphasis on human rights in his foreign policy, for example, coupled with congressional hearings and adverse publicity in the American mass media, must have had some effect in moderating the late President Park's behavior in the domestic arena.

Not to be overlooked is the role of Japan, which not only has managed to nurture and preserve the only democratic government in

---

90. A minor personality cult appeared to be developing in South Korea after Chun Doo Hwan's assumption of the presidency in the summer of 1980. Article after article in the controlled press extolled the virtues of Chun; the government hastily put together a documentary film on "the path of our new leader"; and his new policy lines—notably his massive anticorruption drive and educational reform (e.g., the proposed abolition of college entrance examinations)—and his "democratic style of leadership" were being praised and applauded from all quarters, or so the readers of the controlled press were told. All this could be viewed as a part of Chun's attempt to bolster his legitimacy, given the manner in which he had seized power. Nonetheless, the situation in South Korea is child's play compared to what is happening in North Korea. In the North, it is not simply Kim Il Sung who has been deified and is literally worshipped; his entire clan and immediate family members, with a few notable exceptions, are also idolized. North Korea has advanced the phenomenon of the Kim cult, already unparalleled in political history, to new heights with the appointment of Kim's son, Jong Il, as his "only successor." After elevating the junior Kim to the number two position in the Secretariat of the ruling Workers Party of Korea (WPK), as well as to the fourth position in the WPK Politburo, where he is outranked only by his father and two of Kim Il Sung's aging comrades from the anti-Japanese guerrilla days, and to the third position in the WPK Military Committee at the Sixth Congress of the party in October 1980, Kim Il Sung has launched an intensive indoctrination campaign to legitimize the hereditary succession. All North Korean citizens, with particular emphasis on children and youth, are required to study Kim Jong Il's "thoughts" (*sasang*), "theory" (*iron*), and "virtues" (*tŏksŏng*); and his picture, typically taken with his father, is found in the homes of cadres and schools. The junior Kim is referred to as "the glorious party center" (in public speeches and official publications), "the dear (or beloved) comrade leader" (*ch'inae hanŭn chidoja tongji*), or "the great leader's only successor." I obtained the preceding information during my visit to North Korea from July 14 to August 1, 1981.

East Asia but also remains one of the major centers of political opposition and criticism, on a nongovernmental level, vis-à-vis Seoul.

In contrast, North Korea was not only patterned on the Soviet model of "proletarian dictatorship" and "democratic centralism," but is apparently immune to any external pressure for political liberalization. Nor is there any evidence that either the PRC or the Soviet Union has attempted or has any reason to exert pressure on Pyongyang to change its internal political practices.

In short, while the two Koreas have in common the extraordinary concentration of political power in the hands of their respective rulers, their political experiences have thus far been significantly divergent, most notably in terms of articulating dissenting political views. This suggests that, in terms of political dynamics, the role of counter-elites cannot be brushed aside in South Korea and that its ruling elite operates under a set of internal political constraints that are potentially far more crippling than anything its counterpart in North Korea faces.

5 PSYCHOLOGICAL ENVIRONMENT: ATTITUDINAL PRISM

No matter how important the operational environment may be, it becomes a relevant factor in the formulation of foreign policy only to the extent to which, and in the form in which, it is perceived by the decision-making elite. How the operational environment is actually perceived, therefore, is as crucial as the objective attributes of the environment itself. The lens or screen through which the operational environment is filtered to the elite is conceptualized as an "attitudinal prism," of which three interrelated dimensions will be discussed in this chapter—ideology, historical legacy, and personality predispositions.

IDEOLOGY

There is a dominant ideology that unites the two Koreas, namely, nationalism. Manifested in the Korean people's pride in and devotion to their common ancestral origins, language, and cultural heritage, this attitude is fueled by their historical experiences—particularly their painful and humiliating experiences as a pawn of big-power rivalry and, most recently, as a Japanese colony. The quest for political, economic, and military independence on the part of the two Koreas can be understood largely as an expression of Korean nationalism. So, too, can the oscillating behavior of North Korea vis-à-vis Beijing and Moscow. The continuing salience of national reunification in the language and behavior of Korean politics both at home and abroad likewise bespeaks the potency and hence political utility of nationalistic sentiment.

Let us examine the specific contents of nationalism as articulated by the respective political leaders of the two Koreas. A convenient way of doing this is to focus on *chuch'e*. *Chuch'e sasang* (the ideology of *chuch'e*) has been formally elevated to the official ideology of the DPRK: its new constitution, adopted in December 1972, proclaims that North Korea "is guided in its activity by the Juche [*chuch'e*] idea of the Workers' Party of Korea, a creative application of Marxism-Leninism to the conditions of our country" (Article 4). The concept of *chuch'e* was first articulated by Kim Il Sung in a speech to party propaganda and agitation workers in December 1955. In his words:

> To establish *chuch'e* [self-identity or autonomy] is not to preclude the need to learn from foreign countries, as some of our comrades may erroneously infer through simplistic thinking. Far from it. We must learn good experiences from all socialist countries.
> What is important is to know the purpose of our learning. It is to make good use of advanced experiences of the Soviet Union and other socialist countries.
> . . . Some people say that the Soviet way is good, and others say that the Chinese way is good. But isn't it about time that we created our own way?
> It is absolutely futile to follow the forms of other people without learning the truths of Marxism-Leninism. While steadfastly adhering to the principles of Marxism-Leninism in revolution and construction alike, we must nonetheless creatively apply them to the concrete conditions of our country and to the peculiarities of our people.[1]

Kim went on to say that it would be an error of dogmatism to "mechanically apply the experiences of others without due regard to our country's history, our people's tradition, our realities, and our people's level of commitment." "Marxism-Leninism is not a dogma but a guide to action and a creative theory," he said. As such, its "invincible, great power" will materialize "only when it is creatively applied to the concrete conditions of each country."[2]

After nearly two decades of trying to implement the *chuch'e*

1. Kim Il Sung, *Uri hyŏngmyŏng esŏŭi chuch'e e taehayŏ* [On *Chuch'e* in Our Revolution] (Pyongyang: Chosŏn Nodongdang Ch'ulp'an-sa, 1970), pp. 39–40.
2. Ibid., pp. 40–41.

idea, Kim, in September 1972, summed up its essence to Japanese journalists in these terms:

> In a word, the idea of *chuch'e* means that the masters of revolution and construction are the masses of the people and that they are also the motive force of revolution and construction. (In other words, it is an idea that one is the master of one's own destiny and has the power to shape it oneself.) *We are by no means the first to discover this idea. Anyone who is a Marxist-Leninist thinks this way. I have merely laid a special emphasis on this idea.*[3]

Kim attributed the origins of the *chuch'e* idea in the North Korean context to the need to cope with a unique set of problems for which there were no ready-made answers and said that many of the approaches he used were "original." He cited such examples as the decision "boldly to push ahead with the socialist tranformation of agriculture without waiting first for the realization of industrialization" and the decision not to expropriate the property of middle and small entrepreneurs and rich peasants but to embrace them in cooperatives and remold them along socialist lines. Finally, he stated that *chuch'e* finds expression in "independence [*chaju*] in politics, self-reliance [*charip*] in the economy, and self-defense [*chawi*] in national defense."[4]

Three years later, however, Kim Il Sung introduced new elements in his exposition of *chuch'e*. In a speech commemorating the thirtieth anniversary of the founding of the Workers' Party of Korea on October 9, 1975, Kim said that *chuch'e* was adopted as the "revolutionary line" by "Korea's true Communists" in the early 1930s. He further stated that *chuch'e* was "invented" (*ch'angsi*), developed, and systematized during the "long and hard anti-Japanese revolutionary struggle." As far as can be determined, this was the first time that Kim Il Sung traced the genesis of *chuch'e* to the 1930s and claimed, albeit inferentially, authorship of the idea. Kim further stated that *chuch'e sasang* is based on "the philosophical principle that man is the master of everything and decides everything." Moreover, he went on, it "scientifically clarifies the position and role of man in the world, provides the most correct viewpoint regarding nature and society, and furnishes a powerful weapon for understanding and transforming [*kaejo*] the world." Kim claimed for the idea of *chuch'e* the

---

3. See the lead article on the front page of *Mainichi shimbun*, September 19, 1972 as well as the transcripts of the four-hour interview in ibid., pp. 4–5. The Japanese newsmen were led by Takahashi Takehiko, chief editorial writer for the paper. For the Korean text of the interview, see *Nodong sinmun*, September 19, 1972; for an English version, see *Pyongyang Times*, September 23, 1972. The sentence in parentheses do not appear in the Japanese text. Emphasis has been added by the author.

4. *Mainichi shimbun*, September 19, 1972, pp. 4–5.

status of theory, strategy, and tactic all at the same time. Not only does it provide "correct answers to all problems that arise in revolution and construction," but it also illuminates for the working masses a "fundamental standpoint" (*kŭnbon ipchang*) and a "fundamental method" (*kŭnbon pangbŏp*). The former refers to the attitude of the master and independence in revolution and construction, while the latter refers to the "creative standpoint" that the working masses must adopt in their struggle to transform nature and society.[5]

Given the dynamics of the cult of personality that prevails in North Korea, it was but a short step from Kim's pronouncements given above to the heaping of extravagant praise on *chuch'e* by his propagandists. They called it an "immortal" idea that constitutes the guiding ideology of the new era, the "era of *chuch'e*." They argued that it provides guidance not only to the "revolutionary struggle of the working class" but also to the "great task of the liberation of mankind." In their words, it has "captured the hearts of the revolutionaries and progressive peoples of the entire world"; indeed, its "invention" by Kim Il Sung is said to have marked "a turning point in the history of human ideas." It allegedly "constitutes the highest stage in the development of the revolutionary ideas of the working class."[6]

Then, in his main report to the WPK Sixth Congress in October 1980, Kim Il Sung injected a sense of urgency to the quest for *chuch'e*: he devoted a major portion of his four-hour long speech to the theme "Let Us Model the Entire Society on the Idea of *Chuch'e*" (*On sahoerŭl chuch'e sasanghwa haja*). He defined the task as one of turning all members of the society into Communists of the *chuch'e* type, transforming all facets of life in accordance with the requirements of the *chuch'e* idea, and attaining the complete independence of the working masses. Kim stressed that *chuch'e sasang* is synonymous with a *weltanschauung* (*segyekwan*) that squarely places man in the center of all things and with a theory of revolution that aims at the attainment of independence for the working masses. It in effect provides the key to the conquest of the "ideological and material fortresses of communism"—that is, to the transition from socialism to communism. The conquest of the "ideological fortress of communism" would entail the stepped-up implementation of the three revolutionary lines—ideological, technical, and cultural revolutions; it would also require accelerating the struggle to transform all mem-

5. *Kim Il-sŏng chŏjak sŏnjip*, vol. 7 (Hanyang Ch'ul-p'ansa edition), pp. 234–236.
6. "Kyŏng'ae hanŭn suryŏng Kim Il-sŏng tongjinŭn chuch'e sidaeŭi hyŏngmyŏng sasang ŭl ch'angsi hasin widaehan sasang iron'ga isida" [The Respected and Beloved Leader Comrade Kim Il Sung Is A Great Thinker and Theoretician Who Invented the Revolutionary Idea for the Era of *Chuch'e*], *Kŭlloja*, January, 1976, pp. 18–28.

bers of the society into revolutionaries, proletarians, and intellectuals (*On sahoeŭi hyŏngmyŏng-hwa, nodong kyegŭp-hwa, interi-hwa*). What Kim wants is not only to change the attitude and values of all North Korean citizens so that they all think and act like the masters of revolution but also to raise their level of knowledge, skills, and culture. The conquest of the "material fortress of communism" would necessitate redoubled efforts in economic construction, with particular emphasis on "*chuch'e*-orientation, modernization, and science-orientation" (*chuch'e-hwa, hyŏndae-hwa, kwahak-hwa*) (see chapter 4). Kim also set forth ambitious targets in ten key areas of the North Korean economy for the 1980s (see Table 6 in chapter 4). What is particularly noteworthy is that insofar as Kim Il Sung and North Korea are concerned, *chuch'e* has superceded Marxism-Leninism; in fact, Kim's main report contains not a single reference to the latter.[7]

In sum, *chuch'e* has indeed become the national obsession of North Korea. It is not only a political slogan but also an all-encompassing philosophy of life as well as a guide to practical action. The visitor to North Korea learns that the label *chuch'e* is applied to virtually everything that happens in that country—from agriculture to zoology. While such a preoccupation with *chuch'e* entails certain questionable consequences—such as a propensity toward chauvinism, bragging, and even deception—its tangible results in the areas of economic construction, education, health care, and performing arts are quite impressive.

Since the term *chuch'e* symbolizes the yearning for national pride, self-identity, and independence, its magnetic appeal to Korean political leaders is amply understandable. Inasmuch as Kim Il Sung did not coin the term, the mere fact that he had turned it into his ideological trademark could not and did not reduce its perceived utility as a political symbol to his sworn enemies in South Korea. Indeed, one need not search long to discover that not only its underlying ideas but the term itself were very much in the minds of Park Chung Hee and his colleagues when they executed the historic coup d'etat of May 16, 1961.

Thus, in a book published in February 1962, Park deplored "our lack of national consciousness, an extreme deficiency in the national awareness of the fact that we live together; we die together." He then underscored the importance of "establishing one's ego" saying that the "establishment of the ego means the establishment of independence and spontaneity." He also wrote:

---

7. Kim Il Sung, *Chosŏn Nodongdang cheyukch'a taehoe esŏ han chung'ang wiwonhoe saŏp ch'onghwa pogo*, pp. 31–65. See note 51 in chapter 4.

Now is [the] time for us to take a new view of Korean history. We must grasp the subjectivity [or self-identity, i.e., *chuch'e*] of the Korean nation, restore the spiritual pillar of Korean history and establish a critical but receptive posture for the introduction of foreign culture.[8]

In his first inaugural speech as the duly elected president of the ROK on December 17, 1963, Park said:

In order to carry out a great renovation movement in search of political liberty, economic self-reliance, and social harmony and stability, we must first of all wage a spiritual revolution on the individual level. Every citizen must inculcate in himself an independent *chuch'e* consciousness, firmly establish the spirit of self-reliance and self-help whereby one becomes the master of one's own destiny, and achieve the correct spiritual posture of national self-identity.[9]

Chuch'e or its basic underlying idea subsequently became one of the recurrent themes in Park's speeches. In a Liberation Day address in August 1971, for example, Park once again spoke of the regained "national self-identity," which, in his words, signifies "independence, self-reliance, and self-defense," emphasizing the particular importance of *chuch'e* in times of significant change in big-power relations.[10] But the most significant articulation of *chuch'e* ideology came late in 1972 when the series of traumatic events known as *Siwol Yusin* (officially translated as the "October Revitalizing Reforms") erupted.

The guiding ideology of *Siwol Yusin* was *chuch'e*, as President Park articulated on the occasion of declaring martial law on October 17, 1972, and made more explicit during his press conference on January 12, 1973. The principal theme of his October 17 declaration was that given the profound changes in the internal and, more importantly, the external situation, South Korea had to find its own solutions to its pressing problems—solutions tailored to its own needs and requirements. This entailed a drastic restructuring of political institutions, including a fortiori the jettisoning of a Western-type democracy and its replacement by a "Koreanized democracy." On a more concrete level, the need to carry on the dialogue with North

---

8. Park Chung Hee, *Our Nation's Path* (Seoul: Hollym Corporation, 1962, 1970), pp. 20–21; 28–29; 119.

9. *Minju Konghwadang sanyŏn-sa* [Four-Year History of the Democratic-Republican Party] (Seoul: Minju Konghwadang Kihoek Chosabu, 1967), p. 153.

10. For the text of his speech, in which Park used the term *chuch'e* four times, see *Tong'a ilbo* (Seoul), August 16, 1971.

Korea for the eventual goal of reunification was invoked as the major justification for the perpetuation of his rule, accompanied by a prodigious aggrandizement of formal authority vested in the office of the president.[11]

In his press conference on January 12, 1973, Park specifically stressed the linkage between the "October Revitalizing Reforms" and *chuch'e* ideology. The fundamental objective of the "reforms," he said, "is to achieve both national stability and prosperity and reunification with our own strength and wisdom and on the basis of an accurate awareness of . . . national history." He then added that the "ideology of the October Revitalizing Reforms is identical to that of the May 16 Revolution [i.e., his seizure of power in the May 1961 coup] in that it lays special emphasis on our national self-identity."[12] The renewed emphasis given to *chuch'e* was reflected in the name of the newly created electoral college—*T'ong'il Chuch'e Kungmin Hoeŭi* (officially translated as the National Council for Unification)—which, on December 23, 1972, dutifully elected Park to a new six-year term as president by a vote of 2,357 to 0 with two invalid votes.[13] It was also manifested in the new educational policy of the ROK government, which decreed extensive revisions of all precollegiate textbooks to stress both "*chuch'e* consciousness" and a "correct national viewpoint."

In sum, both Kim Il Sung and Park Chung Hee defined *chuch'e* in terms of Korea's need, and indeed right, to seek its own solutions to its own problems. Both saw *chuch'e* as signifying and necessitating the assertion of Korea's national pride and self-identity. Convinced that a modernizing nation greatly needed a unifying symbol and a guiding ideology, both took steps not only to enshrine the term but to indoctrinate the youth, in their respective domains, to its underlying concepts and values. Finally, both used the term to legitimize, consolidate, and perpetuate their respective political controls. Park's successor, Chun Doo Hwan, has not explicitly embraced *chuch'e* ideology. He has nonetheless laid a great deal of emphasis on the need to find Korean solutions to Korean problems, to shape the destiny of the Korean people with their own hands, and to enhance Korea's national power.[14] Notwithstanding all this, it must be stressed emphatically that *chuch'e* is an all-pervasive phenomenon in North Korea, whereas it is little more than a political slogan in South Korea. The

11. For the text of the October 17 declaration, see ibid., October 18, 1972. For the enumeration of presidential powers, see the text of the new ROK Constitution in *Han'guk ilbo*, October 28, 1972.
12. *Tong'a ilbo*, January 12, 1973.
13. Ibid., December 23, 1972.
14. See, for example, his inaugural speech on March 3, 1981 in *Han'guk ilbo*, March 5, 1981 and his speech to the Advisory Council on Peaceful Unification on June 5, 1981 in ibid., June 8, 1981.

South cannot even begin to compare with the North in terms of the scope, intensity, and impact of *chuch'e*. What is common to both halves of Korea, nonetheless, is *chuch'e*'s pronounced accent on nationalism.

If nationalism is such a potent unifying element in Korea's ideological fabric, it is considerably offset by another ideology that stands as an impenetrable barrier between the two Koreas—namely, the ideology of Marxism-Leninism as interpreted by Kim Il Sung. While, as noted previously, Kim Il Sung's *chuch'e sasang* has all but replaced Marxism-Leninism in North Korea's political lexicon, one can nonetheless find distinct echoes of Marxism-Leninism in the rhetoric and behavior of the North Korean leader. First, Kim fully embraces Marx's analysis of capitalism—that it is inherently evil, contains seeds of its own destruction, and hence will inevitably disintegrate. Second, he firmly believes in the notion of class struggle, laying primary emphasis on the struggle between exploiting and exploited classes. Convinced that not all capitalists are exploiters and further that they can be remolded through indoctrination, Kim would gladly welcome them into his revolutionary ranks. Those against whom the class struggle must be waged relentlessly, then, are the die-hard reactionaries, the counterrevolutionaries, and all others who would not recant their past sins and crimes.[15]

Third, Kim enshrines the doctrine of the dictatorship of the proletariat, which, he says, provides democracy to the proletariat on the one hand and dictatorship to the bourgeoisie on the other. Fourth, Kim is a faithful adherent of Lenin's organizational principle of democratic centralism, which, in effect, means an oligarchical control of rank-and-file members by the Political Bureau of the WPK Central Committee. Fifth, he is a practitioner of the Stalinist approach to socialist construction, pursuing industrialization through a series of multiyear economic plans stressing heavy industry and aimed at the building of an independent national economy capable of producing all or most of the essential goods at home. Structurally, this means that the North Korean economy is a Soviet-type command economy with centralized planning playing the pivotal role. Sixth, there is a strongly voluntaristic tinge to Kim's brand of Marxism-Leninism—namely, a heavy emphasis on conscious action. While it does not emanate from Marx, this is eminently compatible with the views and practices of Lenin, Stalin, and Mao Zedong.

Finally, Kim is one of the most vigorous and, in his view, faithful disciples of Lenin's theory of imperialism. Not only does Kim at-

15. This exposition of the Marxist-Leninist components in Kim Il Sung thought is adapted from B. C. Koh, "Ideology and Political Control in North Korea," *Journal of Politics* 32, 3 (August 1970): 668–671.

tribute all the miseries and troubles of Korea, the Third World, and the entire globe to imperialism led by the United States, but he flatly asserts that its eventual demise is preordained. Nevertheless, in keeping with a voluntaristic orientation, he would not sit with folded arms until imperialism dies a natural death according to the laws of history. Instead, he urges all socialist nations to wage a fierce struggle against it both individually and, particularly, as a unified camp. Nothing, in his view, is more alien to Marxism-Leninism than to compromise with the imperialists. Against this backdrop, it is not difficult to surmise the depth of disappointment, chagrin, and even outrage with which Kim must have greeted the advent of détente between his major ally, Beijing, and his archenemy, Washington.

To all the components of Marxism-Leninism a la Kim Il Sung noted above, South Korea is adamantly opposed. Not only does Seoul categorically reject the Marxian interpretation of capitalism, it has embraced capitalism, pursuing economic development based on the twin pillars of private initiative and international capital, tempered by a significant intrusion and guidance from the government. Nor is there any tolerance for the notion of class struggle in South Korea, although the goal of social justice has officially been endorsed.

While even a lip service to the concept of proletarian dictatorship is out of the question, there is no explicit apotheosis of the privileges of the bourgeoisie. Although, as was adumbrated earlier, the South Korean polity as a whole may have a functional equivalent of "democratic centralism"—in the sense that effective political power is concentrated at the top and that those who are in the middle and at the bottom of the politico-socioeconomic pyramid must dance to the tune of the top leadership—it is nonetheless a relatively open and moderately "free" society.

A strong superficial resemblance between the economies of the two Koreas is that they both rely on multiyear economic plans, but the resemblance ends there. In terms of the degree of control exercised by the government over the economy and of the role of private initiative, the two are poles apart. Finally, it is clear that South Korea does not subscribe to Lenin's theory of imperialism. Most important, it regards the United States, not as the leader of the imperialist camp, but as Seoul's foremost ally, benefactor, and partner. If there are villains among contemporary foreign powers, they include most probably the Soviet Union and the People's Republic of China, although, since 1973, Seoul has eschewed any overtly hostile references to these Communist powers.

In short, anticommunism—in the sense of opposing the North Korean brand of communism—is a striking, albeit a negative, feature of South Korea's ideological fabric. Indeed, it has become such an ingrained part of South Korea's national consciousness that the political elites, notably Syngman Rhee and Park Chung Hee, have found it expedient to use it as the major rationale for political repression. No matter how disenchanted segments of the South Korean populace were by Park's repressive rule, they were solidly behind their government in opposing North Korean-style communism. This is attributable to the combined impact of anti-Communist indoctrination, harsh anti-Communist and national security laws, and, above all, the lingering memories of the atrocities committed by the North Korean Communists in the South during the Korean War.

HISTORICAL LEGACY

The most important historical legacy that continues to color the perceptions and behaviors of the Korean people pertains to Korea's interaction with big powers, notably the four Pacific powers. From their long experience of being squeezed and exploited, invaded and subjugated, and pampered and protected by the powers surrounding their peninsula, the Koreans have developed two contradictory attitudes toward them—distrust and dependence. These two attitudes, one may argue, underpinned *sadae chuūi* (roughly translated as "sycophancy" or, in North Korean parlance, "flunkyism"). Despite their categoric repudiation of it in rhetoric, both Pyongyang and Seoul continue to profit by it in practice. On one hand, so the reasoning goes, the big powers are not to be trusted, for when the chips are down, they are after one and the same thing—the unscrupulous pursuit of their selfish interest at the expense of the weaker Korea. On the other hand, they are to be depended on and played off against one another, for none of them wants any one power to achieve hegemony over the entire Korean peninsula, and hence the key to Korea's survival lies in capitalizing upon the reciprocal jealousy and fear among the big powers.

The more recent events must no doubt have influenced the perceptions of both Koreas. For North Korea, Moscow's failure to provide an all-out support during the Korean War must have been profoundly disillusioning. Nor does it seem that Pyongyang has interpreted Beijing's decision to intervene in the war as a gesture of fraternal friendship pure and simple. From their wartime collaboration with the Chinese, during which they were distinctly subordinate to the latter, the North Koreans appear to have learned the value of independence.

For South Korea's part, the value, indeed the indispensability, of the United States was sharply underlined by the war. The images of the Soviet Union and the People's Republic of China as hostile powers with aggressive designs were hardened. Most importantly, the credibility of North Korea's Kim Il Sung plummeted in the eyes of the South Korean people, a situation that has been aggravated by his complete and categorical disavowal of any responsibility for the outbreak of the war. For those who have experienced the horrors of the war and witnessed the rapidity with which the North Korean armed forces overran South Korea in the early days of the war, North Korea's claim that the war was started by the South Korean and American troops evokes not only disbelief but a sense of indignation as well. The deep-seated skepticism of the South Korean people toward North Korea's affirmation of peaceful intentions and the success with which Park Chung Hee used the northern threat to perpetuate his dictatorial rule testify to the resilience of the traumas of the Korean War.

PERSONALITY PREDISPOSITIONS

The final component of the attitudinal prism of the foreign policy elite is at once most important and least illuminating. For although we are quite certain that the elite's personality predispositions help to shape and mold their perception of the operational environment, we are woefully ignorant about them. Nonetheless, I shall venture to offer some speculative hypotheses about selected aspects of the personality predispositions of Kim Il Sung and the late Park Chung Hee. While a focus on Kim Il Sung requires no justification, a lengthy discussion of Park Chung Hee does: owing to the longevity of his rule (1961–1979) and the magnitude of his power, Park's impact on South Korea's foreign policy remains unsurpassed. It therefore makes sense to probe the late Park's personality predispositions and their probable effects on Seoul's foreign policy during his tenure of office.

Kim Il Sung

Kim Il Sung's obsession with national pride, his apotheosis of *chuch'e*, and the frenzied personality cult surrounding him may be traced to compensatory craving for deference and power on his part. As conceptualized by Harold D. Lasswell, the "political type" pursues power as a means of compensation against deprivation. *Power is expected to overcome low estimates of the self*, by changing either the traits of the self or the environment in which it functions."[16] In the early stages of his career, Kim Il Sung appears to have suffered considerable deprivation. Not only did he experience ridicule and isolation in Chinese schools in Manchuria, but he served under Chinese superiors in a Chinese Communist guerrilla force.[17]

Moreover, his seizure of power in North Korea with the blessings and help of the Soviet occupation authorities may have engendered not only doubts about his legitimacy in the eyes of his counter-elites and compatriots but also a gnawing sense of inadequacy and insecurity on his own part. The prodigious attempt to beef up his revolutionary credentials and the attendant propagation of a personality cult may well have emanated from his compensatory cravings for deference. The gargantuan effort to project an image of a sagacious leader with authorship of hundreds of articles and scores of books may also be related to the fact that Kim's formal schooling ended at the tenth grade; it "may be viewed as a compensatory response of an educationally deprived but deference-seeking political leader."[18]

Kim's predominantly Chinese background also helps to explain the striking similarities between the operative components of his political thought and those of Mao Zedong thought. This and the related fact that Kim has "emulated" a sizable proportion of Mao's policies over the years become eminently comprehensible when they are set against the twin backdrops of his long association with Chinese communism and his fluency in the Chinese language. Given that Chinese is either the only foreign language in Kim's repertoire or the foreign language with which he is most familiar, he may be an avid reader of Chinese publications. Kim's Chinese background also goes a long way toward explaining Pyongyang's special ties with Beijing.[19]

16. Harold D. Lasswell, *Power and Personality* (New York: Viking Press, 1962), p. 39. I first advanced this line of argument in my paper "Political Leadership in North Korea: Toward a Conceptual Understanding of Kim Il-sŏng's Leadership Behavior," which was presented to the Conference on North Korea, Center for Korean Studies, University of Hawaii, Honolulu, Hawaii, June 10–14, 1974. See my article under the same title in *Korean Studies* (Honolulu) 2 (1978): 139–158.

17. Ibid., p. 147. For authoritative accounts of Kim's background, see Dae-Sook Suh, *The Korean Communist Movement, 1918–1948* (Princeton: Princeton University Press, 1967), part 5; Robert A. Scalapino and Chong-Sik Lee, *Communism in Korea*, vol. 1 (Berkeley: University of California Press, 1972), pp. 202–230.

18. Koh, "Political Leadership in North Korea," p. 148.

19. On the similarities between Kim's and Mao's thoughts, see Koh, "Ideology and Political Control in North Korea," pp. 655–674; on North Korea's emulation of Beijing, consult Glenn D. Paige, "North Korea and the Emulation of Russian and Chinese Behavior," in A. Doak Barnett (ed.), *Communist Strategies in Asia* (New York: Praeger, 1963), pp. 228–262; as for Kim's linguistic skills, one of his biographies states: "In fact, [Kim Il Sung] already had at that time [in his fifth grade] outstanding talents

Park Chung Hee

The overwhelming impression of Park Chung Hee that emerges from a scrutiny of the available biographical information, combined with reflections about his style of leadership, is that he manifested what may be called a *mobŏmsaeng* (model student) syndrome.[20] Born in September 1917 to a poor peasant family in Sŏnsan County, North Kyŏngsang Province, Park learned the virtues of obedience, discipline, and hard work early in his life. Park's father was fifty-four, and his mother forty-four, when he was born. He was the last of seven children. Although he was said to have been the object of special attention in his family, it is likely that being the youngest member of a large family in a status-bound traditional village may have instilled in him the habit of deference to authority figures early in his life. By the time Park started school at the age of nine, his father had died. The grinding poverty at home made him particularly appreciative of the value and privilege of schooling. He had to walk 30 *ri* (approximately 12 kilometers) to and from school but rarely missed his classes. At school, he was a serious and hard-working student who "always sat erect and motionless," "never engaging in frivolous talks with classmates during class sessions." He scrupulously fulfilled his duties, including payment of tuition on time. From the fourth grade on, he began to excel in schoolwork, graduating (i.e., finishing the sixth grade) at the top of his class.[21]

It is notable that in his sixth grade report card Park received the maximum possible score of ten for all but two of his twelve subjects.

---

in literary Chinese [*hanmun*] and the Chinese language [*chungguk mal*]. His spoken Chinese was so fluent that even the Chinese could not tell that he was a Korean. Yun Pok-jin, *Kim Il Sung wonsunim ŭi ŏrin sijŏl iyagi* [Tales of Marshall Kim Il Sung's Childhood] (Tokyo: Minch'ŏng Ch'ulp'an-sa, 1963), p. 77. Despite his alleged service in the Soviet Red Army during World War II, Kim's command of Russian is believed to be marginal. Nor does he appear to have a working knowledge of Japanese, for he told Professor Nishikawa Jun of Waseda University in November 1975 that he was a regular reader of the Japanese magazine *Sekai* in Korean translation. See Kim Il Sung, "Kakumei to kensetsu no dōtei" [Paths of Revolution and Construction], *Sekai* (Tokyo), February 1976, p. 187.

20. This argument was first presented in my paper "The Foreign Policies of the Two Koreas: Sources, Patterns, and Consequences," submitted to the workshop on comparative study of North and South Korea, sponsored by the Joint Committee on Korean Studies, the Social Science Research Council and the American Council of Learned Societies, January 16–17, 1976, San Juan, Puerto Rico.

21. Han Ch'ang-wan, *Pak Chŏng-hŭi taet'ongnyŏng, Kim Chong-p'il paksa* [President Park Chung Hee, Dr. Kim Jong Pil] (Seoul: Chŏnggyŏng Podosa, 1967), pp. 20–24. The quoted passages are from p. 24. I have also examined: Chŏng Kwang-mo, *Ch'ŏngwadae* [Blue House] (Seoul: Ōmun'gak, 1967); Kim Yŏng-t'ae, *Memarŭn choguge tanbinŭn naeryŏtta: Pak taet'ongnyŏng ŭi palchach'wi* [Rain Falls on the Barren Father-

He received nine in both physical exercises and "home economics" (*kasa chaebong*). Although a score of nine on a ten-point scale is impressive, it must be seen in conjunction with a "poor" rating he received on his physical development.[22] He was a small and frail youth, and his determination to excel in sports and, particularly, his later decision to pursue a military career may be interpreted as a compensatory response.

Park passed the entrance examination for Taegu Normal School in 1932. Since students of normal schools were not only on full government scholarships, but also guaranteed teaching positions upon graduation, Park thus became the pride and envy of his village. He had beaten the stiff hundred-to-one odds. It is significant that Park went to a normal school rather than a regular middle school, for the training in normal schools was particularly rigorous. In fact, it was so rigorous, arduous, and heavily oriented toward indoctrination of proper thought and behavior that the attrition rate was said to be 20 to 30 percent. Students were required to live in dormitories where they were subject to military-like discipline and regimentation. Not only did Park survive such austere life, he thrived on it.[23] He was a model student in a thoroughgoing way.

The three-year interlude between his graduation from normal school and the beginning of a military career may have reinforced Park's *mobŏmsaeng* syndrome. As a novice teacher in an elementary school, Park had the responsibility of not only imparting knowledge to his pupils but also of instilling in them the habits of discipline and obedience. Perhaps for the first time in his life he also found himself issuing orders and instructions to other people, which were, in all probability, scrupulously obeyed. His *mobŏmsaeng* traits were further strengthened and graphically demonstrated during his subsequent career in the Japanese Imperial Army. That he graduated at the top of his class from the Manchukuo Military Academy after three years of rigorous military training speaks for itself. Thanks to his outstanding record, he was given the rare privilege of attending the Japanese Military Academy in Tokyo for one year, from which he graduated in 1944 as the third-ranking member of his class—another remarkable tribute to his fortitude, self-discipline, and model behavior.

From such early life experiences and the subsequent military ca-

---

land: The Footsteps of President Park], 2 vols. (Ch'unch'ŏn, Kangwon-do: Yongjin Ch'ulp'an-sa, 1969); and Kim Chong-sin, *Pak Chŏng-hŭi taet'ongnyŏng* [President Park Chung Hee] (Seoul: Hallim Ch'ulp'an-sa, 1970). The last-named book is intended for children. These sources agree on the basic outline of Park's career, although there are some minor discrepancies.

22. Chŏng Kwang-mo, *Ch'ŏngwadae*, p. 139.
23. Kim Yŏng-t'ae, *Memarŭn choguge*, pp. 72–77.

reer, I submit, Park developed a *mobŏmsaeng* syndrome, with its accent on discipline, unquestioning obedience, duty, and self-sacrifice. The corollary of such a syndrome is that once one achieves a position of authority, one expects *mobŏmsaeng*-like behavior from one's subordinates. The teacher or commander instructs and issues orders; the pupils (or men under his command) listen, obey, and carry out orders. There is no room for disagreement or squabble, let alone disobedience. This may help to explain not only Park's well-known intolerance of political dissent by opposition politicians, intellectuals, and students but also his singularly harsh reactions to any signs of disloyalty within his own political party.

Other aspects of his early life that may have helped to mold Park's predispositions include the abject poverty of his family and his experiences with the Japanese. Poverty may have taught him the blessings of affluence, and his experiences with the Japanese must surely have exposed him to the humiliations of second-class citizenship. His single-minded commitment to the goal of modernizing Korea and his dedication to *charip* (self-reliance), *pŏnyŏng* (prosperity), and *chuch'esŏng* (autonomy or self-identity) may be appreciated in this light. His public statements indicated that he saw himself performing a supreme duty to his nation and people by prolonging his tenure of office. He spoke of "faithfully shouldering the burden which the people have imposed" on him and of "leading the nation through a tortuous path" as the "loyal servant of the people."[24] Indeed, he justified his May 16, 1961 coup on the grounds of saving the nation from the brink of disaster brought about by rampant corruption, injustice, and disorder. It could be argued that his coup d'etat, an act of overt rebellion against a constituted authority as well as his hierarchical superiors, was incongruent with his *mobŏmsaeng* syndrome. On the other hand, it is possible that given the chaotic situation in South Korea at the time and the apparent inability of the ruling politicians to cope with the problems of the day, Park may indeed have perceived, as he claimed to have done, a higher duty to "save the nation."[25]

In a poem he wrote to his brother-in-law, Han Sang-bong (husband of his second eldest sister), on the eve of the coup, Park intimated that he was prepared to die, should his plan "to bring order to the fatherland" fail. He bade goodbye to Kŭmo Mountain in his native Yŏngnam region, promising that he would not return home but

---

24. See in particular his first inaugural address in December 1963 and his special statement accompanying the proclamation of martial law on October 17, 1972. Han Ch'ang-wan, *Pak Chŏng-hŭi*, pp. 51–58 and *Tong'a ilbo*, October 18, 1972.

25. For an articulation of his views along these lines, see Park Chung Hee, *The Country, the Revolution, and I* (Seoul: Hollym Corporation, 1962).

commit suicide in the event that his "unswerving determination should fail to bear fruit."[26] The fact that he took pains to justify the coup as a "radical but unavoidable surgery to save the life" of Korea may also have reflected his gnawing realization that his actions represented deviations from model behavior as normally understood. Almost apologetic, he pledged to dedicate his life to fulfill the goals of his "revolution"—"to construct a fatherland that is prosperous and free from humiliation and poverty."[27] In a sense, his dogged determination to cling to power to the bitter end could be interpreted as an attempt to vindicate his coup d'etat by presiding over the completion of a substantial portion of his modernization program.

The implications of Park's personality predispositions for foreign policy need to be specified briefly. The chief implication of his *mobŏmsaeng* syndrome is rather indirect: by contributing to his dictatorial style of leadership, perpetuation of power, and political repression, one may argue, the syndrome helped to generate unnecessary strains in Seoul's relations with its major allies. The mounting chorus of criticisms in Tokyo and Washington necessitated an expenditure of an inordinate amount of time, money, and effort in propaganda and lobbying on Seoul's part. The abduction, in August 1973, of the opposition leader Kim Dae Jung from Tokyo by agents of South Korea's Central Intelligence Agency (KCIA) is but one example of the manner in which South Korea's domestic political dynamics, shaped and molded by Park's personality predispositions, could affect and constrain Seoul's international behavior.[28]

As already noted, Park's early exposure to the ills of poverty may have contributed to his decision to elevate the goal of economic development to the supreme national objective. Much of Seoul's foreign policy is linked to that goal, notably its pursuit of strong ties with Japan and the United States and its efforts to expand trade and other ties with Third World as well as Communist countries. Additionally, Park's Japanese background may be viewed as a notable element in his evolving ties with Japan, beginning with his successful bid to normalize relations with Tokyo in 1964 amid bitter political controversy at home. Finally, one may speculate that his dictatorial style and intolerance for dissent may have adversely affected the foreign policy decision-making process.

    26. For the Korean text of the poem, see Han Ch'ang-wan, *Pak Chŏng-hŭi*, pp. 30–31.
    27. He made these remarks in a speech marking his retirement from active military duty on August 30, 1963. Ibid., pp. 34–39.
    28. See "Dokyumento: Kim Tae-jung shi rachi jiken" [Document: the Kim Dae Jung Kidnapping Incident], *Sekai*, November 1973, pp. 137–173.

6 PSYCHOLOGICAL ENVIRONMENT: ELITE IMAGES

In the preceding chapter we focused on the screen or filter through which the operational environment is likely to be perceived by the foreign policy elites in the two Koreas. It now remains to discuss briefly what actual images such an attitudinal prism projects. In other words, what pictures do the elites have in their heads that are likely to influence their foreign policy behavior?

One knotty analytic problem presents itself at once: How does one differentiate between verbalized images and images qua decision premises? This problem essentially boils down to one of ascertaining *true* images of the foreign policy elite. It is plain that verbalized images—images that are reflected in public statements—may frequently diverge from the true images that are used as decision premises by the elite. On the other hand, it would be erroneous to dismiss all verbalized images as rhetoric aimed only at public consumption, for they may well be congruent with true images. This consideration, coupled with the fact that verbalized images are relatively easy to ascertain, leads us primarily to examine the elite's public statements. To the extent that the latter do not conflict with subsequent actions taken by the elite, they may be viewed as prima facie valid, that is, accurately reflecting images qua decision premises.[1]

Another analytic problem pertains to the scope of the foreign

---

1. After lengthy discussions with members of North Korea's elite—academics, cadres, government officials—during my visit to the DPRK in July–August, 1981, I became convinced that their published views were remarkably close to their sincerely held beliefs.

policy elite. As will be noted in the following chapter, the nature of foreign policy decision making is such that regardless of the degree of centralization and concentration of political power, it cannot be monopolized by the top political leader. There are bound to be other relevant actors who can and do contribute to the decision-making process. Nonetheless, due to the constraints of available information, I shall focus primarily on the top leaders in the two Koreas. This means that in the case of North Korea we shall examine the statements of Kim Il Sung, supplementing them, if necessary, with those of other top leaders and commentaries from *Nodong sinmun*, the WPK organ, which serves as the authoritative mouthpiece for the supreme leader. In the case of South Korea, we shall rely primarily on the pronouncements of the late Park Chung Hee. In a strict sense, what is presented below are not elite images but "leadership" images.

NORTH KOREA

Perceptions of the Sino-American Rapprochement

Since the most outstanding aspect of Korea's external setting is the easing of tensions among the big powers, with the notable exception of Sino-Soviet relations, it may be appropriate to examine Kim Il Sung's images of that phenomenon. Although he promptly called Nixon's July 1971 announcement that he would visit Beijing a sign of capitulation—"a trip of the defeated [that] fully reflects the declining fate of US imperialism"[2]—Kim appeared to look upon the development with a mixture of alarm and jealousy. On one hand, he struck a note of caution:

> As historical experiences show, the aggressive nature of imperialism never changes even when its strength has become weak and the imperialists refuse to withdraw from their old position of their own accord. The deeper the imperialists sink into a quagmire, the more persistently they cling to the "double-dealing tactics" of holding an olive branch in one hand and brandishing a bayonet in the other and the more vicious they become in their manoeuvres of aggression and war under the cloak of "peace."[3]

He then called on "the peoples of the revolutionary Asian countries" to "completely bury moribund imperialism by always maintaining a

2. *Pyongyang Times*, August 14, 1971. Kim made these remarks on August 6, 1971.
3. Ibid.

high vigilance against the desperate 'double-dealing tactics' of the enemy and by smashing all his sinister schemes" and to "strengthen [their] antiimperialist, anti-US united front" with a view to chasing out the "US imperialists aggressors" from "South Korea, Taiwan, Indochina, . . . Japan, and all other parts of Asia where they have set foot."[4]

On the other hand, Kim betrayed undercurrents of jealousy when he told *New York Times* correspondents Harrison E. Salisbury and John M. Lee in May 1972 that "the US government should improve relations not only with big countries but with small countries as well." "We do not think," he said, "the improvement of the US relations with big countries will greatly influence its relations with small countries. But the US government has not yet changed its former attitude in its relations with small countries."[5]

Images of the United States

In Kim's images of the external setting, the pivotal element is his perception that the United States is the main stumbling block to Korean reunification as well as North Korea's number one enemy. While his verbalized image of the "aggressive designs of US imperialism" may be deliberately exaggerated, it seems to reflect his genuine conviction that American military power not only thwarted his previous attempt to unify Korea by force but still remains the primary deterrent to the Communist takeover of South Korea. Most important, Kim's image of "US imperialism" must be understood from the perspective of Pyongyang's security needs. What is intended by both Seoul and Washington as a defensive or a deterrent move may well be seen by Pyongyang as a threatening, or even an aggressive, one.

In a lengthy memorandum issued on June 26, 1978, the DPRK Foreign Ministry cited specific measures that were being taken to beef up South Korea's military capabilities and to compensate for the planned gradual withdrawal of American ground troops from South Korea. It expressed alarm at the increasing frequency and scale of joint military exercises between ROK and US forces:

> The United States conducted the joint US-South Korean military exercise dubbed "Team Spirit '78," the largest in scale since the Korean War, from 10 to 17 March 1978. According to an official announcement by the U.S. Defense Department spokesman and the South Korean side, 118,000 troops including 73,000

---
4. Ibid.
5. Ibid., June 10, 1972. The interview took place in Pyongyang on May 26, 1972. See also the *New York Times*, May 31, 1972.

South Korean puppet ground, naval, and air force troops, 23,000 reinforcement troops from the US mainland and the Pacific area and 22,000 US troops stationed in South Korea, participated in this large-scale exercise. Also participating were more than 200 US Air Force planes of 12 kinds, including B-52 strategic bombers, F-111 swing-wing fighter-bombers, F-4 Phantoms and A-7 close air support planes. Also mobilized were US naval forces comprising 12 warships, including the carrier Midway, various landing boats and ships and naval vessels for logistic support. "Team Spirit '78," which mobilized all services and arms of the US and puppet armed forces and included all operations, including ground operations, landing operations, bombing exercises, and paratroop and heavy equipment air-drop exercises, was a frenzied war racket to invade the northern half of the republic and a full-scale preparatory and experimental war against the DPRK. Mobilizing and conducting launching exercises of the Lance missile, which can carry nuclear warheads, particularly bared the US imperialists' dark intention to provoke even nuclear war in Korea.[6]

The North Korean Foreign Ministry went on to charge that the US side had violated the armistice agreement and committed "military provocations" 9,500 times during the first five months of 1978.[7] If true, this would mean that the average number of provocations and violations per day was sixty-three. While this portion of the memorandum clearly strains the reader's imagination, the bulk of the facts and figures cited in the remainder of the memorandum are based on published reports in South Korean, Japanese, and US media and appear to be reliable. In short, it is public knowledge that South Korea's military arsenal is being fortified on a large scale and that joint military exercises by US and ROK troops do sometimes simulate an invasion of North Korea. The "team spirit" exercises mentioned above have been conducted every year since 1976. In 1981 the joint exercise lasted two months, from February to April. It simulated an invasion of North Korea, mobilizing a total of 161,500 troops. Of the 61,500 US troops who participated, more than a half were airlifted from Okinawa and the continental United States.[8]

"Team Spirit 82" exercises, held from February to April 1982, were the largest ever: even though the number of soldiers mobilized remained about the same as in the previous year, the aircraft carrier *Midway* participated for the first time in two years, and the equip-

6. *Pyongyang Radio*, June 26, 1978, as monitored by FBIS.
7. Ibid.
8. *Korea Herald*, January 8, 1981; *Korea Newsreview*, February 14, 1981, p. 4.

ment deployed and operations performed were more sophisticated than ever. To underscore the defensive nature of the exercises, however, the United States and South Korea invited North Korea to send observers, but the North Koreans declined.[9]

The North Korean reaction to "Team Spirit 82" was a predictable one. On February 14, one day after the exercises began, the spokesman of the DPRK Foreign Ministry issued a statement sharply denouncing the US and the ROK for conducting a "test war" and a "preliminary war" and expressing a sense of outrage at the fact that they had invited North Korea to send observers. The spokesman characterized the invitation as "a ridiculous act which can be committed only by the most brazen-faced provocateur and an intolerable insult to the Korean people and the world peace-loving people."[10]

Articles, commentaries, and editorials denouncing the joint exercises appeared almost daily in the North Korean press, and mass rallies were held throughout North Korea. In one of the rallies held in Pyongyang on March 9, Ho Jong Suk, secretary of the WPK Central Committee and the highest ranking woman in the North Korean power hierarchy, charged that the United States and South Korea were preparing for a nuclear war. She noted that such aircraft as A-4 Skyhawks, F-15s, and F-16s, which are "capable of carrying nuclear shells and bombs," were being deployed and that the "US imperialists are hurling into the military rehearsals nuclear weapons belonging to US troops occupying South Korea and several hundred missiles with nuclear warheads and troops of the unit specializing in nuclear weapons belonging to the US Third Marine Division in Okinawa." "Judging from all indications," she said, "the current war racket called 'Team Spirit 1982' is not a repetition of the usual exercises which have been staged consecutively for the past seven years since 1976, but a new test war and a preliminary nuclear war for the completion of nuclear war preparations in Korea and the invasion of our republic at any time they please. In fact, nobody can guarantee that this unprecedentedly large-scale war exercise staged with many nuclear weapons will not escalate into a full-scale nuclear war against our republic."[11]

One may justifiably question whether North Korean statements regarding the threat of invasion by the United States and South Korea reflect genuine convictions of its decision-making elite. Direct exposure to the mood of Pyongyang's elite and lengthy talks with offi-

9. *Korea Herald,* February 20, 1982; *Korea Newsreview,* March 20, 1982, p. 7; *New York Times,* April 1, 1982.
10. KCNA, Pyongyang, February 15, 1982, as monitored by FBIS.
11. *Pyongyang Radio,* March 10, 1982, as monitored by FBIS.

cials, cadres, and academics in Pyongyang in the summer of 1981 gave me the strong impression that North Korea does indeed feel insecure and that it sees a real possibility of attack from the South. To the North Korean leaders the American intervention in Vietnam is a vivid reminder that the United States is fully capable of aggression. They justify their own military preparedness in terms of self-defense and flatly disclaim any aggressive designs on their part. The North Korean perceptions become a little more comprehensible when they are viewed against the backdrop of Pyongyang's delicate relations with Beijing and Moscow, neither of which appears to be perceived by the North Koreans as a truly reliable ally. It may even be argued that Pyongyang is gripped by a "siege mentality." The sense of urgency with which the goal of self-reliance (*chuch'e*) in all domains is being pursued may be related in part to this gnawing fear. In sum, it would be a mistake to dismiss North Korean rhetoric on threats to its security as propaganda pure and simple; it should be construed as reflecting not only propaganda but also deep-seated anxiety.

Apart from America's military threat, Kim Il Sung harps on the theme that the United States has turned South Korea into a colony and the South Korean people into slaves of American monopoly capital. His strategy of the southern revolution is predicated on the assumption that there is a large amount of anti-American sentiment in South Korea stemming from America's alleged colonial exploitation of the latter. Kim Il Sung's apparent overestimation of the degree of American influence in South Korea flows logically from the preceding image.

In an interview with the Japanese magazine *Sekai* in March 1976, Kim said:

> The US imperialists want to keep south Korea under their thumb partly because they want to make south Korea their permanent raw material base. It is a fact that they lust for the materials in south Korea. . . .
>
> To the US imperialists it is also essential to have control over south Korea as a military base. They want to seize the whole of Korea and, further, realize their world domination by using south Korea as their military, strategic base. They want south Korea as a military base to deter the Soviet Union and China and tighten their control of Japan.[12]

12. Kim Il Sung, *For the Independent Peaceful Reunification of Korea*, Rev. ed. (New York: Guardian Associates, Inc., 1976), p. 219. For the Japanese version of the interview, see Kim Il Sung, "Chōsen no heiwa to tōitsu" [Peace and Reunification in Korea], *Sekai*, July 1976, pp. 120–135; for the Korean version, see *Kim Il-sŏng chŏjak sŏnjip*, vol. 7 (Hanyang Ch'ulp'ansa edition), pp. 266–286.

Kim then stated that the "present south Korean rulers are acting strictly on orders from the US Central Intelligence Agency."[13] It was consistent with such North Korean perception that *Nodong sinmun* characterized Washington's recall of its ambassador to South Korea in protest against the Park regime's expulsion of its opposition leader from the National Assembly in October 1979 as "a political trick stemming from Carter's crafty nature." According to the WPK organ:

> Collusion with the South Korean puppet clique by the Carter Administration [such as continuing military aid and the impending visit of Defense Secretary Brown to South Korea] has inspired the puppets to be outrageous in their intensified repression of the opposition party.... The US imperialist aggressors, including Carter, greatly fear that the political tension [in South Korea] will develop into an explosive situation. Therefore, by expressing ... regret over the fascist oppression by the Pak Chong-hui puppet clique and pretending to disagree with the infringement of human rights, the Carter Administration is scheming to placate the indignation of the opposition party and people of all strata and to block their antigovernment advance.[14]

That Kim does appreciate the difficulty of arousing anti-American sentiment in South Korea was revealed by these remarks:

> However, the south Korean people and a considerable number of Asian people are not yet sufficiently awakened to the sinister aggressive activities of the US imperialists and they do not wage a vigorous struggle against their presence in Asia and their domination and control of Asian nations. Some south Koreans do hate US imperialism, but there are still some others who regard US imperialism as the "benefactor" who gives them some sort of "favor" and think that only when they cling to the US can they be given rice to eat.[15]

Given his images of the degree to which the United States controls South Korea, it was natural for Kim Il Sung to place the blame for the lack of progress in the Seoul-Pyongyang dialogue squarely on Washington.[16] North Korea's proposals for direct negotiations with the United States, to the exclusion of South Korea, first made in 1974 and reiterated in subsequent years, were likewise consistent with

13. Kim Il Sung, *For the Independent Peaceful Reunification of Korea*, p. 220.
14. *Nodong sinmun*, October 17, 1979, as translated by FBIS.
15. Kim Il Sung, *For the Independent Peaceful Reunification of Korea*, pp. 220–221.
16. Ibid., p. 221.

such perceptions, even though they may also reflect Pyongyang's desire simultaneously to undercut Seoul's international standing and to drive a wedge between Seoul and Washington.[17]

In the summer of 1981 North Korean leaders I talked with, from academics to a vice-premier, noted with approval signs of a growing anti-American sentiment in the South in the wake of the May 1980 Kwangju Uprising. They characterized the US role in the latter (which consisted, inter alia, of permitting ROK troops under the command of General John A. Wickham, Jr. to be used by ROK General Chun Doo Hwan to suppress the rebellion) as "a tactical victory coupled with a strategic defeat." When, in a dramatic display of anti-Americanism, a group of dissident students set fire to the American Cultural Center in Pusan in March 1982, North Korea was understandably buoyed. *Nodong sinmun*, noting that the arsonists had scattered leaflets condemning "the US imperialists' crimes of scheming to divide Korea permanently and the US neocolonial policy against South Korea" and demanding both the withdrawal of US troops from Korea and the overthrow of the Chun Doo Hwan regime, called the incident "an explosion of the anti-US sentiment deeply stored up in the hearts of the South Korean people for a long time." The paper also hailed it as an expression of the patriotism and the determination of the South Korean people to drive out the US troops and to restore national dignity and sovereignty.[18]

Images of Japan

Kim Il Sung's image of the threat of "Japanese militarism" may also be genuine, even though it too contains an element of overestimation. Here the three components of the attitudinal prism discussed earlier become germane. For the ideology of Marxism-Leninism, particularly Lenin's theory of imperialism, the historical legacy of Japanese colonial rule over Korea, and Kim Il Sung's personal experiences in the anti-Japanese guerrilla struggle in Manchuria combine to underline the perceived danger of Japan's growing economic might. The latter's military alliance with the United States,

---

17. For Kim Il Sung's explanation of the proposals, see ibid., pp. 225–227; 233–234. For recent reiterations of them, see Vice Premier Chong Jun Gi's report to a Pyongyang meeting on June 23, 1978 in *KCNA*, Pyongyang, June 23, 1978, as monitored by FBIS; Kim Il Sung's speech commemorating the thirtieth anniversary of the founding of the DPRK on September 9, 1978 in ibid., September 9, 1978; and Kim Il Sung's report to the Sixth Congress of the WPK on October 10, 1980 in *Choguk ŭi chajujŏk p'yŏnghwa t'ong'irul irukhaja* [Let Us Achieve the Independent and Peaceful Reunification of the Fatherland] (Pyongyang: Chosŏn Nodong-dang Ch'ulp'an-sa, 1980), p. 9. This pamphlet reproduces the section on reunification policy from Kim's report.

18. *Nodong sinmun*, March 22, 1982, as translated by FBIS.

deepening economic ties with South Korea, and, above all, explicit linking of Seoul's security with its own thus become a matter of increasing concern for North Korea.

It is notable that while continuing its diatribes against "the revival of Japanese militarism," Pyongyang has not only taken pains to differentiate between the Japanese government and the Japanese people but has also sought consistently to improve its ties with Tokyo. Kim Il Sung has thus tried to portray Japan as being under the control, if not domination, of the United States, urging the Japanese people to "awaken and wage a joint struggle [with the Korean people] against US imperialist aggression and interference."[19]

On the other hand, Kim has indicated that Japan's recognition of the Seoul government's claim to exclusive legitimacy in the Korean peninsula embodied in the 1965 ROK-Japan Basic Treaty of Normalization would not pose a barrier to normalization of relations between North Korea and Japan.[20] In April 1977 Kim also said:

> We will not demand unreasonably that the Japanese government have ties only with us and sever ties with the south Korean authorities. We need not make this sort of demand, and even if we do so our demand will not be met. If such a demand is put forward when our country is not yet reunified, it will put the Japanese government in an awkward situation. We, therefore, do not pin great hopes on the Japanese government in connection with the question of [North] Korea-Japan relations.[21]

Images of South Korea

Kim Il Sung's image of South Korea is a blend of both realism and wishful thinking. That his incessant rhetoric about the abject poverty and unspeakable sufferings of the South Korean people diverge from his image qua decision premises is suggested by the absence of any rash moves to capitalize on such alleged weaknesses. In fact, there is reason to suspect that firsthand exposure on the part of some North Korean leaders to the sights and sounds of South Korea, the alleged hell on earth, may have led to a more realistic appreciation of the strengths as well as weaknesses of Seoul's economic capabilities.

Whether Kim Il Sung has also modified his image of the revolu-

19. Kim Il Sung, "Chōsen no heiwa to tōitsu," pp. 128–130.
20. See Kim Il Sung's interview with Ebata Kiyoshi, chief editorial writer for *Asahi shimbun* in the April 28, 1972 issue of the Japanese newspaper. See also *Asahi Evening News*, April 29, 1972 and May 1, 1972 (editorial).
21. Kim Il Sung, *Talks With Executive Managing Editor of Japanese Yomiuri Shimbun and His Party* (Pyongyang: Foreign Languages Publishing House, 1977), p. 12.

tionary potential of the South Korean masses is problematic. I am inclined to believe that he still underestimates the depth and tenacity of anti-Communist sentiment in South Korea and that he deludes himself when he equates opposition to political repression with support for the North Korean formula for reunification. In fact, he seriously undermines the cause of South Korea's political dissidents when he openly supports them because it only bolsters the South Korean regime's claim that political dissidents either aid and abet or are aided and abetted by the North Korean Communists. On the other hand, it is possible that North Korea may be perfectly aware of what it is doing and that its covert objective in expressing solidarity with South Korean dissidents is not to aid their cause in the short run but to help accelerate the vicious circle of repression–opposition–further repression–further opposition. Pyongyang may calculate that such a vicious circle will promote its strategy of southern revolution in the long run. In Pyongyang's view, the more viciously the South Korean government suppresses political dissent, the more aroused the South Korean people will become. According to Kim Il Sung:

> It cannot be said that the struggle of the south Korean people for democracy has been totally squashed. The south Korean people keep on struggling with a hope to free themselves from the fascist suppression of the enemy and his tyranny. . . .
>
> The south Korean rulers now resort to a most unscrupulous fascist rule. But such a fascist suppression cannot work. The lessons of history show that a tyrant cannot stay long. No nation's history knows as yet an instance of a tyrant lasting long and there is no such instance in our time either. In the past the dynasties of feudal society and the rulers of capitalist society tried to improve their position by repression. But all of them met their doom in the face of the resistance of the popular masses. Therefore, we think that if the south Korean people awaken and the entire people in north and south Korea fight in unity, Korea can surely be reunified independently.[22]

When Park Chung Hee's abrupt assassination was announced in October 1979, North Korea reacted in a predictable fashion. *Nodong sinmun* saw Park's violent death as proof of "how serious the political crisis and social disorder in South Korea are" and as evidence that "a traitor who betrays the nation and is engaged in treachery is bound to meet an unenviable end."[23] In a front-page editorial on November 9, 1979, the paper summed up the "lesson" of Park's demise:

22. Ibid., pp. 9–10.
23. *Nodong sinmun*, October 28, 1979, as translated by FBIS.

The masters he had served through his flunkeyist betrayal to the country never proved to be a protector or saviour. When one indulges in treacheries, turning one's back on one's own nation and clinging to the coattails of foreign forces, one is, needless to say, repudiated by the people and when one becomes no longer necessary as a confidant, one is bound to be forsaken also by one's masters.[24]

In short, just as North Korea saw the United States as the mastermind of Park's repressive policies during his lifetime, so it viewed Washington as the silent coconspirator in his assassination.

Images of the Internal Setting

As far as North Korea's internal setting is concerned, Kim Il Sung has consistently articulated the view that economic power, military power, and internal political cohesion are interrelated and interdependent, and that they are all necessary to underpin not only North Korea's independence but also its strategy of reunification. Although his periodic assessments of the progress North Korea is making in the fields of economic and defense construction and political indoctrination are conspicuous for their self-praise and exaggerations, they also contain significant revelations of problems and weaknesses.

Kim's speech to a national agricultural conference in January 1974 is a case in point. After proclaiming that in 1973 North Korea had compiled a record "unprecedented in the history of world agriculture" by "doubling or more than doubling the 1972 agricultural output" in "many cooperative farms," Kim went on to reveal that sizable numbers of North Korea's cadres, scientists, and technicians were "performing their jobs haphazardly, contaminated by worn-out ideas" and "not knowing what they are doing right and what they are doing wrong." He also deplored the fact that North Korean scientists and technicians had been unable to improve seeds at a time when many other nations were undergoing the so-called green revolution. "Unless [they] are told unequivocally what problems to do research on and what books to read," he said, "they will not study diligently. . . . Today a sizable number of them are idling away their time."[25] Kim also indirectly conceded the limits of political indoctrination, by revealing that many of North Korea's agricultural projects were plagued by "the lack of party spirit, proletarian class spirit, and people's spirit on the part of cadres in the agricultural management

24. Ibid., November 9, 1979, as translated by FBIS.
25. *Nodong sinmun*, January 13, 1974.

field" and that "the life style of the old society" still pervaded North Korea's rural areas.[26]

Kim Il Sung's speech to North Korea's first national conference of "labor administration workers" in September 1979 revealed the persistence of problems in the domestic arena. Following the customary format, he first heaped extravagant praise on the accomplishments of his people and, by implication, on his leadership:

> Today our people are leading a happy life without worry about food, clothing, their children's education, medical treatment, taxation or debt. Our country has become a superior socialist nation where all workers enjoy a happy life to their heart's content, without material or mental anxiety or suffering. From ancient times, our forefathers desired to build *a paradise on earth. This desire has been fulfilled in the era of our Workers' Party*. This is the greatest achievement and most brilliant victory attained by our people.[27]

Kim then proceeded to reveal that precisely because "the life of our people has become affluent and daily worries have been eliminated, the practice of refusing to work assiduously and trying to evade hard work for easy work has emerged among some workers"; that workers in quite a few plants and enterprises fail to put in eight hours of work a day as required by law; and that despite a serious shortage of labor at the national level, "the local industry sector has a manpower surplus of more than 25 percent." Kim also deplored the finding that in factories and enterprises workers do not exert themselves until the last ten days of each month, when a frantic effort is made to fulfill the monthly production quota. The implication of such practice, in Kim's view, was that "factories and enterprises have more manpower than they actually need and are wasting it." Moreover, he continued, "we waste a lot of manpower, put a heavy strain on machines and equipment and are unable to upgrade the quality of products." As causes of such practice, Kim cited the chronic tardiness in the supply of raw materials to factories and the nonobservance of "the rule of cooperative production."

Kim also took "economic guidance functionaries" to task for failing to keep workers at the same position for a sufficient length of time and to help raise the workers' level of technical expertise. He pointed to the lack of proper maintenance for production facilities

---

26. Ibid.
27. *Pyongyang Times*, October 6, 1979. Kim made the speech on September 27, 1979. Emphasis added.

and equipment, blaming "the late or insufficient delivery of repair materials" to the factories concerned. Other problems that Kim cited included the failure fully to implement the "socialist principle of distribution and the socialist system of labor remuneration" (which decree that distribution and compensation shall be commensurate with one's actual contribution to the productive process) and the "bureaucratism" and "subjectivism" of cadres, who were accused of issuing unreasonable orders and failing to work among the masses, to make a realistic assessment of the work situation, and to provide guidance to the workers.[28]

In short, it appears that Kim's images of the internal setting are realistic, although one may question the feasibility of some of his goals, notably that of totally remaking the North Korean people and society.

SOUTH KOREA

Images of Détente

Park Chung Hee's perception of the implications of détente for Korea bore a striking resemblance to that of Kim Il Sung in one major respect: he, too, expressed caution. Specifically, Park warned against the danger that big powers might sacrifice the interests of small and medium states under the pretext of easing tensions. Détente, he argued, had set in motion the process of "prodigious change in the existing power balance among the big powers surrounding the Korean peninsula," and such change was likely to undermine seriously South Korea's national security. Under these circumstances, he said, it was imperative that the Korean people "guard and steer our destiny with our own hands." This in turn underscored the importance of dialogue between Seoul and Pyongyang, and it was primarily on the grounds of strengthening Seoul's capacity to carry on that dialogue that a drastic restructuring of South Korea's political system, known as *Siwol Yusin* was justified.[29]

Images of Allies

If Park was alarmed over the possibility of being shortchanged by the big powers, he did not discount their ability to help Korea. In fact, Park's images of the United States and Japan as the main sources

28. Ibid.
29. See Park's special proclamation in *Tong'a ilbo*, October 18, 1972.

of assistance remained intact. He thus vigorously sought and received repeated reaffirmations of US commitments to South Korea's security as well as assistance in the modernization of the ROK armed forces. He also insisted that since Japan was constrained by its constitution and internal political considerations not to provide any military aid to South Korea, it should "strengthen economic cooperation" with Seoul. In doing all this, he took pains to stress the reciprocal nature of Seoul's ties with both Washington and Tokyo—that the latter two had vital stakes in the security of South Korea and in the peace and stability of the Korean peninsula—a view that was fully embraced by the two powers.[30]

Notwithstanding all this, Park kept underscoring the importance of self-reliance. In his words:

> A multipolar world is certainly not a simple international environment. Unlike the Cold War days when dependence on the power of an ally was possible, we now have only ourselves to rely on, and at the same time we must carefully watch the moves of the United States, Japan, China, the Soviet Union and many other countries as well. This requires a high level of adaptability and creativeness.[31]

He cautioned against the hazards of "the games that Big Powers play," in which "yesterday's friend can be abandoned without consideration, yesterday's adversary can be today's friend, and today's enemy can become tomorrow's negotiating partner." The principal lesson of all this, in his view, is that "we have only our own power to safeguard security and independence. Help is offered only when one helps oneself. When each country is concerned with its own interests, in the end, it is often the question of who is winning rather than who is right that decides the final outcome." He added that "our allies will begin to help us only after they are convinced that we, and not the north Korean Communists, are overwhelmingly superior."[32]

These images have apparently been inherited by Park's successors. For the Chun Doo Hwan government, in its quest for a $6 billion loan to help finance its fifth Five-Year Plan (1982–1986), put forth the argument of reciprocal benefit: since South Korea was making substantial contributions to Japan's security requirements, it was amply justified in requesting economic assistance. Tokyo's initial reluctance to embrace Seoul's argument temporarily strained relations

30. For reaffirmations of the preceding views, see Park's interviews with *Mainichi shimbun* and the *Agence France Presse* in *Han'guk ilbo*, November 16 and 27, 1975.
31. Park Chung Hee, *Korea Reborn: A Model for Development* (Englewood Cliffs, NJ: Prentice-Hall, 1979), p. 128.
32. Ibid., p. 129 and p. 132.

between the two countries, but by mid-1982 the two sides were moving toward a compromise solution of the dispute.[33]

Images of Moscow and Beijing

Seoul's efforts to improve relations with Moscow and Beijing on the heels of the Sino-American opening and the Sino-Japanese normalization reflected some modification in Park's previously held image that the two Communist powers were implacably hostile toward South Korea and posed direct and indirect threats to its security. What was notable was that his image of the PRC had always been markedly hostile, while the Soviet Union had not been salient in his thinking. For example, in defending his decision to send ROK troops to Vietnam in February 1965, he said:

> It is Communist China which supports and incites the North Vietnamese guerrillas behind the scenes. We all well know that it was also Communist China that supported and incited the North Korean Communists. Communist China is playing with fire in South Vietnam, just as she did in Korea 15 years ago.[34]

He was conspicuously silent on Moscow's role in both the Korean War and the Vietnam conflict.

To cite another example, Park expressed "deep concern" over "the threat from Communist China, which has developed nuclear weapons":

> Encouraged by [the] nuclear capability of Red China, . . . some Communist elements in Asian countries . . . may attempt indirect invasions to expand the influence of the Communists. As a nation which is near Communist China, the Republic of Korea should work out flexible policy to cope with any possible new trends which may influence the security of Korea.[35]

It is, of course, possible that change in Seoul's policy toward Communist nations was neither preceded nor accompanied by any change in Park's images of their potential threat. In fact, the consistently hostile posture of Beijing toward Seoul may simply have reinforced Park's preconceptions.

In an interview with the French paper *Le Soir* in November 1975,

---

33. More on this in chapter 10.
34. "To Help a Neighbor is To Defend Oneself," speech to a national rally to send off ROK expeditionary forces to South Vietnam on February 9, 1965, in *Major Speeches by Korea's Park Chung Hee* (Seoul: Hollym Corp., 1970), p. 238.
35. "Self-reliant Defense and Economic Construction," press conference on January 10, 1969, in ibid., p. 212.

however, Park stated that there were significant differences between North Korea and the other Communist countries:

> (1) They [other Communist countries] accept peaceful coexistence; (2) they are ready to cooperate in the interest of prosperity and progress of mankind in spite of differences in ideologies and systems; and (3) they accept the principle that resolution of conflicting interests must be achieved through negotiation and not through resort to arms or violence.

He further noted that South Korea and other Communist countries share "the fundamental objective of pursuing human progress and prosperity" and added:

> In this light, if Communist China should open their doors to us and make the move for establishment of friendly relations for mutual benefit, in accordance with the principle of equality and reciprocity, we shall respond accordingly and in a positive manner. This is our basic position.[36]

Images of North Korea

There is considerable evidence that Park's image of North Korea remained intact throughout his long tenure in power. Within three months of the publication of the July 4, 1972 North-South joint statement, Park called for stepped-up anti-Communist indoctrination, saying that "the covert objective of the [North Korean] Communist party is to induce the [South Korean] people to . . . lower their guards and then launch an invasion anew."[37] Indeed, the painfully slow pace of the North-South dialogue and its deterioration in the span of a year into a shouting match was attributable, in the final analysis, to the total lack of mutual trust between the two sides, neither of which appears to have modified either their strategic objectives or their images of each other's ultimate goals.

Park continued to portray North Korea as being "bent on reckless schemes for Communization of the whole of Korea"[38] and as "the most isolated and irrational of all the countries of the world."[39] "The north Korean Communists," Park told Alain Vernay, deputy editor of *Le Figaro*, in October 1978, "will try to overrun us militarily, when

36. Park Chung Hee, *Toward Peaceful Unification: Selected Speeches by President Park Chung Hee* (Seoul: Kwangmyong Publishing Co., 1976), p. 168.
37. *Tong'a ilbo*, October 2, 1972.
38. *New Year Press Conference by President Park Chung Hee, January 1977* (Seoul: Korean Overseas Information Service, 1977), p. 37.
39. "Text of President's Interview With *Le Figaro*," *Korea Herald*, October 27, 1978.

they decide they stand a good chance, and they will offer to talk when they think they are in a weaker position. This is their standing modus operandi." He added:

> When we achieve firm superiority over north Korea in such areas as economic development, military strength, and political viability, the north Korean Communists will be induced to reconcile themselves to the futility of a military takeover of the south and will have no alternative but to respond to our peaceful unification formula.[40]

In January 1979, Park reiterated his conviction that North Korea "has not yet given up its policy of unification by force" and asserted that it was capable of attacking South Korea without the endorsement or support of Moscow or Beijing. He thus discounted the speculation that improved relations between the United States and Japan on one hand and the PRC on the other might help moderate Pyongyang's policy.[41]

Images of the Internal Setting

Park Chung Hee's images of South Korea's internal setting were directly related to those of its external setting. In assessing the implications of the Communist takeover in Indochina, he remarked on April 29, 1975:

> The Indochina development teaches us some valuable lessons. First, it shows that negotiations, detente or deals with the Communists are possible only when [a] balance of power is there.
> Second, the time when a country could rely on other nations for its security has passed. Today a nation can survive and expect assistance from others only when it has the determination and ability to safeguard its own security by itself. This is a cruel reality. Third, the Indochina situation shows that a country, even if it has such ability, could not defend itself properly in emergency if its public opinion is split and it is plunged into confusion.[42]

The view that South Korea's twin requirements of economic modernization and national security necessitated unity of the people, their unswerving support for their goals, and their discipline and self-

40. Ibid.
41. *New Year Press Conference by President Park Chung Hee, January 19, 1979* (Seoul: KOIS, 1979), pp. 23–26.
42. *Korean News*, no. 153 (April 29, 1975) (Washington: Korean Information Office, Embassy of Korea), p. 1.

sacrifice was a recurrent theme in Park's public statements throughout his political career. The corollary of this view was that political dissent and partisan bickering directly undermined South Korea's national interests, as perceived by Park. Thus he told *Newsweek* magazine in October 1974:

> I also felt it important to continue in office to totally mobilize our national strength by eliminating waste and inefficiency in our society; to wipe out the defects caused by a dangerous laissez-faire attitude among our people in order to engage in a peaceful competition with North Korea. I therefore instituted the October [1972] reforms which some people criticize because they do not understand their purpose. I decided to bear the cross and leave it to history to judge whether I was right or wrong.[43]

In the same interview, Park denied that there was political repression in South Korea, pointing to the existence of "free debate" in the National Assembly and of the right of the press to criticize government policies. But he added that his government only acknowledged "the right of minor dissent" and "cannot tolerate demonstrations that can bring about social confusion or adversely affect the economic development of the nation." He indirectly admitted the limited success of his effort, when he said that he had found it "most difficult . . . to promote the unity of our people; to create an atmosphere of harmony where our nation's potential can be utilized to the fullest degree." "Once that is achieved," he added, "all other problems will solve themselves."[44]

In his October 1978 interview with *Le Figaro*, Park stated that although "all the basic rights including the freedom of the press are . . . guaranteed" in South Korea, they "may, however, be partially restricted in accordance with the Constitution and the laws of the land when these restrictions are necessary to defend basic and essential national interests such as the maintenance of public order and national security." He added:

> We are locked in a tense confrontation with the north Korean Communists across the Demilitarized Zone only 24 miles away from our capital city of Seoul. The aggressive north Korean Communists are ready to grab any chance to unleash an invasion as they did in 1950. As the survival of the nation and the lives of our people are at stake, we cannot afford to be as liberal with our freedoms and rights as the people of Western Europe are.[45]

43. *Newsweek*, November 4, 1974, p. 15.
44. Ibid.   45. *Korea Herald*, October 27, 1978.

It is, of course, difficult to tell whether the above was more a verbalized justification for the type of political system Park had imposed on his people than a faithful reflection of his true convictions. Given that both the confrontation between the two Koreas and the proximity of the DMZ to Seoul are real rather than imaginary, there is a high probability that the preceding statements may indeed have been Park's true images.

Chun Doo Hwan's Images of the Operational Environment

Images of Korea's internal and external setting articulated by Park's successor, Chun Doo Hwan, contain a basic continuity in one important respect: like his predecessor, Chun is profoundly distrustful of North Korea and argues that the goal of national security must override all others. As he put it in his inaugural speech on March 3, 1981:

> No matter how fine our goals, they are meaningless unless our national security is unflinchingly preserved. We must not relax our guard for even the most fleeting of moments; in light of our unique geopolitical position, we must keep an unblinking watch on the volatile situations surrounding the Korean peninsula, as well as on the unpredictable global scene in the 1980s. There is no substitute for national security: it is fundamental to national survival. The overriding importance of national security must be indelibly ingrained in our minds.[46]

Regarding the perceived North Korean threat, Chun told the National Press Club in Washington on February 2, 1981:

> We live under constant threat of military invasion from the north. During the past 10 years, north Korea has aggressively built up arms, dug infiltration tunnels, and sent guerrillas and provocateurs into the south. North Korea remains the most tightly closed, highly regimented, and ideologically militant Communist regime in the world today. . . . It is unpredictable, uncompromising and dangerous.[47]

Chun is nonetheless critical of the manner in which the late Park Chung Hee cloaked his repressive measures in the mantle of national security. In his words: "political strife in Korea in the 1970s resulted mainly because one person held the reins of power for too long. Even the Constitutional Order was arbitrarily changed for this end." Equating the essence of democracy with "the guarantee of a peaceful trans-

---

46. *Korea Newsreview*, March 7, 1981, p. 8.
47. *Korea Herald*, February 4, 1981.

fer of power," Chun pledged to "work toward bringing about such a Constitutional order." He said:

> When this principle is established and adhered to, other disputes can be resolved creatively and productively within the Constitutional framework. I shall work toward bringing about such a Constitutional order. We are striving to create a political order within which more freedom will ensure greater political and social stability. We will then have more democratic and stable domestic politics in Korea.[48]

In his inaugural speech mentioned earlier, Chun made a solemn pledge: "I will not fail to establish the tradition of peaceful transfer of power, a long-delayed national task."[49]

If Chun's insistence on the peaceful transfer of power sets him apart from the late Park Chung Hee, there is nonetheless a remarkable continuity in one crucial aspect. Chun, too, believes that Western-style democracy is not suitable for Korean soil and needs to be adapted to Korea's peculiar "history, culture and values." The needs of the country, in his view, are "stability, security and economic and social development"; those of the people are "freedom and the right to maximum health and happiness." To meet both sets of these needs, he believes that it is necessary to devise a political system that will root out corruption and abuse of power and promote justice for all in the political, social, and economic sense.[50]

Also reminiscent of the late Park is Chun's insistence to foreign journalists that there is indeed freedom of expression and political dissent under his rule. Asked by an American reporter at the National Press Club in February 1981 why there was press censorship in South Korea contrary to his claim that information was freely available there, Chun answered: "That is behind us. That is not current information. The censorship existed under martial law, which has been lifted as you know, and I am pleased to inform you . . . that there is no press censorship. There is no need for it."[51]

Later in the year, Chun told Gilbert E. Kaplan, editor-in-chief of the American business magazine *Institutional Investor*, that there was freedom of political dissent in South Korea:

> Currently, four major parties, including the Democratic Socialist Party, are represented in the National Assembly. The Demo-

48. Ibid.
49. *Korea Newsreview*, March 7, 1981, p. 9.
50. *Forging A New Era: The Fifth Republic of Korea* (Seoul: Korean Overseas Information Service, 1981), p. 20; these views were expressed in an interview with *Kyŏnghyang sinmun*, a Seoul daily, on August 27, 1980.
51. Ibid., p. 79.

cratic Justice Party, the majority party, holds 55 percent of the Assembly seats. All discussions are freely conducted in the National Assembly. And yet some ask whether Korea has real opposition parties. In my opinion, such a question is raised by people who are not familiar with the state of affairs in Korea. Or it may be that since they do not know Korean, they simply cannot read the vernacular press to learn what is being discussed in the National Assembly.[52]

Finally, Chun echoes the view of the late Park that America's alliance with Seoul is mutually beneficial. Asked, during his February 1981 appearance at the National Press Club, to explain "the function of the 39,000 American troops in your country in light of South Korea's far larger standing army," Chun replied:

Let me first point out that peace and stability on the Korean peninsula is indispensable to peace and tranquility in the Northeast Asian region, which in turn is essential to the global peace structure. The right to exist of the Republic of Korea must be defended in this way, but that is not all.
Korea is after all a bulwark of defense for the Free World, especially Japan and the United States in the Pacific Basin. So, working together, we and the US forces serve to restrain, serve to stay the hands of Soviet expansionism in Northeast Asia, and particularly to diminish the possibility of Soviet Russia using North Korea as a proxy and creating major strife in that critically important region. That is the role, that is the strategic role, that the United States forces are playing.[53]

Chun added that the American military presence in Korea also "compels the Soviet ground forces to disperse and to overextend in Europe, in the Middle East and in the Far East." "Their forces," he said, "are considerable in number and we serve to keep a portion of those forces tied down in our region, and this denies them the possibility of concentrating their power in one particular region."[54]

Implicit in the preceding view is the image of the Soviet Union as a hostile power. In fact, Chun was specifically asked which of the two Communist powers, the Soviet Union or the PRC, he considers "the greater threat to peace and stability in your region." Chun replied: "If the People's Republic of China is a friend of the United

52. "The World According to Chun Doo Hwan," *Institutional Investor*, February 1982, p. 76.
53. *Forging A New Era*, p. 79.
54. Ibid.

States, I think I can extend the logic and say a friend of a friend is less of a threat to us than the other power you have mentioned."[55]

These, then, are selected images of the operational environment articulated by the top political leaders of the two Korean states. We shall now turn to that important but elusive dimension of foreign policy—decision making.

55. Ibid., p. 78.

7 DECISION MAKING: STRUCTURES AND ROUTINES

Ideally, foreign policy analysis must encompass a thoroughgoing description and explanation of the structure and processes of decision making, illuminating, at a bare minimum, who makes what decision, how, and why. In reality, such a task remains singularly elusive. For the data requirements are truly formidable. In the words of the pioneering proponents of the decision-making framework, Snyder, Bruck, and Sapin:

> About the decision-makers in any decisional system concerned with any particular problem we want to know: what are the characteristics and relationships of the spheres of competence? what are the motivational influences at work? what is the nature of the communication network? what is the nature, amount and distribution of information? and, finally, what is the reciprocal impact of these on each other? Answers to these questions should provide a basis for adequately describing and explaining state action.[1]

Due to practical constraints on data gathering, the decision-making framework first proposed by Snyder and his colleagues a quarter century ago has thus far generated but one empirical application,[2] and it is plain that the framework is largely inapplicable,

---

1. Richard C. Snyder, H. W. Bruck, B. Sapin (eds.), *Foreign Policy Decision-Making* (New York: Free Press, 1962), p. 174.
2. Richard C. Snyder, H. W. Bruck, and B. Sapin, *Decision-Making as an Approach to the Study of International Politics* (Princeton: Princeton University, Organiza-

even irrelevant, to such closed political systems as North and South Korea. As already noted, the DPRK is one of the most closed countries in the world in terms of accessibility to outsiders and of the quantity and quality of information emanating from it. The ROK, while markedly more open than its northern rival, is nonetheless a closed society from the point of view of the flow of information, which is both controlled and manipulated by the government to a striking degree.

Within the context of the crude analytic scheme employed in this study, decision-making is construed in a narrow sense to refer primarily to the structures and routines, both formal and informal, of foreign policy decision making. Among the four components of decision making, formal structure is the only one that can be identified without difficulty. The remainder is, by and large, shrouded in secrecy; all that can be essayed here, therefore, is speculation, informed by a limited knowledge of the political systems of the two Koreas.

NORTH KOREA

Several things are noteworthy regarding the structures of foreign policy decision making in North Korea. First, like most Communist political systems, the North Korean system is characterzied by the prepotent role of the party—the Workers' Party of Korea (KWP). Although a considerable overlap of personnel in the top echelons of party and government blurs the distinction somewhat, it is clear that in terms of both formal and actual power the government is subordinate to the party. Second, a situation which is unique to North Korea pertains to the Central People's Committee (CPC), a supercabinet that was created by the DPRK Constitution of 1972. Its importance is indicated by the fact that nearly all of its members are either full or candidate members of the Political Bureau of the WPK Central Committee. Third, the Ministry of Foreign Affairs (*Oegyo-bu*), as a part of the State Administration Council (*Chŏngmu-won*), is given primarily administrative functions—the responsibility of implementing, rather than formulating, foreign policy. Finally, there is a division of labor in the conduct of North Korean diplomacy: whereas the Ministry of Foreign Affairs is responsible for foreign relations at the official level (i.e., government-to-government relations), another organization, the Committee for Cultural Relations With Foreign Countries, is charged

---

tional Behavior Section, 1954). The lone empirical application of the framework is Glenn D. Paige, *The Korean Decision* (New York: Free Press, 1968).

with the task of conducting people-to-people diplomacy and cultural exchanges. The committee is believed to be accountable to the WPK: as of mid-1982, the deputy-director of the International Department of the WPK Central Committee (Hyon Jun Kuk) served concurrently as the vice-chairman of the committee.

Insofar as formal authority for foreign policy making is concerned, the president (*chusŏk*) of the DPRK is supreme. The Constitution stipulates that the president "shall directly guide the Central People's Committee" (Art. 91), which is empowered to "formulate domestic and foreign policies of the nation" (Art. 103, para. 1). Additional foreign policy powers that the Constitution grants to the president include the power to "ratify or terminate treaties with other nations" (Art. 96) and the power to "receive the credentials and recall orders of the diplomatic representatives of other nations" (Art. 97). Also enjoying a formal role in North Korea's foreign policy making process is the Supreme People's Assembly, to which the Constitution assigns the power to "formulate the basic principles of the nation's domestic and foreign policies" (Art. 76, para. 2).

As noted, the Ministry of Foreign Affairs enjoys a distinctly subordinate status in North Korea's formal foreign policy machinery. That it is eclipsed in actual practice by the WPK, not to mention the CPC, is suggested by the fact that the head of the International Department of the WPK Central Committee, Kim Yong Nam, outranks the minister of foreign affairs, Ho Dam, in North Korea's power hierarchy, as measured by the order in which names are mentioned on ceremonial occasions as well as by membership in the all-powerful Political Bureau of the WPK Central Committee. Whereas Kim is a full member of the politburo and ranks twelfth in the power hierarchy, Ho is only an alternate member and ranks twentieth.[3]

Nonetheless, one should not downgrade the role of the Foreign Ministry both in the formulation and the conduct of North Korean foreign policy. For it is an important collector and generator of information for Pyongyang's foreign policy making elite; moreover, as is well known, policy may be substantially affected, even transformed, in the course of implementation. One should, therefore, at least take note of the basic structure of the Foreign Ministry. Like its counterparts in other countries, including South Korea, the DPRK Foreign Ministry consists of both functional and geographical bureaus. The former encompass protocol, financial affairs, treaties and other laws, international organizations, publicity (*podo-guk*), consular affairs, external propaganda, and documents; the geographical bureaus are designated by numbers ranging from one to eight.[4]

    3. *Nodong sinmun*, October 15, 1980.
    4. *Kita Chōsen kenkyū* 5, 55 (January 1979): 15; *Pukhan chŏngch'i-ron* [On North Korean Politics] (Seoul: Kŭktong Munje Yŏn'guso, 1976), p. 609.

Figure 2 displays most of the party and government organs in North Korea that are in a position, both in a formal and a functional sense, to play some role in the foreign policy process. They are (1) the Presidency of the DPRK, (2) the Supreme People's Assembly, (3) the Central People's Committee (CPC), (4) the CPC Foreign Policy Commission, (5) the CPC National Defense Commission, (6) the Ministry of Foreign Affairs of the State Administration Council (SAC), (7) the Ministry of the People's Armed Forces of the SAC, (8) the Ministry of External Economic Relations of the SAC, (9) the Ministry of Foreign Trade of the SAC, (10) the Central Committee (CC) of the WPK, (11) the Politburo of the WPK-CC, (12) the Secretariat of the WPK-CC, (13) the CC International Department, (14) the CC External Activities Department, (15) the CC Propaganda and Agitation Department, (16) the CC Military Committee, and (17) the National Party Congress of the WPK. Although not shown in Figure 2, the DPRK Academy of Social Science (*Sahoe Kwahagwon*) may also play a part in the foreign policy making process. During my 1981 visit to North Korea, I had many hours of discussion with members of the academy and obtained the impression that they had some role to play in the foreign policy process. I learned, for example, that the academy had at least two offices or institutes (*yŏn'gusil*) devoted to the reunification problem. Finally, one may also add the Committee for the Reunification of the Fatherland to the list of organs that may participate in the implementation, if not the formulation, of reunification policy.

Whether or not any of these organs will actually participate in foreign policy decision making and implementation—and, if so, what its relative influence will be—will depend on such variables as issue areas, the decision time available, the stakes involved, and the political clout of the organizational elites involved, which in turn is a function of many other factors. It has nevertheless been adumbrated that apart from the president, the two most influential organs are likely to be the Central People's Committee and the WPK politburo, whose memberships overlap to a striking degree.[5] Since 1979 these two organs have periodically held joint meetings. In April 1982, the WPK Central Committee and the Supreme People's Assembly held a joint session for the first time in North Korean history. There is a high probability that in a crisis situation an ad hoc group may be formed whose membership may not correspond exactly to that of any formal standing body.

As Graham T. Allison has shown, established routines of bu-

5. As of June 1982, all but one of CPC members were either full or candidate members of the WPK Politburo. The lone exception was Kang Ryang Uk, one of the three vice presidents of the DPRK. Kang, who is believed to be related to Kim Il Sung on his mother's side, is not a member of the WPK but chairman of the Central Committee of the Korea Social Democratic party.

FIGURE 2 · North Korean Party and Government Organs with Possible Inputs into Foreign Policy

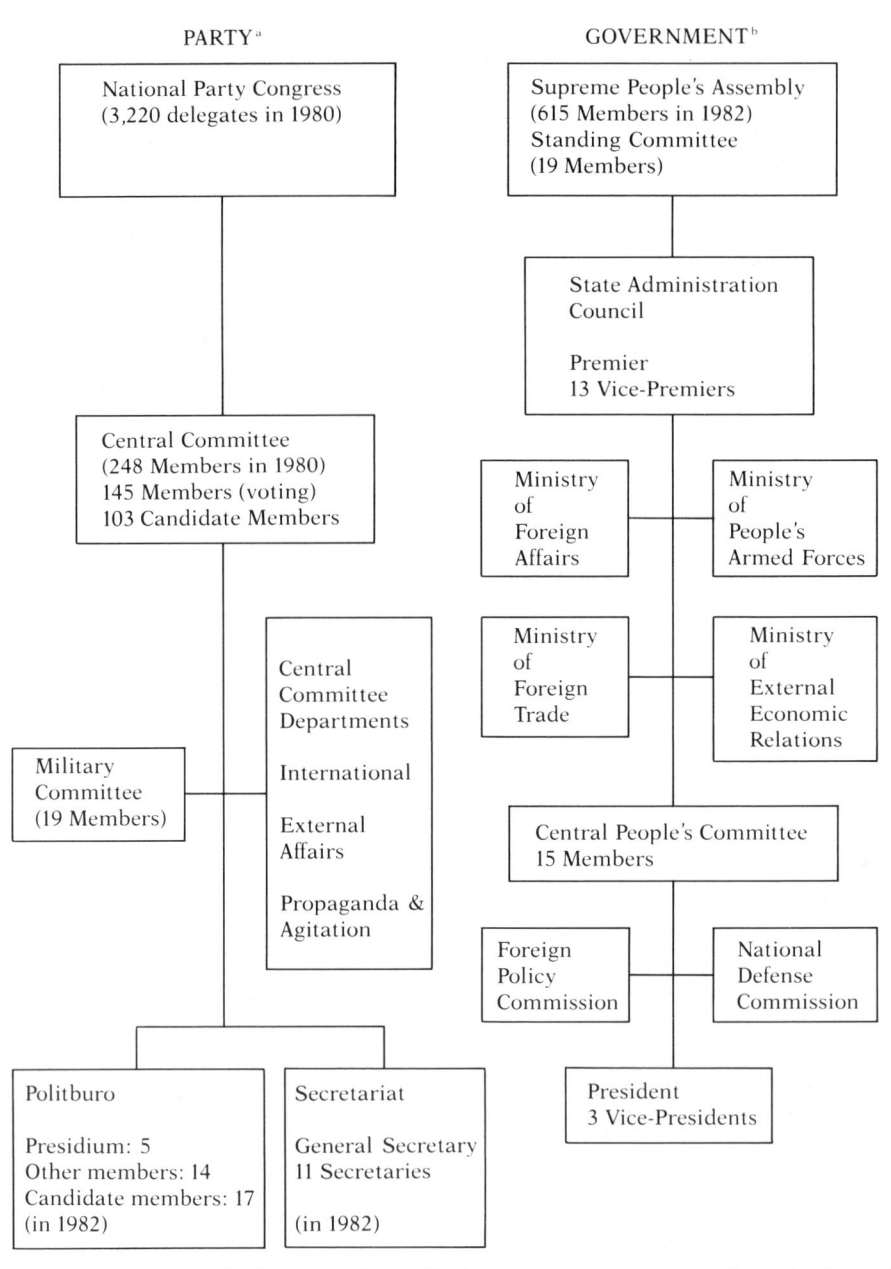

PARTY[a]

- National Party Congress (3,220 delegates in 1980)
- Central Committee (248 Members in 1980) 145 Members (voting) 103 Candidate Members
- Military Committee (19 Members)
- Central Committee Departments
  - International
  - External Affairs
  - Propaganda & Agitation
- Politburo
  - Presidium: 5
  - Other members: 14
  - Candidate members: 17
  - (in 1982)
- Secretariat
  - General Secretary
  - 11 Secretaries
  - (in 1982)

GOVERNMENT[b]

- Supreme People's Assembly (615 Members in 1982) Standing Committee (19 Members)
- State Administration Council
  - Premier
  - 13 Vice-Premiers
- Ministry of Foreign Affairs
- Ministry of People's Armed Forces
- Ministry of Foreign Trade
- Ministry of External Economic Relations
- Central People's Committee 15 Members
- Foreign Policy Commission
- National Defense Commission
- President
- 3 Vice-Presidents

[a] NPC elects CC, which in turn elects all other organs. In practice, the flow of influence is reversed—that is, from the Politburo to CC and NPC.
[b] SPA elects all other organs.

reaucratic organizations have a notable impact both on the formulation and implementation of foreign policy.[6] While most of the organs mentioned above are most likely to have developed a set of standard operating procedures their substantive contents remain by and large unknown to the outside world. From the discernible characteristics of the North Korean political system, however, one may surmise that the supreme leader, Kim Il Sung, is most likely to play the pivotal, probably the decisive, role insofar as key foreign policy decisions are concerned. One may further hypothesize that given the imperatives of the personality cult permeating the entire North Korean polity and society, an adversary process is likely to be absent in the policy process: interpretations, contingencies, and options that are perceived to be unacceptable to the supreme leader are most likely to be suppressed, thus magnifying Kim Il Sung's influence manifold. That such a situation, if it actually exists, has negative implications for the efficacy of North Korean foreign policy is obvious.[7]

No matter what the structure and routines of decision making may be, the strategic importance of information cannot be overemphasized. Insight into how information is generated, processed, and transmitted to decision points will go a long way toward elucidating the foreign policy making process. Fragmentary evidence suggests that there may exist a North Korean counterpart to America's FBIS (Foreign Broadcast Information Service) Daily Report, which contains selections of translated texts or excerpts of foreign broadcast or press material.[8] Given the need for information as deci-

    6. Allison, *Essence of Decision: Explaining the Cuban Missile Crisis* (Boston: Little, Brown, 1971).

    7. Since there are notable parallels between Stalin and Kim Il Sung—such as the personality cult, authorship of innumerable articles and pamphlets, "theoretical" and otherwise, the longevity of rule, and the scope and magnitude of power exercised—it is instructive to learn that Stalin could and did ignore other organs of power, especially in his last years. In the words of Khrushchev: "Stalin did everything himself, bypassing the Central Committee and using the Politbureau as little more than a rubber stamp. Stalin rarely bothered to ask the opinion of Politbureau members about a given measure. He would just make a decision and issue a decree. . . . When Stalin proposed something, there were no questions, no comments. A 'proposal' from Stalin was a God-given command, and you don't haggle about what God tells you to do—you just offer thanks and obey." *Khrushchev Remembers*, with an introduction, commentary, and notes by Edward Crankshaw, translated by Strobe Talbott (New York: Bantam Books, 1971), pp. 294–297.

    8. During my 1981 visit to North Korea, I was able to confirm the existence of such material. They include *Tangbo* [Party News] and *Ch'amgo sinmun* [Reference News]. I was told that access to such material was determined on a "need-to-know" basis. I found that the higher one's rank and position in the North Korean hierarchy, the better informed one was of the events outside of North Korea. Nonetheless, the North Korean elite's understanding of the intricacies of the external situation was appallingly low.

sion premises and given the considerable leeway that the editor of such a series is bound to be granted, one can surmise that the editor wields appreciable influence in North Korean foreign policy making.

Finally, another systemic constraint on foreign policy making in North Korea should be noted briefly. During my nineteen-day visit to that country in the summer of 1981, I learned that North Korean diplomats posted in foreign countries follow the same schedule of work and study that is prescribed for their compatriots at home. The schedule calls for, among other things, lecture and/or film meetings on Wednesday evenings, manual labor for all white-collar and professional people on Fridays (they are expected to do manual labor for the entire day), and political study sessions on Saturday afternoons. When one adds to the above the special demands on the time of North Korean diplomats imposed by their cardinal duty to propagate the works of Kim Il Sung—through mailings, advertisements, organization and support of various pro-North Korean organizations in their host countries—it becomes clear that their ability to collect, analyze, and report information on important developments abroad is substantially undercut.

SOUTH KOREA

Unlike North Korea, South Korea has experienced change in top political leadership. This means that one must differentiate between the various regimes (or republics) in discussing foreign policy decision making. It is generally believed that both the Syngman Rhee (1948–1960) and Park Chung Hee (1961–1979) regimes featured the phenomenon of presidential predominance in foreign policy making not only in a personal sense but also in an institutional sense. That is to say, the president and his top aides apparently eclipsed all others in terms of foreign policy making power.

On the other hand, the Fifth Republic of Chun Doo Hwan appears to allow a slightly wider sharing of power among the various government organs than was true previously. It is also speculated in informed circles that there may exist an informal junta consisting of military leaders, either on active duty or on reserve, who engineered the December 12, 1979 coup and the subsequent takeover of power by the Chun Doo Hwan group. Core members of the covert junta are believed to be members of the seventeenth class of the ROK Military Academy. President Chun is a member of the eleventh class.

If the preceding speculation is valid, then it is clear that "formalism"—a discrepancy between form and reality—is even more marked in the Fifth Republic than was the case in the preceding republics. Formalism manifests itself in more obvious ways, too. Just as the Supreme People's Assembly of the DPRK is a rubber-stamp body not only in the realm of foreign policy but in other areas as well, so the National Assembly of the ROK is relegated to the peripheral, albeit symbolically important, status of a debating society.

Nor does the ROK Ministry of Foreign Affairs seem to carry any more weight in foreign policy making than does its counterpart in North Korea. If, as I have surmised, the key foreign policy decision making elites in North Korea are members of the Political Bureau of the WPK Central Committee and the Central People's Committee, who, then, are their counterparts in South Korea? In the Park regime, they included the director of the ROK Central Intelligence Agency (KCIA) and the top echelons of the Presidential Secretariat in the Blue House—notably, the director-general of the Secretariat and the chief presidential secretaries. The National Security Council (NSC) appeared to have been a pivotal body. Composed of the president, the prime minister, the deputy prime minister, the foreign minister, the defense minister, the director of the KCIA, and others whom the president might designate, the NSC was empowered by the Constitution to provide advice to the president on issues of foreign, military, and domestic policies bearing on national security prior to their consideration by the State Council.[9]

The main changes that President Chun Doo Hwan has introduced appear to be (1) reorganization of the Presidential Secretariat with the manifest goal of making the president more accessible to his cabinet ministers and (2) renaming the KCIA the "Agency for National Security Planning" (ANSP). The composition of the NSC during the first year of the Fifth Republic strongly suggested its continuing importance.[10] It is noteworthy that all three persons who have

9. Gregory F. T. Winn, "Korean Foreign Policy Decision Making: Process and Structure," *Colloquium Paper*, no. 4, Center for Korean Studies, University of Hawaii, Honolulu, 1976, pp. 14–15.

10. Another indication of the NSC's importance was provided by the appointment of No Tae Woo to the council by President Chun in September 1981. No, who retired as the commander of the ROK Defense Security Command and immediately joined Chun's cabinet as a minister of state for political affairs in July 1981, is widely regarded as one of the key figures in the December 12, 1979 coup which led to the emergence of Chun Doo Hwan as the top leader of South Korea. A former classmate of Chun at the ROK Military Academy, No may very well emerge as Chun's successor to the presidency in 1988. On No's background, see Shim Jae Hoon, "The Answer is No," *Far Eastern Economic Review*, July 31, 1981, p. 22. No was named to head the newly created Ministry of Sports in March 1982 and then, in May 1982, moved to the post of Home Minister. Both of these positions are key posts. The former is responsible for the preparations for the 1988 Olympic Games scheduled to be held in Seoul, while the latter oversees all local government units and police.

FIGURE 3 · South Korean Government Organs with Possible Inputs into Foreign Policy

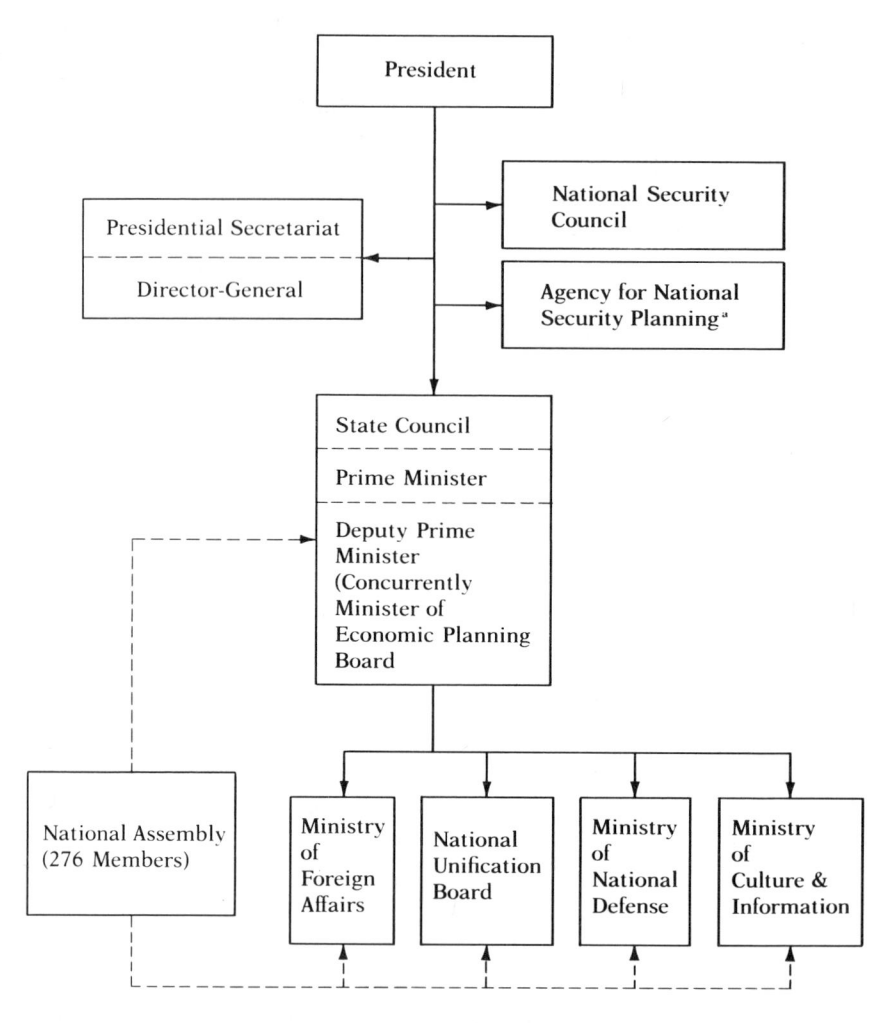

```
                        ┌─────────────────┐
                        │   President     │
                        └────────┬────────┘
                                 │
                  ┌──────────────┼──────────────────────────┐
                  │              │                          │
                  │              ▼                          │
                  │    ┌─────────────────────┐              │
                  │    │ National Security   │              │
┌─────────────────┴─┐  │ Council             │              │
│ Presidential      │  └─────────────────────┘              │
│ Secretariat       │◄─                                     │
│ ─ ─ ─ ─ ─ ─ ─ ─ ─ │   ┌─────────────────────┐             │
│ Director-General  │   │ Agency for National │             │
└───────────────────┘   │ Security Planning ª │             │
                        └─────────────────────┘             │
                                 │                          │
                                 ▼                          │
                    ┌──────────────────────┐
                    │  State Council       │
                    │ ─ ─ ─ ─ ─ ─ ─ ─ ─ ─  │
                    │  Prime Minister      │
                    │ ─ ─ ─ ─ ─ ─ ─ ─ ─ ─  │
         ┌ ─ ─ ─ ─ ►│  Deputy Prime        │
         │          │  Minister            │
         │          │  (Concurrently       │
         │          │  Minister of         │
         │          │  Economic Planning   │
         │          │  Board)              │
         │          └──────────┬───────────┘
         │              ┌──────┼──────┬─────────┐
         │              ▼      ▼      ▼         ▼
┌────────┴────────┐ ┌───────┐┌──────┐┌───────┐┌──────────┐
│ National Assembly│ │Ministry││Nation-││Ministry││Ministry  │
│ (276 Members)    │ │of     ││al Uni-││of      ││of        │
│                  │ │Foreign││fication││National││Culture & │
│                  │ │Affairs││Board  ││Defense ││Information│
└──────────────────┘ └───▲───┘└──▲───┘└───▲────┘└────▲─────┘
         └ ─ ─ ─ ─ ─ ─ ─ ┴ ─ ─ ─ ┴ ─ ─ ─ ─┴ ─ ─ ─ ─ ─┘
```

NOTE: Solid arrows indicate the direction of control, while dotted arrows merely suggest the possibility of some inputs from the National Assembly.
ª Previously known as the Central Intelligence Agency.

served as the director-general of the Presidential Secretariat under Chun (up to June 1982) have significant links with foreign policy. The first incumbent, Kim Kyung Won, had served as a special assistant for international politics to the late Park and later became Chun's ambassador to the United Nations. The second incumbent, Lee Bum Suk, had served as the minister of the National Unification Board under Chun and left the Blue House to become the minister of foreign affairs. Finally, the third and current (as of June 1982) incumbent, Hahm Pyong-choon, was the late Park's ambassador to the United States. Given their expertise in foreign affairs, it is reasonable to surmise that these people may have had some inputs into foreign policy decisions during their tenures in the Blue House. Even if the hypothesis about the existence of an invisible junta as the supreme decision-making body is true, there nonetheless remains the possibility that its main preoccupations are domestic, rather than foreign policy, issues. For none of the presumed members of such a junta has any expertise in foreign policy.

Another possible similarity between North and South Korea pertains to the routines of decision making. Given the marked concentration of power in the hands of the top leader and his close associates, both formal and informal, one may surmise that there is likely to be a significant constraint on the flow of ideas and information in South Korea as well. In other words, the hypothesized absence of an adversary process in North Korea may be equally germane in the case of South Korea. One must hasten to add, however, that there may be a significant difference in the relative severity of the problem in the two Korean states. Various factors—the conditions under which the Chun regime emerged, the absence of a personality cult, and the probable sharing of power among the members of the inner circle—suggest the possibility that the social distance between the president and his subordinates may be considerably less than that between Kim Il Sung and other members of the North Korean elite. Vertical flow of information and ideas, in short, will most probably be inhibited in the South but not to the same degree as in the North. This problem was apparently more severe under Syngman Rhee and Park Chung Hee than it is under Chun Doo Hwan.[11] In this connection, it should be pointed out that public opinion plays little or no part in the formulation of foreign policy. The public, however, are mobilized to bolster or legitimize government positions dealing with foreign and, especially, security policies.[12]

11. Winn, "Korean Foreign Policy," pp. 9–10; *Han'guk ilbo*, August 18, 1981.
12. Chae-Jin Lee, "The Direction of South Korea's Foreign Policy," *Korean Studies* 2 (1978): 102–103.

If there are standard operating procedures (SOPs) in South Korea's foreign policy organs, as there must be, their specific contents are difficult to ascertain. One knowledgeable observer has hypothesized that whereas the standard operating procedures have resulted in the bureaucratization of policy making *within* organizations, patterns of interaction *between* organizations remain by and large uncharted, thereby impeding horizontal communication and bargaining. He further speculates that since the policy making elite, who play an "overwhelming role in collecting information related to foreign policy and in defining important issues," have formed a "consensus regarding anticommunism and national security," a measure of "group thinking" may be feasible in coping with foreign policy problems. Finally, he notes the absence of any mechanism for long-range planning in foreign policy and the markedly ad hoc and crisis-oriented nature of foreign policy making in South Korea.[13]

Figure 3 lists most of the organs that have either a potential or an actual role in the conduct of South Korean foreign policy. The relevant structures and officials appear to be (1) the president, (2) the Presidential Secretariat, especially its director-general, (3) the National Security Council, (4) the Agency for National Security Planning, (5) the State Council, (6) the prime minister, (7) the deputy prime minister (who concurrently serves as the minister of the Economic Planning Board), (8) the Ministry of Foreign Affairs, (9) the National Unification Board, (10) the Ministry of National Defense, (11) the Ministry of Culture and Information, and (12) the National Assembly.

Although we have used the term *formalism* to stress the discrepancy between form and reality, there is nonetheless an important sense in which form does accurately reflect the reality. For example, the president is given a dazzling array of powers in the Constitution. Under the 1972 ROK Constitution, in addition to the customary powers to "represent the nation vis-à-vis foreign nations," to conclude and ratify treaties, to accredit, receive, or send diplomatic envoys, and to declare wars, the president was empowered to issue "emergency decrees" pertaining to domestic politics, diplomacy, national defense, the economy, finance, or any matter connected with government, whenever he deems it necessary in order to cope with or avert threats to national security, law and order or any other serious crisis (Arts.

---

13. Ahn Byung-Joon, "Wolnamjŏn ihu Han'guk-kwa Miguk ŭi oegyo chŏngch'aek kyŏlchŏng kwajŏng pigyo" [A Comparison of the Foreign Policy Making Processes in South Korea and the US in the post-Vietnam War Period], paper presented to the third joint conference of the Korean Political Science Association and the Association of Korean Political Scientists in North America, June 18–20, 1979, Seoul, Korea, pp. 172–173. The page numbers refer to the proceedings of the conference.

43, 50, and 53). His powers were further enhanced by the stipulation that he "shall be the presiding officer of the State Council," which was given the authority to consider all important foreign policy matters (Arts. 65 and 66).

The 1980 ROK Constitution retains all of these powers. Two relatively minor differences, however, pertain to the new power of the president to "submit important policies relating to diplomacy, national defense, unification, and other matters relating to diplomacy, national defense, unification, and other matters relating to the national destiny to a national referendum, if he deems it necessary" (Art. 47) and to a check on emergency powers. Unlike the 1972 document, the new charter stipulates that "the President shall notify the National Assembly [of emergency measures] without delay and shall obtain the concurrence of the National Assembly" and that "in case no concurrence is obtained, the measures shall lose effect forthwith" (Art. 51, para. 3). The ability of the National Assembly to restrain the exercise of presidential powers, however, is diluted by the provision that the president has the power unilaterally to dissolve the assembly (Art. 57) and by the further fact that the electoral system makes it exceedingly difficult for political parties other than the president's own to gain control of the assembly.

The influence of the director-general of the Presidential Secretariat and the chief presidential secretaries is linked inseparably to their access to the president as well as the latter's dependence on the former on a daily basis. We have also noted that the expertise of the person who happens to be serving as director-general in foreign affairs may serve to enhance his role in foreign policy making. President Chun Doo Hwan has abolished the positions of special assistants with a view to enhancing individual cabinet members' access to him,[14] and he is known to make a special effort to maintain direct channels of information from multiple sources.

The strategic role of the ANSP—formerly KCIA—stems not only from its capability to collect, interpret, and transmit foreign-policy-related information but also from its unique function in the South Korea polity: it has served, since its inception in 1963, as an indispensable tool of political power and governance for the president.

As the nation's top administrator as well as the ranking member of the president's cabinet, the prime minister is a logical member of South Korea's foreign policy making elite. His actual impact on foreign policy, needless to say, will vary with his expertise, rapport with the president, and other factors. Even though the Ministry of Foreign Affairs may be viewed primarily as an executor, rather than a for-

---

14. *Haptong News Agency*, September 9, 1980, as monitored by FBIS.

mulator, of foreign policy, its importance should not be minimized for reasons already noted. Its salient organizational characteristics are as follows: In addition to the minister, the vice-minister, and two assistant ministers (for political affairs and for economic affairs), the ministry has two offices (planning and management, and protocol) and nine bureaus. Of the latter, four are functional bureaus (consular affairs and overseas residents, international economic affairs, information and culture, treaties and international organizations), while the remainder are geographic ones (Asia, the Americas, Europe, the Middle East, and Africa). The Foreign Ministry also has an Institute of Foreign Affairs and National Security, which performs the twin functions of training and research. One noteworthy feature of the ROK Foreign Ministry is that it has almost twice as many people in overseas missions as it does in its home office.[15]

Inasmuch as national reunification is a pivotal issue in South Korea's foreign policy, the National Unification Board may play some role in it. In practice, the board appears essentially to be a research and training organization. Given the relative weight of both national security and economic development in Seoul's overall policy framework, the ministries concerned with these functions—especially the Ministry of National Defense and the Economic Planning Board—are in a position to provide some inputs into, or otherwise help shape, foreign policy.

The primarily ceremonial character of the National Assembly has already been noted. That it has the potential to play some role in foreign policy making is suggested by the constitutional stipulation that the assembly shall have the power to give and, by implication, to withhold consent to treaties, declarations of war, the dispatch of ROK troops to foreign countries, and the stationing of foreign troops within the territory of the ROK (Art. 96). More important in practice is the assembly's power of interpellation, under which members of the cabinet may be questioned regarding policy matters, both domestic and foreign (Art. 98). Whether such a procedure has any tangible impact on the substance or style of foreign policy, however, is debatable. Indeed, under the conditions where the government almost automatically controls an absolute majority in the assembly, interpellations, no matter how vociferous, take on a predominantly ritualistic character.

15. As of March 1979, there were 829 foreign service officers stationed abroad, as opposed to 442 in Seoul. Republic of Korea, Ministry of Foreign Affairs, *Hyŏnhwang* [Current Situation] (Seoul: Committee on Foreign Affairs, the National Assembly, the 101st extraordinary session, March, 1979), pp. 3–4. The number of bureaus was reduced from 12 to 9 in October 1981, as part of a large-scale retrenchment program. *Han'guk ilbo*, October 17, 1981.

In sum, there are multiple structures in both Koreas which are potentially capable of participating in their respective foreign policy making processes. There is, however, ground for surmising that only a few institutions with strategic access to the top leaders may play the pivotal role in them. While the contents of the decision-making routines of Seoul and Pyongyang alike are elusive, one can nonetheless infer from the salient characteristics of the political systems that the processing of information and the exploration of policy options may be somewhat constrained, particularly in the cult-dominated North.

8   FOREIGN POLICY OUTPUTS: STRATEGIC AND OPERATIONAL DECISIONS

Although we have posited analytic distinctions among the inputs, conversion process, and outputs of foreign policy, their empirical boundaries remain rather hazy. In fact, there is substantial overlap among them. For example, "bilateral systems" of the external setting of the operational environment encompass a nation's bilateral relations with, and hence policies toward, other nations in its geographic region. What is more, our discussion of the psychological environment of foreign policy, particularly of the elite images of the operational environment, has adumbrated many facets of the actual foreign policies of the two Koreas. Our purpose in this chapter, then, is to describe in more detail selected foreign policy outputs of Seoul and Pyongyang, probe their linkage to the input variables, and compare them. Our discussion will be guided by a crude typology of foreign policy outputs that consists of strategic, operational, and tactical decisions and that differentiates between symbolic and substantive actions. Of these, strategic and operational decisions will be examined in this chapter, and the remainder will be taken up in the following chapter.

STRATEGIC DECISIONS

Strategic decisions are marked by their relatively long time frame; they are designed to endure over time and expected to generate payoffs in a slow, incremental fashion. They tend to be relatively abstract. Since both Koreas have embraced national reunification as their respective strategic objectives and since that goal does indeed present a convenient framework within which to analyze their respective foreign policy behaviors, it may be fruitful to focus on their overall strategies of national reunification. Such strategies may have evolved over time, rather than being adopted suddenly; hence it may not be possible to pinpoint the time when "strategic decisions" regarding reunification were made. What is feasible, however, is to examine public statements by the top decision makers in the two Koreas with a view to ascertaining their strategic thinking.

North Korea's Reunification Strategy

Since the early 1960s North Korea has been pursuing what may be called the "strategy of triple revolutions." Components of that strategy began to take form in the late 1950s. For example, in his report at the tenth anniversary celebration of the founding of the DPRK on September 8, 1958, Premier Kim Il Sung stated that "the peaceful reunification of the country will certainly be achieved" when two conditions are met: (1) consolidation of the "socialist forces in the northern half" and (2) the waging of a "national salvation struggle" by "all the patriotic, democratic forces in south Korea" against "the US imperialists and traitorous Syngman Rhee clique."[1] These ideas were reiterated in Kim's report on the work of the Central Committee to the Fourth Congress of the WPK on September 11, 1961,[2] and again in his speech to the first session of the Third Supreme National Assembly of the DPRK on October 23, 1962.[3] In the latter speech, Kim also suggested the third component of the strategy: the need to unite with all exploited and oppressed peoples in a struggle against the imperialists, particularly the "US imperialists."[4]

It was, however, not until February 1964 that Kim Il Sung explicitly articulated the three-pronged strategy, clearly revealing the internal logic and interrelationship of its parts. In a concluding speech delivered to the Eighth Plenum of the Fourth Central Committee of the WPK on February 27, 1964, which dealt specifically with the question of how to achieve national reunification, Kim expounded on the theme of developing "revolutionary forces" (*hyŏngmyŏng yŏngnyang*) on three fronts: (1) North Korea, (2) South Korea, and (3) the world at large.[5]

1. Kim Il Sung, *Selected Works*, vol. 2 (Pyongyang: Foreign Languages Publishing House, 1971), p. 223.
2. *Kim Il Sung chŏjak sŏnjip* [Selected Works of Kim Il Sung], vol. 3 (Pyongyang: Chosŏn Nodong-dang Ch'ul-p'an-sa, 1968), pp. 150–151.
3. Ibid., pp. 399–411.   4. Ibid., pp. 413–416.
5. *Kim Il Sung chŏjak sŏnjip*, vol. 4, pp. 77–96.

The first component of the strategy is to turn North Korea into a powerful revolutionary base by fortifying its political, economic, and military capabilities. To bolster political capability means to strengthen the Workers Party of Korea, the vanguard of the revolution, and then to rally the popular masses behind its banner. It entails stepped-up efforts at political indoctrination with a view to "educating and remolding" (*kyoyang kaejo*) the North Korean people in all walks of life. No less important is the task of enhancing the economic capability of North Korea. Not only is economic power a sine qua non for strengthening political and military capabilities, it is also prerequisite for strengthening the revolutionary capability of the South Korean people. For the sharper the contrast between the economic conditions of the North and the South, with the North enjoying the edge, the more attractive the North will become to the South Korean people, and the more determined they will become in their struggle against "colonial rule" in the South. Kim Il Sung also sees linkage between enhanced economic capability and the progress of the "world revolution": with a powerful economic capability, North Korea will be in a position to contribute significantly to the strengthening of the might of the socialist camp.[6] The last leg in the tripod of power is military capability, which is a "powerful means of smashing counterrevolutionary forces and of guaranteeing the victory of the revolution." Without it, North Korea "can neither preserve the fruits of revolution against an aggression by the enemy nor protect, let alone strengthen, political and economic capabilities." Stressing that military might is necessary regardless of whether the revolution is conducted in a peaceful or violent way, Kim summarized five specific goals which the party had previously adopted: (1) upgrading the political and technical training of the Korean People's Army (KPA) so that all KPA soldiers may become "cadres"; (2) modernizing its arms and equipment; (3) turning all miltiary bases into impregnable "fortresses"; (4) arming the entire people; and (5) turning the entire country into a fortress.[7]

The second component of the reunification strategy is to foster the revolutionary capability of South Korea. Conceding that the capability was "very weak," Kim Il Sung saw a profound gap between the objective reality of South Korea and the subjective consciousness of the South Korean people. The reality, in his view, was marked by appalling social and economic conditions in which the masses were on the verge of starvation and which were caused by the "colonial rule of the American imperialists and their lackeys." However, the subjective consciousness of the South Korean masses, according to Kim, lagged behind the reality, for they failed to grasp who their real

6. Ibid., pp. 82–85.   7. Ibid., pp. 85–87.

enemy was and lacked revolutionary consciousness. "The North Korean people can assist the South Korean people but cannot wage the [anti-imperialist] struggle for them," Kim said. Hence the need for developing the revolutionary capability of the South Korean people. This would require the following steps:

First, the "main force of revolution" must be developed. This means organizing a Marxist-Leninist party, awakening the proletariat, and forging a solid link between the two. Second, the peasant masses must be won over to the revolutionary cause. Together with the proletariat, the peasantry will form the backbone of the southern revolution. Third, it is necessary to build a powerful leadership core for the party. The core must consist of "outstanding persons who are both armed with the Marxist-Leninist *weltanschauung* and capable of formulating revolutionary strategies and tactics on their own." Both of these qualifications, in Kim's view, need to be "tempered in the flames of revolutionary struggle." Fourth, such a revolutionary core must organize a wide array of mass organizations, leading them in all manner of struggle, be it large or small, economic or political, covert or legitimate, violent or nonviolent; the specific form of struggle at any given moment must hinge on the prevailing circumstances and conditions. Such a process, Kim argues, is bound to swell the ranks of revolutionaries and to intensify the struggle of the masses.[8]

Fifth, it is important to form a united front encompassing many different types of people—intellectuals, students, petite bourgeoisie, national bourgeoisie, and all other "democracy-oriented" people. The success in forming a united front will not only create favorable conditions for the development of the main force of revolution but also provide powerful auxiliary personnel to the latter. Such a united front takes two forms: lower level and upper level. While the "lower-level united front" involves uniting with the masses, the "upper-level united front" entails winning over the hearts and minds of segments of the ruling class—the "progressive persons" in the "ruling class party" and leaders of the "intermediate parties." Finally, Kim Il Sung underlines the importance of weakening counterrevolutionary forces. An important target here is the enemy's armed forces. Since, in Kim's view, the ruling class depends on the support of the armed forces, the former is bound to crumble when and if the latter takes up the people's cause. Although the high echelons of the South Korean armed forces come from reactionary classes, the "absolute majority of its enlisted men and low-ranking officers come from basic classes [the proletariat and peasantry]." To Kim, this means that they are susceptible to conversion.[9]

The final component of the reunification strategy calls for the

8. Ibid., pp. 88–91.   9. Ibid., pp. 91–93.

strengthening of "international revolutionary forces." Kim Il Sung emphasizes the need to cultivate the support of Third World nations. North Korea, he urges, should not only publicize its "legitimate" positions and win their support but also unite with and support their anti-American struggle. It should also exploit "frictions and contradictions" among imperialist nations. The ultimate goal is to isolate the United States in the international arena and drive it to the precipice in all parts of the globe. Interestingly, Kim extolls the virtue of humility in the conduct of diplomacy. "We should not only display respect and hospitality to our foreign guests but also show them unadorned truth about our country," he says.[10]

In sum, the logic of Kim's reunification strategy is as follows: the North will serve as the base for stirring up both the South Korean people and antiimperialist forces throughout the world, but the brunt of the struggle to oust the American troops from South Korea and to topple the South Korean regime must be borne by the South Korean people themselves. Should the latter rise up in a massive revolt and should there be a concerted pressure on the United States in the rest of the world, the US will be compelled to withdraw its troops from South Korea. And without the American military presence to prop it up, the South Korean regime will collapse, paving the way for the emergence of a "progressive" regime. It will then become possible for North Korea and the new South Korean regime to work out a formula for reunification.

What are the probable sources of the preceding strategy? Some of the input variables we enumerated earlier in the book appear to be relevant. To begin with the operational environment, there were two important developments in North Korea's external setting that appear to have stimulated Kim Il Sung's strategic thinking. One was the Vietnam War, which Kim may have perceived as evidence of the vulnerability of US and US-backed troops to a guerrilla-type "people's war." The other was the April 19, 1960 student uprising in South Korea that led to the overthrow of the Syngman Rhee regime, which seemed to Kim to be proof of the tremendous revolutionary potential of the South Korean people. Insofar as North Korea's internal setting

---

10. Ibid., pp. 94–95. Such a stricture seems to belie North Korea's actual behavior, notably the spectacular personality cult centering about Kim Il Sung, which spills over to the international arena with paid advertisements of Kim's words of wisdom in the foreign press around the world. I found during my 1981 visit to the DPRK that humility and candor were not among North Korea's virtues. The North Koreans were eager to advertise their accomplishments and to downplay, gloss over, or even conceal evidence of foreign assistance. For accounts of similar experiences by other visitors, see Mark Gayn, "The Cult of Kim," *New York Times Magazine*, October 1, 1972, pp. 16–32 and Suzuki Kenji, "Kita Chōsen mita mama" [North Korea Observed], *Kokusai kankei shiryō*, no. 4 (October 25, 1975) (Tokyo: Kokusai Kankei Kyōdō Kenkyūsho), pp. 1–8.

was concerned, significant gains in economic construction may have given Kim confidence in the ability of North Korea to aid and abet revolution in South Korea. Politically, linking economic and military construction in the North to the goal of national reunification may conceivably bolster Kim's ability to spur his people on toward greater efforts and sacrifices.

Turning to the psychological environment, we note the probable role of "historical legacy." For example, his bitter experiences during the Korean War may have underscored the futility of an outright invasion in a situation where the United States is likely to intervene directly. In fact, Kim explicitly stated that had the South Korean people organized an uprising behind the enemy lines and shared the fighting with the Korean People's Army during the Korean War, the "problem of our fatherland's reunification would have been solved a long time ago." He also lamented that the fragility of "revolutionary forces in South Korea" had resulted in the loss of numerous opportunities to "expedite the victory of the South Korean revolution."[11] Hence the urgency of the need to organize "revolutionary forces" in the South. With respect to the removal of US troops from South Korea, a top priority goal for North Korea, the ideological component of Kim's attitudinal prism may also be germane: his belief in the Leninist doctrine of imperialism may not only have colored his perception of a causal link between America's "colonial rule" in the South and the "plight of the South Korean people" but also buttressed his view that the South Korean people need only to be aroused in order for North Korea to win them over to the revolutionary cause. His belief in the superiority of socialism over capitalism may have further fueled this line of thinking.

South Korea's Reunification Strategy

South Korea's strategy of national reunification has several noteworthy aspects. First, it has not been as clearly articulated as that of North Korea. In fact, one may even question whether a conscious strategic decision has ever been made in Seoul with specific reference to reunification. Second, to the extent that a coherent strategy of national reunification exists, its principal thrust is strikingly similar to that of North Korea. For, stripped to its bare essentials, the strategy consists of building up national power with a view to prevailing over the North. Finally, if there is a significant difference between the approaches of the two Koreas, it is that North Korea's clar-

11. *Kim Il Sung chōjak sōnjip*, vol. 4, pp. 80–81. Kim made these remarks in his speech to the eighth plenum of the Fourth WPK Central Committee on February 27, 1964.

ion call for a revolutionary overthrow of the South Korean regime is not matched by any revolutionary rhetoric emanating from the South. Notwithstanding this contrast, South Korea's antipathy towards the North Korean regime is no less intense than that of North Korea toward Seoul.

South Korea's reunification strategy, as articulated by the late Park Chung Hee shortly after his seizure of power in a military coup in May 1961, may be characterized as the strategy of fostering national power (*kungnyŏk paeyang*). That strategy was pursued throughout his eighteen-year rule and has not been repudiated by his successors. Essentially it calls for an all-out effort at building national power, of which economic power is the backbone. Any serious effort toward reunification must be postponed until the intermediate goal of building up national power in all fields, economic, military, political, cultural, and social, is attained to such an extent that the South is placed in an absolutely superior position vis-à-vis the North. Exactly how reunification is to be achieved once this goal is attained remains unclear. What is clear, however, is that there is no room for Communist influence in the reunified Korea as envisioned by South Korea.

As Park Chung Hee put it in June 1966: "I, together with all you fellow citizens, reaffirm that unification through victory over communism [*sung'gong t'ong'il*] is our supreme task and that we will march forward together toward the construction of self-reliant economy and modernization."[12] In the same speech, Park predicted that "positive approaches" toward reunification by South Korea might become feasible in "the second-half of the decade of the 1970s by which time we anticipate to have solidified the foundation of a self-reliant economy as the national base for unification, to have fully developed the democratic potentials, and to have seized a complete initiative in all respects."[13]

It should not be overlooked that the successive ROK governments have officially embraced the United Nations formula for reunification—the holding of UN-supervised elections in all of Korea

12. "Statement by President Park Chung Hee on Unification, June 25, 1966," in Se-Jin Kim (ed.), *Korean Unification: Source Materials With an Introduction* (Seoul: Research Center for Peace and Unification, 1976), p. 282.
13. For a summary and discussion of Park's views on reunification in the 1960s, see Hak-Joon Kim, *The Unification Policy of South and North Korea* (Seoul: Seoul National University Press, 1977), pp. 194–207; for Park's views during the first half of the 1970s, see *Toward Peaceful Unification: Selected Speeches by President Park Chung Hee* (Seoul: Kwangmyong Publishing Co., 1976); for a selection of his speeches bearing on reunification in the 1976–1978 period, see Chong-Shik Chung (ed.), *Korean Unification: Source Materials With an Introduction*, vol. 2 (Seoul: Research Center for Peace and Unification, 1979).

based on the principle of proportional representation as a preliminary step toward the establishment of a unified government. In view of North Korea's categorical rejection of the formula, which is undoubtedly linked to the simple statistical fact that the South Korean population outnumbers that of the North by two to one, it cannot be viewed as a realistic option. In the absence of radical change in the operational environment, the probability of its realization is as low as that of the success of the southern revolution in Pyongyang's strategy. Whether it should be treated as a distinct component of Seoul's "strategy" of reunification is debatable.

To speculate briefly on the probable sources of Park's strategic thinking regarding reunification, one may readily link his emphasis on building up national power to his military background: throughout much of his adult life he had been exposed to the stark realities of power. The fact that the adversary is a Communist state dedicated to the revolutionary overthrow of the South Korean government and engaged in a frenetic program of economic and defense construction must have bolstered Park's belief in the need to surpass the North in indexes of power. The historical legacy of the Korean War, a war in which Park participated as a high-ranking officer in the ROK Army, may have been an important factor in Park's calculus. If his alleged involvement in an abortive Communist uprising in the southeastern part of Korea in the late 1940s is true, it may help to explain both his pronounced anticommunism and his frequently expressed view that the Communists are not to be trusted. For, not only did he possess a firsthand experience in the workings of communism, but he must have felt an acute need to atone for his past transgressions with an uncompromising hostility toward the Communists.

Finally, his single-minded quest for modernization may have been fueled not only by his early exposure to abject poverty but also by his desire to vindicate his coup d'etat. If he were to succeed in transforming South Korea from a poor, underdeveloped country into a modern, industrialized nation, he would have accomplished a feat that none of his predecessors had been able to accomplish. His place in history would then be secure, and his 1961 coup would be hailed as a turning point in the turbulent annals of South Korea. All of this implies that modernization was more than an intermediate goal for Park and that he would have been content to have achieved it without making any headway toward reunification. In sum, he appeared to have lacked the kind of intense personal desire to be the "respected and beloved leader of the 50 million Korean people" which his archrival in the North displayed.

OPERATIONAL DECISIONS

Operational decisions are those shaping "operational directions." As defined by Jan F. Triska, "*operational direction* is subordinate to strategy and concerns the direction and unification of tactical episodes. It is more flexible than strategy, but less so than tactics. Its range of duration is shorter than strategy: it changes with new clusters of tactics, which it funnels along the lines established by strategy."[14]

Operational decisions are needed to implement each of the three principal components of North Korea's reunification strategy. In overall terms, while North Korea has continued to view the goal of strengthening the revolutionary capability of the North as pivotal and hence meriting the highest priority, the vigor with which the other two goals are pursued has varied over the years. For example, while the southern revolution appeared to receive a top priority in the 1960s, the goal of strengthening international "revolutionary forces" became highly salient in the 1970s.

Revolution in the North

Because its resources are limited, Pyongyang is compelled to assign priorities among diverse programs in implementing the goal of beefing up the revolutionary capability of the North. For although a balanced growth—equal distribution of available human and material resources among the economic, defense, and political sectors—is a possible option in theory, in reality, it means sacrificing the speed of growth, something the North Korean leadership has thus far been unwilling to do.

In the early part of the 1960s emphasis appeared to be on economic construction, but in the mid 1960s defense construction emerged as a top priority goal. In terms of the distribution of the available resources, economic construction continued to eclipse all other programs, but military expenditures began to increase sharply beginning in 1964. As Table 6 shows, military expenditures as a percentage of total government expenditures leaped from 2.1 percent in 1963 to 7.5 percent in 1964. Another big jump came in 1967, when the proportion of military to total government expenditures more than doubled over the previous year, hitting the 30 percent mark. All this was accompanied by Pyongyang's official explanation that significant change in its operational environment had necessitated a diversion of

14. Jan F. Triska, "A Model for Study of Soviet Foreign Policy," *American Political Science Review* 52, 1 (March 1958): 67–69.

growing amounts of resources from economic to defense sectors and that that in turn had slowed down the pace of economic construction, making it necessary for North Korea to extend the Seven-Year Economic Plan of 1961–1967 for three years.[15]

As explained by Kim Il Sung, the rationale for adjusting "the Party's internal and external operational direction" (*tang'ŭi taenae'oe hwaltong bangch'im*)[16] included the following: First, the American intervention in Vietnam had demonstrated beyond doubt the aggressive nature of "US imperialism." "While taking pains not to exacerbate their relations with big countries, the American imperialists have directed their torch of aggression primarily to Vietnam and are scheming to swallow one by one such divided or small countries as [North] Korea, Cuba, and East Germany," Kim said.[17] Second, there was a growing threat of resurgent "Japanese militarism." Specifically, Kim perceived the emergence of a de facto tripartite military alliance among the United States, Japan, and South Korea through a set of bilateral military agreements.[18] Third, given the above, there was an urgent need for united action on the part of all socialist countries and "peace-loving" peoples to oppose the "imperialist aggression." Calling upon the "fraternal socialist countries" to send "volunteer soldiers" to Vietnam, Kim declared that North Korea was prepared to send such soldiers at anytime, should Hanoi request such assistance.[19] Finally, Kim made a thinly veiled criticism of both Beijing and Moscow for their continuing dispute, arguing that commonalities eclipsed differences among socialist countries. He also extolled the virtue of independence in both intrabloc and international affairs, adding that North Korea was completely independent of any external control or influence.[20]

The temporary easing of tensions in the Korean peninsula in 1972, epitomized by the publication of the North-South joint communiqué on July 4, 1972, reversed the trend in military spending: the proportion of North Korea's military to total government expenditures declined from 31 percent in 1971 to 17 percent in 1972, stabilizing near the 16 percent mark in the ensuing period. As we noted previously, however, such dramatic changes in the official statistics relating to defense spending can be misleading. For most countries hide the true magnitude of their military expenditures from the public view. A more credible gauge of North Korea's operational direction may be found in its relations with South Korea.

15. See Kim Il Sung's report to the Representatives' Conference of the WPK on October 5, 1966 in *Kim Il Sung chŏjak sŏnjip*, vol. 4, pp. 317–403.
16. Ibid., p. 317.   17. Ibid., p. 322.   18. Ibid., p. 323.
19. Ibid., pp. 326–329.   20. Ibid., pp. 333–353.

Fostering Revolutionary Forces in the South

The goal of strengthening the revolutionary capability of the South appeared to have received a great deal of attention from North Korea throughout the 1960s. Pyongyang's initial operational direction may be characterized as a combination of propaganda and organization. On one hand, North Korea continued to generate and, particularly, reiterate proposals for "peaceful reunification." For example, Kim Il Sung proposed on August 14, 1960 that North and South Korea should form a "confederation." In essence, the plan envisaged the formation of a "Supreme National Council" (*tae minjok hoeŭi*) consisting of representatives of the two Korean governments and charged with the function of coordinating economic and cultural intercourse between the two sides. This would be a strictly provisional measure, and the two governments would remain fully autonomous.[21] This proposal has since been repeated many times. In June 1962 North Korea repeated its proposal for reciprocal reduction of armed forces, a meeting of North and South Korean leaders to discuss reunification, and a mutual nonaggression treaty, coupled with the withdrawal of US troops from South Korea.[22] In March 1964 the DPRK Supreme People's Assembly sent an urgent appeal to the ROK National Assembly as well as to major social organizations in South Korea, calling for an immediate overthrow of the Park Chung Hee government, which, in Pyongyang's view, was on the verge of capitulating to the "Japanese militarists" in the South Korea-Japan normalization talks then under way. It also proposed the convening of an all-Korea conference to discuss ways of "saving our fatherland from the impending disaster" and offered to provide economic aid to South Korea as well as jobs to any South Korean who would defect to the North.[23]

On the other hand, North Korea never ceased to dispatch highly trained agents, frequently of South Korean origin, to the South with the mission of laying the groundwork for organization of a Marxist-Leninist party. But the North Korean effort in the South encountered nearly insurmountable barriers in the form of deep-seated anticommunism, harsh anti-Communist laws, and the efficiency of South Korea's antisubversive and counterespionage apparatus. North Korean agents and their converts found it exceedingly difficult to sur-

21. *Chosŏn chung'ang yŏn'gam* [Korean Central Yearbook], 1960 (Pyongyang: Chosŏn Chung'ang T'ongsin-sa, 1961), p. 25.
22. *Tōitsu Chōsen nenkan* [One Korea Yearbook], 1965–66 (Tokyo: Tōitsu Chōsen Shimbun-sha, 1966), p. 252.
23. Ibid., p. 253; *Chosŏn chung'ang yŏn'gam*, 1965 (Pyongyang, 1966), p. 111.

vive, let alone operate effectively. In fact, Pyongyang's hopes for organizing a South-based underground party all but evaporated in 1968 with the arrest of 158 persons on charges of violating South Korea's anti-Communist and national security laws by trying to organize a "Revolutionary Party for Reunification" (*T'ong'il Hyŏngmyŏng-dang*). Of this total, 73 were tried, and nine were executed.[24] In June 1970, however, North Korea claimed that "South Korean revolutionaries who are faithful soldiers of Kim Il Sung" had succeeded in forming the "Central Committee" of the "Revolutionary Party for Reunification" (RPR) and in proclaiming the party's "Manifesto and Programme" in August, 1969. The party itself, Pyongyang claimed, was organized in March 1964.[25] North Korea continued to insist that the RPR was alive and well by regularly publishing statements in the North Korean press that were attributed to it, by producing an "RPR delegation" on ceremonial occasions in North Korea, by operating a "clandestine radio station" alleged to be the voice of the RPR broadcast from South Korea (the South Korean government claims the station is located in Haeju, North Korea), and by publishing a weekly newspaper, *Hyŏngmyŏng chŏnsŏn* (Revolutionary Front), and other publications. Nevertheless, the party appeared to be more a figment of North Korean imagination than a functioning apparatus worthy of the name.[26]

In the mid 1960s Pyongyang's operational direction appeared to change somewhat: in its southern strategy, there was a sudden increase in the use of violence, as measured by the number of significant incidents south of the military demarcation line in the Demilitarized Zone and within South Korea. Whereas there were 59 such incidents in 1965 and 50 in 1966, the number leaped to 566 in 1967—an eleven-fold increase over the previous year. The following year not only saw a continuation of the trend, with 629 incidents,[27] but also the most daring display of North Korean violence: on January 21, a thirty-one man commando unit consisting entirely of officers in the KPA came within several hundred feet of the presidential mansion in

24. *T'ong'il Hyŏngmyŏng-dang chuyo munsŏ-jip* [Principal Documents of the Revolutionary Party for Reunification] (no publisher listed, 1979), pp. 367–368.
25. For the texts of the Manifesto and Programme, see ibid.
26. A careful reading of documents purported to be those of the RPR and the weekly "organ of the Central Committee of the RPR," *Hyŏngmyŏng chŏnsŏn*, bolsters the suspicion that they are written and produced in North Korea. Apart from the use of Chinese ideographs and the expression "Han'guk" in lieu of "Chosŏn," they contain numerous expressions which are peculiar to North Korea. See ibid., passim and *Hyŏngmyŏng chŏnsŏn*, October 1979–March 1980.
27. See Rinn-sup Shinn, "Foreign and Reunification Policies," *Problems of Communism*, 22, 1 (January–February 1973): 61.

Seoul in an abortive attempt to assassinate President Park Chung Hee. The lone survivor of the ill-fated mission, Lieutenant Kim Sin-jo, revealed that his unit had trained for two years for the mission and that there were an estimated 2,400 North Korean commandos undergoing special training in North Korea for guerrilla missions in the South.[28]

It is possible that the increase in the use of violence by North Korean agents in the South may have reflected not a change in Pyongyang's operational direction but a simple acceleration of the old. Eager to pave the way for organization of a revolutionary party in the South, Pyongyang may have significantly increased the number of infiltrators to the South, which in turn increased the probability of their detection by the South Korean authorities. An equally plausible explanation points to a number of factors. In the external setting, there were two ominous developments from Pyongyang's point of view: the normalization of relations between South Korea and Japan (the agreements were signed in December 1964 and put in force a year later) and South Korea's decision to dispatch troops to Vietnam (a mobile army surgical hospital was sent in September 1964, and combat troops followed in 1965). In the internal setting, North Korea had begun to experience slowdowns and bottlenecks in economic construction, and needed to explain them away in part by citing the need to divert resources to military buildup. All this meant that by stirring up trouble in the South, North Korea could underscore the vulnerability and instability of the South Korean regime, which in turn may put a brake on South Korea's military intervention in Vietnam and Japan's investment in South Korea. Had the commando mission succeeded, North Korea could have gone a long way toward achieving one of its two principal aims in the southern strategy: the overthrow of the Park Chung Hee regime.

A precipitous decline in the number of violent incidents in 1969 (from 629 in the previous year to 111) suggested still another shift in Pyongyang's operational direction: substitution of peaceful overtures to the ROK regime for subversive operations against it. The number of incidents remained at the relatively modest level of 113 in 1970 and then plummeted to forty-seven in 1971. In 1972 the incidents disappeared altogether.[29] As we shall see below, all this was accompanied by further adjustment in North Korea's operational direction. The moderation of Pyongyang's posture toward Seoul, insofar as the use of violence was concerned, may have been a function, primarily, of North Korea's realization that its bellicose operational direction had

28. B. C. Koh, *The Foreign Policy of North Korea* (New York: Praeger Publishers, 1969), pp. 146–147.
29. Rinn-sup Shinn, "Foreign and Reunification Policies," pp. 62–63.

been counterproductive. For not only had Pyongyang failed to make any headway in its southern strategy, but it had helped to heighten the vigilance of both Seoul and Washington, which in turn had led to the beefing up of their arsenal in the South.

Dialogue With the South

The change in North Korea's operational direction in 1971 took the following form. First, in April, North Korea dropped its previous precondition for negotiation with South Korea—withdrawal of US troops. In a report to the Fifth Session of the Fourth Supreme People's Assembly, DPRK Foreign Minister Ho Dam declared, as a part of a new eight-point program for reunification, that North Korea would be willing to hold "a political consultative meeting of North and South Korea with the attendance of all political parties and public organizations and all *patriotic* persons to negotiate" the various problems confronting the two sides, including the withdrawal of US troops, "at any mutually agreeable time and place."[30]

Then, on August 6, three weeks after the dramatic announcement by President Nixon that he would visit the PRC, the DPRK made a further concession: Kim Il Sung stated that North Korea was willing to negotiate with "all political parties, including the Democratic-Republican party, all social organizations, and all individuals" in South Korea.[31] The omission of the adjective "patriotic" from the scope of potential parties to negotiation as well as the explicit inclusion of South Korea's ruling political party were extremely significant: Pyongyang was sending a clear signal to Seoul that it meant business and would welcome discussion with any and everybody. This eventually led to the initiation of the short-lived dialogue.

How may one account for Pyongyang's new operational direction? First and foremost, we need to note the backdrop against which North Korea's most conciliatory gesture toward South Korea was made: the Sino-American opening. The stunning news that its foremost ally and worst enemy were moving toward a rapprochement must have confronted Pyongyang with an urgent need to initiate some moves of its own. Clearly, the status quo of unremitting hostility between the two Koreas could not continue in the face of such a dramatic change in the operational environment. No less important was another change in the external setting: obviously stimulated by the emerging Sino-American détente, South Korea, too, had changed its operational direction and had proposed, for the first time since the

30. *Nodong sinmun*, April 13, 1971. Emphasis added.
31. Ibid., August 7, 1971.

partition, to talk directly with North Korea, albeit through ostensibly nongovernmental channels.

Also germane was the singularly slow pace of the southern revolution. The RPR, as noted, was more symbolic than real, insofar as its efficacy in the South was concerned. On the other hand, dialogue with Seoul would have the potential of opening up channels of communication and intercourse with the South, thus enabling the North to gain a valuable access to the South Korean people. Additionally, there was a distinct possibility that dialogue, by reducing tensions and dispelling Seoul's fear of Pyongyang's aggressive designs, might help achieve the foremost intermediate goal in North Korea's strategy of reunification, namely, the withdrawal of US troops. Finally, reduction of tensions would also have beneficial effects on North Korea's economic construction: it would allow North Korea to reduce both its military expenditures and its force level. The latter in turn would help alleviate a serious bottleneck in Pyongyang's economy: a shortage of manpower.

Two rival hypotheses should be noted briefly. First, it is possible that the removal of preconditions for negotiation with the South may have reflected not a change in Pyongyang's operational direction but simply a tactical adjustment—a propaganda ploy. According to this view, North Korea was subsequently caught off guard by South Korea's unexpected response—a call for Red Cross talks on the question of separated families. Coming within five days of Kim Il Sung's remarkably open-ended proposal for dialogue, the South Korean offer may have left North Korea very little leeway. Second, it may be argued that what North Korea did was not merely to change its operational direction but to modify its strategy in a significant way. That is to say, it may have jettisoned the goal of revolutionary overthrow of the South Korean regime in favor of coexistence and negotiation.

The plausibility of the second hypothesis, however, is substantially undercut by the discovery of an underground tunnel in the western sector of the DMZ by the ROK troops in November 1974. Equipped with a narrow-gauge railway, the tunnel measured 122 centimeters in height and 90 centimeters in width, and extended 3.5 kilometers from North Korea, with 1.2 kilometers of the tunnel being located south of the DMZ. According to the UN Command, it was of sufficient size to allow the infiltration of an entire regiment in an hour. The ROK authorities surmised that work on the tunnel was done while the North-South dialogue was in progress. In March 1975, the ROK troops discovered a second tunnel, which was said to be even bigger and more sophisticated than the first one—that is, capable of handling the passage of small armored vehicles as well as a division of armed men in an hour. Finally, in October 1978, a third tunnel was discovered, which was about the same size as the second in height and width but much shorter in length (1.6 kilometers).[32]

From Dialogue to Diatribe

Still another adjustment in Pyongyang's operational direction occurred in August 1973. Apparently concluding that the dialogue with Seoul was getting nowhere, Pyongyang must have decided to either discontinue or downgrade it drastically. Citing the kidnapping of South Korea's opposition leader Kim Dae Jung from Japan by agents of the South Korean Central Intelligence Agency (KCIA) on August 8, 1973 as an excuse, Pyongyang demanded that Seoul replace the cochairman and other members of the North-South Coordinating Committee (NSCC) who were affiliated with KCIA with people "with national conscience" and genuine desire for a peaceful reunification. Since South Korea had flatly denied any responsibility for the kidnapping incident, it was in no position to accede to the North Korean demand; hence the latter was tantamount to a unilateral notice by Pyongyang that it would suspend the dialogue. In fact, even though Seoul later expressed a willingness to accede to the North Korean demand for a reshuffle of the NSCC, Pyongyang erected a new hurdle: it insisted that as a precondition for resuming the NSCC talks, Seoul should (1) renounce President Park Chung Hee's "special statement" of June 23, 1973, in which he had proposed, inter alia, the simultaneous entry of North and South Korea into the United Nations, and (2) release all political prisoners. What Pyongyang ultimately achieved was not a total suspension but a downgrading of the dialogue. For it allowed the NSCC talks to continue in the form of vice chairmen's meetings until March 1975, and the Red Cross talks were kept alive in the form of "working-level meetings" until March 1978.

More than anything else, Pyongyang's sense of betrayal by Seoul helps to account for the preceding operational direction. The publication of the North-South joint statement on July 4, 1972 had been hailed by North Korea as a significant milestone. Pyongyang made it plain that the enunciation of three principles of reunification would pave the way toward the removal of US troops from South Korea: (1) reunification shall be attained independently without either relying upon or tolerating interference from any external power; (2) reunification shall be realized through peaceful means rather than

---

32. For details, see *Tunnels of War* (Seoul: Korean Overseas Information Service, 1978).

through the use of force against each other; and (3) both sides shall promote a great national unity as a homogeneous people, transcending differences in ideas, ideologies, and systems.[33] In a news conference held on the date of the statement's publication in Pyongyang, DPRK Vice Premier Pak Sung Chol stressed that the most important element of the new accord was the joint commitment "to solve the problems of our own country by ourselves according to the principle of national self-determination, rejecting outside forces." He also said that the joint statement was intended to deal "a powerful blow to those who try to obstruct Korea's reunification," adding:

> Now it is clear that none of the outside forces can find any excuse for interfering in the internal affairs of our nation. Now that there exists no threat of aggression in south Korea from the north, nor . . . any need of protection and [since] our nation is settling its internal problems according to its own faith, the US imperialists must no longer meddle in the domestic affairs of our country; they must withdraw at once, taking with them all their forces of aggression.[34]

If Pyongyang's official statements reflected its true expectations, it was to be rudely disillusioned. From the inception, Seoul insisted that neither the United Nations nor the US troops in South Korea were "outside forces" within the meaning of the joint statement. Nor did the statement and the subsequent talks reduce tensions in the Korean peninsula sufficiently to induce or warrant mutual arms reduction. In sum, nothing much changed. If anything, the dialogue was used by President Park Chung Hee to bolster his own political position at home, for he invoked it as the main justification for his "October [1972] Reforms" whose transparent goal was to strengthen his political power and to enable him to stay in power indefinitely.

Apart from the preceding considerations, North Korea may have perceived that the continuation of the dialogue would not really serve its interest. For one of the by-products of the dialogue for North Korea may have been the discovery that South Korea was a far cry from the kind of a living hell that the North Korean propagandists had previously protrayed it to be and that even the decision-making elite may have been predisposed to believe. On the contrary, what the handful of North Koreans who were allowed to visit South Korea during the first year of the dialogue found was a surprisingly dynamic economy, visible signs of an economic boom, and a standard of living that seemed to be higher than that of North Korea. In short, the pre-

33. This is my own translation of the Korean text of the joint statement as published in *Nodong sinmun*, July 5, 1972 and *Tong'a ilbo*, July 4, 1972.
34. *Pyongyang Times*, July 6, 1972.

vious estimate that increased contacts between the two Koreas would enhance the opportunity for converting the South Korean people to Pyongyang's cause may have been revised somewhat.

Pyongyang's Quest for a Political Conference

Another possibility is that a key aim of North Korea may have been to bring about a political conference of all political parties, social organizations, and other leaders of both the North and the South and that its inability to attain that aim may have contributed to the adoption of its new operational direction. This hypothesis is buttressed by the following facts: First, ever since April 1948, when the first "joint conference of representatives of political parties and social organizations of north and south Korea" was held in Pyongyang,[35] North Korea has periodically revived the proposal for a similar conference. In fact, it is significant that in its eight-point program for reunification unveiled in April 1971, North Korea called for the holding of "a political consultative meeting of North and South Korea with the attendance of all political parties and public organizations and all patriotic persons."[36] While further softening Pyongyang's position four months later, Kim Il Sung indicated a willingness to negotiate with "all political parties, including the Democratic-Republican party, all social organizations, and all individuals."[37]

As noted, these developments set the stage for Seoul's dramatic proposal for Red Cross talks, ushering in the North-South dialogue. In January 1972, Kim Il Sung told the *Yomiuri shimbun* of Japan that the peaceful solution of the reunification question "required" the holding of "bilateral or multilateral negotiations" among "various political parties of north and south Korea."[38] Five months later, he reiterated his position to *The New York Times*:

> We want contacts not only with south Korean "national assemblymen" but also with a broad spectrum of political and public figures in south Korea. In other words, we hold that all the political parties and social organizations of north and south Korea should get together in a political consultative conference and exchange wide-ranging views on the question of national reunification.[39]

---

35. Kim Il Sung, *For the Independent Peaceful Reunification of Korea* (New York: International Publishers, 1975), p. 26. This volume should not be confused with the revised edition published by Guardian Associates, Inc. of New York in 1976, which was cited earlier in the book.

36. *Nodong sinmun*, April 13, 1971.   37. Ibid., August 7, 1971.

38. Kim Il Sung, *For the Independent Peaceful Reunification of Korea*, 1975, p. 155.

39. Ibid., p. 167. See also *New York Times*, May 31, 1972.

What is significant about Kim's statement is that it was made on the heels of KCIA Director Lee Hu Rak's secret visit to Pyongyang to pave the way for the publication of the North-South joint statement on July 4, 1972.[40]

Then, during the twenty-fourth preparatory meeting of North and South Korean Red Cross representatives on July 26, 1972, North Korea specifically raised the issue of inviting representatives of political parties and social organizations to the forthcoming full-dress Red Cross talks. More important, it referred to specific political parties in both North and South Korea, including the Revolutionary Party for Reunification.[41] From then on North Korea was to raise the issue with dogged persistence both in the Red Cross and in Coordinating Committee talks. Finally, when Kim Yong Ju announced Pyongyang's intention to suspend the NSCC talks on August 28, 1973, thus signaling a new operational direction, he cited, as one of the numerous reasons, Seoul's opposition to the proposal to expand the NSCC talks to include representatives of political parties and social organizations.[42]

Why has North Korea steadfastly insisted on the necessity for a comprehensive political conference in subsequent years? What does it hope to accomplish in such a conference? Pyongyang's major aim appears to be to obtain an opportunity and a forum to convey its message—its positions, proposals, and arguments regarding reunification—to the widest possible audience from the South. Underlying such an aim may be the conviction that its own proposals and ideas are reasonable, just, and compelling, since they are based on the imperatives of primordial sentiments—a sense of national pride; the need to exclude foreign influence and interference from one's own affairs; and the imperative necessity for self-determination, for finding solution to one's problems, standing on one's own feet. The principal barrier that Pyongyang faces, in its own view, is the refusal of the South Korean authorities to allow the North Korean message to get through. In addition, Pyongyang's explicit inclusion of the Revolutionary Party for Reunification in the category of South Korean political parties suggests that it may hope to help legitimize or, at least, rejuvenate the virtually moribund organization. For if it were allowed to participate in the proposed conference, the RPR would certainly attract attention from the South Korean people. Moreover, it might greatly complicate the task of coordination for the South Korean delegation. North Korea's tactical response to South Korea's new initiatives in early 1979 may be appreciated from the preceding

40. Kim met with the two *New York Times* reporters on May 26, 1972; Lee Hu Rak had visited Pyongyang from May 2 to 5, 1972.
41. *Nodong sinmun*, July 27, 1972.
42. Ibid., August 29, 1973.

perspective, as we shall see shortly. Finally, in the latter part of the 1970s, North Korea appeared to have become increasingly confident in and proud of its achievements in economic construction and social programs (e.g., its health care system and educational system), and this may have led to the belief that an opportunity to observe the North firsthand would be an eye-opening experience for most South Korean people, who have been led by their own propaganda apparatus to equate North Korea with a veritable hell on earth.

Pyongyang's Attempt to Revive the Dialogue in 1980

North Korea's own initiatives in January 1980, on the other hand, may signify not a tactical adjustment but a new operational direction, although the boundary line between the two is admittedly hazy. On January 11, North Korea broadcast a message to South Korea over Pyongyang radio: it would dispatch two liaison personnel to the conference room of the Neutral Nations Supervisory Commission in Panmunjom at 2:00 P.M. the following day to deliver to the South Korean side a letter containing an important message concerning national reunification. As things turned out, North Korea delivered not one but twelve letters. The most significant of them was the one signed by DPRK Premier Li Jong Ok and addressed to "Mr. Sin Hyŏn-hwak, Prime Minister, The Republic of Korea, Seoul."[43] What was remarkable about the letter was that for the first time since the establishment of two rival regimes in the Korean peninsula in 1948, one side had referred to the other by its official name. Even at the height of North-South amity—when they had reached an agreement on a joint statement in July 1972—they had carefully refrained from using each other's official names. Substantively, the letter proposed that dialogue be resumed as soon as possible: "we are ready to have talks between the authorities of the North and the South and, furthermore, bring to maturity talks between the high-level authorities, along with the comprehensive political consultative conference already called for by us." As for the site of the talks, Li suggested Panmunjom, Pyongyang, or Seoul, adding that "we have no objection to a third country either."[44]

The remaining eleven letters were all signed by "Kim Il, Vice-President, The Democratic People's Republic of Korea; Secretary of the Central Committee, the Workers' Party of Korea; and Chairman, the Committee for the Peaceful Reunification of the Fatherland" and addressed to the top leaders of all political parties—the ruling

---

43. For the Korean text of the letter, see *Han'guk ilbo*, January 21, 1980; for an English version, see *KCNA*, Pyongyang, January 12, 1980, as monitored by FBIS.

44. *KCNA*, Pyongyang, January 12, 1980.

Democratic-Republican party, the opposition New Democratic party, the Democratic Unification party, the United Socialist party—and other prominent individuals, notably, General Yi Hŭi-song, ROK Army Chief of Staff and Martial Law Commander; Stephen Cardinal Kim, Archbishop of Seoul; and Yun Po Sun, former president of the ROK. Although the letters varied slightly in content, they all contained the same proposal: to hold a meeting of politicians and other leaders of the North and the South.[45]

It was clear that all this reflected Pyongyang's desire to generate a positive response from Seoul. In other words, it signaled a new operational direction: to earnestly seek the resumption of dialogue. On the other hand, the move also bespoke the tenacity of the North Korean quest for a comprehensive political conference. Mindful of the experience of only a year ago, when its attempt to initiate such a conference failed due to Seoul's insistence on negotiations between the "responsible authorities" of the two sides, North Korea chose a different tactic. It not only merged the proposal for a meeting of responsible authorities with that for a comprehensive political conference but also relied on two persons with impeccable credentials to represent the "responsible authorities" in the North—the premier of the Administration Council of the DPRK and the vice-president of the DPRK. It took pains to remind South Korea that Kim Il held the concurrent titles of Secretary of the WPK Central Committee and Chairman of the Committee for the Peaceful Reunification of the Fatherland. And, as noted, in order to make its proposals more palatable, North Korea took the unprecedented step of referring to South Korea as the Republic of Korea.

Two significant developments in North Korea's operational environment may help explain its new overtures toward South Korea. First and foremost, the assassination of ROK President Park Chung Hee on October 26, 1979 had set in motion the process of political change in the South. Not only was the hated adversary gone, but there was serious talk of democratization in the post-Park South. Even though there was considerable uncertainty about the true intentions of the real rulers following the coup on December 12, 1979, it was nonetheless plain that North Korea should test the waters. Second, the Soviet invasion of Afghanistan in December 1979 had added a new dimension to the operational environment. To a regime long wedded to the principle of independence, the blatant intervention by the Soviet Union in a neighboring country, the toppling of a friendly regime, the installation of a puppet government, and the continuing armed occupation of the territory must have come as shocking news.

45. Ibid. and ibid., January 14, 1980, as monitored by FBIS.

Not only did the Soviet action epitomize "dominationism," to which North Korea is uncompromisingly opposed,[46] but it must also have constrained Pyongyang to ponder its own vulnerability to similar intervention. The Soviet action also served to strengthen ties between the PRC and the US, both of which became acutely aware of the degree to which their strategic interests converged vis-à-vis the Soviet Union. This development had a significant implication for North Korea, for it regarded the PRC as its foremost ally, while viewing the US as its worst enemy. Clearly, the status quo in the Korean peninsula could not continue indefinitely in the face of such a fluid situation surrounding it.

The new North Korean overtures evoked a favorable response from South Korea. On January 18, President Choi Kyu Hah termed them "the first affirmative response to our proposal for dialogue between the responsible authorities of the North and the South," implying that Seoul would accept Pyongyang's new proposal.[47] Then on January 24, Prime Minister Shin Hyon Hwack (Sin Hyŏn-hwak) sent a reply to DPRK Premier Li's January 12 letter, agreeing to a meeting with Li and proposing contacts between working-level representatives of both sides in Panmunjom to arrange the details of the summit meeting. Reciprocating the North Korean action, Shin addressed Li as "Premier, the Administration Council, the Democratic People's Republic of Korea." It marked the first time that an official of the ROK Government ever used North Korea's official name. Then followed a series of contacts between working-level delegates of the two sides at two-week intervals. The contacts revealed that there were still many obstacles to be overcome. The two sides disagreed on three issues: the site of the proposed meeting, its agenda, and its nature. North Korea insisted that the meeting should be held in Pyongyang and Seoul on an alternating basis, not have any specific agenda, and should be characterized as an "encounter" (*sangbong*) or "contacts" (*chŏpch'ok*). South Korea expressed a strong preference for Geneva, Switzerland or any other place outside of Korea so that the meeting could not be exploited for propaganda purposes by either side, for having a specific agenda, and for calling it a "conference" (*hoedam*). At their fourth contact on March 18, the two sides reached a compromise

---

46. According to Kim Il Sung: "It is in the nature of dominationism to override the independence of other countries and oppress and control other nations and peoples. Dominationism means openly colonizing other countries and oppressing and exploiting them undisguisedly and . . . putting other countries under the yoke of slavery by various crafty methods to dominate and control them." See his speech commemorating the thirtieth anniversary of the DPRK's founding on September 9, 1978, in *KCNA*, Pyongyang, September 9, 1978, as monitored by FBIS.

47. *Han'guk ilbo*, January 21, 1980.

agreement on the site of the proposed meeting: Panmunjom, or more specifically "P'anmun'gak" (controlled by North Korea), and "Freedom House" (controlled by South Korea) on an alternating basis.[48]

As things turned out, this was the only agreement the two sides were able to reach. Subsequent contacts were marked by mutual recriminations; some even bordered on shouting matches. The contacts finally ended in a complete deadlock on August 20.[49] The dismal failure of the new round of contacts reflected not only the depth of mutual distrust but also the unwillingness or inability of both sides to make any concessions, given the extraordinary volatility of the political situation in the South. The continuing social unrest, the extension of martial law, the bloody uprising in Kwangju and its brutal suppression by the military, the emergence of a parallel military government, and, finally, the formal seizure of power by Chun Doo Hwan—all of this turmoil made it impossible for North Korea to approach the preliminary negotiations in Panmunjom with a coherent strategy. Nor did it facilitate the formulation of clear guidelines for the South Korean negotiators.

The Proposal for a Democratic Confederal Republic of Koryŏ

Later in the year North Korea unveiled still another operational direction. In his report to the Sixth Congress of the WPK on October 10, President Kim Il Sung put forth a comprehensive proposal for the establishment of a Democratic Confederal Republic of Koryŏ (DCRK). What was new and significant about the proposal was that it characterized a confederation of North and South Korea not as a transitional measure but as the unified state itself. Under the proposal, "on condition that the north and the south recognize and tolerate each other's ideas and social systems," "a unified national government" would be established "in which the two sides are represented on an equal footing and under which they exercise regional autonomy respectively with equal rights and duties." Two main organs of the DCRK would be "a supreme national confederal assembly [consisting of] an equal number of representatives from north and south and an appropriate number of representatives of overseas nationals" and "a confederal standing committee [empowered] to guide the regional governments in north and south and to administer all affairs of the confederal state." "Under the leadership of the confederal government the regional governments in north and south should follow an independent policy within the limits consistent with the fundamental interests and demands of the whole nation, and

48. Ibid., February 8 and 21, March 6 and 20, 1980.
49. Ibid., April 3 and 21, May 8 and 26, June 26, and August 21, 1980.

strive to narrow down the differences between north and south in all spheres and to achieve a uniform development of the country and the nation."[50]

Kim Il Sung argued that the "DCRK, as a unified state embracing the whole of the territory and people of our country, should pursue a policy which agrees with the fundamental interests and demands of the entire Korean people." He then went on to enumerate ten specific points that the confederal state should adopt as its policy:

> First, the DCRK should adhere to independence in all state activities and follow an independent policy. . . .
> Second, the DCRK should effect democracy throughout the country and in all spheres of society and promote great national unity. . . .
> Third, the DCRK should bring about economic cooperation and exchange between north and south and ensure the development of an independent national economy. . . .
> Fourth, the DCRK should realize north-south exchange and cooperation in the spheres of science, culture and education and ensure uniform progress in the country's science and technology, national culture and arts, and national education. . . .
> Fifth, the DCRK should reopen the suspended transport and communications between north and south and ensure free utilization of the means of transport and communications in all parts of the country. . . .
> Sixth, the DCRK should ensure a stable livelihood for the entire people including the workers, peasants and other working masses and promote their welfare systematically. . . .
> Seventh, the DCRK should remove military confrontation between north and south and form a combined national army to defend the nation against invasion from outside. . . .
> Eighth, the DCRK should defend and protect the national rights and interests of all Koreans overseas. . . .
> Ninth, the DCRK should handle properly the foreign relations established by the north and the south prior to reunification, and should coordinate the foreign activities of the two regional governments in a unified way. . . .
> Tenth, the DCRK should, as a unified state representing the whole nation, develop friendly relations with all countries of the world and pursue a peaceful foreign policy. . . .[51]

---

50. Kim Il Sung, *Report to the Sixth Congress of the Workers' Party of Korea on the Work of the Central Committee, October 10, 1980* (Pyongyang: Foreign Languages Publishing House, 1980), pp. 69–71.
51. Ibid., pp. 71–79.

If all of these ideas are to be implemented, what is likely to emerge is not merely a confederation but something resembling a federal republic. For there will be combined armed forces, unified foreign and defense policies, and a central direction of important aspects of government and administration. This raises the question of the feasibility of the DCRK proposal. Does North Korea seriously believe that it has the chance of being accepted by South Korea?

Clues to North Korean aims are provided by the other parts of Kim's report to the Sixth WPK Congress as well as by his subsequent pronouncements. Nowhere in his report does Kim suggest a willingness to negotiate with the South Korean authorities regarding his proposal. In fact, he spares no words in denouncing the latter:

> For the sheer brutality of the despotic repressions they are perpetrating, the present military fascists of south Korea have put all the fascist dictators of the world in the shade. History has not known to this day such hangmen as the south Korean military fascist rulers who massacred thousands of their countrymen at a time with rifle and bayonet and cruelly removed their political opponents.[52]

Kim then calls for the overthrow of "the colonial fascist rule of the US imperialists and their stooges in south Korea." As for the implementation of the DCRK proposal, Kim exhorts "all the Korean nationals in north and south and abroad" to "fight firmly rallied together in a grand national front under the banner of national reunification, regardless of the difference in ideology, social system, party affiliation and political views."[53] In short, the new North Korean proposal is aimed not at inducing South Korea's governing elite to a conference table but at arousing the Korean people to revolutionary action against the South Korean regime.

The proposal was also designed as a major tool of international propaganda, for North Korea expended a massive effort to publicize it throughout the world. Kim Il Sung himself stressed the importance of generating support for the DCRK idea both in Korea and in the world at large. In an interview with the visiting delegation of the Chinese *Xinhua* New Agency, Kim first reiterated the need to "liquidate the present fascist ruling system [in South Korea] which is reinforcing the foothold of one-man dictatorship" in order to "achieve the grand unity of our nation" as a prelude to the implementation of the DCRK proposal. He then noted:

> Not only the entire Korean people in the north and south but also the peace-loving people of the world warmly support and

52. Ibid., p. 63.   53. Ibid., p. 64 and p. 81.

hail this proposal. With the active support and encouragement of the Chinese people and peoples all over the world, our whole nation, by uniting and fighting powerfully, will surely check and frustrate the "two Koreas" plot of the partitionists and establish the Democratic Confederal Republic of Koryo and thus achieve the independent and peaceful reunification of the country.[54]

What are the probable sources of this operational direction? First, the elevation of the confederation idea from a way station to a destination may reflect Kim's gnawing realization that reunification in its pure form is all but unattainable within his lifetime. In lengthy discussions with a visiting group of Korean-American scholars in Pyongyang in July 1981, North Korean academics and officials stressed the degree of systemic differences between the North and the South as the main variable in the evolution of Pyongyang's proposals for reunification. In 1949, for example, systemic differences were relatively small or within manageable limits; hence North Korea proposed free elections throughout Korea for the purpose of setting up a centralized government. What was sought in 1949, in other words, was a unification of *systems* (*chedo ŭi t'ong'il*). By 1960, however, systemic differences had widened to such an extent that the immediate establishment of a unified government became an unrealistic goal; hence North Korea proposed a system of confederation as a transitional measure. After the passage of a sufficient preparatory period, free elections would be held, and a central government symbolizing a systemic unification of Korea would emerge. By 1980, the gap between the two systems had widened still further so that the idea of an eventual systemic unification had to be abandoned. Hence a confederation of two separate systems was proposed as the most appropriate form of a unified state. In lieu of systemic unification, the North Koreans explained, the DCRK proposal aims to achieve *national* unification (*minjokchŏk t'ong'il*) entailing wide-ranging collaboration and contacts among the entire Korean people.

Second, the convening of the Sixth Congress of the WPK, a major event in North Korea and, quite possibly, the last party congress for the aging leader,[55] called for the unveiling of some new ideas, rather than a rehash of old ones. As things turned out, the only thing that was really new proved to be the decision to equate confederation with reunification. However, whatever novelty the idea may have had

54. *KCNA*, Pyongyang, April 26, 1981. Press Release of the DPRK Permanent Observer Mission to the United Nations, no. 30, April 27, 1981.
55. There was a nine-year interval between the Fourth and Fifth Congresses and a ten-year interval between the Fifth and Sixth Congresses. If the same pattern holds, then the Seventh Congress will be held in 1989 or 1990, when Kim Il Sung will be 77 or 78.

was somewhat blunted by the sweeping nature of the proposed confederation, which would embrace practically all the ideas about reunification that North Korea had previously articulated. Third, given the manner in which the new South Korean leader came to power and especially given what Pyongyang viewed as his brutal suppression of the Kwangju rebellion, Kim Il Sung had nothing but contempt for Chun Doo Hwan. It was therefore inconceivable for Kim to enter into negotiations with the Chun regime. Finally, notwithstanding setbacks in the South, Kim does not appear to have modified his strategic thinking about the need for a southern revolution. In fact, the Kwangju uprising may have reinforced his confidence in the revolutionary potential and capabilities of the South Korean masses.[56]

Generating Support in the World Arena

Insofar as Pyongyang's operational direction of building up "international revolutionary forces" is concerned, three specific goals may be identified: (1) to generate support for North Korea, (2) to isolate both South Korea and the United States, and (3) to exert direct and indirect pressure on the United States so as to bring about the withdrawal of the American troops from South Korea. While Pyongyang has consistently pursued these goals over the past quarter century, the tempo and magnitude of its efforts and the results attained have been a function of changes in the operational environment. Generally speaking, while the 1960s saw a steady increase in Pyongyang's diplomacy, it was during the 1970s that most impressive gains were registered.

Change in North Korea's international position is most graphically illustrated in table 1. During the first 11 years of its existence, the DPRK established diplomatic relations with thirteen countries, of which only two were non-Communist countries. It should be noted that South Korea's record in this regard was not appreciably better than its northern rival's, having obtained fourteen diplomatic partners during the same period (see Table 2). In the 1960s, North Korea established diplomatic relations with twenty countries. Of this total, only one country, Cuba, belonged to the Communist bloc. All were developing nations of the Third World. An overwhelming majority were in Africa and the Middle East. Pyongyang's considerable achieve-

---

56. In my talks with North Korean scholars, party cadres, and government officials during my trip to the DPRK in the summer of 1981, I repeatedly pressed the issue of North Korea's refusal to deal with the Chun Doo Hwan regime, pointing out that such a posture was tantamount to the acceptance of a stalemate for at least seven years. The North Koreans, however, were unanimous in their argument that given the lack of legitimacy and popular support, the Chun regime would collapse in the not too distant future.

ments in the diplomatic arena in the 1960s, however, were eclipsed by a spectacular increase in the number of Seoul's diplomatic partners in the same period: Seoul added sixty-five countries to the roster—more than three times the number of Pyongyang's diplomatic partners.

It appears that Pyongyang decided in the early part of the 1970s to bridge the gap. A combination of accelerated efforts by Pyongyang, an improvement in its image abroad, and a changed international climate helped to produce a rich payoff: North Korea established diplomatic relations with sixty-four countires, which is more than twice the number (thirty-one) of South Korea's new diplomatic partners during the same period.[57]

Although marginally different from the general policy line, Pyongyang's operational direction during the 1970s was nonetheless significant: it was one of stepping up efforts and diversifying relations in the world arena. In terms of establishing formal diplomatic ties, the three-year period between 1973 and 1975 proved to be most productive for North Korea. Not only did it succeed in establishing diplomatic relations with five Western European countries—Sweden, Denmark, Finland, Norway, and Iceland—but it also won admission to the World Health Organization (WHO) in May 1973, overcoming stiff opposition by the ROK and its allies. This was a significant milestone for North Korean diplomacy, for it gave North Korea the customary right of establishing a permanent observer's mission at the United Nations. Pyongyang promptly set up such a mission first in Geneva and then in New York. Later in the year, North Korea participated as an observer in the UN debate on Korea for the first time in its history. Together with South Korea, which had previously monopolized the right to represent the Korean people, North Korea was allowed not only to observe the proceedings of both the First Committee (Political and Security Affairs) and the General Assembly but also to make speeches in the First Committee. After intensive behind-the-scenes maneuvers and bargaining, in which the representatives of the two Koreas negotiated, not face-to-face but through intermediaries— Algeria for North Korea and the Netherlands for South Korea—a compromise "consensus" statement was adopted without a vote by the First Committee and later by the General Assembly.[58]

In 1974, North Korea almost succeeded in obtaining a favorable UN resolution when a draft resolution calling for withdrawal of UN

57. Here I am referring to *net* gains in diplomatic partners, rather than to the number of countries with which diplomatic relations were established. See tables 1 and 2.

58. For details, see B. C. Koh, "The United Nations and the Politics of Korean Reunification," *Journal of Korean Affairs* 3, 4 (January 1974): 37–56.

forces from South Korea was narrowly defeated in the First Committee by a vote of 48 to 48 with 38 abstentions. Then, in 1975, it scored a symbolic victory of sorts, when the UN—both its First Committee and the General Assembly—took the unprecedented step of passing two contradictory resolutions on Korea, one favorable to North Korea and the other supportive of South Korea. The net effect of the UN action was therefore neutral: neither Pyongyang nor Seoul gained anything substantive. Nonetheless, the symbolic gain for North Korea was considerable, since it marked the first time that the United Nations had passed a resolution that had been cosponsored by North Korea's allies. By conveniently ignoring the pro-South Korea resolution that the same General Assembly had also passed, North Korea could claim a victory and urge the United States to honor the pro-North Korea resolution. In its operative part, the latter called for dissolution of the UN Command in South Korea, withdrawal of "all the foreign troops stationed in South Korea under the flag of the United Nations," and replacement of the armistice agreement with a peace agreement.[59]

Pyongyang's Quest for Dialogue With the United States

In March, 1974, North Korea unveiled another operational direction—an active quest for direct negotiations with the United States. On March 25, 1974, the third session of the Fifth Supreme People's Assembly of the DPRK adopted an open letter to the US Congress proposing that direct negotiations be held between North Korea and the United States on the question of replacing the existing armistice agreement with a peace treaty between the two countries. Two most noteworthy aspects of this overture were, first, North Korea's insistence on bilateral talks and, second, its expectation that the centerpiece of the proposed peace treaty would be withdrawal of US troops and weapons from South Korea.[60] The proposal has since been repeated on numerous occasions both in public and in private.

Pyongyang's probable motives appeared to include the following: First and foremost, its hope that the North-South dialogue would pave the way for withdrawal of US troops from South Korea had been shattered. It must have concluded that further talks with Seoul would be completely sterile in terms of attaining that overriding goal. Furthermore, Pyongyang appeared to be genuinely convinced that the

---

59. See B. C. Koh, "The Battle Without Victors: The Korean Question in the 30th Session of the UN General Assembly," *Journal of Korean Affairs* 5, 4 (January 1976): 43–63.

60. For the text of the March 25, 1974 letter, see *Pyongyang Times*, March 30, 1974.

United States was the real power in South Korea—a conviction that is buttressed by Pyongyang's perception of US aims in Korea and that buttresses its claim that the ROK is not a legitimate political entity but a "puppet of US imperialism."

In addition, should the North Korean overtures bear any fruit, they were likely to produce a number of payoffs to Pyongyang. They would enhance the DPRK's international prestige and perhaps indirectly bolster its claim to exclusive legitimacy in the Korean peninsula. They might also cause some strain in US-ROK relations. At the very least, bilateral talks between North Korea and the United States over the head of South Korea would undercut the ROK's prestige both in South Korea and abroad. Finally, it is worth noting that nine months earlier North Korea had proposed the conclusion of a bilateral peace treaty with South Korea that would pave the way for the withdrawal of US troops from South Korea. However, South Korea had countered in January 1974 with a proposal for a mutual nonaggression agreement, contingent upon the continuation of the armistice agreement. The new North Korean move was, in a sense, a tactical response to the South Korean counterproposal.

South Korea's Operational Direction

South Korea's operational direction in the 1960s concentrated on the building of economic power at home and international support abroad while simultaneously ignoring all overtures from North Korea. In other words, South Korea set out to translate into action its strategy of "economic construction first, reunification later" (*sŏn kŏnsŏl hu t'ong'il*). Its developmental strategy, however, had a predominantly international orientation, for it consisted of relying heavily on foreign capital and international trade. It was necessary not only to maintain the alliance with the United States as the cornerstone of Seoul's foreign policy but also to cultivate a new relationship with its erstwhile enemy and colonial master, Japan. Normalization of diplomatic relations with Tokyo, in short, became a matter of utmost urgency for Seoul.

Normalization of Relations With Japan

Although preliminary discussions for normalization of relations between South Korea and Japan began as early as October 1951, at the height of the Korean War, it was not until the advent of military rule in 1961 that Seoul started to make an all-out effort. Among the principal issues of contention were (1) the status of Korean residents in Japan, (2) problems concerning property claims, (3) problems concerning the "Rhee Line" (which extended South Korea's jurisdiction to 50 nautical miles from its coastline, thus barring Japanese fishermen from fishing within these waters), (4) Japanese possession of Korean art treasures, (5) conflicting territorial claims to Tokto (or Takeshima) Island, and (6) Japan's policy of repatriation of Korean residents to North Korea.[61] Compromise was reached on most of these issues (with the notable exception of the Tokto issue), and five agreements were signed in June 1965. Instruments of ratification were exchanged six months later, and the agreements entered into force on January 17, 1966.[62]

A diplomatic breakthrough of major proportions, the settlement had implications for South Korea's reunification strategy in at least two ways: First, the Treaty of Basic Relations Between the Republic of Korea and Japan "confirmed" in Article 3 that "the Government of the Republic of Korea is the only lawful Government in Korea as specified in the Resolution 195 (III) of the United Nations General Assembly."[63] The ambiguity of the UN resolution[64] allowed South Korea to construe Article 3 of the basic treaty to signify Japan's recognition of the exclusive legitimacy of the ROK government in the entire peninsula, while simultaneously permitting Japan to state a different interpretation—that the U.N. resolution simply declared the ROK government to be the only lawful government "having effective control and jurisdiction over that part of Korea where the [UN] Temporary Commission was able to observe and consult" in 1948, which was the southern half of the Korean peninsula.

The second and, no doubt, far more significant implication of the rapprochement pertained to "economic cooperation" between the two countries. With Japan's commitment to provide a total of $800 million to South Korea over a ten-year period ($300 million in grants,

61. Youngnok Koo, "The Conduct of Foreign Affairs," in Edward R. Wright (ed.), *Korean Politics in Transition* (Seattle: University of Washington Press, 1975), p. 221.

62. Republic of Korea, Ministry of Foreign Affairs, *Han'guk oegyo samsimnyŏn* [Thirty Years of South Korean Diplomacy], *1948–1978* (Seoul: Oemubu, 1979), pp. 117–118.

63. Se-Jin Kim (ed.), *Korean Unification: Source Materials With An Introduction* (Seoul: Research Center for Peace and Unification, 1976), p. 281.

64. It declared that "there has been established a lawful government (the Government of the Republic of Korea) having effective control and jurisdiction over that part of Korea where the Temporary Commission was able to observe and consult and in which the great majority of the people of all Korea reside; that this Government is based on elections which were a valid expression of the free will of the electorate of that part of Korea and which were observed by the Temporary Commission; and that this is the only such Government in Korea." Ibid., pp. 109–110. The resolution was passed on December 12, 1948 by a vote of 48 to 6, with 1 abstention and 3 absences. Han K. Kim (ed.), *Reunification of Korea: 50 Basic Documents* (Washington, DC: Institute for Asian Studies, 1972), p. 18.

$200 million in government loans, and $300 million in private commercial credits),[65] the diplomatic settlement laid the groundwork for the influx of Japanese capital and technology into South Korea. In fact, the United States and Japan became not only the principal sources of investment capital in South Korea's drive for accelerated economic development but also its main trading partners. For example, during the first Five-Year Plan period (1962–1966), the United States and Japan together accounted for the annual average of 62 percent of South Korean exports and 77 percent of its imports. During the second Five-Year Plan period (1967–1971), South Korea's dependence on the two countries as export markets increased to 73 percent on the average, while their share of South Korean imports declined slightly to 72 percent on the average. In the third Five-Year Plan period (1972–1976), the two countries together accounted for the annual average of 64 percent of South Korean exports, while enjoying nearly the same share of South Korea's import market. While there has been a steady decline in South Korea's dependence on these two trading partners in recent years, they still remain South Korea's foremost export markets as well as its primary sources of import goods.[66] In 1981, Japan and the United States together accounted for 43 percent of South Korea's commodity exports and 48 percent of its imports.[67]

In sum, South Korea's decision to normalize relations with Japan in the mid-1960s was a momentous one. Indeed, given its significance and impact, it could very well be characterized as a strategic decision. That it is treated as an operational decision here is justifiable only in the context of South Korea's reunification strategy. The sources of the operational decision overlap with those of Park Chung Hee's decision to pursue economic modernization with all deliberate speed: his early exposure to abject poverty and his desire to vindicate his coup d'etat. Additionally, his predominantly Japanese background—education in Japanese-run schools, including the Japanese Military Academy, service in the Japanese Imperial Army, and open admiration for the Meiji Restoration—may help account for his tenacious quest for a compromise settlement, notwithstanding fervent opposition from large segments of the South Korean citizenry.[68]

65. Yung-Hwan Jo, "Japanese-Korean Relations and Asian Diplomacy," *Orbis* 11, 2 (Summer 1967): p. 587.
66. Republic of Korea, Economic Planning Board, *Major Statistics of Korean Economy, 1979* (Seoul: EPB, 1979), pp. 200–201.
67. *Korea Herald*, February 3, 1982.
68. See Kwan Bong Kim, *The Korea-Japan Treaty Crisis and the Instability of the Korean Political System* (New York: Praeger Publishers, 1971).

Participation in the Vietnam War

Another significant operational decision, which had huge implications not only for Seoul's security but also for its modernization program, was its decision to dispatch combat troops to South Vietnam. Although South Korean participation in the Vietnam conflict began in September 1964, when "a ROK Mobile Army Surgical Hospital (MASH) and ten Taekwondo instructors were dispatched to Vietnam," it was not until October 1965 that the first ROK combat troops arrived there. The decision to become a cobelligerent in the war was not made by Seoul on its own initiative but only after considerable pressure was exerted by the United States on South Korea. Nonetheless, it was an autonomous decision on the part of the ROK government, for which US pressure alone provides an insufficient explanation.[69]

The ROK troops, whose peak strength stood at approximately 50,000 men, became the next to largest foreign contingent in the Vietnam conflict, second only to the US troops. During the seven and a half years of their participation in the war (from October 1965 to March 1973), the ROK troops reportedly "caused 41,000 enemy deaths, and 'pacified' a 7,438-square-kilometer area . . . where approximately 870,000 people . . . lived. Total Korean battle deaths are estimated to have been about 4,000."[70]

If explanation for the South Korean decision can be inferred from its actual consequences, two factors emerge as most noteworthy: the strengthening of the Seoul-Washington alliance and economic gains. By agreeing to dispatch combat troops on a significant scale, South Korea helped to fulfill a number of functions for the United States: (1) it promoted the goal of bringing "more flags" to Vietnam, thereby further internationalizing the conflict; (2) it considerably lessened the US military burden; (3) it helped to reduce the cost of the war to the United States; and (4) it contributed to the American military objectives in Vietnam. The upshot of all this was to improve appreciably the bilateral relations between South Korea and the United States. Not only did Seoul succeed in obtaining from Washington a commitment not to reduce its troop level in Korea, but Washington reciprocated by increasing its military assistance to South Korea and by expediting delivery of advanced weapons and equipment. The successful conclusion of a long-sought Status of the United States Armed Forces Agreement between the two coun-

69. For an informative analysis of the sources and consequences of the decision, see Sungjoo Han, "South Korea's Participation in the Vietnam Conflict: An Analysis of the U.S.-Korean Alliance," *Orbis* 21, 4 (Winter 1978): 893–912.

70. Ibid., p. 893.

tries was most probably related to the invigoration of the ROK–US alliance.[71]

Not to be overlooked are economic gains. According to Sung-joo Han:

> Between 1965 and 1969 [South Korea's] total Vietnam earnings from such sources as military commodity procurement, war risk insurance premiums, contracts for services, construction contracts, remittances of military and civilian personnel, and commercial exports, amounted to $546 million, some 16 percent of total foreign receipts or about 2 percent of GNP for the same period. Earnings for the entire period of Korean participation (1965–1973) are estimated to have been at least $1 billion, without counting the increase in direct US economic and military aid to Korea. The "Vietnam earnings" became available during a critical stage in Korea's economic development, when large amounts of international liquidity were needed for the rapid expansion of export industries.[72]

In addition, a sizable number of South Korean men received a valuable combat experience, thus bolstering South Korea's overall military capability. A listing of gains, however, should not obscure the fact that South Korea had to pay a high price for them. Apart from combat casualties, South Korea's international prestige suffered a setback because of the widespread unpopularity of the American intervention in the conflict. ROK troops sent to Vietnam were disparagingly referred to as "mercenaries" in the pay of "American imperialism." South Korea's credibility may have declined most sharply among the Third World nations.[73]

Expansion of Diplomatic Partners

Supplementing the operational decisions discussed above was the decision to increase the number of trading and diplomatic partners. One of the first diplomatic moves ever made by the coup leaders in 1961 was to dispatch five good-will delegations to all corners of the globe—the Americas, Southeast Asia, the Middle and Near East, Europe, and Africa. The delegations visited a total of 76 countries. The effort was repeated in the latter part of 1962 with the focus on Africa, Latin America, and the Middle and Near East. The most tangible result of such diplomacy was the addition of 36 diplomatic partners be-

71. Ibid., pp. 903–904.
72. Ibid., p. 898.
73. See Frank Baldwin (ed.), *Without Parallel: The American-Korean Relationship Since 1945* (New York: Pantheon Books, 1974), pp. 27–31 and p. 207.

tween July 1961 and the end of 1962.[74] Of the 36 countries, 15 were in Latin America, 11 in Africa, 5 in the Middle and Near East, 3 in Europe, and 2 in Oceania (Australia and New Zealand). By broadening its diplomatic base, Seoul hoped to gain not only economic payoffs but also international support—specifically, support for its positions in the annual UN debate on Korea.

Seoul's Pursuit of Dialogue With Pyongyang

A significant change in South Korea's operational direction occurred in mid-1970: instead of completely ignoring North Korea's propaganda offensive, Seoul decided to meet it head-on. In a speech on August 15, President Park Chung Hee unveiled a new operational decision. He was prepared, he stated, to propose "epochal and . . . realistic measures" aimed at removing step by step the "various artificial barriers between South and North Korea" and he would not oppose Pyongyang's participation in the annual UN debate on Korea, provided Pyongyang recognized the UN's authority to deal with the Korean question. Finally, Park challenged "the North Korean Communists" to "a bona fide competition in development, in construction and in creativity to prove which system, Democracy or Communist Totalitarianism, can provide better living for the people and which society is a better place to live in."[75]

If Park's proposals signaled a notable departure from Seoul's previous policy, they also fell considerably short of being an olive branch to Pyongyang. For not only was the offer of reconciliation contingent on conditions to which North Korea could not readily accede,[76] but the manner in which the proposals were made was hardly calculated to evoke a positive North Korean response. Aside from the fact that Seoul's proposals were couched in the form of an open challenge to Pyongyang, they contained a denunciation of Kim Il Sung as well as references to the "North Korean puppets." Predictably, North Korea categorically rejected Park's proposals, calling them "nonsense

74. Republic of Korea, Ministry of Foreign Affairs, *Han'guk oegyo samsimnyŏn*, p. 114. See also table 2.
75. For excerpts from Park's speech, see Han K. Kim, *Reunification of Korea*, pp. 60–61.
76. For Pyongyang to renounce aggressive aims toward Seoul, for example, would be tantamount to admitting that it had indeed harbored such aims, which North Korea had steadfastly denied. As for the UN, Pyongyang had consistently maintained that the world organization had forfeited its moral and legal authority as an impartial arbiter on the Korean question because of its participation as a belligerent in the Korean War. More important, Park's "concession" was identical in substance to the idea of "conditional invitation" that the ROK's allies had been supporting at the UN since 1961. See B. C. Koh, "The Korean Workers' Party and Detente," *Journal of International Affairs* 28, 2 (1974): 181–185.

uttered by the traitor, Park Chung Hee, [which] is filled with falsehood and deception and [which] contains no realistic plan for reunification." Pyongyang added that Park's speech constitutes "nothing but a masquerade of the previous plots for 'unification through northward march' in a new garb of 'peaceful unification.'"[77]

A dramatic change in Korea's operational environment, triggered by the Sino-American rapprochement in mid-1971, however, led to the modification of North Korea's own operational direction: it now signaled a willingness to negotiate with the Park Chung Hee government. Seoul then took the initiative of proposing "humanitarian talks" between Red Cross representatives of the two Koreas, and the North-South dialogue finally materialized in September 1971. Just as the change in the external setting appeared to be the key factor underlying the softening of the North Korean posture toward the South, so the perceived need to respond positively to new external stimuli may have played a pivotal role in changing South Korea's operational direction. No less important was Seoul's growing confidence, fueled by its spectacular economic gains. Its national power, of which economic power is the backbone, had grown so much that it could bargain with the North from a position of strength. Finally, if nothing substantive should come out of the dialogue, South Korea would at least have neutralized North Korean propaganda.

The initiation of Red Cross talks, which were conducted ostensibly by nongovernmental representatives but in fact under governmental direction, paved the way for a potentially momentous development: the initiation of political talks. According to the revelations of DPRK Vice-Premier Pak Sung Chol on July 4, 1972, soon after the initiation of the preliminary Red Cross talks in Panmunjom, Seoul and Pyongyang agreed to hold "high-level talks." "In order to prepare for the high-level talks," Pak said, "unofficial contacts of liaison delegates from the north and south were realized in November [1971] and they visited Pyongyang and Seoul."[78] If Pak's account is true, then it serves to undercut the credibility of the ROK government, which, at the very moment when it was engaged in secret negotiations with the DPRK, declared an "emergency decree" (*wisuryŏng*) aimed at expanding the powers of President Park Chung Hee and curtailing civil liberties on the ground that there was an imminent danger of invasion from North Korea. On the other hand, the move can be interpreted as an attempt by the Seoul government to ensure its security before facing the risks of negotiations with Pyongyang. More important, Park Chung Hee faced the twin challenges of increased opposi-

77. The North Korean reply was contained in an editorial in the WPK organ, *Nodong sinmun*, August 22, 1970.
78. *Pyongyang Times*, July 6, 1972.

tion strength in the National Assembly and growing social unrest at home, and the emergency decree may be viewed as a predominantly political move aimed at consolidating his position.

From May 2 to 5, 1972, Lee Hu Rak, director of the KCIA and widely regarded at the time as the second most powerful man in South Korea, visited Pyongyang in utmost secrecy. He met separately with Premier Kim Il Sung and his younger brother, Kim Yong Ju, twice. The latter, who served at the time as director of the Organization and Guidance Department of the WPK Central Committee, was Lee's principal negotiating partner. Although Kim Yong Ju was invited to visit Seoul for further negotiations, he declined the offer for health reasons and sent Vice-Premier Pak Sung Chol in his place. Pak visited Seoul from May 29 to June 1 and met with President Park Chung Hee, Lee Hu Rak, and other leaders.[79]

These secret, high-level contacts led to the publication of a North-South joint statement on July 4, 1972. The statement, issued in the names of Kim Yong Ju and Lee Hu Rak "pursuant to the intention of their respective superiors," declared that the two sides had reached an agreement on three "principles for the reunification of our fatherland": (1) independence and exclusion of "external powers," (2) nonuse of force, and (3) great national unity "transcending differences in ideas, ideologies, and systems."[80] According to the statement, the two sides had further agreed to refrain from slandering or defaming each other as well as from committing armed provocations, great or small. They had also agreed to (1) promote intercourse in various fields, (2) expedite the Red Cross talks, (3) install a "hot line" between Seoul and Pyongyang, and (4) establish a "North-South Coordinating Committee," with Kim Yong Ju and Lee Hu Rak serving as cochairmen "for the purpose of promoting the implementation of the preceding points of agreement."[81]

We have already discussed Pyongyang's probable motives for agreeing to the dialogue: among other things, it anticipated huge payoffs in terms of the eventual withdrawal of U.S. troops from South Korea. What, then, were Seoul's motives? To ask this question raises the intriguing question, was the July 4 joint statement a truthful document worthy of being taken seriously? Even at the time of its publication, the document appeared to experienced observers of the Korean scene to be too good to be true. It somehow strained one's imagination to believe that two parties that would neither explicitly recognize each other's existence nor call each other by their proper

79. For Seoul's version of these contacts, see *Confrontation With Dialogue*, Korea Policy Series, No. 5, July 1972 (Seoul: Korean Overseas Information Service, 1972).
80. *Tong'a ilbo*, July 4, 1972.
81. Ibid.

names had successfully reached an agreement on the principles of their political integration in such sweeping terms.[82]

More important, there were ominous signs of a fundamental disagreement between the two sides on the very day the joint statement was being published. In sharp contrast to the unmistakable optimism of Pak Sung Chol, Lee Hu Rak was singularly restrained. Whereas Pak characterized the publication of the statement as "a great historic event which puts an end to the 27-year-long split and antagonism of the north and the south and heralds the dawn of reunification to our people,"[83] Lee merely saw it as the beginning of "confrontation with a dialogue" between Seoul and Pyongyang. In his words, "dialogue does not necessarily mean peace itself. Dialogue is no more than one of the wise means of seeking peace." Urging the South Korean people not to harbor any illusions about the probable payoffs of the dialogue, Lee underscored the need for strengthening South Korea's security posture and institutional framework. In fact, he clearly stated that a fundamental restructuring of South Korea's political system might be necessary in order to carry on the dialogue.[84]

With the benefit of hindsight, it can be hypothesized that domestic political considerations may have been primarily responsible for the unusual promptness with which Seoul agreed to the three principles of reunification embodied in the North-South joint statement. For not only were the principles clearly of North Korean origin both in phraseology and in substance, but the first principle—particularly the pledge to exclude "external powers" from the reunification process—was manifestly at variance with the ROK's long-standing policy as well as with its security interests. Given the political uses to which the beginning of the political dialogue was subsequently put by Park—it was used as the main justification for the "October [1972] Revitalizing Reforms"—it is tempting to speculate that there may even have been an elaborate scenario worked out in advance. According to such a scenario, the foremost consideration was the generation of a grand rationale (*taeŭi myŏngbun*) for extending Park's tenure in office. A combination of factors—the extraordinary controversy surrounding the 1969 constitutional amendment lifting a ban on Park's third term, Park's dramatic pledge on the eve of the 1971 presidential election that he would not seek a fourth term, the increased strength of the opposition New Democratic party in the National Assembly—

82. The joint statement conspicuously avoided any references to "the Republic of Korea" and "the Democratic People's Republic of Korea." Instead, it used such neutral terms as Seoul and Pyongyang, North and South, and the "two sides."

83. *Pyongyang Times*, July 6, 1972. These remarks were made by Pak in a news conference on July 4, 1972 in Pyongyang.

84. *Confrontation With Dialogue*, pp. 12–32. During his news conference on July 4, 1972, Lee Hu Rak referred to the need for structural change at least four times.

made it impractical to attempt another constitutional amendment within the framework of the existing constitution. Hence an extraordinary circumstance justifying extraconstitutional measures was needed. The initiation of the dialogue provided precisely such an excuse. The ominous frequency with which Lee Hu Rak mentioned the need for a fundamental restructuring of institutions on July 4, 1972, coupled with the actual developments since October 1972, serves to bolster the preceding interpretation.

A plausible rival hypothesis is that Park's own version of what happened and why should be taken at its face value, that he may have taken the extraconstitutional measures in the sincere belief that they would enable him to conduct the dialogue in earnest and from a position of strength, and that the impasse and the subsequent rupture of the dialogue may be attributed to North Korea's dogged adherence to its revolutionary strategy and failure to compromise its positions at the conference table.

Finally, there is a third hypothesis that seeks to integrate the first two. It speculates that the truth may lie somewhere in between, that while the initiatives for dialogue may have been taken without any clearly formulated scenario for political exploitation at home, they nevertheless lent themselves to such uses, and that the October "reforms" may have been intended not simply to extend the tenure and powers of Park but also to enable his regime to conduct the dialogue more efficaciously.

None of the preceding hypotheses precludes the possibility that once the dialogue got under way, Seoul sincerely sought to keep it going and to attain tangible results in terms of reducing tensions and promoting interchanges between the two halves of Korea. Indeed, a careful review of the available records of the two-pronged dialogue suggests that Seoul's approach was consistently incrementalistic, pragmatic, and conciliatory, while that of Pyongyang manifested a substantial degree of impatience, dogmatism, and abrasiveness (more on this in chapter 9).

Seoul's "Open Door" Policy

South Korea signaled still another change in its operational direction in June 1973 when it published a "special statement regarding foreign policy for peace and unification" by President Park Chung Hee. Most noteworthy of the seven points contained in the special statements were the following:

> 4. We shall not oppose north Korea's participation with us in international organizations, if it is conducive to the easing of tension and the furtherance of international cooperation.

5. We shall not object to our admittance into the United Nations together with north Korea, if the majority of the member-states of the United Nations so wish, provided that it does not cause hindrance to our national unification.

Even before our admittance into the United Nations as a member, we shall not be opposed to north Korea also being invited at the time of the UN General Assembly's deliberation of "the Korean question" in which the representative of the Republic of Korea is invited to participate.

6. The Republic of Korea will open its door to all the nations of the world on the basis of the principles of reciprocity and equality. At the same time, we urge those countries whose ideologies and social institutions are different from ours to open their doors likewise to us.

Park hastened to add that the policy statements regarding North Korea should be construed as "interim measures during the transition period pending the achievement of our national unification" and that "the taking of these measures does not signify our recognition of north Korea as a state."[85]

The timing, and perhaps even the content, of the "special statement" needs to be understood against the backdrop of a few significant developments in Seoul's operational environment. In the one-year period since the publication of the North-South joint statement, North Korea had scored sizable gains in the international arena: it had established diplomatic relations with twelve countries, including Sweden, Denmark, Finland, and Norway (compared with a gain of two diplomatic partners for South Korea in the same period). More important, it had cracked the wall of the UN system by winning a hard-fought battle to join the WHO in May 1973. All this meant that the gap between Seoul and Pyongyang at the UN in terms of ability to generate support for their respective positions had been substantially narrowed. Seoul's newly announced policy of not opposing North Korea's participation in international organizations in general and in the UN General Assembly's deliberation of the Korean question in particular, then, was partly an acknowledgment of a fait accompli and partly an acceptance of what appeared to be an ineluctable outcome.

What was new, however, was Seoul's bold proposal for a simultaneous entry of both North and South Korea into the UN as full-fledged members. The proposal clearly reflected Seoul's assessment that reunification remained but a distant goal, that its interests would be best served by membership in the world organization, and

---

85. Park Chung Hee, *Toward Peaceful Unification* (Seoul: Kwangmyong Publishing Co., 1976), pp. 78–79.

that, given the veto power of Pyongyang's principal allies in the UN Security Council, it would be all but impossible for Seoul to gain entry into the world body alone or without North Korean cooperation.

No less significant was the "open door" policy enunciated in the special statement. Strictly speaking, however, it was by no means the first time that South Korea had declared a willingness to deal with any and all countries regardless of ideology. In his New Year's news conference on January 11, 1971, President Park had stated his desire to "improve relations with nonhostile Communist countries." In September of that year, a "nongovernmental economic delegation" led by the president of the Korea Trade Promotion Corporation visited Yugoslavia, thus marking the first time that South Korean citizens visited a Communist country with government approval. In May 1973, a South Korean citizen was admitted into the Soviet Union for the first time for the purpose of attending an international meeting.[86] Nonetheless, it was significant that Seoul's softening of posture toward Communist countries was elevated to the level of major foreign policy: Seoul served notice to the entire world that it would welcome contacts with all countries on the basis of reciprocity and equality. Although no significant change materialized in the realm of state-to-state relations, nongovernmental contacts and indirect trade between South Korea and Eastern European countries increased appreciably.

Seoul's New Offensive in 1982

In January 1982 South Korea launched a massive diplomatic offensive in the area of reunification policy that clearly bespoke a new operational direction. In his New Year's policy statement to the National Assembly on January 22, President Chun Doo Hwan unveiled a comprehensive proposal for the solution of the reunification problem. He proposed the formation of a "Consultative Conference for National Reunification" consisting of representatives of North and South Korea with the aim of drafting a constitution for a unified Korea, the conclusion of a provisional agreement on basic relations between the two Korean states, and the establishment of "resident liaison missions" headed by cabinet-rank plenipotentiaries in each other's capitals. Chun also reiterated his 1981 proposals for a summit meeting and exchange of visits between the heads of the two Korean governments.[87]

86. Republic of Korea, Ministry of Foreign Affairs, *Han'guk oegyo samsimnyŏn*, pp. 242–244.
87. For the text of his statement, see *Han'guk ilbo*, January 25, 1982 and *New Year Policy Statement by President Chun Do Hwan Before the National Assembly*, January 22 (Seoul: Korean Overseas Information Service, 1982).

Unlike his 1981 overtures toward Pyongyang, this action bore earmarks of an operational direction. First, it was the first time that South Korea had ever unveiled such a comprehensive blueprint for national reunification. Second, the plan, together with supplementary proposals unveiled ten days later, contained some new ideas as well as a rehash of old ones, including some ideas that Pyongyang had previously proposed. Third, the Chun statement was followed by a barrage of supplementary proposals containing concrete ideas spanning the whole gamut of inter-Korean relations. Fourth, the ROK government made it clear that the top priority of its diplomacy in 1982 would be to seek international support for its new initiatives regarding reunification.[88]

Chun disclosed that his proposals had originally been prepared for the summit meeting he had proposed in January and June 1981; he was making them public, he said, to provide "the North Korean authorities and the rest of the world with an opportunity to comprehend our genuine intent." He suggested that when the proposed Consultative Conference for National Reunification agrees upon the text of a draft constitution for a unified Korea, it should be submitted to "free, democratic referendums held throughout the whole peninsula." Then a general election should be held, in accordance with the constitution, to elect a unified legislature and establish a unified government.[89]

The proposed "provisional agreement on basic relations between South and North Korea," according to Chun, is aimed at promoting mutual confidence and trust and normalizing relations between the two sides. The agreement would incorporate the following principles: (1) equality and reciprocity; (2) seeking peaceful solutions to all problems through dialogue and negotiation; (3) recognition of each other's existing political order and social institutions, and non-interference in each other's internal affairs; (4) maintenance of the existing regime of armistice, coupled with the search for measures to end the arms race and military confrontation; (5) opening up each other's society through various forms of exchange and cooperation; (6) respect for each other's bilateral and multilateral treaties and agreements pending unification; and (7) exchange of resident liaison missions headed by plenipotentiary envoys with the rank of cabinet minister.[90]

Chun proposed that "high-level delegations from the South and the North, headed by cabinet-rank chief delegates, meet together at the earliest possible date in a preparatory conference to work out the

---

88. *Han'guk ilbo*, January 25, 1982.
89. *New Year Policy Statement by President Chun Doo Hwan*, p. 13.
90. Ibid., pp. 14–16.

necessary procedures for a South-North summit meeting." He added that his government had already made the necessary preparations to send a delegation.[91]

Although North Korea rejected Chun's proposals on January 26, Seoul unveiled a twenty-point proposal for inter-Korean cooperation on February 1. In a statement issued by ROK Minister of National Unification Son Chae-sik, Seoul proposed the opening of a Seoul-Pyongyang highway, the joint development and operation of tourist facilities on *Sŏrak* (located in the South) and *Kŭmgang* (located in the North) Mountains, mail exchanges between family members and reunions of separated families, mutual visits by newsmen and other personnel, the dispatch of single teams to international sports competitions, joint research in the DMZ, removal of military facilities in the DMZ, the opening of free ports in both parts, trade of consumer goods, and other measures. Son explained that some of these measures had been proposed by the North previously and urged Pyongyang to show its sincerity by accepting them. He stressed that nearly all of the ideas were capable of being implemented promptly without any prolonged negotiations.[92]

Then, on February 18, Seoul announced that it had decided to propose to Pyongyang the convening of a North-South conference on sports to discuss problems relating to the 1988 Olympic Games scheduled to be held in Seoul.[93] Finally, on February 25, Son proposed to North Korea the convening of a "high-level conference" between the two sides in Seoul, Pyongyang, or Panmunjom in March for the purpose of discussing Seoul's proposals as well as the counterproposal unveiled by Pyongyang on February 10. Son then disclosed the identities of a nine-member ROK delegation to the proposed conference headed by then Minister of State for Political Affairs No Tae Woo.[94]

In sum, in the span of five weeks, Seoul had literally bombarded Pyongyang with proposals covering every conceivable aspect of inter-Korean relations. What did Seoul hope to accomplish with these initiatives? Given the stridency with which Pyongyang had previously denounced Chun Doo Hwan and rejected his proposals for a summit meeting, Seoul was probably under no illusion that the new set of proposals would strike a responsive chord in its adversary. The new overtures can therefore be viewed as signaling a new phase in Seoul's international public relations or psychological warfare against Pyongyang.

They served notice that Seoul would take an offensive, rather

91. Ibid., p. 16.   92. *Han'guk ilbo*, February 3, 1982.
93. Ibid., February 20, 1982.   94. Ibid., February 27, 1982.

than a defensive, posture in the war of words. Furthermore, if Chun's 1981 proposals for mutual visits by top leaders had failed to neutralize Kim Il Sung's 1980 proposal for a DCRK, the new set of proposals emanating from Seoul were designed to accomplish that goal. If Pyongyang vigorously pursued the goal of generating international support for its own proposal, Seoul set out to prove that it could play that game, too. In fact, in assessing President Chun's first year in office under the new Constitution, The *New York Times* on March 4, 1982 gave him high marks for his moves in the reunification field. In the words of its correspondent, Henry Scott Stokes: "For years, Kim Il Sung carried the torch of reunification; Mr. Park [Chung Hee], by contrast, seemed to lack confidence in dealing directly with the Communists. The torch may now have passed to Mr. Chun."[95]

95. Henry Scott Stokes, "South Korea Under Chun: New Vigor But Little Shift Toward Democracy," *New York Times*, March 4, 1982.

9 FOREIGN POLICY OUTPUTS: TACTICAL DECISIONS, SYMBOLIC AND SUBSTANTIVE ACTIONS

Tactical decisions are subordinate to strategic or operational decisions and may either precede or follow the latter. They are frequently precipitated by specific challenges or stimuli in the operational environment. They are more flexible and less abstract than either strategic or operational decisions. Their range of duration is relatively short, and their impact typically modest. Because they are so numerous, all that can be essayed here is to provide some examples. In the following survey, we shall move back and forth between North and South Korea to provide a semblance of chronological order.

NORTH KOREA'S TACTICAL DECISIONS

To begin with North Korea, the barrage of propaganda that preceded the North Korean invasion of South Korea in June 1950 clearly bespoke Pyongyang's tactical decision to camouflage the impending invasion. On June 7, 1950, eighteen days before the invasion, North Korea, speaking through the Democratic Front for the Reunification of the Fatherland, proposed the holding of all-Korean elections from August 5 to 8 for the purpose of electing a unified national legislative assembly, which would convene in Seoul on August 15, 1950, the fifth anniversary of Korea's Liberation. It also proposed the holding of a conference of representatives from all political parties and social organizations from June 15 to 17. Finally, on June 19, the DPRK Supreme People's Assembly proposed to the ROK National Assembly that the two rival assemblies be merged to form a single legislative body for all of Korea. That all this was a tactical move aimed at concealing Pyongyang's aggressive designs is suggested by the following factors: First, given the amount of planning and preparation that preceded the invasion, it is clear that by the time these proposals were made, North Korea was poised for war. Its foremost concern must have been to safeguard the advantage of a surprise attack. Second, the unrealistically short lead time the proposals contained—only a week's notice for the convening of a North-South conference—and the unacceptable preconditions that Pyongyang set—specific individuals, for example, including President Syngman Rhee and virtually all prominent political leaders in South Korea, were excluded from the conference on the ground that they were "traitors"—made it unlikely that North Korea was seriously seeking a negotiated solution to the problem of territorial division.[1]

Some of the more celebrated tactical episodes reflective of North Korea's bellicose operational direction in the late 1960s were the abortive commando raid on the South Korean presidential mansion on January 21, 1968, the seizure of the USS *Pueblo* and its eighty-three man crew in Wonsan Bay on January 23, 1968, and the downing of the EC-121 US naval reconnaissance plane on April 15, 1969. These moves were fueled by a complex array of motives: Pyongyang's desire to eliminate its archenemy, President Park Chung Hee, destabilize South Korean society, and trigger a revolutionary situation; its concern for security; its desire to humiliate and harass the United States; its need to demonstrate both the reality of the American threat to its security and its ability to counter it; and the imperative of North Korea's internal politics, particularly the intense personality cult centering around Premier Kim Il Sung.[2]

The publication of a "special statement regarding foreign policy for peace and unification" by President Park on June 23, 1973 presented Pyongyang with the need for a tactical decision, and it was made with unusual speed: in a speech welcoming the visit of Gustav Husak, general secretary of the Czechoslovak Communist Party Central Committee, only several hours after the publication of Park's statement, President Kim Il Sung—his title changed from premier to president in December 1972—made a counterproposal. Kim said that North and South Korea should enter the United Nations, not as separate entities, but as "one state under the name of the Confederal Republic of Koryo" and revived his earlier proposal for a North-South

---

1. B. C. Koh, *The Foreign Policy of North Korea* (New York: Praeger, 1969), pp. 120–121.
2. B. C. Koh, "The *Pueblo* Incident in Perspective," *Asian Survey* 9, 4 (April 1969): 264–280.

confederation as an intermediate step toward reunification. All this was presented as a part of a newly formulated five-point proposal on reunification. The other points in the package dealt with (1) the removal of the state of military confrontation between the North and the South, which in turn encompassed an earlier five-point proposal —(a) to stop arms reinforcement and the arms race, (b) to cut the army strength of both sides to 100,000 men or less, (c) to stop the introduction from foreign countries of all weapons, combat equipment, and war supplies, (d) to make the US forces and other foreign troops withdraw from Korea, and (e) to conclude a peace agreement guaranteeing that the foregoing points would be fulfilled and that the North and the South would not use arms against each other; (2) North-South cooperation in political, military, diplomatic, economic, and cultural fields; and (3) the convening of a "great national conference" involving the people in all walks of life from both sides.[3]

A major factor underlying North Korea's tactical response to Park's proposals may be found in the internal setting of the operational environment. A political system whose most salient characteristic is the exaltation of its supreme leader can ill afford to create the impression of meekly accepting its adversary's proposals, however alluring they may be. It must take the initiative at all times. To do otherwise is not only to betray the principle of *chuch'e*, the lifeblood of Kim Il Sung's political teachings as well as North Korea's national ideology, but to undercut the stature of the supreme leader, the putative fountainhead of all wisdom. Furthermore, by insisting upon the formation of a confederal state of the two Koreas for the purpose of UN membership, North Korea could flaunt the consistency of its policy, for it had advocated the idea of confederation since 1960. Equally consistent with Pyongyang's previous stand was the idea of a "great national conference" encompassing a cross section of the Korean people; it was first proposed on the eve of the Korean War and had been periodically reiterated. Finally, there remains the possibility that Kim Il Sung's rejection of the proposal for a simultaneous entry of the two Koreas into the UN may be based in part on his genuine conviction that such a move may have the effect of legitimizing and prolonging the status quo—the partition of the Korean peninsula. In fact, North Korea was to denounce the separate membership idea as a "sinister scheme to perpetuate the division of Korea" with singular frequency and vehemence. As noted, it was cited, together with the Kim Dae Jung kidnapping incident of August 1973, as the pretext for breaking up the North-South Coordinating Committee talks in August 1973.

3. Kim Il Sung, *For the Independent Peaceful Reunification of Korea* (New York: International Publishers, 1975), pp. 201–207.

If the ax killing of two American army officers by North Korean soldiers in the Joint Security Area of Panmunjom on August 18, 1976 was a premeditated act, rather than a spontaneous reaction of fiercely anti-American North Korean soldiers to what they had perceived as a provocation, then it must have been preceded by a calculation of tactical advantages by North Korea. The timing of the incident is suggestive: it coincided with two events that were of more than passing interest to North Korea—the conference of heads of state or governments of the nonaligned countries in Colombo, Sri Lanka, and the Republican National Convention in Kansas City, Missouri. The incident may have had the dual aim of focusing world attention on the increased danger of a war in Korea and underscoring the costs of the American military presence in Korea to the leaders and people of the United States in an election year. The Colombo conference adopted a "resolution on the Korean question" endorsing North Korean demands for the immediate cessation of "the imperialist war provocation maneuvers in South Korea," removal of nuclear weapons and foreign troops from South Korea, and replacement of the Korean armistice agreement by a peace agreement. It also adopted a "political declaration" that included an expression of support for North Korea.[4] The possibility nonetheless remains that the incident may have been caused by a spontaneous reaction of North Korean soldiers on the scene of the tree-cutting operation by ROK and US soldiers.

North Korea's subsequent actions vis-à-vis the United States reflected a series of tactical decisions in pursuit of its operational direction of seeking dialogue with Washington. For example, Pyongyang apparently greeted the advent of the Carter Administration in 1977 with cautious optimism and considerable restraint. Thus, in an unusual gesture, Kim Il Sung took pains in his New Year's message of 1977 to differentiate between the old and new administrations in Washington. In denouncing the "aggressive machinations" of the "US imperialists" against North Korea, Kim twice specifically referred to the "Ford Administration of the United States."[5]

It was not until April 23 that North Korea offered its comments on the Carter Administration. In an interview with the *Yomiuri shimbun* of Japan, Kim Il Sung stated that while North Korea was taking a "wait and see" attitude toward President Carter, it was nonetheless disturbed by what it perceived as a discrepancy between Carter's campaign pledges and his actions since taking office. Specifically,

---

4. North Korea, however, fell short of accomplishing its goal at Colombo, for about twenty-five countries reportedly expressed their reservations to the resolution endorsing North Korea's positions. See B. C. Koh, "North Korea 1976: Under Stress," *Asian Survey* 17, 1 (January 1977): 64–65.

5. *Pyongyang Times*, January 1, 1977.

Kim expressed reservations about the slow pace of the proposed withdrawal of US troops (for he saw the possibility that it might not be completed during Carter's tenure of office), its incomplete nature (i.e., Carter's plan to keep the US Air Force contingents in South Korea indefinitely), and Washington's intention to consult with both Seoul and Tokyo about the process. Finally, Kim accused Carter of failing to implement the latter's "campaign pledge" not to support "a regime [that suppresses] human rights" and of continuing to provide military aid to Seoul.[6]

Another noteworthy tactical decision occurred in July 1977 when a crisis erupted over the downing of a US Army CH-47 helicopter by North Korean troops over the North Korean side of the DMZ; three crewmen were killed and a fourth was wounded and captured. The downing of the aircraft itself reflected less a tactical decision than an implementation of standard operating procedure on the part of the North Korean troops concerned. The handling of the crisis, however, required a tactical decision. North Korea appears to have perceived a stake in not jeopardizing Carter's announced plan to withdraw US ground troops from South Korea, although the plan fell short of North Korea's expectations. Not only was Pyongyang's official account of the incident low-keyed, but North Koreans displayed a businesslike attitude in their negotiations with Americans in Panmunjom over the return of three bodies and the release of the wounded survivor. That an agreement was reached and implemented within three days of the incident marked a milestone of sorts in North Korean-American relations.[7]

Another milestone was reached on September 28, 1977 when Ho Dam, vice-premier and foreign minister of the DPRK, arrived in New York to attend an emergency meeting of foreign ministers of the non-aligned countries. Given the significance of his visit—he became the highest-ranking North Korean official ever to set foot in the United States—it reflected an important tactical decision on Pyongyang's part. Although the ostensible aim of his visit was to attend an international meeting, and despite public disavowal of any ulterior motives, it was clear that he had hopes of meeting with officials of the US government, for Ho's visit coincided with the receipt by President Carter of two "indirect requests from North Korea for a meeting with US officials."[8] The latter development, needless to say, signified a diversification of North Korean tactics in pursuit of its operational direction.

The first of the two indirect requests was reportedly contained

6. *Yomiuri shimbun* (Tokyo), April 28, 1977.
7. *New York Times*, July 16 and 17, 1977. For North Korean accounts, see *Pyongyang Times*, July 23, 1977.
8. *Korea Herald*, October 2, 1977.

in a letter to Carter from President Bongo of Gabon, who had earlier paid a state visit to the DPRK. The idea was broached again in a "letter from President Tito of Yugoslavia, delivered to Carter personally by Yugoslav Vice-President Edvard Kardelj." Tito, too, had visited North Korea earlier in the year. President Carter and his aides expressed "willingness to meet [with North Koreans] provided that South Korea is present as an equal participant," describing the position as "unshakable."[9] In a series of interviews with foreign (particularly Japanese) newsmen in New York, Ho Dam reiterated North Korea's proposals for direct negotiations with the United States and specifically suggested that the two countries hold "a preliminary meeting in which . . . the question of including South Korean representatives in the US-North Korean talks could be discussed."[10]

Shortly after his return to North Korea, Ho Dam told the Yugoslav News Agency TANJUG that although North Korea had not received a direct answer to its proposal for direct talks with the United States, a statement by Carter's press secretary to the effect that the US would not negotiate with North Korea without South Korean participation was tantamount to America's rejection of "our proposals for direct negotiations." Ho stressed that the proposed "peace treaty and reunification are two separate questions." North Korea, he said, wanted to negotiate with the United States for the former only "while the central problem, Korea's reunification, would be settled subsequently 'by peaceful means, on the basis of democracy, after the withdrawal of foreign troops and without external interference in our internal affairs.' That would be the theme of the talks between north and south."[11]

As it became clear that Washington's policy toward Korea did not and would not change in the direction desired by Pyongyang, the latter made the tactical decision to resume attacks on the United States. One of the most vicious attacks was contained in a *Nodong sinmun* commentary of March 28, 1978:

> The US imperialists' aggressive policy against Korea has not changed, but has continued since Carter became President. This policy has become more ominous with the passage of time. In the United States, presidents can be changed but not policies. It is actually monopolistic capital which handles politics, and the administrator is nothing but a means used by the monopolistic capitalists to realize their policy of aggression and war. Carter is

9. Ibid.
10. *Kyōdō News Agency*, New York, September 30, 1977, as monitored by FBIS; *Asahi shimbun* (Tokyo), October 1, 1977; and *Korea Herald*, October 8, 1977.
11. TANJUG, Belgrade, October 22, 1977, as monitored by FBIS.

pushing a more cunning policy of aggression against Korea than that of his predecessors in a most sinister and wicked way. The US imperialists' new war maneuvers, now proceeding in South Korea under the signboard of a "troop withdrawal," bears witness to this, and the US-Korea joint military exercise is clear proof. The present US ruling circles, like those in the past, want war in Korea, not peace; division, not reunification.

Two things are noteworthy: First, although *Nodong sinmun* is the official mouthpiece of the ruling WPK, of which Kim Il Sung is the undisputed leader, it was the former, not the latter, which carried out such a frontal attack on the Carter policy. Second, harsh as the preceding attack may sound, it is relatively restrained compared to North Korea's diatribe against Park Chung Hee contained in the same commentary. Whereas the object of attack is Carter's *policy* in the foregoing example, it is Park's *person and character* that are attacked later in the commentary. This is not to suggest that Kim Il Sung has refrained from making any adverse comments on Carter. In an interview with the Japanese magazine *Sekai* published in January 1979, Kim repeated the essence of the North Korean criticism of the Carter policy and charged that Carter was being hypocritical, for Kim saw a discrepancy between Carter's words and deeds as well as between his stated and real objectives. Kim further accused Carter of intimidating both the South Korean and the Japanese people.[12]

SOUTH KOREA'S TACTICAL DECISIONS

South Korea's decision on August 12, 1971 to propose Red Cross talks with North Korea was a tactical one in a dual sense. First, it was made within the overall context of the new operational direction, unveiled on August 15, 1970, of countering North Korean propaganda head-on and of working toward the removal of "artificial barriers" between the two halves of Korea. Second, it was a tactical response to the move made by Pyongyang six days earlier, namely, Kim Il Sung's flat declaration that North Korea was willing to talk with "all political parties, including the Democratic-Republican party, all social organizations, and all individuals" in South Korea. We have already seen that the single most important factor helping to explain the ap-

12. Kim Il Sung, "Chōsen no tōitsu to kokusai jōsei" [Korean Reunification and the International Situation], *Sekai*, January 1979, pp. 146–157. The interview was conducted in Pyongyang on October 21, 1978 by Yasue Ryokai, editor of the Japanese magazine.

parent eagerness of both Pyongyang and Seoul to start a dialogue in the summer of 1971 was the dramatic change in their common external setting—the rapprochement between Washington and Beijing. The tactical calculus underlying Seoul's proposal for Red Cross talks needs to be examined briefly.

While Pyongyang's overtures had clearly been political, Seoul seemed anxious to eliminate or minimize political overtones from its own overtures toward the North. Probably Seoul did not wish to do anything that would in any way enhance the legitimacy of its archrival. It was not yet prepared to signal a change in its long-standing position that there was no autonomous government worthy of the name in the northern half of the peninsula. Hence the ROK government opted for a medium and agenda of dialogue that could be regarded as primarily humanitarian. It was not anyone formally connected with the ROK government but the president of the ROK National Red Cross who made the stunning proposal. He proposed to his counterpart in North Korea that representatives of the two Red Cross organizations hold discussions on the problem of the estimated ten million Koreans whose families had been broken up due to the division of the peninsula. Should the North Korean side accept the proposal, what would materialize would be a dialogue, not between any official representatives of the two Koreas, but between two ostensibly nongovernmental organizations.

Neither side was under any illusion that the reality would be congruent with the form: given the character of the political systems on both sides, no organization, no matter what its avowed aims or international affiliations, was immune from governmental control. Insofar as the dialogue was concerned, it could be safely assumed that the Red Cross organizations were completely subservient to their respective governments. In fact, even the composition of the two delegations was deceptive: they both included persons who were not bona fide members of the Red Cross organizations. Notwithstanding all this, what mattered a great deal to Seoul was the facade—that the parties to the dialogue would be Red Cross personnel and that the agenda would be an unmistakably humanitarian one.

Once preparatory talks between representatives of the Red Cross organizations of North and South Korea got under way, however, South Korea appears to have made another tactical decision—that is, to pursue contacts with the North at the political level. Not only was this decision implemented under the utmost secrecy, but, when it culminated in the publication of the North-South joint statement on July 4, 1972, care was taken to gloss over the fact that unlike the Red Cross talks, what had taken place were the patently government-to-government contacts between the two Koreas. We have already speculated about the probable motives of both Seoul and Pyongyang with respect to that momentous development. Suffice it here to consider one tactical dimension of Seoul's behavior. An intriguing question is just why Seoul had agreed to the three principles of reunification that formed the core of the joint statement. At first glance, they seem eminently sensible: independence, the renunciation of force, and great national unity. However, as already noted, the seemingly innocuous principle of independent reunification proved to be the focus of fundamental disagreement between the two sides.

The principle states: "Reunification shall be attained independently without either relying upon or tolerating interference from any external force." Is it possible that Seoul was unaware of the implications of the phraseology of this principle? Not only had the principle, and particularly its wording, been a prominent part of North Korean rhetoric concerning reunification for a long time, but it had been invariably mentioned in the context of North Korea's call for the withdrawal of US troops from South Korea. To Pyongyang, the mere presence of US troops and weapons in the South constituted a flagrant interference by an external power in the internal affairs of the Korean people. It therefore strains one's imagination to believe that Seoul had failed to anticipate Pyongyang's argument that the principle of independence, together with the other principles, had removed the rationale for the continued stationing of US troops in South Korea.[13] It appears that the need to produce a joint statement proved to be so compelling as to eclipse Seoul's probable misgivings about the principle's implications. As we have seen previously, Seoul was promptly to dismiss Pyongyang's interpretation and to argue that US troops in no way constituted an "external force." This line of reasoning is interlocked with the hypothesis, advanced earlier, that internal political considerations may have figured prominently in Park Chung Hee's calculations.

CONDUCT OF THE DIALOGUE

The actual conduct of negotiations necessitated tactical adjustments on the part of both parties. Notwithstanding, and perhaps because of, the fact that the Park regime capitalized on the dialogue in order to bolster its power at home, its tactics at the conference table bespoke a dogged determination to keep the dialogue going and to seek incre-

13. During my 1981 trip I was told by a member of the DPRK Academy of Social Science that Kim Il Sung had personally explained the meaning of this principle to Lee Hu Rak and that Lee had not only understood but also pledged to honor it.

mental change in North-South relations. During the preparatory stage of the Red Cross talks, disagreement immediately arose regarding the agenda of the full-dress talks: the North insisted on "the question of realizing free travel and mutual visits among family members, relatives, and friends who are dispersed between the North and the South." The South argued that the scope of the dispersed persons should be restricted to family members and that mutual visits should be preceded by the confirmation of their current status and whereabouts and correspondence between them.[14]

After ten meetings spanning two months, Seoul proposed to add "relatives" to the scope of dispersed persons, and Pyongyang agreed to drop "friends." Seoul's next tactical move was to propose, at the nineteenth preparatory meeting, the convening of "working-level" meetings. It was during the latter that Seoul proposed a revised version of the agenda that, in effect, incorporated the substance of Pyongyang's proposal. It should not be overlooked, however, that all this was happening against the backdrop of secret political contacts between the two sides which eventually produced the North-South joint statement on July 4, 1972.

At the twenty-second preparatory meeting, held only ten days after the publication of the joint statement, the North erected yet another hurdle: it demanded that the delegations to the full-dress talks be accompanied by "advisors consisting of representatives of the government, the Supreme People's Assembly [or the National Assembly in the case of South Korea], political parties, and social organizations." In subsequent meetings, the North made it clear that "political parties" in South Korea encompassed the Revolutionary Party for Reunification. The South was plainly not prepared to accede to such a demand but, faced with an impasse, proposed the convening of another round of "working-level" meetings. In the end, Seoul opted for the tactic of ignoring the issue and of not contesting Pyongyang's insistence that its own Red Cross delegation include advisors representing not only political parties and social organizations but also *Ch'ongnyŏn*, the North Korea-oriented Korean residents' association in Japan. The South also yielded to the North's insistence that the

14. This and the following discussion of the conduct of North-South negotiations draws on: *Han'guk ilbo, Nodong sinmun, Pyongyang Times, KCNA, How the Political Talks Between the North and the South Have Proceeded* (Pyongyang: Central Committee of the Korean Journalists Union, September 25, 1973); *South-North Dialogue in Korea*, nos. 5–10 (Seoul: International Cultural Society of Korea, 1964–1976); *South and North Korea: Differing Approaches to Dialogue* (Seoul: Research Center for Peace and Unification [RCPU], no date); *The Republic of Korea's Basic Position on South-North Dialogue* (Seoul: RCPU, 1979); *A Handbook on (Inter-Korean) South-North Dialogue* (Seoul: RCPU, 1979); *Pukhan chŏnsŏ* [North Korean Handbook], *1945–1980* (Seoul: Kŭktong Munje Yŏn'guso, 1980), pp. 762–786.

first full-dress meeting be held in Pyongyang. In short, it is plain that South Korea made more concessions than its northern rival in order to pave the way for the full-dress Red Cross talks, which finally began on August 30, 1972.

The beginning of the full-dress talks, however, in no way signaled the end of tactical challenges from the North, for Pyongyang insisted that the main task of the talks was not simply to find solutions to the problem of dispersed family members and relatives but to bring about territorial reunification based on patriotism, nationalism, and the North-South joint statement. At the third meeting, held in Pyongyang on Octber 24, 1972, the North made a startling argument: as a precondition for resolving the problem of dispersed persons, the South must create a "free atmosphere." Specifically, Pyongyang demanded that Seoul cease all "anti-Communist policies, activities, education and propaganda." At the fourth meeting, held in Seoul on November 22, 1972, the North reiterated its position, specifically demanding the repeal of anti-Communist laws by South Korea. It also argued that confirmation of the status and location of dispersed families should be done not through the exchange of tracing cards as proposed by the South, but through free travel by the persons concerned. The South, however, refused to yield to the North's demands, insisting that the Red Cross talks should focus on the practical, humanitarian problem of alleviating the hardships of the dispersed families and relatives and stick to the procedure for locating missing persons established by the International Red Cross.

The North kept on escalating its demands. At the sixth meeting held in Seoul from May 9 to 10, 1973, for example, it demanded that the individuals concerned be given not only the right of free travel but also freedom of the press and of assembly. It also called on the South to guarantee the right of political parties, social organizations, public organs, and individuals to participate in the activities of the Red Cross. In the seventh and final meeting of the full-dress Red Cross talks, the South countered by proposing the establishment of "working-level meetings" as well as the exchange of delegations to visit the ancestral graves during the forthcoming *ch'usŏk*, the traditional Korean holiday celebrating the harvest. In sum, Seoul's tactics revealed that it was determined to minimize the potential political fallout of contacts among dispersed family members and relatives, whereas Pyongyang appeared to be intent on opening up channels of contact with the South that would facilitate its efforts to win the hearts and minds of the South Korean brethren. While Seoul was clearly anxious to continue the talks and to generate positive results, it was not willing to make concessions on larger issues. Finally, Seoul tried in vain to maintain a strict distinction between the Red Cross talks and the political talks, the latter of which began on October 12, 1972, following the publication of the North-South joint statement.

The conduct of the political talks was no less plagued by problems and hurdles. Apart from the fundamental incompatibility of the strategic interests of the two sides and their deep-seated mutual distrust, the sources of the difficulties included two specific developments: First, Seoul's declaration on July 4, 1972 that the principle of independence embodied in the joint statement did not preclude the American military presence in South Korea irked and disillusioned Pyongyang. Second, President Park's invocation of the dialogue as the main justification for his "October [1972] reforms" may have made Pyongyang realize that it had become an unwitting accessory to Park's scheme to bolster his own political power at home.

At the first meeting of the cochairmen of the North-South Coordinating Committee (NSCC), which had not yet been formally established, on October 12, 1972, North Korea called on South Korea to jettison the policies of "relying on outside forces" and suppressing communism and to lift the state of emergency that had been in effect for nearly a year. At the second meeting of the cochairmen, held in Pyongyang from November 2 to 3, 1972, North Korea made its demands more specific: among other things, it wanted the withdrawal of US troops stationed in South Korea, the cessation of Japan's "aggressive maneuvers," the release of all political prisoners including Communists, the realization of a North-South confederation through negotiations "at the highest levels," and the implementation of "many-sided collaboration and interchange." Meanwhile, South Korea advocated the establishment of the North-South Coordinating Committee in an operational form at the earliest possible date and the policy of noninterference in each other's political system. Both of these points were agreed upon at the meeting.

But the meetings of the NSCC[15] continued to highlight deep divisions between the two sides. The North argued that the whole range of problems facing the divided Korea should be attacked simultaneously, with top priority being given to the problem of easing military tensions. The latter, it insisted, called for the cessation of arms reinforcement and the arms race, mutual reduction of their respective troops strengths to 100,000 or less, the withdrawal of US troops from South Korea, and the conclusion of a peace treaty between the two sides. The North further pressed for the simultaneous formation of five subcommittees within the NSCC on (1) economic, (2) cultural,

15. The third and final meeting of the cochairmen of the NSCC was held on November 20, 1972, at which time the committee was formally inaugurated. On the same day, the first meeting of the NSCC per se was convened.

(3) military, (4) diplomatic, and (5) political collaboration. Finally, it advocated the convening of a conference of political parties and social organizations in order to promote national unity.

The South's approach was markedly restrained and cautious. Arguing that the building of mutual trust necessitated a gradual approach, it proposed the establishment of two subcommittees first: one on economic, the other on sociocultural issues. The former would explore the possibilities of setting up facilities on both sides to handle exchange of goods and of launching joint projects for exploration or operation in selected fields. The latter would deal with multifaceted contacts and exchanges between artistic, scholarly, athletic, and social organizations. Notwithstanding the lack of progress and, particularly, Pyongyang's decision in August 1973 to downgrade the talks on both fronts—the Red Cross and the NSCC—Seoul tried very hard to keep the dialogue alive. Its apparent eagerness to pursue the dialogue, however, was tempered by its unwillingness to yield to the North Korean demands. For Seoul must have perceived that what Pyongyang was after was nothing less than a drastic change in the military balance in the peninsula through the removal of US troops and arms from the South. Furthermore, South Korea's profound distrust of North Korea had in no way abated. On the contrary, the dialogue must have deepened it. Under these conditions, Seoul's basic tactical orientation in the two-pronged talks with Pyongyang was to make only minor concessions. Its desire to keep the dialogue alive may have been linked to the internal political uses to which the dialogue had been put. Having justified profound political changes at home in terms of the imperatives of the dialogue, the Park regime had a stake in its continuation.

Seoul departed from its policy of maintaining a distinction between the Red Cross and NSCC talks in the wake of a traumatic event—the attempted assassination of President Park Chung Hee and the murder of his wife in Seoul on August 15, 1974 by a Korean resident in Japan who allegedly acted under the guidance of the North Korea-oriented *Ch'ongnyŏn*. In both of the downgraded versions of the dialogue—the eighth meeting of the deputy cochairmen of the NSCC on September 21, 1974 and the fourth meeting of the working-level delegates of the North and South Korean Red Cross organizations on September 25, 1974—Seoul demanded that Pyongyang punish those responsible for the event. This departure may be explained by the gravity of the event, the profound sense of outrage felt in Seoul, and the desire of Park's top subordinates to express their loyalty and sympathy to the bereaved leader. One cannot, of course, rule out the possibility that it may have been Park's own decision.

Also noteworthy is Seoul's tactical response to Pyongyang's proposal, first made in June 1973, that the two sides conclude a peace treaty. Had the proposal been simply one of concluding a peace treaty, Seoul would have had no reasons to object. However, the North Korean proposal was an integral part of a package containing, among other things, the demand for the withdrawal of US troops from South Korea and the prohibition of arms buildup. Seoul's initial reaction was to ignore it. Faced with Pyongyang's continuing propaganda barrage, however, which portrayed Seoul as being opposed to a peace treaty pure and simple, Seoul must have made a tactical decision to mount a counteroffensive. In a news conference on January 18, 1974, President Park Chung Hee proposed that North and South Korea conclude a "mutual nonaggression agreement." Under such an agreement, the two sides would pledge not to resort to invasion or any other use of force against each other and not to interfere in each other's internal affairs. The existing armistice agreement would remain in effect. Conspicuously absent was any reference to the American military presence in South Korea.[16] As noted previously, North Korea's overtures to the United States, initiated in March 1974, while signaling a new operational direction, could also be viewed as a tactical response to Seoul's counterproposal. Pyongyang's new operational direction marked the jettisoning of its previous position regarding a peace treaty with Seoul. For its part, however, Seoul has never withdrawn its proposal for a nonaggression agreement and has periodically reaffirmed it.

In mid 1975 South Korea and its principal allies were confronted with a tactical challenge: North Korea had been vigorously pressing for the dissolution of the United Nations Command in South Korea and the replacement of the armistice agreement with a peace agreement between North Korea and the United States. It was expected to have its allies in the UN submit a draft resolution incorporating its demands to the thirtieth session of the UN General Assembly. In collaboration with the United States and other allies, South Korea worked out a tactic consisting of the following components: (1) they would agree to dissolve the UN Command provided that alternative arrangements for the maintenance of the armistice agreement can be worked out among "all the parties directly concerned," namely, the two Koreas, the US, and the PRC; (2) all the parties directly concerned should enter into negotiations as soon as possible "on new arrangements designed to replace the armistice agreement, reduce tensions and ensure lasting peace in the Korean peninsula"; and (3) they would clearly differentiate the issue of the American military presence in South Korea from that of the UN Command, pointing out that

16. *Tong'a ilbo*, January 18, 1974.

the stationing of US troops in South Korea is based on a bilateral agreement between Seoul and Washington. Although the tactic was effective insofar as blunting the propaganda offensive of Pyongyang and its allies was concerned, it failed to prevent the passage of a pro-North Korean resolution in the General Assembly for the first time in the history of the UN debate on Korea. The practical impact of the latter, however, was neutralized by the simultaneous adoption by the General Assembly of a pro-South Korean resolution.[17]

We have already seen that South Korea made an unsuccessful attempt in early 1979 to revive dialogue with North Korea. What was the tactical calculus underlying President Park's January 19 proposal for an unconditional meeting of the "authorities of the South and the North"? There had been a significant development in the external setting: the normalization of diplomatic relations between the US and the PRC. In fact, PRC Vice-Premier Deng Xiaoping was scheduled to visit the United States in a few weeks, and there was a high probability that he might try to persuade Washington to soften its posture toward Pyongyang. There was a clear and urgent need for Seoul to reaffirm to the world its commitment to the easing of tensions in the peninsula and to indicate both its sincerity and flexibility in the quest for dialogue. Should the North reject the overtures, that would undercut its claim that the impasse in the dialogue was due solely to the South's lack of sincerity. Finally, there was a possibility that North Korea might be ready to resume the dialogue in light of the changed international situation.

Pyongyang's Response to Seoul's 1979 Initiative

North Korea's tactical decision regarding Park's proposal was unveiled on January 24. In a statement issued in the name of the Central Committee of the Democratic Front for the Reunification of the Fatherland (DFRF) on January 23, North Korea first characterized the proposal as a "positive response to our unchanging and consistent stand of keeping open the door to dialogue" as well as an indication that "the South Korean authorities have abandoned their previous policy of perpetuating 'the two Koreas' and are willing to make a fresh start." It then put forth a four-point proposal:

First, the North and the South should adhere to the ideals and principles embodied in the July 4, 1972 joint statement. Specifically, both sides should publicly declare on February 1 that they reaffirm and shall solemnly observe those ideals and principles, notably, (1) re-

---

17. For details, see B. C. Koh, "The Battle Without Victors: The Korean Question in the 30th Session of the U.N. General Assembly," *Journal of Korean Affairs* 5, 4 (January 1976): 43–63.

unification by independent means, without relying upon external forces, (2) reunification by peaceful means, and (3) the principle of great national unity transcending differences in ideologies, ideas, and systems.

Second, both sides should immediately cease defaming or slandering each other.

Third, both sides should stop immediately and unconditionally all hostile military acts against each other. Specifically, both sides should stop all hostile military acts along the DMZ, including the reinforcement of their forces, military operations, the construction of military facilities, and all military exercises as of March 1.

Fourth, a great national conference consisting of representatives of all political parties, social organizations, patriotic personages from all walks of life, and Korean residents in foreign countries should be convened. A preliminary meeting of working-level representatives should be held in early June in Pyongyang with a view to convening the conference in early September either in Pyongyang or in Seoul.[18]

Several aspects of the North Korean response are noteworthy. First, North Korea took pains to downgrade the Park proposal: not only did it characterize the latter as a response to its own standing offer rather than as an initiative in its own right, but it also chose the medium of the DFRF to put forth its own proposals. In other words, Pyongyang implied that Park's proposal did not merit a response from Kim Il Sung, or the Workers' Party of Korea, or any organ of the DPRK Government. Second, none of the principal points were new; Pyongyang simply reiterated its previous positions, thereby safeguarding both its consistency and initiative. Third, the idea of a great national conference contained a trojan horse: since it must include representatives of *all* political parties from both sides, Pyongyang could insist that representatives of the Revolutionary Party for Reunification be included in the South Korean delegation. In fact, the RPR promptly asserted its right to attend the proposed conference in the capacity of the "defender and spokesman of the true interests of the broad working masses of *the Republic of Korea*."[19] If Seoul were to accede to such a demand, it would have the effect of indirectly legitimizing the RPR. More important, the ability of the South Korean side to conduct negotiations with one voice would be hopelessly compromised. Should South Korea refuse to allow the RPR to be represented in the proposed conference, that could be used by North Korea at any time to torpedo the talks while laying the blame squarely on

18. *Nodong sinmun*, January 24, 1979.
19. The assertion was contained in a statement issued by the RPR Central Committee one day after the North Korean response was published. The statement was published in *Nodong sinmun*, January 24, 1979. Emphasis added.

South Korea. In sum, it was a no-win situation for South Korea. Moreover, the size of the proposed conference made it exceedingly unlikely that any real negotiations could take place; it would most probably emerge as a propaganda forum. Finally, Pyongyang's proposal that all hostile military acts, including military exercises, should stop effective March 1 appeared to have a specific aim: to stop the massive joint military exercise by the US and ROK troops codenamed "Team Spirit '79," which had been scheduled to begin on that very day.

Given all these considerations, Seoul's response was predictable. Reminding North Korea that all previous agreements between the North and the South, including the July 4 joint statement, had resulted from "dialogue between the responsible authorities of both sides," ROK Minister of Public Information Kim Sŏng-jin proposed that a preliminary meeting of representatives of the "responsible authorities of North and South Korea" be held as soon as possible either in Seoul or in Pyongyang.[20] What ensued thereafter was a bizarre sequence of events. While neither side made any concession whatsoever, a meeting of sorts nonetheless materialized in Panmunjom on February 17. However, the four-man delegation from the North insisted that it represented the DFRF, while the four-man delegation from the South claimed to represent the NSCC. Although the two delegations managed to meet two more times—on March 7 and 14—their positions remained adamant, and nothing was accomplished. Finally, the feeble attempt to revive the dialogue collapsed ignominiously, with both sides blaming each other for their insincerity and inflexibility.

The Proposal for Tripartite Talks: Seoul's Aims

In July 1979, Presidents Park and Carter jointly proposed to Pyongyang the convening of a tripartite conference. It clearly signaled a tactical move on the part of both Seoul and Washington aimed simultaneously at blunting North Korea's undaunted quest for direct contacts with the United States and easing tensions in the Korean peninsula. As far as Washington was concerned, the substantive idea embodied in the proposal—three-way talks—was not new. For it had repeatedly stated that it would not talk with North Korea without direct participation of South Korea. The proposal nonetheless had novel features. First, it was the first time that the idea of three-way talks had been explicitly endorsed by the United States. All the previous signals had been implicit. Second, it was a joint pro-

20. *Tong'a ilbo*, January 26, 1979.

posal by both the US and South Korea. Finally, the publication of the proposal in the joint communiqué emanating from a summit meeting enhanced its importance.

As far as South Korea was concerned, the proposal marked a definite change in its posture. For it had never endorsed the idea of three-way talks either directly or indirectly. On the contrary, it had been known to be opposed to the idea. The first hint of change came two days before President Carter's state visit to South Korea: on July 27, 1979 Foreign Minister Park Tong Jin said that the ROK government's position on tripartite talks was "flexible."[21] Since preparations, including the drafting of a joint communiqué, had been under way for some time, it is fair to assume that Park was aware of the impending joint proposal at the time. The ROK government's behavior on the heels of the publication of the joint proposal, coupled with its previous lack of enthusiasm for the idea of three-way talks, strongly suggests that initiative for the proposal came from the United States.

How then may one account for Seoul's tactical decision to embrace the idea and make the joint proposal? Having just tested Pyongyang's intentions through "irregular contacts" (*pyŏnch'ŭk chŏpch'ok*) between representatives of the two sides in Panmunjom, following President Park's January 27 proposal, Seoul was far from sanguine about the chances of any new overtures being successful. Nonetheless, it clearly valued its alliance with the United States and amply understood Washington's desire to produce some tangible results during the Seoul summit. A joint proposal by the two presidents would not only symbolize their solidarity but also demonstrate their common determination to seek a peaceful solution of the Korean problem. On the other hand, the ROK government faced the problem of dispelling the impression that it may have succumbed to US pressure. In a carefully coordinated program of public relations,[22] the Seoul government took pains to differentiate between the proposed "*samdangguk hoeŭi*" (meeting of the responsible authorities of the three countries) and "*samja hoedam*" (tripartite conference), insisting that the former would feature North and South Korea as the real parties, with the United States playing the role of a helper (*hyŏmnyŏkja*). In Seoul's view, in other words, what was being proposed was three-way talks in form but bilateral talks in substance. Whether such a perception was shared by Washington is problematical, however,

21. *Chosŏn ilbo*, June 28, 1979.
22. Both journalists and scholars were briefed by government officials on the points that needed to be stressed in their reporting and commentaries about the proposal as well as other aspects of the Carter-Park joint communiqué. I was in Seoul at the time and was able to confirm this with participants, who must remain anonymous.

since US officials gave no indication whatever of a secondary role for the United States in the proposed conference.[23] What seemed plain, nevertheless, is that Seoul's explicit downplaying of the prospective role of Washington in the talks helped to make the proposal less enticing to Pyongyang than would have been the case otherwise. For Pyongyang had shown ample signs that it was more interested in contacts with the United States than in talking with South Korea.

Pyongyang and the Proposal for Tripartite Talks

North Korea apparently made the tactical decision to reject the proposal. In a statement by a spokesman for the DPRK Foreign Ministry broadcast over Pyongyang Radio on July 10, North Korea described the proposal as "extremely unrealistic, inconsistent, and confused" and reiterated its own proposal for direct talks with the United States to discuss the question of US troop withdrawal from South Korea as well as the replacement of the Korean armistice agreement by a peace treaty between Pyongyang and Washington. These issues, Pyongyang insisted, needed to be separated from those relating to reunification; they concern only North Korea and the United States. "Because it is not a signatory to the armistice agreement," said Pyongyang, South Korea is not entitled to participate in the talks. Should the United States persist in requesting South Korean participation, however, North Korea would "allow the South Korean authorities to participate as an observer in the talks between us and the United States," provided that the latter get started first.[24]

On the other hand, North Korea would be willing to hold separate talks with South Korea on the various problems of national reunification; the United States has no right to participate in such talks, because national reunification is an internal question to be solved by the Koreans themselves without any interference from external forces. The North Korean statement also included a strong denunciation of President Carter's state visit to South Korea from June 29 to July 1, 1979, calling it "a powder-reeking trip of a hypocrite agitating for aggression and war." It continued:

> The whole course of Carter's trip to South Korea gave ample proof that the US ruling circles had not yet given up their wild design to keep hold of South Korea as their permanent colony and military base. Further, judging Carter's South Korean visit in combination with his earlier Japan trip, we can see that his South Korean trip was a part of the scheme to accelerate the

23. *New York Times*, July 2 and 4, 1979.
24. *KCNA*, Pyongyang, July 10, 1979, as monitored by FBIS.

"US-Japan-South Korea military integration" which the United States had been promoting from long ago as its basic strategy of Asian aggression.

Finally, the statement condemned the joint reaffirmation by Presidents Carter and Park of the principles of simultaneous admission of the two Koreas to the United Nations and "cross recognition" (the idea that recognition of North Korea by the United States and other allies of South Korea should be contingent upon recognition of South Korea by the Soviet Union and the PRC) as "insidious schemes to freeze forever the division of Korea into 'two Koreas.'"[25]

How may one explain the internal logic of North Korea's tactical decision? To the extent that a subjectively rational calculation of the probable costs and benefits of its options has ocurred in Pyongyang, it may have involved some of the following considerations. The probable costs of accepting the joint US-ROK proposal were numerous: (1) acceptance may have projected an image of North Korea reacting passively to an external stimulus rather than taking an initiative, an image that would have undercut both the *chuch'e* ideology and Kim Il Sung's self-esteem; (2) given the publicity about Washington's request for the assistance of Beijing and Moscow in persuading Pyongyang, a positive response would have detracted from North Korea's national pride; (3) an acceptance of trilateral talks means a reversal of Pyongyang's previous insistence on bilateral talks, which would not only create an image of inconsistency and vacillation on Pyongyang's part but also would symbolize North Korea's implicit acceptance of South Korea as a coequal partner in negotiations; (4) substantively, North Korea could anticipate very few payoffs in terms of attaining its strategic objectives regarding reunification; and, finally, (5) there was a danger that the talks might undermine the North Korean political system, by facilitating an influx of information that is inconsistent with North Korea's "party line"—for example, the truth about South Korea's economic progress and standard of living.

Against these costs were arrayed a cluster of probable benefits: (1) an acceptance of the proposal might help pave the way for a gradual improvement of relations with the United States, which would have long-term benefits, such as economic intercourse; (2) it might possibly influence the US decision on troop withdrawal from South Korea, for Washington could equate the initiation of three-way talks with a reduction of tensions in the Korean peninsula and proceed to implement its earlier decision to withdraw US ground troops from Korea in stages; (3) if tensions in the peninsula should indeed abate, that would enable North Korea to reallocate its resources, both hu-

25. Ibid.

man and material, from defense to economic construction, thus helping to alleviate its economic difficulties; and, finally, (4) depending on the level of the three-way talks, North Korea, including its supreme leader, would have an opportunity to bask in the glow of international limelight. That there would be a sharing of such limelight, especially with the despised South Korean regime, probably diluted the attractiveness of this last-mentioned incentive to North Korea. Pyongyang's actual response suggests that the probable costs outweighed the probable benefits in its tactical calculus.

Seoul's Response to North Korean Overtures in 1980

We may now turn to South Korea's tactical decision to respond positively to North Korea's overtures for the resumption of dialogue in January 1980. As noted, North Korea delivered two sets of letters to South Korea on January 12. One was from DPRK Premier Li Jong Ok to "Mr. Shin Hyon Hwack, Prime Minister, the Republic of Korea," while the remainder was from DPRK Vice-President Kim Il to eleven political, military, and religious leaders of South Korea. All the letters contained the same message: let us resume dialogue. The main difference was that while the Li letter called for a meeting of responsible authorities, the Kim Il letters proposed a meeting of representatives of political parties, social organizations, and other leaders. Seoul's tactical decision was to respond only to the Li letter. Prime Minister Shin Hyon Hwack wrote to his North Korean counterpart, "Mr. Li Jong Ok, Premier of the Administration Council, the Democratic People's Republic of Korea," proposing that preparatory meetings be held in Panmunjom between working-level delegates of the two sides with a view to arranging a meeting between the two premiers.

The following considerations may have been instrumental in generating South Korea's response. First, as President Choi Kyu Hah stated, Li Jong Ok's proposal signaled in a substantive sense North Korea's acceptance of the idea of a meeting of the responsible authorities of the two sides, which South Korea had been pursuing since January 1979. Second, Li's use of the term "the Republic of Korea" was of symbolic significance, marking a milestone in inter-Korean relations; it was a tremendous gesture of reconciliation on Pyongyang's part, a gesture that Seoul could ill afford not to reciprocate. Third, experience had taught South Korea that acceptance of the North Korean proposal would merely mark the first step in a long journey, that the necessary preparatory stage was likely to be long, arduous, and even acrimonious, and that the actual meeting of the two premiers might not even materialize. In short, South Korea had nothing to lose by testing North Korea's intentions anew. Finally, there is a remote possibility that Shin Hyon Hwack may have seized upon the opportunity to bolster his own image. For, should the effort succeed, Shin was likely to bask in the limelight of publicity and, depending upon the outcome of the talks, might even emerge as a national hero. This hypothesis is predicated on the premise that Shin had a major role to play in the decision-making process. Given the fluidity of the political situation in South Korea, that assumption is a credible one.

Chun Doo Hwan's Proposals for a Summit Meeting

In January 1981, the new ruler of South Korea, President Chun Doo Hwan, made a dramatic proposal to "President Kim Il Sung" to visit Seoul for a summit meeting. Chun also indicated a willingness to visit Pyongyang if invited.[26] What are some of the factors that may have entered into Chun's tactical calculations? First, it is obvious that Chun's overtures were consistent with the operational direction set by his predecessor—to vigorously pursue the resumption of dialogue and to take initiatives at periodic intervals. In January 1979, for example, Park Chung Hee had proposed an unconditional resumption of dialogue. Second, the Chun proposal could also be construed as his administration's tactical response to the much-vaunted proposal for the formation of a confederal republic made by Kim Il Sung three months earlier. Although Kim's proposal pointedly ruled out the Chun regime as a participant in the proposed confederation, it nonetheless required a response of sorts from Chun so as to counter Pyongyang's propaganda campaign. Third, having consolidated his power beyond challenge, Chun was in a position to enunciate a foreign policy position for the first time. By going a step further than his mentor, the late President Park, Chun succeeded in demonstrating not only the basic continuity in the reunification policy of the Republic of Korea but also political courage and imagination. Whereas Park had merely implied a willingness to talk with Kim Il Sung, Chun explicitly invited Kim to visit Seoul, referring to him as "President."

Fourth, there is a possibility that Chun's bold overtures toward Pyongyang were linked to his subsequent visit to Washington. Although the announcement of Chun's planned visit was not made until January 22, negotiations were most probably under way when Chun made his proposal to Kim Il Sung on January 12. The latter may have been a part of Chun's effort to lay the groundwork for the summit meeting with the new US president. Other preparatory measures that followed included the commutation of the death sentence to the opposition leader Kim Dae Jung on January 23 and the lifting of martial law on January 24.

Finally, one may ask whether Chun's proposal was more sym-

26. *Han'guk ilbo*, January 14, 1981.

bolic than serious. Given North Korea's previously enunciated position, Chun must have known that there was but a slim chance of a favorable response from Kim Il Sung. The fact that Chun took the unprecedented step of referring to Kim by his official title, however, suggests that Chun was eager to break the impasse in inter-Korean relations. On the other hand, whatever inducement this step may have offered North Korea was somewhat diluted by the prompt disclaimer by the South Korean authorities of any legal significance of Chun's act or any change in South Korea's anti-Communist policy. Furthermore, Chun himself pointed out in the same speech that unveiled his proposal that "the North Korean Communists have not abandoned their objective of Communizing the South by force in violation of the various agreements embodied in the July 4 joint statement...."[27]

Notwithstanding all this, the symbolic significance of Chun's gesture was plain: it marked the first time in the annals of inter-Korean relations that a head of state of one side referred to his counterpart by the latter's official title. Should North Korea reciprocate such an unprecedented gesture, as South Korea had done a year ago with regard to Premier Li Jong Ok's letter to his South Korean counterpart? More important, should Pyongyang grab this opportunity to resume dialogue with Seoul?

After mulling over the proposal for a week, North Korea rejected it in singularly harsh terms:

> How dare this man, known as a devilish murderer to his fellow countrymen and a traitor selling the country to foreign forces, attempt to attend the sacred table of dialogue to discuss the important question of the fatherland's reunification? We cannot have a dialogue with traitor Chon Tu-hwan [Chun Doo Hwan] as our partner in discussing reunification because he is an illegal self-styled president, a murderous rogue who drenched the country with the blood of his fellow countrymen and a traitor who is surrendering the nation's destiny to foreign forces.
> If we sit face to face with traitor Chon Tu-hwan, it will only result in justifying and encouraging his treacherous crimes against the nation. A dialogue must promote reunification. It must not be a dialogue for division. With someone who does not rely on foreign forces in South Korea, and does not seek division, fascism and anticommunist confrontation, we will discuss the reunification problem and other problems related to the future of the nation without any hindrance, irrespective of his ideas and his ideology. We will never sit at the same table with the butcher of the nation. Although the Chon Tu-hwan ring talks

27. Ibid.

about reunification and dialogue, it is not interested in them at all. It seeks only division.[28]

In short, North Korea's reasons for the rejection of Chun's overtures are, first, that he is not qualified to represent South Korea in talks with the North; second, that he is insincere; and, third, that acceptance of the proposal would have the effect of legitimizing Chun's seizure of power and his claims to speak for the South Korean people. Additionally, North Korea took pains to point out that the idea of a summit conference between the heads of state of the two Korean regimes was nothing new but had in fact been first proposed by North Korea as early as November 1972, and that Chun Doo Hwan "only reveals his political ignorance" by saying that he is making a new proposal. For, in the words of *Nodong sinmun*, "as a low-ranking officer involved in repression and massacres, he has no knowledge of the history of contacts and dialogue between the North and the South."[29]

On June 5, Chun renewed his January 12 proposal. In a speech to the inaugural session of the Advisory Council on Peaceful Unification Policy, Chun called on Kim Il Sung to accept his earlier invitation to visit Seoul, reiterating his own willingness to visit Pyongyang. Chun expanded the proposal by proffering the option of Panmunjom or a third country as the site of a summit meeting. Chun also urged North Korea to open up its society to the outside world, and advocated the early initiation of North-South contacts in the athletic, cultural, postal, and economic fields. The tone of Chun's speech was notably conciliatory, and he made no adverse reference to North Korea. Finally, Chun repeated his earlier gesture of referring to Kim Il Sung as "President."[30]

The fact that reaction to his January 12 proposal had by and large been favorable, notwithstanding Pyongyang's categorical rejection of it, must have been a key factor in Chun's decision to renew and expand it. The timing of Chun's reaffirmation of his previous proposal may have been linked with his planned tour of the five ASEAN (the Association of Southeast Asian Nations) countries (more on this in chapter 10). Another consideration may have been the markedly enhanced status of Chun Doo Hwan. After concluding a triumphant visit to the United States and a fruitful summit meeting with President Reagan, Chun was reelected president under the new Constitu-

28. *Nodong sinmun*, January 21, 1981, as translated by FBIS. The preceding quotes are from a *Nodong sinmun* commentary, not from North Korea's official response to the Chun proposal. The latter was contained in a statement issued on January 19, 1981 by the Chairman of the Committee for the Peaceful Reunification of the Fatherland.
29. Ibid.
30. *Han'guk ilbo*, June 8, 1981; *Korea Herald*, June 6, 1981.

tion. His own political party won a comfortable majority in the election for the new National Assembly. All this had made his position secure enough to pursue policy goals with vigor. Additionally, Chun's diplomatic initiative could be and was indeed used to mobilize the South Korean people in anti-North Korean rallies.[31]

Finally, North Korea's official interpretation of Chun's aims in making the June 5 proposal is worth noting. After reiterating its flat rejection of any notion of dialogue with Chun on the ground that as "a murderer whose hands are stained with the blood of people," Chun "is not qualified nor entitled to talk about the reunification question," *Minju Chosŏn*, the daily organ of the DPRK government, commented on June 11:

> He came out with the "unification proposal" this time again in a crafty attempt to lull the discontent of the people, prop up the shaking fascist dictatorial "regime" and, furthermore, gain recognition from the people by deluding the world public opinion. . . . The "new proposal" brought by him is a despicable third-rate drama only for a propaganda effect.[32]

Pyongyang's Response to Seoul's Overtures in 1982

As noted in the preceding chapter, Seoul renewed its overtures toward Pyongyang in early 1982. First, President Chun unveiled a comprehensive blueprint for reunification containing, inter alia, plans for the drafting of a constitution for a unified Korea and the proposal for the conclusion of a provisional agreement on basic relations between North and South Korea. This was followed by the publication of a twenty-point proposal for North-South collaboration and intercourse. What was Pyongyang's tactical response to these overtures?

The first indication that it would reject Chun's new overtures came within two days of his policy speech to the National Assembly: On January 24, the Voice of the Revolutionary Party for Reunification, an unofficial but nonetheless authoritative transmitter of Pyongyang's thinking, called Chun's January 22 speech "gibberish" and said that he "is not entitled to discuss reunification, the nation's common cause." For, in its view, Chun "is a fascist murderer who ruthlessly massacred those patriotic people who called for reunification, a vicious splittist who is trying to make the nation's division perma-

---

31. A rally held in Seoul's Yoŭido Plaza on June 24 called on North Korea to abandon its aggressive aims against the South and accept Chun's June 5 proposal. The rally, which was reportedly attended by two million people, also featured the burning of Kim Il Sung's effigy. *Han'guk ilbo*, June 26, 1981.

32. *KCNA*, Pyongyang, June 11, 1981, as monitored by FBIS.

nent and a war fanatic who is trying to drive this land into the flames of war."[33]

Two days later, Pyongyang Radio broadcast the text of the *Nodong sinmun* commentary scheduled to be published on the following day, which categorically rejected the new proposals. Pyongyang called the idea of holding a general election for the purpose of organizing a consultative conference for national reunification totally unrealistic, because the political leaders who can really represent the views of the South Korean people were either imprisoned or banned from political activity by the Chun regime. Pyongyang further expressed concern that the proposed Provisional Agreement on Basic Relations would help perpetuate the division of the peninsula. According to *Nodong sinmun*, the fraudulent nature of Chun's proposals was revealed by the fact that they glossed over such fundamental issues as the withdrawal of US troops from South Korea, democratization of South Korean society, and abandoning the policy of anti-Communist confrontation. The WPK organ called on the Chun regime to "apologize to the people for its crimes and immediately step down from power."[34]

Then, in a statement issued on January 27 in the name of the Democratic Front for the Reunification of the Fatherland, Pyongyang indicated for the first time its willingness to talk with Chun Doo Hwan, provided a number of conditions were met: the Chun regime was to (1) give up the two Koreas policy; (2) demand the withdrawal of US troops; (3) establish democracy; (4) renounce the anti-Communist confrontation policy; (5) apologize to the whole nation for the massacre in Kwangju; and (6) release all political prisoners, including Kim Dae Jung. Since these preconditions were tantamount to a demand for Chun's capitulation, they in no way signaled any softening of Pyongyang's posture.[35]

Finally, on February 10, North Korea took a counteroffensive. Its Committee for the Peaceful Reunification of the Fatherland (CPRF) proposed that a joint conference of politicians in the North and the South and abroad be convened as a consultative body for Korean reunification. Referring to President Chun's January 22 proposals, the CPRF statement characterized the idea of general elections as "an empty theory copied from a textbook on politics" and the idea of a provisional agreement between North and South Korea as a carbon copy of a formula adopted by others—namely, the two Germanys. The statement further noted that most of the twenty-point proposal

---

33. *Voice of the Revolutionary Party for Reunification*, January 24, 1982, as monitored by FBIS.
34. *Nodong sinmun*, January 27, 1982.
35. *Pyongyang Radio*, January 27, 1982, as monitored by FBIS.

put forth by Seoul had previously been advocated by Pyongyang and that Seoul's proposals had merely scratched the surface of the wide array of ideas that the DPRK had originated over the years. The bottom line, however, was that no fruitful negotiation for reunification can take place unless both parties sincerely desire reunification, the CPRF statement said. What is more, such negotiation constitutes a sacred task in which no "murderer" and "strangler of democracy" can take part. Notwithstanding all this, the statement continued, North Korea had shown "the leniency of giving [Chun Doo Hwan] an opportunity to atone for his crimes and take the road of patriotism."[36]

Since Chun had failed to respond positively to its gesture, however, Pyongyang was now prepared to propose a joint conference of politicians from North and South Korea and abroad who are truly desirous of reunification. Then the CPRF proceeded to name a hundred delegates to the conference. Fifty of the delegates were from the North; they included all of the prominent figures, with the conspicuous exception of Kim Il Sung and Kim Jong Il. While four leaders of *Ch'ongnyŏn*, the North Korea-oriented Korean residents association in Japan, were included in the roster of delegates from the North, all other overseas Koreans were listed as part of the southern delegation. There were ten such persons, all of whom were prominent dissidents. Many of them had openly endorsed President Kim Il Sung's DCRK proposal. Also included in the southern roster was Yi Chong-sang, vice-chairman of the Central Committee of the Revolutionary Party for Reunification. The remaining names on the roster included many prominent dissidents in the South, including Kim Dae Jung and the poet Kim Chi Ha.[37] What was unusual about this tactical move was that North Korea insisted on its right to select all the delegates to the proposed conference; in so doing, it insured that, should the move succeed, the outcome of the conference would reflect fully its own positions on reunification.

In sum, Pyongyang's response to Seoul's new overtures consisted of rejecting them categorically, reiterating its own views, and making what amounted to a counterproposal for a conference to which only individuals acceptable to North Korea would be invited. Its public statements reveal much about the rationale behind these tactical moves. Pyongyang appears to be genuinely convinced that President Chun Doo Hwan is not qualified to sit face to face with its own "Great Leader" to discuss the lofty issues of national reunification. Moreover, Pyongyang saw ulterior motives in Chun's moves: (1) the desire to neutralize "growing support for the DCRK proposal both in Korea

36. *KCNA*, Pyongyang, February 10, 1982, as monitored by FBIS.
37. Ibid.

and abroad" and (2) the attempt to stem the mounting tide of internal and external opposition to him and his regime.[38]

Given such perceptions, Pyongyang was not prepared to play into Chun's hands. On the contrary, by changing its position on the possibility of negotiation with Chun from a categorical no to a conditional yes, Pyongyang hoped to counter the charge of inflexibility. It is highly improbable that Pyongyang really expected Chun to respond positively to its offer of "leniency." Nor does it appear that Pyongyang's proposal for a joint conference of a hundred politicians from the North, the South, and abroad was calculated to produce substantive results. In a word, all of these were tactical moves in the continuing war of words between North and South Korea.

SYMBOLIC AND SUBSTANTIVE ACTIONS

The preceding discussion makes it plain that foreign policy behavior, like internally directed state behavior, has both symbolic and substantive dimensions. The two are not mutually exclusive but eminently compatible. Hence any given act on the stage of diplomacy can contain both symbolic and substantive dimensions. It can, of course, take on a purely symbolic meaning or, conversely, may only carry substantive implications. Sometimes, seemingly substantive acts may only possess symbolic significance, or, conversely, what is originally intended as a symbolic act may turn out to have substantive value. Although these twin dimensions of foreign policy behavior have already been adumbrated in the preceding analysis, it may be useful to examine them in a more explicit fashion.

Let us begin with Park Chung Hee's August 15, 1970 speech unveiling Seoul's new operational direction. Was it primarily symbolic or substantive? If it was intended as a serious proposition to North Korea, then it obviously contained more than symbols. A close reading of the speech, however, makes one wonder, for it is liberally sprinkled with provocative expressions: "a group of national traitors led by Kim Il Sung and his clique"; "Kim Il Sung and his clique are war criminals who should be put to the rigorous judgment of history and the nation"; "this clique has repeatedly engaged in unscrupulous

38. *Nam Chosŏn chipkwonjaga tŭlko naon irŭnba "t'ong'il minju konghwaguk" surip pang'an'ŭn minjogŭi yŏnggu punnyŏl pang'an ida* [The So-called Proposal for the Establishment of a "Unified Democratic Republic" Put Forth by the Ruler of South Korea Is a Proposal for the Perpetual Division of the Nation] (Pyongyang: Choguk P'yŏnghwa T'ong'il Wiwonhoe, 1982), pp. 15–21.

stereotyped propaganda campaigns"; and "the northern part of Korea is now reduced to a military camp, fanatically gripped with war preparations, where despotism and terror predominate."[39] Regardless of the accuracy or inaccuracy of these expressions, it is clear that they are not calculated to evoke a favorable response from North Korea. It seems reasonable to infer that the speech was primarily a symbolic move to offset or counter North Korea's equally symbolic "peace" offensive. It nonetheless bespoke a change in Seoul's operational direction from completely ignoring North Korean propaganda to generating counterpropaganda.

As noted previously, a major milestone in North-South relations was achieved on August 6, 1971 when Kim Il Sung declared that North Korea was "ready to establish contact at any time with all political parties, including the Democratic Republican party, and all social organizations and individual personages in south Korea." By explicitly mentioning the ruling party of South Korea and by broadening the scope of potential parties to negotiations to include "all individual personages in south Korea," Kim clearly signaled a willingness to talk with leaders of the Park Chung Hee regime, including Park himself. The same speech, however, also contained the customary denunciations of the Park regime, calling the latter the "puppet clique of south Korea [that] clings as always to the coattails of the US imperialists and relies all the more on the Japanese militarists in a vain attempt to put off their doom." Kim added:

> In an attempt to cover up their treacherous nature and stifle the movement for peaceful reunification, mounting with irresistible force among the south Korean people, they are noisily advertising their fraudulent "peaceful reunification programme." This stupid ruse, however, can fool no one, nor can it save the south Korean puppet clique from a doom already sealed.[40]

It is clear that, taken as a whole, Kim Il Sung's speech was far from conciliatory; he made no effort to sweeten his proposal with temperate language. From a substantive point of view, however, the speech offered something new—namely, a concrete proposal for unconditional and open-ended contacts with any person or group in the South. It would therefore be erroneous to dismiss it as a purely symbolic gesture. A more plausible interpretation would be that it was a substantive proposal tempered by symbolic pronouncements of self-righteousness and scorn. When South Korea countered the move with

39. *Major Speeches by President Park Chung Hee, Republic of Korea* (Seoul: Samhwa Publishing Co., no date), pp. 14–15.
40. Kim Il Sung, *For the Independent Peaceful Reunification of Korea*, rev. ed. (1976), pp. 84–85.

a proposal of its own six days later, it not only ignored Kim Il Sung's overtures altogether but successfully projected an image of taking a completely new initiative with imagination and boldness.

How may one assess North Korea's proposal for direct talks with the United States, which was first made in March 1974 and which has been repeated frequently since then? That it has a substantive dimension can be inferred from the persistence with which Pyongyang has been pursuing the goal. Particularly revealing in this respect are North Korea's use of third parties to convey its message to Washington and Foreign Minister Ho Dam's visit to the UN. In short, it is reasonable to infer that North Korea sincerely wants a direct dialogue with the United States.

Nonetheless, the proposal clearly has a symbolic angle in that it is aimed at producing certain propaganda effects. For one thing, it is designed symbolically to upgrade North Korea at the expense of South Korea by publicly underscoring the fact that North Korea and the United States are coequal signatories to the armistice agreement. Such a gesture conveniently overlooks the fact that there is another signatory to the agreement, namely the Commander of the Chinese People's Volunteers (CPV). This oversight, of course, is congruent with the fiction, maintained by Beijing and Pyongyang alike, that the CPV is not to be equated with the People's Liberation Army of the PRC and that the CPV has officially been disbanded. Another symbolic effect of the North Korean proposal is to portray North Korea as a peace-loving and peace-seeking nation, while simultaneously depicting South Korea as an obstacle to peace in the Korean peninsula.

Whether the substantive or symbolic aspect is primary hinges on the degree to which the North Korean intentions materialize. If they do to any measurable degree, then the substantive dimension will become primary. In terms of the meager results achieved thus far, however, the symbolic dimension appears to be more salient. This is not to suggest that the symbolic effects described above have been realized; rather, it is to argue that the most Pyongyang can hope for at this stage is the attainment of some of its propaganda goals.

An example of a manifestly substantive foreign policy action is the establishment of diplomatic relations. In the case of both North and South Korea, however, this type of eminently substantive act has thus far had profoundly symbolic dimensions. For one of the major considerations in seeking diplomatic ties with other countries has been to secure potential allies or supporters in the UN, where the Korean question is periodically debated in typically symbolic and highly ritualistic fashion. At stake are the perceived legitimacy and prestige of both Seoul and Pyongyang. It should be kept in mind that even the passage of a favorable resolution—such as one rec-

TABLE 10 · Diplomatic Relations and UN Vote on Korea, 1975

	First Committee Vote			
Diplomatic Relations with:	Pro-N. Korea N %	Pro-S. Korea N %	Neutral N %	Total N %
North Korea only	37 (94.9)		2 (5.1)	39 (100.0)
South Korea only		37 (88.1)	5 (11.9)	42 (100.0)
Both	11 (23.9)	19 (41.3)	16 (34.8)	46 (100.0)
Neither	3 (20.0)	3 (20.0)	9 (60.0)	15 (100.0)
Total	51 (35.9)	59 (41.6)	32 (22.5)	142 (100.0)

ommending the separate admission of the two Koreas to the UN, or one endorsing the immediate withdrawal of all foreign troops from Korea—has little or no substantive effect. The UN, for example, is not empowered to admit a country over that country's objections. Nor can it compel the US troops to withdraw from South Korea in the face of the argument by Seoul and Washington that their presence is ordained by bilateral agreement.

Pyongyang's vehement denunciation of Seoul's espousal of the concept of simultaneous admission of the two Koreas to the UN is therefore a symbolic act par excellence. Similarly, Pyongyang's principal gain when the thirtieth session of the UN General Assembly adopted a resolution calling for, inter alia, the withdrawal of all foreign troops from Korea was symbolic. For the resolution gave Pyongyang the first victory of any sorts during the two decades of UN involvement in Korea. If the victory was offset by the simultaneous adoption by the world body of a contradictory resolution favoring South Korea, North Korea chose simply to ignore the contradiction and to advertise that part of the UN action which bolstered its own position. In fact, the bulk of the North Korean people never learned of the existence of a contradictory resolution.

Pyongyang's sense of elation, nevertheless, was by no means entirely illusory. For what happened signaled the end of an era—an era of South Korean dominance in the UN's handling of the Korean question. In the words of President Park Chung Hee: "This [the passage of two rival resolutions on Korea] caused great disappointment to us, and I think it seriously undermined the authority and prestige of the United Nations."[41]

How realistic is the perception, shared by Seoul and Pyongyang alike, that the establishment of diplomatic relations with another

---

41. Park made these remarks in his New Year news conference on January 15, 1976. See Park Chung Hee, *Toward Peaceful Unification* (Seoul: Kwangmyong Publishing Co., 1976), p. 134.

TABLE 11 · Diplomatic Relations and UN Vote on Korea, 1975 (Percentages)

Diplomatic Relations with:	Pro-N. Korea	Pro-S. Korea	Neutral	Total
North Korea only	72.5		6.3	27.5
South Korea only		62.7	15.6	29.6
Both	21.6	32.2	50.0	32.4
Neither	5.9	5.1	28.1	10.5
Total	100.0	100.0	100.0	100.0

country helps to secure support for its respective positions in the United Nations? Tables 10 and 11 suggest some clues to this question. Table 10 shows that as of 1975, there were forty-six UN member states that had ambassadorial-level diplomatic relations with both North and South Korea. Fifteen UN member states had relations with neither. As might be expected, none of the UN members that had diplomatic relations with only one part of Korea voted *against* a draft resolution favorable to that part. Nonetheless, some chose to remain neutral, either by abstaining or by being absent. This suggests that the support of those states could not be taken for granted. South Korea appears to have been less successful in preventing "desertions"— if neutral votes can be so regarded—than did its northern rival. From the countries having relations with both Koreas, South Korea won nineteen votes (41.3 percent) as opposed to North Korea's eleven votes (23.9 percent). The two sides were even with respect to the fourth group of countries—those having relations with neither Korea.[42]

Table 11 presents the same data in a slightly different form. It shows percentages vertically, thus enabling us to break down pro-Pyongyang, pro-Seoul, and neutral votes and to ascertain the relative importance of diplomatic relations for North and South Korea in the context of the United Nations. The first column shows that 72.5 percent of pro-North Korean votes came from those states that have diplomatic relations with North Korea only, while 21.6 percent came from those that simultaneously recognize both North and South Korea. The second column shows that South Korea worked very hard to generate support, for over 37 percent of the votes it received emanated from countries that are not firmly allied with it. Unlike the countries that only recognize Seoul, these countries had no predisposition to support South Korea. The third column shows that the expected pattern holds: those countries that either have diplomatic ties with both Seoul and Pyongyang or do not recognize either of

42. Koh, "The Battle Without Victors," pp. 61–62.

them tend to remain neutral in the Korean controversy. Nearly 80 percent of neutral votes came from these two groups. The column also discloses that better than 20 percent of the neutral votes came from countries supposedly friendly to either Seoul or Pyongyang, with Seoul incurring a substantially larger loss than its rival.

In sum, the preceding analysis suggests that while the establishment of diplomatic relations is a valuable asset for the two Koreas in the UN battle, its positive effect on UN diplomacy can be assured only by preventing the rival regime from also establishing diplomatic relations with the same country. When the other payoffs of diplomatic relations such as trade and cultural intercourse are considered, it becomes obvious that cultivating and maintaining friendly ties with other countries emerge as amply rewarding activities for both Koreas, not only symbolically but substantively as well.

10   IMPACT OF FOREIGN POLICY

Thus far we have examined the sources of the foreign policies of the two Koreas, aspects of their decision-making processes, and their outputs in the form of strategic, operational, and tactical decisions. No picture of foreign policy is complete, however, without some delineation of the actual consequences of foreign policy decisions. What impact, if any, do these decisions have on the operational and psychological environment? To what extent do anticipated consequences materialize? What are some of the major unanticipated consequences? Is there a net balance of gains over losses?

    Despite their obvious importance, these questions are not easy to answer. The main difficulty has to do with the establishment of causal nexuses. Barring a controlled experiment, it is all but impossible to establish conclusively causal links between a given foreign policy decision and a set of consequences. This means that once again we have little choice but to operate on an impressionistic and speculative plane. Such a handicap, however, need not doom our exercise to complete sterility. For example, if a manifestly intended consequence does not occur, this in itself goes a long way toward elucidating the nature of a decision's impact.

PYONGYANG'S REUNIFICATION POLICY

Let us begin by assessing the impact of Pyongyang's operational decision in the early 1970s to shift emphasis from revolution to dialogue,

199

presumably in pursuit of the same strategy of reunification. The new operational direction was most probably the product of the North Korean elite's images of the changing external and internal milieu—most notably, the emerging détente between Washington and Beijing and the impasse regarding the southern revolution as originally conceived. In other words, it was a partial manifestation of the impact of its previous foreign policy output, combined with environmental change.

What changes, if any, did the new operational direction help to produce in the environment, both operational and psychological? In the global system, there was clear growth in North Korea's international standing, as measured by its successful entry into the UN system (not to be confused with the UN itself);[1] its growing number of diplomatic partners, including Western European countries; and its steady gains on the UN scoreboard, to the point where the General Assembly passed a resolution in its favor for the first time in the annals of that world body. All these gains may be attributable to the toning down of overt violence, which the new operational direction foreshadowed, as well as to the facelifting Pyongyang received from the appearance of détente in the Korean peninsula.

We have previously speculated that the new operational direction had the twin goals of paving the way for the withdrawal of US troops from South Korea and of facilitating the campaign to convert the South Korean people to Pyongyang's revolutionary cause. It is plain that these intended consequences have yet to materialize. Not only are the American troops still in South Korea in strength, but Washington's commitment to Seoul's security has been unmistakably reaffirmed. Nor is there any sign that North Korea has succeeded in changing the staunchly anti-Communist attitude of the South Korean people to the slightest degree.

Did North Korea perceive the futility of its operational direction? For the concept of feedback posits that perception of unanticipated consequences contributes to a reassessment and an eventual modification or abandonment of a previous policy. The virtual deadlock of dialogue since August 1973 may reflect a possible modification of the operational direction. In fact, a new operational direction supplementing, if not supplanting, the previous one did emerge in March 1974, when North Korea proposed direct talks with the United States for the first time.

1. In May 1980 North Korea hosted a regional conference of the United Nations Educational Scientific and Cultural Organization in Pyongyang. In addition to the acting secretary-general of the UNESCO and other officials, representatives of India, the Philippines, Sri Lanka, Indonesia, Thailand, and the PRC participated in the five-day-long event. The agenda of the conference was regional cooperation regarding the integration of education in schools and society. *Kita Chōsen kenkyū* 7, 71 (June 1980): 19.

What of the impact of the new operational direction? Had it been successful, it would have produced significant changes in North Korea's operational environment. Insofar as the external setting was concerned, it would have created a strain in Seoul-Washington relations; downgraded and possibly humiliated South Korea; neutralized the perceived threat of American military might to North Korean security; and improved Pyongyang's relations with Washington. In terms of the internal setting of North Korea, its economic capabilities would have been enhanced, at least indirectly, thanks to the probable reallocation of resources from defense to economic construction. Even Pyongyang's military situation might have benefited, since the removal or significant downgrading of the American military presence in South Korea would certainly have affected the military balance in the peninsula. In terms of North Korea's political dynamics, the success of its overtures toward the United States could have been seized upon as a major victory for Kim Il Sung's foreign policy and exploited for internal propaganda purposes. On the other hand, the publicized dilution of the American menace to North Korea would have removed the major object of political indoctrination in North Korea.

The stark reality, however, is that none of the postulated results has actually occurred. In terms of the principal stated objective—namely, inducing the US to come to a conference table with North Korea alone—the new operational direction has thus far been a complete failure. In one sense, it has proved to be counterproductive. For while covert, behind-the-scenes maneuvers may have left North Korea at least where it started, publicized efforts to persuade Washington to talk directly with Pyongyang have forced the United States to take a position. And the frequency of the North Korean attempts has been paralleled by the frequency of Washington's reaffirmation that it would not negotiate directly with North Korea without the participation of South Korea. This means that Washington has been forced to make a specific commitment to South Korea, thus all but dashing North Korean hopes for a breakthrough.

From a tactical point of view, North Korean actions have a tendency to work at cross-purposes. On one hand, Pyongyang has reiterated the manifest goal of negotiating directly with the United States with a remarkable degree of persistence. On the other hand, it has for the most part not offered any inducements to Washington in terms, for example, of conciliatory rhetoric. Take the following characterization of President Reagan, with whose administration North Korea wants to have a direct dialogue:

> The world jeers at the mean act of Reagan who, as soon as he became president, summoned the atrocious, murderous thug to

embrace and caress him. All the dirty acts committed by Reagan in a few days since he took office in the White House remind the people of a report in the Western press that there is no man of large caliber in the United States in connection with the inauguration of Reagan, of clown origin, as the US president succeeding Carter, the owner of a peanut farm. Reagan seems to be unfit for a politician of a country styling itself a big power, though he may be fit as a gangster on the theatrical stage.[2]

To be sure, North Korea was reacting angrily to Reagan's invitation to ROK President Chun Doo Hwan to visit the United States. Nevertheless, its unrestrained rhetoric had an adverse consequence for North Korea a month later, when the Reagan Administration rejected the request of the DPRK Observer Mission to the UN for permission to travel from New York to Washington, DC to attend an international trade conference jointly sponsored by the UN and the World Bank. The State Department spokesman specifically cited as one of the grounds for its action "the extraordinary level of crude invective being hurled at the US administration and President Reagan personally by the North Korean government."[3] Undaunted, Pyongyang continued to denounce Reagan as "a war-thirsty element,"[4] and "a die-hard defender of racism."[5] In talking with Vice Premier Chong Jun Gi, on July 31, 1981, I raised the issue of the efficacy of Pyongyang's policy toward the United States, with specific reference to North Korea's quest for direct talks. He responded in two parts. First, he denied that North Korea had engaged in any *personal* attacks on President Reagan, insisting that only his policies and actions had been the objects of criticism. Second, he made it clear that North Korea had no intention of making any tactical adjustments—such as ceasing anti-US statements—since it valued its national dignity and independence more than anything else. Whether there would be any improvement in North Korean-American relations in the future would depend entirely on the attitude and actions of the US government, he said.

SEOUL'S REUNIFICATION POLICY

The shift in Pyongyang's operational direction in the early 1970s coincided with a similar shift in Seoul's posture toward the North. Both

2. *Nodong sinmun*, February 10, 1981, as translated by FBIS.
3. *Korea Herald*, March 17, 1981.
4. *KCNA*, Pyongyang, March 20, 1981, as monitored by FBIS.
5. *Nodong sinmun*, March 23, 1981.

were rooted in the dramatic change in Korea's immediate external setting. How shall we assess the impact of Seoul's operational decision to seek dialogue with Pyongyang? Did it achieve its intended goals? The manifest goal of easing tensions in the peninsula and improving inter-Korean relations was obviously thwarted. For the dialogue ended in an impasse, and no measurable reduction in tensions has occurred. The probable latent goal of using the dialogue as a pretext to execute a wholesale restructuring of the political system to enhance the powers of President Park Chung Hee, however, was attained, although its long-term consequences turned out to be counterproductive.

While a complex array of factors enter into the equation, it is nonetheless clear that Seoul's own actions have contributed to the failure of the dialogue. The unabashedly political uses to which the Park regime put the dialogue did not help its actual conduct in any way. Nor did Seoul's failure to reach an ample understanding about the meaning of the three principles of reunification embodied in the July 4 joint statement improve prospects for the easing of North-South tensions. Nevertheless, one should not overlook the fact that the fundamental cause of the early demise of the dialogue was the deep-seated mutual distrust, coupled with the incompatibility of the strategic goals of both sides.

A major milestone in the evolution of Seoul's reunification policy was the enunciation of "foreign policy for peace and unification" by President Park in June 1973; it signaled a new operational direction which not only acknowledged North Korea's right to participate in international organizations together with South Korea but also sought to have the two gain admission to the UN simultaneously as separate members. Additionally, the new operational direction purported to open Seoul's door to "all the nations of the world on the basis of the principles of reciprocity and equality." What impact did the new operational direction have?

As we have noted previously, Park's June 1973 policy statement reflected the impact of environmental change on his government's thinking. The DPRK had already made significant gains in the arena of world diplomacy, becoming a member of the WHO as well as an observer at the United Nations. Hence Seoul did not yield anything substantive when it proclaimed "we shall not oppose north Korea's participation with us in international organizations." The proposal for a simultaneous entry of the two Koreas into the United Nations reflected Seoul's conviction, reinforced by its frustrating experience in the dialogue with Pyongyang, that the chances of an early reunification were extremely slim and that it would be advantageous to become a full-fledged member of the world body as soon as possible.

As things turned out, the manifest goal of paving the way for UN membership proved to be unattainable. More important, North Korea reacted in a way Park and his aides had most probably failed to anticipate: it not only denounced the proposal for simultaneous entry to the UN as a scheme to perpetuate the division of the Korean peninsula, but also used it as a pretext to suspend the North-South dialogue. Furthermore, North Korea made a counterproposal—that the two Koreas enter the UN as a single entity under the rubric of the "Confederal Republic of Koryŏ." The only part of the new operational direction that has had a modicum of success is the open door policy. South Korean citizens were allowed to visit the Soviet Union and Eastern European countries with increasing frequency, usually to attend international events, and citizens of these Communist countries began to visit South Korea in growing numbers.[6] Economic relations in the form of indirect trade also began to expand; within five years of the enunciation of the open door policy, South Korea was engaged in indirect trade with all but two of the Communist nations (the exceptions were North Korea and Albania).[7]

Seoul's attempts to resuscitate dialogue with Pyongyang—notably the late President Park Chung Hee's January 1979 proposal; the joint Park-Carter proposal of July, 1979; and President Chun Doo Hwan's 1981 and 1982 proposals—have thus far been sterile. The failure to realize the manifest objective, however, does not mean that these efforts have had no impact. For, at the least, they have performed the important function of testing North Korea's intentions. No less useful for Seoul have been the propaganda payoffs of the overtures, which have helped to portray South Korea as flexible and eager for dialogue both in the domestic and international arenas. Finally, we must not overlook the possibility that Chun's 1981 proposals may have helped to bolster his perceived legitimacy and improve his image both at home and abroad.

PYONGYANG'S POLICY TOWARD MOSCOW AND BEIJING

The DPRK has forged special ties with its two northern neighbors, the Soviet Union and the People's Republic of China. It was under the aegis of the former that the North Korean regime came into being;

---

6. Republic of Korea, Ministry of Foreign Affairs, *Han'guk oegyo samsimnyŏn* [Thirty Years of South Korean Diplomacy], *1948–1978* (Seoul: Oemubu, Oegyo Yŏn'guwon, 1979), pp. 242–245.

7. The value of two-way trade between South Korea and thirteen Communist nations totaled $40 million in 1978. *Hapdong News Agency*, Seoul, September 28, 1979, as monitored by FBIS.

more important, Kim Il Sung's rise to power in the 1940s was possible primarily because of the conspicuous patronage of the Soviet occupation authorities. Nonetheless, it was the PRC, barely a year old and beset with the monumental tasks of economic rehabilitation and political consolidation at home, that rescued the Kim Il Sung regime from the brink of a total defeat in the Korean War. In the post-Korean War period, the two Communist giants have continued to be the principal sources of economic, technical, and military aid to North Korea. With the conclusion of mutual defense treaties in 1961, the two have also become the allies of the DPRK in a military sense.

Given all this, Pyongyang has had to pay particular attention to the maintenance of friendly relations with Moscow and Beijing. As long as the latter two remained fraternal allies themselves, Pyongyang's task was relatively easy. However, the beginning of a quarrel between them in 1956 posed new problems for Pyongyang. In essence, the challenge confronting North Korea was how to maintain a semblance of neutrality in the face of mounting pressure for support from both of the feuding allies. In time, Pyongyang managed to turn the challenge into an opportunity to maximize its leverage and, eventually, its independence.

Pyongyang's initial response, from 1956 to 1961, was to straddle the fence. Although it clearly sympathized with Beijing with respect to major issues—such as de-Stalinization, the cult of the individual, and the policy toward imperialism—it nonetheless paid lip service to the new lines emanating from Moscow. At the same time, Pyongyang continued to strengthen its ties with Beijing. For example, North Korea paid China the ultimate compliment of emulating the latter's economic policies in 1958: its *Ch'ŏllima* (Legendary Flying Horse) movement was apparently inspired by the Great Leap Forward, and its integration of agricultural cooperatives was patterned after the commune movement. More important, Premier Zhou Enlai visited Pyongyang in February 1958, and Premier Kim Il Sung made a return visit to Beijing in November and December of the same year; that was Kim's third visit to China since 1953.[8]

Meanwhile, the abrupt cancellation of Premier Nikita Khrushchev's plan to visit North Korea in 1960 suggested that all was not well in Pyongyang-Moscow relations. First Deputy Premier Alexei Kosygin, however, did visit Pyongyang in May 1961, two weeks after a military takeover in Seoul. In July of the same year, Kim Il Sung flew to both Moscow and Beijing to conclude mutual defense treaties with both. Symbolically, North Korea acknowledged not only its dependence on both Moscow and Beijing but also the Soviet Union's pre-

8. For details, see B. C. Koh, "North Korea and the Sino-Soviet Schism," *Western Political Quarterly* 22, 4 (December 1969): 940–962.

eminent position as its number one ally and protector by going to the Soviet capital first.

By late 1962, however, North Korea found itself solidly allied with the PRC; Pyongyang unequivocally supported Beijing in the Sino-Indian border clash of October 1962, and indirectly criticized Moscow for backing down in the Cuban missile crisis in the same month. More important, representatives of the WPK suffered humiliating rebuffs at the congresses of Eastern European Communist parties in November and December 1962. Finally, in January 1963, the WPK organ *Nodong sinmun* published an editorial that explicitly defended the Chinese Communist party for the first time.[9] Relations with Moscow steadily deteriorated, and by September, *Nodong sinmun* was openly criticizing the Soviet Union, accusing the latter of having exploited North Korea economically and of practicing "big-power chauvinism" and "xenophobia."[10]

Part of the price Pyongyang had to pay for its ideological solidarity with Beijing was a sharp decline in Soviet aid, which in turn had an adverse effect on North Korea's implementation of its Seven-Year Plan. Since Beijing was having its own economic problems, it was in no position to compensate for Pyongyang's losses. The emergence of a new leadership in the Kremlin in late 1964, therefore, provided Pyongyang with a welcome opportunity to reassess its policy toward the Soviet Union. A change in Soviet-North Korean relations was signaled, first, by the visit of a high-level North Korean delegation led by First Vice Premier Kim Il to Moscow in November 1964 and then by Premier Kosygin's four-day visit to the DPRK in February 1965. Soviet military aid to Pyongyang resumed, and economic and cultural contacts increased appreciably.

Meanwhile, the eruption of the Cultural Revolution in China led to a notable cooling of Sino-North Korean relations. Preoccupied with domestic upheavals, China virtually withdrew from the international scene; moreover, Red Guards reportedly labeled Kim Il Sung a "fat revisionist" leading a luxurious life at the expense of the working masses. In July 1966, *Nodong sinmun* even published an article criticizing Chinese ideographs, saying that they symbolized backwardness and that Koreans should be proud of their phonetic alphabet and should not waste their time in trying to learn the Chinese characters.[11]

Still, lest it be perceived as having joined the Soviet camp, North Korea proclaimed in August 1966 its independence of both Moscow and Beijing. In a two-and-a-half-page editorial entitled "Let Us Defend Our Independence," *Nodong sinmun* extolled the virtues of

9. *Nodong sinmun*, January 30, 1963.
10. Ibid., September 7, 1974.   11. Ibid., July 27, 1966.

independence (*chajusŏng*) and *chuch'esŏng*, and rejected the right of any outside power to dictate its policies. The WPK organ also indirectly criticized Beijing's rigid attitude toward forming a socialist united front in Vietnam, arguing that Communists should set aside all their differences to join their efforts in helping the Vietnamese people resist the "imperialist aggressors."[12]

The goal of independence, however, called for a policy of equidistance toward Moscow and Beijing, and the conclusion of the most violent phase of the Cultural Revolution in China provided Pyongyang with an opportunity to correct the appearance of a tilt toward Moscow. In October 1969, Choi Yong Gon, president of the Presidium of the DPRK Supreme People's Assembly and the number two man in the WPK power hierarchy, visited Beijing to participate in the celebration of the twentieth anniversary of the founding of the PRC. In April 1970, Premier Zhou Enlai made his second visit to the DPRK. Statements made by Zhou as well as a joint communiqué issued in the name of Zhou and Kim Il Sung stressed the threat of the "resurgence of Japanese militarism." The latter document even contained a veiled criticism of Moscow for failing to see the dangers of Japanese militarism and for fraternizing with the Sato government.

From this point on, North Korea was able to maintain cordial, if not warm, relations with both Moscow and Beijing, notwithstanding the continuation of the rift between the two. Exchange of visits by athletic, cultural, and other groups increased sharply, and cooperation in the economic, technical, and military fields was stepped up. Measured by the yardstick of mutual visits by top-level political leaders, however, Pyongyang-Beijing relations appeared to be on firmer ground than Pyongyang-Moscow relations. Noteworthy in this connection are Kim Il Sung's visit to the PRC in April 1975 and September 1982, Premier Hua Guofeng's visit to the DPRK in May 1978, Deng Xiaoping's visit to the DPRK in September 1978 and April 1982, Premier Li Jong Ok's visit to the PRC in January 1981, Premier Zhao Ziyang's visit to the DPRK in December 1981, CCP General Secretary Hu Yaobang's visit to the DPRK in April 1982, and Defense Minister Geng Biao's visit to the DPRK in June 1982. It was during Kim Il Sung's 1975 visit to Beijing that North Korea obtained from China the first official acknowledgment that the DPRK is "the sole legal sovereign state of the Korean nation."[13] Significantly, the Soviet Union has yet to grant such a concession. Nor had any top-level Soviet leader set foot in North Korea since 1965.

On the other hand, neither Hua Guofeng's 1978 visit nor Zhao Ziyang's 1981 visit to North Korea produced a joint communiqué.

12. Ibid., August 12, 1966.
13. See the text of the joint communiqué in *Peking Review*, May 2, 1975, pp. 8–11.

North Korea's insistence on neutrality in the Sino-Soviet dispute and the subsequent failure of both sides to agree on the issue of Soviet "hegemonism" may have been responsible for the outcome. Significantly, however, Geng Biao, during his June 1982 visit, proposed a toast to "the good health and longevity of Comrade Secretary Kim Jong Il," thus helping to dispel the rumor that Beijing disapproved of the unprecedented hereditary succession that Kim Il Sung has initiated in North Korea.[14]

Given the preceding record, how shall we assess the impact of Pyongyang's policy toward Moscow and Beijing? Its track record appears to be quite good. Not only has North Korea succeeded in preserving its independence but it has also managed to obtain both symbolic and substantive support of sizable proportions from both of its Communist neighbors over the years. In one sense, Pyongyang's has been a delicate balancing act, and its success may have been a function not simply of its own diplomatic acrobatics but also of the intensity of competition between Moscow and Beijing for Pyongyang's favors.

Symptomatic of this phenomenon are efforts by both Communist giants not only to publicize the nature and extent of Pyongyang's indebtedness to them but also to drive a wedge between Pyongyang and their adversary. Faced with Moscow's persistent practice of publishing details about Soviet aid to North Korea, on, for example, the anniversary of the Soviet-North Korean treaty of friendship, cooperation, and mutual assistance in July, Beijing began in October 1979 to reveal details about Chinese assistance to North Korea. In an article ostensibly devoted to the theme of Sino-North Korean friendship and solidarity, *Renmin Ribao*, the organ of the Chinese Communist Party, disclosed for the first time that the PRC had assisted in building an oil refinery, the Pyongyang subway, a thermal electric power plant, a chemical fertilizer plant, and other projects in North Korea.[15]

To cite an example of open polemics between Moscow and Beijing over Korea, the Soviet government newspaper *Izvestia* charged in March 1981 that the PRC "was promoting cooperation and trade" with South Korea on an official basis and that "China was betraying the Korean people's interests by welcoming a strengthened military presence in Korea by the new US administration." *Renmin Ribao* promptly denied these charges, saying that they reflected the Soviet aim to "stick its sinister hand into the Korean peninsula." It said that China has fully supported Pyongyang's proposals for "independent,

14. *Nodong sinmun*, June 15 and 17, 1982.
15. *Renmin Ribao*, October 19, 1979, as summarized in *Kita Chōsen kenkyū* 6, 66 (December 1979): 6.

peaceful reunification of the country" and demanded immediate withdrawal of US troops from Korea. The Chinese daily pointed out that the Soviet Union had allowed South Korean government ministers, representatives of economic organizations, and academic and sports delegations to visit the Soviet Union "under various pretexts." On the other hand, the paper added, the "militant friendship [between North Korea and China] has weathered severe tests," and the Soviet efforts to wreck it with rumors would be in vain.[16]

For Pyongyang's part, it has taken pains not to identify completely with either Beijing's or Moscow's position in their acrimonious dispute. For example, Pyongyang has studiously avoided using the term "hegemonism," which is the well-known Chinese code word for Soviet attempts to project and expand its power in the world arena. Instead, Pyongyang has coined the phrase "dominationism" (*chibae chuŭi*). As noted, the conspicuous absence of joint communiqués at the end of Hua Guofeng's visit to the DPRK in May 1978 and Zhao Ziyang's visit in December 1981 may have been related to the inability of both sides to resolve this sticky issue.[17] With respect to other sensitive issues, North Korea has displayed a judicious balance of criticism and caution. In January 1979 it criticized the Soviet-backed Vietnamese invasion of Cambodia as a manifestation of "dominationism by a relatively small country," but, when China waged its "punitive preemptive attack" against Vietnam a month later, Pyongyang withheld any comment.[18]

Nor did North Korea offer any public comments on the Soviet invasion and occupation of Afghanistan in January 1980. It did, however, express its displeasure by withholding support for a statement of solidarity with the new Afghan regime at a meeting of the Socialist parliamentary union in Sophia in February 1980. Among the delegations participating in the meeting, only North Korea and Romania failed to sign the statement.[19] A few months later, however, North Korea appeared to acknowledge the fait accompli. In April 1980, Kim Il Sung sent a message to Babrak Karmal, the Soviet-installed chief of Afghanistan, which read in part:

> The Korean people wish the Afghan people great successes in their struggle to overcome all kinds of difficulties lying in the way of advance, safeguard the gains of the April revolution and build a new independent society. I take this opportunity to ex-

16. See the Associated Press dispatch from Beijing in *Korea Herald*, March 14, 1981.
17. For details of the Hua visit, see *Kita Chōsen kenkyū* 4, 47 (May 1978): 5–44.
18. Ibid. 5, 57 (March 1979): 31–36.
19. Ibid. 7, 68 (February 1980): 41.

press my conviction that the friendly and cooperative relations formed between our two countries in the common struggle for independence and against imperialism will further strengthen and develop.[20]

In sum, differences in views and interests on a variety of issues have not prevented Pyongyang from maintaining fairly strong ties with both Moscow and Beijing. While publicly maintaining the position that both the PRC and the Soviet Union are fraternal countries with which the DPRK has bonds of solidarity and friendship, North Korean officials and cadres nonetheless express privately their disappointment over, and even disapproval of, developments in both countries. The turn toward pragmatism, the introduction of various economic measures based on material incentives and free market principles, and the dismantling of the Mao cult and Maoist practices in China appear to generate discomfort and, perhaps, dismay in Pyongyang. On the other hand, neither Beijing nor Moscow has displayed any enthusiasm for Pyongyang's moves to create the first Communist dynasty in history. Notwithstanding all this, both continue to express staunch support for Pyongyang's positions regarding Korean reunification and provide material assistance to the DPRK. In a word, the efficacy of Pyongyang's policy toward Moscow and Beijing will hinge primarily on the dynamics of Sino-Soviet competition.

SEOUL'S POLICY TOWARD THE UNITED STATES

The United States has been the single most important country for the Republic of Korea throughout the latter's short history. Indeed, the ROK owed its birth in August 1948 principally to Washington. Since then its triple requirements of legitimacy, security, and economic development have been met largely through the assistance of the United States. Had it not been for the US military intervention in the Korean War, the ROK would have been conquered by its northern rival. Nor could it have managed the task of postwar economic recovery without the massive infusion of American aid. In addition to spending an estimated $18 billion during the war (and suffering 34,000 battle deaths), the US extended to South Korea economic and military assistance valued at $11 billion between 1953 and 1973. Han Sungjoo estimates that during the period between 1954 and 1970 "American economic and military aid combined accounted for nearly 10% of

---

20. *KCNA*, Pyongyang, April 26, 1980, as monitored by FBIS.

South Korea's GNP."[21] Seventy-seven percent of South Korea's total military expenditures in the 1955–1960 period and 83 percent in the 1961–1968 period came directly from the United States. It was not until 1969 that Seoul's share of its total military expenditures began to surpass the 50 percent mark; in 1978 US direct military assistance to Seoul ceased completely.[22]

These statistics underscore the profoundly asymmetrical nature of Seoul-Washington relations until the early 1970s and suggest the virtual absence of any leverage on the part of South Korea over its principal patron state. Under such circumstances, US policy toward and actions in South Korea were only marginally affected by Seoul's diplomatic efforts; they were shaped primarily by America's own perceptions of its interests and by the dynamics of its policy-making process. Nonetheless, Seoul did strive to attain certain crucial goals, and its efforts had mixed results.

In the 1950s Syngman Rhee's policy of pursuing a bilateral security pact with the United States initially met with a rebuff by President Eisenhower, but it eventually bore fruit due to a combination of factors, of which Rhee's opposition to the proposed armistice and defiant words and actions were probably pivotal. Rhee not only threatened to take unilateral military action against North Korea but also released anti-Communist North Korean prisoners of war. By so doing, Rhee came perilously close to being overthrown in a US-sponsored coup d'etat; the plan to topple Rhee, codenamed "Everready," was never implemented. In the end, Washington decided to barter a security treaty with Seoul for the latter's acceptance of an armistice. Along with the pledge to conclude a security treaty, Rhee extracted from Washington a commitment to provide economic aid and to build up the ROK armed forces to approximately twenty divisions.[23]

In the 1960s Park Chung Hee's initial efforts to secure Washington's support for his interim military regime succeeded, not necessarily because of his diplomatic prowess but because President Kennedy's task force on Korea had recommended acceptance of the fait

21. Han Sungjoo, "South Korea and the United States: the Alliance Survives," *Asian Survey* 20, 11 (November 1980): 1075–1076.

22. Young-Sun Ha, "Korean-American Military Relations: Continuity and Change," paper presented to the Centennial Conference on American-Korean Relations, jointly sponsored by the American Studies Institute, Seoul National University, and the Center for Korean Studies, University of Hawaii, Honolulu, May 21–27, 1982, Tables 1 and 3.

23. Hahn Bae-Ho, "Analysis of Major Issues in the Korean-American Alliance: Ideals and Realities," paper presented to the Centennial Conference on American-Korean Relations, Honolulu, May 21–27, 1982, pp. 11–13. See also John Barry Kotch, "United States Security Policy Toward Korea: 1945–1953," Ph.D. dissertation, Columbia University, 1976.

accompli and use of American influence to steer the military junta in the direction desired by the United States.[24] Park's 1965 decision to send ROK troops to Vietnam under US prodding, as we have already seen, produced substantial payoffs and contributed appreciably to an improvement in Seoul-Washington relations.

However, in the 1970s American-South Korean ties were severely strained due to a series of developments. One was Park's ill-fated attempts to influence American policymakers, notably members of Congress. Alarmed by the implications of President Nixon's Guam Doctrine, in accordance with which 20,000 US troops were withdrawn from South Korea in 1971, the Park regime mounted a massive campaign to win friends and influence people in the United States, using a wide array of means, persons, and organizations. They included Tongsun Park, KCIA agents operating under diplomatic and consular covers in the United States, and a number of front organizations such as the Korean Cultural and Freedom Foundation. These persons and groups made campaign contributions to members of the US Congress and provided numerous favors, both monetary and otherwise. Disclosures of these activities, first in the media and then in congressional and Justice Department investigations, led to the coining of the phrase "Koreagate," and severely tarnished the image of both South Korea and the Korean people as a whole. This was a clear-cut example of a counterproductive policy by the Park Chung Hee regime.[25]

Another development that served to exacerbate Seoul-Washington relations in the second half of the 1970s was President Jimmy Carter's emphasis on human rights in foreign policy. As Park's transparent maneuvers to prolong his tenure in office and expand his power collided with the tenacious and increasingly vocal aspirations of the South Korean citizens—particularly students—for democracy, he further tightened the levers of coercive control, and his regime became markedly repressive. President Carter's injection of human rights into American diplomacy was therefore bound to create problems for the Park regime. The latter responded to increasing American pressure, not by jettisoning its repressive measures, but by making largely symbolic concessions from time to time and by stepping up its publicity campaign. What saved Park, however, was Carter's decision not to press the matter too hard, given America's strategic interests in Korea.

No less irritating than the human rights issue, from Park Chung

24. Hahn Bae-Ho, "Analysis of Major Issues," pp. 17–18.
25. US Senate, Select Committee on Ethics, *Korean Influence Inquiry*, 95th Congress, 2d session, October 10, 1978; Han Sungjoo, "South Korea and the United States," pp. 1077–1079.

Hee's point of view, was Carter's plan to withdraw US ground troops from South Korea. There was a certain amount of high-handedness about the Carter decision, for it was made unilaterally without consulting either South Korea or his own advisers. The only issue Carter left open was *how* to implement a US troop withdrawal, not whether to do it at all. Fortunately for the Park regime, the plan failed to win the support of key actors in the US policy process—influential members of the US Congress, the military establishment, and a sizable part of the foreign policy establishment. The decisive factor in the suspension of the withdrawal plan was a reassessment by the US intelligence community of North Korea's military capability, which showed that it was 30 percent stronger than had been previously estimated. In short, it was not Seoul's policy but the dynamics of Washington's policy process that changed the outcome.[26]

In the 1980s the government of Chun Doo Hwan succeeded in securing Washington's support to a striking extent. A key variable in the equation, however, was a change in the US leadership—the emergence of a Republican administration led by an archconservative, Ronald Reagan, who publicly equated Communism with the most severe deprivation of human rights. Nonetheless, Chun scored a diplomatic victory of immense proportions in February 1981, when he became one of the first heads of state to be invited by President Reagan to Washington. Although the visit was billed as an "official visit"— one notch below a "state visit"—it was a tremendous coup for Chun and his new regime. For the cloud hanging over his seizure of power, particularly in the wake of the Kwangju atrocities in May 1980, underscored the need for an affirmation of support from South Korea's principal guarantor of security. And it was precisely such support that Chun received from Reagan. Not only did Reagan pledge to keep the US security commitment to South Korea embodied in the ROK-US mutual defense treaty of 1954, but he also "assured President Chun that the United States has no plans to withdraw US ground combat forces from the Korean peninsula." Reagan further "commended President Chun for the far-reaching proposal made on January 12, 1981, calling for an exchange of visits by the highest leaders of the south and the north of Korea." The US president also reiterated the long-standing American position that "the Republic of Korea must be a full participant in any US negotiation with North Korea."[27]

26. Ibid., pp. 1079–1080; US Senate, Committee on Foreign Relations, *U.S. Troop Withdrawal from the Republic of Korea*, A Report by Senators Hubert H. Humphrey and John Glenn, 95th Congress, 2d session, January 9, 1978.

27. See the text of the ROK-US joint communiqué issued on February 3, 1981 in *Forging A New Era: The Fifth Republic of Korea* (Seoul: Korean Overseas Information Service, 1981), pp. 62–63.

Additionally, the two presidents agreed to resume "ROK-US security consultative meetings," "annual Korean-US economic consultations," and "annual Korean-US policy planning talks." The United States also pledged to "assist [South] Korea to obtain energy supplies in the event of an emergency affecting our mutual security interests" and to "remain a reliable supplier of nuclear fuel" for Seoul. The latter, for its part, would "explore long-term arrangements for importing American coal." More important, the two presidents underlined the changed nature of US-South Korean relations occasioned by a sharp increase in Seoul's economic capability and activities: they "noted with satisfaction that mutually profitable Korea-US trade had grown dramatically from $531 million in 1970 to $10,000 million in 1980 and that the Republic of Korea is now the United States' twelfth largest trading partner [and] . . . the fifth largest market for American agricultural exports."[28]

In sum, the impact of Seoul's policy toward Washington over the past three decades has varied, depending upon the initiator of that policy, the characteristics of his regime, and, above all, the predispositions of the US government and its top policymakers. Measured by the yardstick of Seoul's triple needs of legitimacy, security, and economic development, US policy toward South Korea has on the whole been positive. The basic character of bilateral relations between Seoul and Washington has been transformed from an asymmetrical dependence to a growing interdependence during the past decade or so. Nonetheless, the asymmetry has by no means disappeared, and the United States continues to play the role of a patron state, albeit to an increasingly diminished degree.

SEOUL'S POLICY TOWARD JAPAN

Japan occupies a special place in the Korean scheme of things. Japan is Korea's former colonial master whose harsh 35-year rule (1910–1945) has left a bitter taste in the mouths of those Koreans who are old enough to remember the ordeal. In other words, there are lingering feelings of animosity and bitterness toward the Japanese in Korea; even those who have learned about Japanese colonial rule through history books appear to be distrustful toward the Japanese for their past record of aggression and plunder against their neighbors. On the other hand, the Koreans are painfully aware that Japan is a next door neighbor with whom they must learn to live in peace. What is more, Japan is an ally of the United States, which happens to

28. Ibid.

be South Korea's foremost ally as well. Then there is the problem of the Korean minority in Japan—the 600,000 persons of Korean descent who constitute Japan's largest minority group. That their allegiance is divided about evenly between Seoul and Pyongyang means that they require special attention. Finally, Japan's phenomenal economic growth has sharply enhanced its value as a trading partner and a source of capital and technology. All of this has meant that the successive South Korean regimes have had to deal with Japan in some way.

During the Syngman Rhee regime (1948–1960), Seoul's policy toward Japan was one of unremitting hostility. Repeated American pressures for improvement of relations led only to halfhearted and intermittent negotiations that proved to be completely sterile. As we have seen, it was Park Chung Hee who succeeded in normalizing relations with Japan in 1965. Although Washington did exert pressure on Park, it was his own dogged determination that led to the historic breakthrough. If the terms of the settlement—Japan's agreement to provide South Korea with $300 million in grants, $200 million in government loans, and $300 million in private commercial credits over a ten-year (1966–1975) period—seemed hardly generous from the Korean people's point of view, given their perception of Japan's exploitive policies and unjust enrichment in Korea, the normalization nonetheless proved to be a major turning point in the annals of South Korea. It paved the way for an influx of Japanese capital and technology, which played a key role in South Korea's economic modernization. By the end of 1979, Japan had extended to Seoul various forms of economic aid (e.g., grants, government loans, export credits, technical assistance, and direct investments) aggregating $3.5 billion.[29]

South Korea's importance to the Japanese economy has steadily grown also. By 1979, South Korea had become Japan's third most important trading partner, next to the United States and Saudi Arabia. It was Japan's second largest export market and the ninth largest source of imported goods.[30] In fact, trade between Seoul and Tokyo was so lopsided that between January 1966 and November 1981 Seoul had incurred a total deficit of $21,638 million. This amounted to 70 percent of all the deficits South Korea had incurred in the same period in its worldwide trade.[31]

29. Gaimu Shō, *Waga gaikō no kinkyō* [Recent Trends in Our Diplomacy], 1980 (Tokyo: Ōkura Shō, Insatsu Kyoku, 1980), pp. 528–529. Japan contributed 29 percent of the total foreign capital requirement in South Korea's First Five-Year Plan (1962–1966), 19.3 percent to the Second Five-Year Plan (1967–1971), and 30 percent to the Third Five-Year Plan (1972–1976). Hahn Bae-ho, "Korea-Japan Relations in the 1970s," *Asian Survey* 20, 11 (November 1980): 1088–1089.
30. Gaimu Shō, *Waga gaikō no kinkyō*, p. 495.
31. *Korea Newsreview*, January 30, 1982, p. 14.

Economic ties, then, are clearly the key dimension of Seoul-Tokyo relations. They simultaneously constitute the sources of mutual benefit and friction. But other equally important sources of strain have been South Korea's internal politics and inter-Korean relations. The former have created problems, primarily because of the repercussions of political repression. When KCIA agents kidnapped Kim Dae Jung, former presidential candidate and leader of Park's opposition forces, from his hotel in Tokyo in August 1973, South Korean-Japanese relations plunged to a new low. Although investigations by the Japanese police implicated a ranking South Korean diplomat (actually a KCIA agent) in the abduction, Seoul refused either to turn over the suspect or to acknowledge any responsibility for the incident. Eventually, a compromise diplomatic settlement was reached whereby ROK Premier Kim Jong Pil personally conveyed expressions of regret to Japanese Prime Minister Tanaka Kakuei without explicitly admitting any wrongdoing on the part of the Seoul government. The incident, nevertheless, cannot be described as a total loss for the Park regime. For while it tarnished the latter's image both in Japan and elsewhere, it also neutralized a key source of vocal opposition as well as a potential challenger to Park.

Two more incidents occurred in 1974 that adversely affected Seoul-Tokyo relations. One was the arrest, trial, and conviction by a South Korean military court of two Japanese citizens on charges of participating in a conspiracy to overthrow the Park regime. The two were eventually released and returned to Japan, but their twenty-year prison terms were nonetheless confirmed by the ROK Supreme Court in May 1975.[32] The other incident was the attempted assassination of President Park and the murder of Mrs. Park in Seoul on August 15, 1974 by a twenty-two-year-old Korean resident of Japan named Mun Se Kwang. He had entered South Korea with an illegally obtained Japanese passport and a handgun that he had previously stolen from a police box in Osaka, Japan. A Japanese national, Mrs. Yoshii Mikiko, had helped Mun to obtain the passport. Moreover, he had allegedly prepared for the terroristic act under the guidance of *Ch'ongnyŏn*, the North Korea-oriented Korean residents' organization. All this meant, in the eyes of the South Korean authorities, that Japan was partially responsible, both morally and substantively, for the tragic outcome.[33]

Although Japan took the conciliatory step of sending its prime minister to the funeral of Mrs. Park, violent anti-Japanese demonstra-

---

32. *Asahi shimbun*, July 16, 1974 and May 28, 1975.
33. B. C. Koh, "South Korea, North Korea, and Japan," *Pacific Community* 6, 2 (January 1975): 205 and 210.

tions erupted in South Korea under apparent guidance from the authorities. The Seoul government demanded not only an official apology from the Japanese government but also the extradition of Mun's alleged collaborators in Japan to South Korea and, failing that, at least their prompt prosecution. It also called on Japan to suppress the activities of *Ch'ongnyŏn*. Aggravating the situation were remarks made in the Japanese Diet by Foreign Minister Kimura Toshio to the effect that the government of the Republic of Korea was not the only legitimate government in the Korean peninsula and that North Korea did not pose a military threat to South Korea. After intense negotiations and mediation efforts by the United States, a compromise was finally reached. Under an elaborate formula worked out by the two sides, Japan dispatched Shiina Etsusaburō, vice president of the Liberal-Democratic party, to Seoul, who delivered Prime Minister Tanaka's personal letter to President Park. The letter expressed Tanaka's condolences and deep regret over the death of Mrs. Park, pledged appropriate measures to prevent similar occurrences in the future, promised full cooperation with Seoul's investigation of the incident, and assured Seoul that Japan would do its best to punish illegal acts aimed at overthrowing the ROK government. In a supplemental verbal explanation, Shiina specifically mentioned *Ch'ongnyŏn* as a possible object of governmental regulation, saying that Japan "understands" the hostile posture of *Ch'ongnyŏn* toward Seoul, frowns upon its utilization by North Korean agents for subversive activities directed against Seoul, and will take stern measures if its members violate Japanese laws. In short, the compromise was a symbolic victory of sorts for South Korea, for which Japan paid a relatively low price from a substantive point of view. What made the compromise solution possible was the perception by both sides that they needed the friendship and good will of each other for the foreseeable future.[34]

Another source of friction in Seoul-Tokyo relations is inter-Korean relations. Seoul's policy since 1965 has been to prevent or discourage Japan from dealing with North Korea in any way that even indirectly bolsters the legitimacy or other policy goals of the Pyongyang government. Seoul's policy has been only moderately successful. While Japan has scrupulously avoided any official contacts with the DPRK, it has nonetheless implemented its long-standing policy of *seikei bunri* (separation of politics from economics) vis-à-vis North Korea. Two-way trade between Japan and North Korea grew from $58 million in 1970 to $600 million in 1980.[35] Had it not been for North Korea's payment problems, the trade volume would probably

34. Ibid., pp. 213–216.
35. *Kita Chōsen kenkyū* 6, 70 (May 1980): 28; *Korea Herald*, January 8, 1981.

have grown at a faster rate. By the mid 1970s, Japan had become North Korea's second largest trading partner.[36]

What irks Seoul is that the idea of *seikei bunri* is a sham; in fact, the government cannot stay totally aloof from trade relations with another country. For example, the ostensibly private agreement, signed in January 1972, between the Dietmen's League for Promotion of Japan-Korea Friendship, led by LDP Dietman Kuno Chūji, and the DPRK Committee for Promotion of International Trade was subsequently endorsed by the Japanese government.[37] Expansion of trade relations has entailed a steady growth in exchange of visitors, and persistent protests by Seoul against the admission of politically oriented North Korean visitors to Japan have thus far had but a limited success. For given the nature of the North Korean political system, the distinction between political and nonpolitical organizations becomes tenuous. Among the recent North Korean visitors to Japan have been delegations representing the League of Socialist Working Youth (February–March 1975 and April 1978); the Federation of Activists in Education and Culture (January–February 1976, January–March 1977, and May–June 1977); the Supreme People's Assembly, led by Hyon Jun Guk, vice-chairman of the DPRK Committee for Cultural Relations with Foreign Countries (May 1977); *Nodong sinmun* (November 1978); youth activists (November 1978); the Federation of Civil Servants (December 1978); and a goodwill delegation led by Hyon Jun Guk (June 1979).[38] Most of these delegations, particularly those led by Hyon Jun Guk, have engaged in patently political activities during their sojourns in Japan, such as holding news conferences and propagating Pyongyang's positions on reunification and other issues. Since the cessation of "protest diplomacy" by Seoul would undoubtedly open the floodgate of visits by all sorts of North Korean groups, it may still be credited with serving Seoul's goal of restraining Tokyo's latent penchant for an "equidistance" policy toward the two Korean states.

Finally, the strain generated by Seoul's request for a $6 billion loan from Tokyo needs to be examined briefly. As noted earlier, Seoul's

36. Indeed, during my 1981 visit to the DPRK, I was struck by signs of the Japanese economic presence. For example, my hotel room in Pyongyang was equipped with Japanese-made air conditioner, television set, and refrigerator; I saw quite a few Japanese bulldozers and trucks in the countryside; and we met a number of Japanese salesmen and engineers. One Japanese salesman told my colleague, Chae-Jin Lee, that since many Japanese companies have their salesmen practically living in Pyongyang, they had de facto branches there. He himself had spent a month in the same Pyongyang hotel we were staying in. However, he complained that he had signed sales contracts for only $800,000 worth of goods, noting that the North Koreans were suffering from a shortage of hard currency.

37. For details of the agreement, see *Pyongyang Times*, February 5, 1972.

38. *Kita Chōsen kenkyū* 6, 63 (September 1979): 66–72.

public posture is that it is entitled to such economic cooperation from Tokyo by virtue of its contributions to Japan's security. Seoul also believes that the magnitude of the deficits in its balance of trade with Japan and Japan's substantial economic stakes in South Korea justify the request for low interest government loans and commodity credits. In April 1982, however, Japan offered a package containing a total of $4 billion, of which only $1.5 billion would be an Official Development Assistance (ODA) loan; the remainder would be Japanese Export-Import Bank credits. South Korea flatly rejected the offer, and negotiations were suspended. But the appointment of a new foreign minister in Seoul in June 1982 led to a minor breakthrough: both sides agreed in July 1982 that the amount of loan would be $4 billion and that the interest rate would be 6.1 percent per annum. Seoul, however, insisted that the ODA portion of the loan package be increased to $2.3 billion. There were also disagreements regarding the form and terms of commodity credits. The prospects for an early settlement of the loan issue were dimmed somewhat by a new controversy surrounding the alleged distortion of historical facts in newly authorized Japanese high school history textbooks. The government censors at the Japanese Education Ministry, it was revealed in late July 1982, had ordered a substantial revision of history textbooks so as to gloss over the aggressive acts and atrocities committed by the Japanese against the Korean and Chinese peoples during and before World War II. Seoul, Pyongyang, and Beijing were in unison in harshly denouncing the Japanese action.[39]

PYONGYANG'S POLICY TOWARD THE NONALIGNED NATIONS

Although it was not until August 1975 that North Korea was admitted to the Nonalignment Movement as a full-fledged member, the movement has nonetheless served as a focal point of Pyongyang's diplomacy for over a decade. The birth of the movement in 1961 coincided with the era of decolonization, and almost all the newly independent countries became its members, thus accounting for its phenomenal growth—from 25 in 1961 to 95 in 1981. This meant that North Korea, which began a concerted effort to expand its diplomatic ties in the Third World in the 1960s, could not avoid being exposed to the rhetoric and politics of the Nonalignment Movement. In fact, all of the twenty nations with which North Korea established diplomatic relations in the 1960s were members of the movement.

39. *Han'guk ilbo*, May 1, May 3 (editorial), and June 5, 1982; *Korea Herald* (International Edition), July 24–28, 1982.

As Pyongyang began to extoll the virtues of independence in the world arena in the mid 1960s, it found the aims and principles of the Nonalignment Movement quite attractive. Indeed, the movement was championing not merely independence but also national liberation and the struggle against neocolonialism and imperialism—precisely the same goals North Korea sought in terms of the Korean question. Finally, Pyongyang probably saw no practical alternative to stepping up its diplomacy vis-à-vis the nonaligned nations, for Seoul, its archrival, was doing the same. Losing the competitive battle in the diplomatic arena would have serious implications for Pyongyang's reunification policy, particularly its strategy of generating international support for its positions.

A turning point in North Korea's relations with the Nonalignment Movement came in September 1971 when it established diplomatic relations with Yugoslavia, the founding member and leader of the movement. But it took Pyongyang four more years of intense diplomatic effort, during which it added nearly forty nonaligned nations to its roster of diplomatic partners, to gain membership in the movement. In December 1975, barely four months after joining the club, Kim Il Sung characterized the Nonalignment Movement as "a mighty antiimperialist revolutionary force reflecting the main trend of the present era," adding that the "emergence of the nonalignment movement has decisively strengthened the revolutionary forces of the world and greatly weakened the reactionary forces of imperialism."[40]

Declaring that neither the safeguarding of national independence nor the building of a new prosperous society could be accomplished "without fighting imperialism," Kim called on the nonaligned countries to "form a broad antiimperialist united front" and to "administer blows at the imperialists and colonialists by concerted efforts." His militancy was explainable in terms of his perception that the "Korean people's struggle to regain the territory and nation usurped by the US imperialists and to reunify the divided country is *the main link* in the antiimperialist national liberation struggle being waged on a worldwide scale."[41]

Such strident militancy, coupled with the single-minded pursuit of the goal of generating maximum support for its reunification policy in the forums of the Nonalignment Movement, appears to have created some difficulty for North Korea. At the Fifth Summit Conference held in Colombo, Sri Lanka in August 1976, Pyongyang's effort

---

40. Kim Il Sung, *The Non-Alignment Movement Is a Mighty Anti-Imperialist Revolutionary Force of Our Times*, treatise published in the inaugural issue of Argentine Magazine, *Guidebook To the Third World*, December 16, 1975 (Pyongyang: Foreign Languages Publishing House, 1976), pp. 1–2.

41. Ibid., p. 3 and pp. 5–6. Emphasis added.

to accentuate political and military issues at the expense of economic and energy problems reportedly annoyed President Tito of Yugoslavia, the elder statesman of the Nonalignment Movement. Nonetheless, as noted previously, the conference did adopt a "resolution on the Korean question" fully endorsing North Korean demands for the immediate cessation of "the imperialist war provocation maneuvers in South Korea," removal of nuclear weapons and foreign troops from South Korea, and replacement of the Korean armistice agreement by a peace agreement; moreover, the intense lobbying by the hundred-man North Korean delegation led by Premier Li Jong Ok paid off in the form of a strong condemnation of American military presence in Korea in a separate political declaration adopted by the conference: "The imperialists have turned South Korea into a military base for aggression, and a base for nuclear attack by extensively introducing more and more armed forces and mass destructive weapons, including nuclear weapons." However, twenty-five nations filed reservations in writing to the wording of this declaration.[42]

At the Fifth Foreign Ministers' Conference held in Belgrade, Yugoslavia, in July 1978, only 19 of the 49 participating countries mentioned the Korean question in their speeches. Of the 19, only 12 voiced unequivocal support for North Korean positions, while the remainder hedged their statements by simply endorsing the peaceful solution of the problem or dialogue between the two parties on the Korean peninsula. The declaration adopted by the conference on the final day (July 31) nonetheless contained a full endorsement of North Korean positions: it welcomed the three principles of reunification enunciated in the North-South joint statement of July 4, 1972 and expressed hope that the foreign troops be withdrawn from South Korea, that the United Nations Command in South Korea be dissolved, and that the armistice agreement be replaced with a peace agreement.[43]

At the Sixth Summit Conference held in Havana, Cuba, in September 1979, Premier Li Jong Ok of the DPRK was elected as one of the twenty vice-chairmen. In addition, North Korea was elected to the Coordinating Committee, which was expanded from twenty-five to thirty-six members. Finally, the conference in its final declaration expressed support for Pyongyang's reunification policy, including its demand for withdrawal of US troops from South Korea.[44]

At the Seventh Foreign Ministers' Conference held in New Delhi,

42. On North Korea's difficulty at the conference, see *Shūkan Asahi*, October 15, 1976, p. 23; for the texts of the resolutions, see *Pyongyang Times*, August 28 and September 4, 1976.
43. *Kita Chōsen kenkyū* 5, 51 (September 1978): 16–19.
44. *Chosŏn chung'ang yŏn'gam*, 1980 (Pyongyang: Chosŏn Chung'ang T'ongsin-sa, 1980), pp. 238–239.

India, in February 1981, North Korea suffered a setback: it was compelled by circumstances to refrain from placing the Korean question on the conference agenda. According to DPRK Foreign Minister Ho Dam, who called a press conference in New Delhi on February 7 to announce the North Korean decision "not to lay the Korean question before the conference," the backdrop of the conference was ominous: "the international tension is becoming more strained and danger of a war is growing day by day due to the big powers' scramble for the sphere of influence." Under such circumstances, Ho said, "the nonaligned countries should uphold the principles of this movement, achieve unity and cohesion and strengthen and develop this movement as an integral force."[45] Although Ho didn't mention any specific problems, two members of the movement, Iran and Iraq, were at war, and other members were deeply divided over the issues of Afghanistan and Cambodia. More important, Iraq had broken off diplomatic relations with North Korea on the ground that the latter had supplied arms to Iran.[46] Finally, South Korea had mounted a strenuous diplomatic campaign to neutralize North Korean influence among the nonaligned countries (more on this in the next section). The implication of all this was that there was high probability that for the first time in the movement's history, any resolution endorsing the North Korean views might be defeated; for under the rule of consensus, opposition by a single member could have that effect.

Pyongyang, in effect, made a virtue out of necessity by describing its decision as "an expression of our broadminded and sincere efforts" to promote unity at the conference. Only ten foreign ministers mentioned the Korean question in their speeches, and only one, from Guinea, explicitly supported the proposal for a Democratic Confederal Republic of Koryŏ, which Kim Il Sung had unveiled in October 1980 and for which the North Koreans had lobbied very hard to generate support.[47] In a postmortem on the conference, on February 19, a joint meeting of the Political Bureau of the WPK Central Committee and the DPRK Central People's Committee made the following statement:

> At the New Delhi foreign ministers conference, the nonaligned countries successfully overcame all factors obstructing unity and pooled their strength in promoting the common cause of antiimperialism and independence in unity. The whole course of the conference showed that the spirit of unity and cooperation is

---

45. *KCNA*, Pyongyang, February 10, 1981, as monitored by FBIS.
46. *Korea Herald*, October 12, 1980.
47. For the gist of the speeches, see *KCNA*, Pyongyang, February 13, 1981, as monitored by FBIS.

stronger than the sentiments of division and antagonism and demonstrated the ability of the nonaligned countries to combine the national and individual interests with the overall interests of the movement.

The Democratic People's Republic of Korea has made a positive contribution to the unity and cohesion of the Nonaligned Movement [sic] by valuing its overall interests and placing them before anything else.[48]

The New Delhi conference did generate symbolic payoffs for North Korea: it picked Pyongyang as the site of two meetings of the Nonalignment Movement scheduled for June and August of 1981. The second conference of the coordinating nations on the nonaligned countries' food and agricultural affairs was held in Pyongyang from June 10 to 12. It was attended by nine coordinating member states (out of thirteen), eight observer countries, and the UN Food and Agriculture Organization. The symbolic significance of the conference for North Korea was that it was the first meeting of the nonalignment movement ever to be held in that country; as such, it signified Pyongyang's growing status in the movement.[49] In August of the same year, Pyongyang hosted a six-day symposium of the nonaligned and other developing countries on increasing food and agricultural production. Attended by representatives of eighty countries and twelve international organizations, the symposium was probably the largest international meeting ever held in North Korea. It provided the North Koreans with an opportunity to show off their achievements in economic construction, to demonstrate their hospitality and friendship to Third World countries, and to drum up support for their proposal for a Democratic Confederal Republic of Koryŏ.[50]

From May 12 to 14, 1982, the seventh meeting of the Coordinating Committee of the News Agencies Pool of Nonaligned Countries was held in Pyongyang. It was attended by fifty-nine delegations representing various news agencies and regional and international organizations. Once again, it provided the North Koreans with a tailor-made opportunity to engage in international public relations, and they made an all-out effort to make the most of it. Premier Li Jong Ok addressed the conference, and President Kim Il Sung hosted a ban-

48. Ibid., Pyongyang, February 20, 1981, as monitored by FBIS. The importance the North Korean leadership attaches to the Nonalignment Movement is suggested by the forum in which the evaluation of the New Delhi conference took place—a joint meeting of the two most powerful political bodies in North Korea, chaired by Kim Il Sung.
49. *Vantage Point* 4, 7 (July 1981), 19.
50. For coverage of the symposium, see *Nodong sinmun*, August 27–September 2, 1981.

quet for the delegates at which he made a lengthy speech reiterating his familiar themes—the imperative of independence, the need for cohesion in the Nonalignment Movement, and the evils of imperialism, particularly "US imperialism." He also set forth his ideas on the ways of improving cooperation among the "information services" of the nonaligned countries. There was even a "meeting for friendship and solidarity" between North Korean journalists and delegates to the meeting, at which a number of delegates praised Kim Il Sung's son and successor-designate Kim Jong Il.[51]

Finally, in June 1982, North Korea suffered a significant setback, when a meeting of the foreign ministers of the Coordinating Committee of Nonaligned Countries in Havana, Cuba, voted down Pyongyang's proposal that called for, among other things, the withdrawal of all foreign troops from South Korea and the dissolution of the UN Command there.[52] This development symbolized the inroads that South Korea had made in the Third World.

In sum, North Korea appears to have obtained mixed results from its participation in the Nonalignment Movement. On the positive side, it succeeded in generating symbolic support from the summit and foreign ministers' conferences for its reunification policy, until it began to encounter difficulty in the early 1980s. It also managed to ward off strenuous efforts by its archrival, the Republic of Korea, to join the movement. That Pyongyang was elected to leading bodies of the movement, notably the vice-chairmanship and the coordinating committee, within four years of becoming a full-fledged member is a tribute to the efficacy of its diplomacy. With their country chosen as the site of a number of conferences related to the movement, North Koreans not only enjoyed enhanced self-esteem, but also had precious opportunities to publicize their achievements and drum up support for their positions on Korean reunification.

On the negative side, the goal enunciated by Kim Il Sung to turn the movement into "a broad antiimperialist united front" has thus far proved to be elusive. The sheer size and diversity of movement membership makes the goal seem all but unattainable. Nor is it likely that Kim Il Sung will emerge as the leader of the movement in the wake of Tito's death. Kim reportedly told a visiting delegation of the Japan Socialist Party in September 1980 that "there is a serious need for a country which could play a central role in the nonaligned [sic] movement."[53] Although this would indicate his readiness to assume a leadership role, the plain fact is that he has not been an active, let alone a prominent, leader in the movement at all. He failed to attend two

51. See *KCNA*, Pyongyang, May 12–16, 1982, as monitored by FBIS.
52. *Han'guk ilbo*, June 10, 1982; *Korea Herald*, June 9, 1982.
53. *NHK* TV Network, Tokyo, September 27, 1980, as monitored by FBIS.

conferences of the heads of state of the nonaligned countries—the Sri Lanka conference of August 1976 and the Havana conference of September 1979—both held since North Korea joined the Movement. A significant variable in the evolution of North Korea's role in the movement will be South Korea, to whose efforts to counter North Korean diplomacy in the Third World we now turn.

SEOUL'S POLICY TOWARD THE THIRD WORLD

By coincidence, the birth of the Nonalignment Movement occurred in the same year that Park Chung Hee took power in South Korea. One of the first conspicuous acts of the Park regime was to launch a vigorous diplomatic campaign in the Third World. With the dual and interrelated aim of lining up votes in the United Nations and expanding diplomatic partners, the military government dispatched five good will delegations to all corners of the globe in the summer of 1961. Three of these delegations visited a total of 30 nonaligned countries: 7 in the Middle East, 7 in Southeast Asia, and 16 in Africa. The effort resulted in the establishment of diplomatic relations with the Ivory Coast, Niger, Benin, Chad, and Cameroon; and in the fall of the same year, it gained the support of 13 newly independent African countries for pro-South Korean resolutions at the UN General Assembly.[54]

The effort continued in 1962 and in subsequent years. Seoul relied increasingly on its good will missions and also invited government leaders and other notables from the various nonaligned countries to visit South Korea. Among the Third World visitors to South Korea were Premier Leabua Jonathan of Lesotho (1966 and 1969), Emperor Haile Selassie I of Ethiopia (1968), and President Diori Hamani of Niger (1969). The pace, vigor, and efficacy of South Korean diplomacy were reflected in the phenomenal growth of its diplomatic partners. In a single year (1962), Seoul established ambassadorial-level diplomatic relations with an astounding 30 countries, most of them in the Third World. By the end of the 1960s, South Korea's diplomatic partners had grown to 80 from a mere 15 in 1960.

Although South Korea's rapidly growing economic capability was a boon to its diplomacy, inasmuch as it was relying on economic and technical cooperation as a major inducement to Third World support, its diplomatic edge began to be blunted by a sharp increase in North Korea's diplomatic efforts in the early 1970s. Pyongyang succeeded in establishing diplomatic relations with many African coun-

---

54. Republic of Korea, Ministry of Foreign Affairs, *Han'guk oegyo samsimnyŏn*, pp. 227–228.

tries that had previously only recognized South Korea: Sierra Leone (1971), Cameroon (1972), Rwanda (1972), Uganda (1972), Senegal (1972), Upper Volta (1972), Madagascar (1972), Zaire (1972), and Gambia (1973). As a result, Seoul was forced to reassess its policy of not dealing with any country that simultaneously recognized North Korea—the so-called Hallstein Doctrine—officially abandoning it in July 1973. Unofficially, the policy became a dead letter in October 1971, when Seoul failed to break off relations with Sierra Leone upon the latter's recognition of the DPRK.

The increasing North Korean challenge was met by a redoubled effort on the part of South Korea in its multifaceted diplomacy vis-à-vis the nonaligned countries: "visitation diplomacy," "invitation diplomacy," and "economic diplomacy" were stepped up. For example, cabinet-level leaders from the nonaligned countries who visited South Korea from 1970 to 1978 numbered more than eighty, among whom were a president (Bongo of Gabon), six prime ministers, and twenty-five foreign ministers.[55]

In Seoul's view, a turning point in its diplomatic competition with Pyongyang in the Third World came in February 1981 when the foreign ministers' conference of the nonaligned countries in New Delhi failed to endorse North Korea's positions on reunification. While South Korea's own efforts do not fully account for what happened or failed to happen there, they are nonetheless noteworthy. In one sense, the timing of President Chun Doo Hwan's dramatic proposal for mutual visits between the heads of the two Korean states was related to Seoul's campaign to undercut Pyongyang at the New Delhi conference, although the most important consideration was no doubt his plans for a summit meeting with the incoming president of the United States. In terms of "visitation diplomacy," two high-level delegations, one led by Choi Kwang Soo, special presidential envoy, and the other led by Foreign Minister Lho Shin-yong, visited nonaligned countries in South Asia, Africa, and the Middle East in November 1980.[56] Additionally, South Korea mobilized its diplomatic missions abroad to lobby against the inclusion of a pro-Pyongyang clause in the final declaration of the forthcoming foreign ministers' conference.[57]

The most successful aspect of Seoul's diplomacy toward the Third World has to do with its relations with the ASEAN. President Chun Doo Hwan's two-week tour of the ASEAN countries in June and July 1981 represented a diplomatic coup of considerable proportions both for himself and his regime. The most notable symbolic payoff of

55. Ibid., pp. 238–240.
56. *Korea Herald*, November 23, 1980 and November 25, 1980.
57. *Korea Newsreview*, February 28, 1981, pp. 8–9.

the trip was that Chun's hosts in all five countries—Indonesia, Malaysia, Singapore, Thailand, and the Philippines—endorsed not only his proposal for mutual visits and dialogue between the presidents of the two Koreas but also the long-standing ROK position on the simultaneous admission of the two Koreas to the United Nations. In so doing, the five ASEAN governments, four of which also have diplomatic relations with Pyongyang, placed themselves solidly in Seoul's camp insofar as the Korean question is concerned. Another symbolic gain for Seoul was the affirmation of common strategic interests between it and the ASEAN. On a personal level, Chun flaunted the firmness of his grip on power at home by showing that his regime was capable of functioning smoothly and without any social or political disturbances during his prolonged absence abroad.[58]

Substantively, the summit meetings between Chun and his hosts paved the way for an expansion of economic and technical cooperation between South Korea and the ASEAN. Economic ties between Seoul and the ASEAN were already substantial. Two-way trade had increased from $195 million in 1971 to $2,614 million in 1980, and the ASEAN had emerged as the key source of important natural resources for Seoul. For example, South Korea depends completely on the ASEAN countries for its domestic requirements for tin—one of the ingredients of its booming electronics industry—rubber, and palm oil. In addition, the "ASEAN countries account for 76 percent of [South] Korea's total import in timber, 49 percent in copper ore, 45 percent in titanium, and 35.2 percent in raw sugar. By far the biggest single import [item] from the region is timber, which accounted for 44.1 percent of [South] Korea's total import from the ASEAN in 1980."[59] During his tour, Chun obtained pledges from the ASEAN governments that the supply of these resources and crude oil would not be interrupted in the future. In return, South Korea pledged to provide its "relatively advanced technical know-how and trained manpower in such sectors as construction, development of energy resources, manufacturing, and processing industries." Chun and the leaders of the ASEAN countries "have also agreed to promote joint ventures, particularly in resource-based industries, and [to] increase cooperation in areas of fishing and marine transportation."[60]

Another important area of cooperation between Seoul and the ASEAN pertains to the military sector. South Korea, which had already been supplying patrol boats, landing craft, small arms, and ammunition to the ASEAN countries, reportedly agreed to step up

58. On the results of Chun's ASEAN tour, see *Korea Herald*, June 25–July 14, 1981; *Asahi shimbun*, July 10, 1981, editorial (p. 5) and news analysis (p. 7).
59. *Korea Herald*, July 10, 1981, special supplement, p. 1.
60. Ibid.

its arms exports to the region. Given Seoul's chronic trade deficit with the ASEAN—$348 million in 1980—and given that its defense industry—comprising eighty companies—had grown so fast as to outpace South Korea's own needs, this appears to have been a mutually beneficial move. Although some of the military equipment is US-licensed (e.g., M-16 rifles, M-1 carbines, and ammunition) and hence requires US congressional approval for export, such approval has been frequently granted in the past.[61]

It should be noted that North Korea did not sit idly by when South Korea was preparing to consolidate its ties with the ASEAN. After the plans for Chun's ASEAN tour became known, Pyongyang dispatched a government delegation headed by Vice Premier Kye Ung Tae to the region. But the mission apparently visited only two of the ASEAN countries—Indonesia and Malaysia—and terse reports in the North Korean press suggested meager results.[62]

When the chips were down, it was pragmatic considerations that prevailed: Chun's diplomatic gains, hence Pyongyang's losses, in the ASEAN countries may be attributed primarily to the complementary economic needs of Seoul and the ASEAN—the former's need for the ASEAN's raw materials and crude oil and the latter's need for Seoul's technical expertise and weapons. The episode demonstrated anew the strategic importance of economic capability in the conduct of foreign policy, particularly in diplomatic competition.

Finally, South Korea's growing ability to drum up support in the Third World was graphically demonstrated in September 1981, when the International Olympic Committee chose Seoul as the site of the 1988 Summer Olympic Games. A key factor in the close contest, in which Nagoya, Japan, competed with Seoul, was the support of Third World nations. The ROK government noted that it would be the first time that the Olympic Games would be hosted by a divided nation. But, more than anything else, the decision was hailed as a symbol of the growing stature of South Korea in the world arena.[63]

61. See "South Korea's Growing Role as a Military Supplier," *Business Week*, June 29, 1981, p. 72; *Asahi shimbun*, July 10, 1981, p. 7.
62. *KCNA*, Pyongyang, May 31 and June 12, 1981, as monitored by FBIS; *Korea Newsreview*, July 25, 1981, pp. 8–9.
63. *Han'guk ilbo*, October 2, 1981.

11 CONCLUSIONS

In the preceding pages we have tried to delineate the salient patterns of the foreign policies of the two Koreas, their probable sources, and their apparent consequences. Although our quest for understanding and insight has been guided by a conceptual map directing us to a number of specific dimensions, we have been hampered by the paucity of data, and the picture we have managed to draw is far from complete. Let us nonetheless recapitulate the principal themes and findings of our study and ponder their implications, both analytical and normative.

PATTERNS OF FOREIGN POLICY

A prolonged exposure to the rhetoric and behavior of the foreign policies of North and South Korea yields the impression that there are more similarities than differences in their basic patterns. For example, both pursue the common strategic goals of legitimacy, security, and development. To be sure, the same goals are also embraced by most of the newly independent nations. Nonetheless, the peculiar circumstances surrounding the two Koreas—the partition of the peninsula at the end of World War II, the unorthodox manner in which the two rival states came into being, the tragedy of a fratricidal war in which other nations also became embroiled, the continuing tensions, and the arms race between the two adversaries—add a sense of urgency to their pursuit.

Most important, two of the three goals are pursued and can only be pursued as a cutthroat zero-sum game. In the eyes of the DPRK and the ROK alike, legitimacy means not simply acceptance by other nations as an international legal personality—an entity possessing the attributes of territory, population, government, and the capacity to enter into international relations—but the acknowledgment of its respective claim that it is the only lawful government in the entire Korean peninsula. Such a goal can only be attained at the expense of the rival party. At a minimum, it requires an effort to undercut the legitimacy of the other state whenever and wherever the opportunity presents itself. While the maximum goal of exclusive legitimacy has become increasingly elusive during the past decade or so, the minimum goal of relative legitimacy continues to be pursued by both sides with unremitting vigor. Not only does the process take on the characteristics of a zero-sum game, it also degenerates into a vicious circle. For the harder one side tries to undercut the other side, the more vigorously the latter must respond to the challenge.

For the two Korean regimes, security is also a mutually exclusive goal that tends to perpetuate a vicious circle. For the foremost threat to each regime's security, both imagined and real, emanates from the other. Unless, and until, mutual distrust is banished and tensions abate measurably, an increase in the perceived security of one side implies a decrease in that of the other. Since that is not a tolerable condition for either regime, stepped-up efforts in arms buildup follow; hence the vicious circle.

The goal of development is closely linked to the other two goals. Inasmuch as economic power constitutes the backbone of national power, it is an indispensable requirement for effective conduct of the competitive diplomacy that the goal of legitimacy dictates. Moreover, bolstering one's sense of security necessitates not merely arms but also an industrial base and a capability to manufacture one's own weapons. Unlike the other goals, however, economic development need not be pursued at the expense of each other; nor does it necessarily precipitate a vicious circle. Whether one's economy is internationally oriented, as Seoul's is, or geared primarily to self-sufficiency, as Pyongyang's is, the pursuit of sustained economic development requires a skill in diplomacy. Both sides have thus far conducted their "economic diplomacy" with varying degrees of success.

If there are thus "shared" goals between the two Koreas, one can nonetheless discern a difference in the priority assigned to each goal by the two sides. For North Korea, legitimacy appears to eclipse the other goals, as far as the conduct of its foreign policy is concerned. South Korea, on the other hand, seems more preoccupied with security and development than with legitimacy per se. It should be stressed, however, that neither side regards any of the three goals as unimportant, for they are closely intertwined.

Another common pattern one can identify in the foreign policies of the two Koreas is their emphasis on self-reliance. In the case of North Korea, its leader Kim Il Sung has elevated *chuch'e* (autonomy or self-reliance) to the pedestal of national ideology and turned its pursuit into a veritable national preoccupation. Self-reliance, however, does not preclude the possibility of cooperation with, and dependence on, other countries. More important, it remains more of a goal than an ongoing reality. Its chief manifestation in Pyongyang's foreign policy behavior, then, is the assertion of the right of North Korea to steer its own destiny even when it seeks and receives valuable economic, technical, and military assistance. The intensity with which Pyongyang has pursued the triple goals of legitimacy, security, and, particularly, development is linked to the apotheosis of self-reliance.

In the case of South Korea, successive leaders have extolled the virtues of self-reliance with varying degrees of enthusiasm. The actual track record, insofar as the practice of self-reliance is concerned, is a mixed one: while there have been some spectacular incidents involving the assertion of independence, such as Syngman Rhee's release of prisoners of war in 1953 and Park Chung Hee's infringement of basic human rights and civil liberties in the face of vocal opposition from the United States, the overriding strategic goals of security and development have constrained Seoul to forge special ties of an asymmetrical alliance with Washington and of economic dependence on both Washington and Tokyo. The strategy of relying on international capital and foreign trade in economic development has further undercut Seoul's ability to manage its own affairs. On the other hand, the phenomenal success of its developmental programs has steadily enhanced Seoul's self-confidence as well as its capacity for autonomy in the world arena. Whatever difference may exist between the North and the South with respect to the degree to which each practices self-reliance may be attributable to the relative size of the two economies, their basic characteristics, and the presence or absence of rivalry among great powers surrounding it. In other words, the single most important variable in explaining the relative success with which Pyongyang has been able to assert independence in its international behavior appears to be the Sino-Soviet conflict.

The third and final pattern that one can identify in the foreign policies of the two Koreas is the blending of rigidity and flexibility. In simple terms, both have adhered rigidly to their basic strategic objectives not only of legitimacy, security, and development but also of national reunification on their own terms, while displaying tactical flexibility as well as a sensitivity to significant changes in their respective operational environments. If the dramatic breakthrough in inter-Korean relations signaled by the initiation of dialogue in the early 1970s bespoke flexibility on the part of both Seoul and Pyongyang, the collapse of the dialogue within three years and the failure of subsequent attempts to revive it reflected the resiliency of their mutually incompatible strategic goals as well as the depth of their mutual distrust. In one sense, the Korean stalemate demonstrates that neither side has been sufficiently flexible. The record shows that most notable changes in the policies of both regimes have occurred as grudging accommodations to faits accomplis.

SOURCES OF FOREIGN POLICY

The operational environment can be viewed not only as the principal source of foreign policy but also as its outcome. The configuration of the external setting—the dynamics of global politics, the attributes of the regional system, and the peculiarities of bilateral relations—no doubt helps to shape and mold the kinds of stimuli to which a nation is constrained to respond. At the same time, it is also susceptible to manipulation and even change by a nation's foreign policy. So, too, can the internal setting of economic power, military power, and political dynamics both structure and be structured by a nation's foreign policy.

From the standpoint of understanding the foreign policy behaviors of the two Koreas, the most important developments in the operational environment over the past few decades have been the emergence of multiple centers of power, the growing potency of the Third World or "nonaligned" countries, the rapprochement between the US and the PRC, the Sino-Soviet conflict, and the growing interdependence of the world. These developments have provided the general context in which both North and South Korea have been able to undertake ambitious programs of economic and defense construction, to expand their respective nets of diplomatic intercourse, to temporarily jettison their policies of unremitting hostility to each other in the interest of dialogue, and to conduct fierce diplomatic and political campaigns aimed at downgrading each other.

The growing economic power of both sides has been both the product and source of their foreign policy behavior. Even the relatively resource-rich and *chuch'e*-oriented North had to rely heavily on the economic and technical assistance of fraternal socialist countries led by the Soviet Union and the PRC in the initial stage of its economic modernization program. The lack of certain key resources, notably crude oil, coupled with the imperative of further modernization, means that foreign trade, and hence foreign policy, will continue to play an important part in North Korea's survival as a nation. On the other hand, the considerable success that Pyongyang has achieved thus far in the realm of economic construction provides it with a valuable resource in the conduct of diplomacy both at the governmental and nongovernmental (including covert) levels. Not only has the capability of North Korea to extend economic assistance to poorer countries in return for, or in anticipation of, diplomatic support been enhanced, but its "invitational diplomacy"—whereby a steady stream of foreign visitors is guided around the showcase museums, theaters, "palaces," and factories in and around Pyongyang and other parts of the country—is a function of growing economic power. Finally, Pyongyang's ability to provide training, arms, and other assistance to guerrilla groups is obviously related to its economic capability.

The linkage between Seoul's strategy of economic development and its foreign policy has already been suggested. As a resource-poor nation, South Korea has opted for the use of foreign capital and foreign trade as the primary weapons in economic modernization, with impressive results. Whether or not it can sustain the momentum of growth hinges crucially on the skill with which it conducts its "economic diplomacy," aimed at securing a stable supply of natural resources and crude oil, diversifying its trade partners, and forging ties of economic and technical cooperation with nations rich and poor. Like its northern rival, South Korea, too, can and does capitalize on its growing economic power to advance its diplomatic aims. If used with tact and finesse, Seoul's apparent edge in economic power over Pyongyang is likely to pay rich dividends in its competition for the support of nonaligned nations.

Political dynamics, a key component of the internal setting, can have tangible effects on a nation's foreign policy. The towering feature of North Korea's political dynamics is the exalted position occupied by its supreme leader Kim Il Sung. A center of an intense personality cult bordering on religion, Kim is portrayed by North Korean propagandists as an outstanding political leader and theoretician whose works and ideas are studied and revered around the world. This necessitates an expenditure of enormous amounts of resources, both material and human, on the propagation of the cult on a global scale. His books, pamphlets, and articles are translated into a multitude of foreign languages and distributed, free of charge, to all corners of the globe, and groups dedicated to the study of his ideas, most notably, *chuch'e sasang*, have sprung up in many countries with the apparent financial subsidy of Pyongyang. In addition, advertisements carrying the entire text of, or excerpts from, his articles or speeches, complete with his portrait, are placed at periodic intervals in publications around the world. In sum, the cult of Kim Il Sung constitutes not only the main pillar of North Korean politics but also the cornerstone of its foreign policy.

The linkage between the two was brought home to me in sharp relief during my visit to the DPRK in the summer of 1981. In the North Korean radio and televised news programs, the major portion of what was billed as "overseas news" was devoted to the reporting of which group held a meeting devoted to the study of the *chuch'e* idea of Kim Il Sung in which country and which newspapers or magazines "published the immortal works of the great leader." The purpose of such reporting was to convince, or reinforce the conviction of, the North Korean populace that theirs was indeed the great leader not only of the Korean people but also of the entire world. This was shown in an unabashed way in a spectacular museum in the beautiful *Myohyang-san* region in the Province of North Pyongan. Known as the International Friendship Exhibition Hall, the museum displays gifts received by Kim Il Sung from various leaders and other people from around the world. The gifts, chosen from nearly 26,000 items that Kim is said to have received as of December 31, 1980, are portrayed by both the official guides and explanatory notes accompanying the displays as "proof" of the "endless love and respect" for the great leader on the part of the world leaders and peoples. They show unmistakably Kim's "greatness," the visitor is told, for whereas Korean rulers in the past used to pay tributes to Chinese emperors, the table has been turned, and Chinese leaders, together with leaders of other countries, "respectfully" bring gifts to Kim Il Sung. What is left unsaid, of course, is that the rules of reciprocity and diplomatic protocol dictate the *exchange* of gifts between heads of state or governments on appropriate occasions. That, coupled with the longevity of Kim's rule, helps to account for the number and variety of gifts. The North Korean people, of whom an average of 500 visit the museum each day during summer months, are thus provided with a dazzling display of what purports to be the international recognition of Kim's alleged greatness.

Turning to South Korea, during much of the 1970s the late Park Chung Hee's repressive measures generated much controversy abroad, and his government was compelled to devote a sizable amount of its resources to defending the measures. President Jimmy Carter's human rights policy, with which Seoul's diplomatic machinery had to cope, was a particular source of irritation to the Park regime. The occasional strains that developed between Seoul and Tokyo frequently had their origins in the domestic politics of South Korea. Witness, for example, the controversy surrounding the kidnapping of the opposition leader Kim Dae Jung in 1973. His threatened execution by the Chun Doo Hwan government in late 1980 and early 1981 also plunged ROK-Japanese relations to a new low, and a major crisis was averted only by President Chun's decision to commute Kim Dae Jung's sentence on the eve of the former's departure for the summit meeting with President Reagan.

The operational environment of the two Koreas sketched above is perceived by their respective decision-making elites through the prism of ideology, historical legacy, and personality predispositions. The single most important ideological dimension for both Koreas is nationalism—the burning desire on the part of leaders and citizens alike to assert their national identity, to determine their own destiny, and to enhance their national prestige abroad in every conceivable way. The much vaunted *chuch'e* idea is but a manifestation of this desire. It is not only in rhetoric but in substance as well that North Korea outperforms South Korea with respect to nationalism. Pyongyang's excessive nationalism, however, also contributes to rigidity in its international behavior. What clearly sets the two Korean states apart ideologically, of course, is the North's commitment to communism and the South's antipathy thereto.

The ideological complexion of the Korean peninsula is clearly traceable to the historical legacy of the Korean people. Their checkered interaction with their giant neighbors, particularly the bitter experience of colonial domination by Japan, goes a long way toward explaining the intensity of nationalist sentiment. If the historical accident of bifurcated military occupation by the Soviet Union and the United States sowed the seeds of clashing ideologies—communism in the Soviet-occupied North and anticommunism in the American-occupied South—the Korean War served to harden the ideological barrier. For most South Koreans who had firsthand exposure to Communist rule during the three-month occupation by the (North) Korean People's Army, anticommunism has become not simply a slogan but an imperative necessity, a sine qua non for survival.

Personality predispositions, the third facet of the attitudinal prism of the decision-making elite, are singularly elusive in the case of the leaders of the two Koreas. Lacking any access to data bearing on their innermost feelings or psychological profiles, one can only make crude inferences from their known backgrounds and behaviors. Kim Il Sung may be characterized as what Harold Lasswell has called the "political type"—a man whose intense cravings for power and deference are seen as compensation for deprivation. Although magnified and distorted beyond recognition by hagiographers, his early life experiences contained deprivations of many sorts—lack of educational opportunities, lack of national pride, the experience of working under Chinese superiors in guerrilla campaigns, and, finally, the questionable circumstances under which he reached the pinnacle of power in North Korea. His apotheosis of *chuch'e* and, particularly, the frenzied personality cult centering around Kim and his family may be viewed, among other things, as compensatory responses to such deprivations.

Park Chung Hee, who ruled South Korea from 1961 to 1979, manifested what may be called a "model student syndrome." Trained in a normal school and military academies under the Japanese, Park learned the habits of stern discipline and unquestioning compliance to superiors' orders. His intolerance of criticism and authoritarian leadership style may have been rooted both in his early training and his long military career. His preoccupation with the goal of economic modernization may have reflected his desire to rid his nation of the stigma of poverty, to which he had been painfully exposed in his childhood.

When the operational environment is filtered through such internal lenses, it is transformed into "elite images," which become decisional premises. While the task of ascertaining such images is no less difficult than that of deciphering personality predispositions, one can gain important clues to the foreign policy elite's thinking from their public statements. A recurrent theme in Kim Il Sung's verbalized images of North Korea's external setting is the threat of "US imperialism." He has made it crystal clear that North Korea regards the United States as its number one enemy, not only because it perpetuates the division of the peninsula through its "colonial occupation" of South Korea and its propping up of "fascist puppet rule," but also because it is constantly scheming to launch a new war in Korea. If his perception that the American military presence in the South hampers his goal of national reunification is realistic, his view that the United States is nothing less than the "colonial master" of the South Korean people who masterminds all the major developments there is farfetched. Likewise, Kim's images of South Korea per se display a large measure of wishful thinking; for example, he appears to equate the South Korean people's struggle for democracy with sympathy for North Korean formulas for reunification.

The late Park Chung Hee's images of South Korea's external setting were dominated by a concern with the balance of power and the perception of a North Korean threat to Seoul's security. While paying the utmost attention to the maintenance and strengthening of security and economic ties with the United States and Japan, Park apparently did not perceive any tangible threat emanating from Pyongyang's two patron states—the Soviet Union and the PRC. His profound distrust of North Korea seems to have been real, even though he clearly exaggerated its danger to South Korea's security as a means of justifying repressive measures at home. The most significant differences between the images of the two leaders pertain to the degree of realism and the influence of ideology. These two factors appear to be related. Ideology appears to color Kim Il Sung's perceptions to a greater degree than it did Park Chung Hee's, resulting in a greater degree of distortion in the former's images than in the latter's.

How do these inputs—the operational and psychological environment of foreign policy—convert to outputs of foreign policy? A basic similarity in the structure of foreign policy decision making in both Koreas is found in the marked degree to which power is concentrated at the top. Neither North nor South Korea has had any significant countervailing forces in their respective political systems; this means that their top leaders play the decisive role in foreign policy making. Nonetheless, given the complexity and volume of foreign policy issues, it is practically impossible for the top leaders to monopolize power in that area. Sharing of power with other elites and institutions is a practical necessity. From the nature of the North Korean polity, however, one can surmise that the flow of information and the airing of contending perspectives may be considerably hampered by systemic constraints—most notably, the deification of the supreme leader. The absence of a similar cult in the South implies that the process there may be slightly more open, although truly adversary decision making probably remains to be approximated. It should be noted, however, that President Chun Doo Hwan may share his power with both his top aides and members of an invisible "junta" to an extent that was unknown during the Park Chung Hee regime.

OUTPUTS OF FOREIGN POLICY

For analytic purposes, outputs of foreign policy may be divided into strategic, operational, and tactical decisions. The most important strategic decisions of the two Koreas pertain to national reunification. North Korea's strategy of reunification, adopted in the early 1960s, consists of fostering "revolutionary forces" on three fronts—North Korea, South Korea, and the world at large. This means, first of all, making an all-out effort to strengthen North Korea's economic, military, and political capabilities. These in turn provide the resources with which to encourage revolutionary forces in the South and to generate support in the world arena. The second component of the strategy is to consolidate revolutionary forces in the South by organizing a Marxist-Leninist party that will serve as the "main force of revolution," winning the support of peasants and industrial workers, uniting the popular masses from all walks of life behind the banner of national reunification, and dealing a crushing blow to counterrevolutionary forces. The dual aim of the southern revolution is to force the US troops to withdraw from South Korea and to replace their "fascist lackeys" with progressive leaders. When these steps are completed, reunification can occur by the simple process of merger or "confederation" of the two governments in Korea.

The third and final component of Pyongyang's reunification strategy is the task of forging bonds and solidarity with all nations and peoples who are opposed to imperialism in general and American imperialism in particular. This entails explaining North Korea's positions and winning support for them on the world stage. It also implies the need to counter South Korea's diplomatic efforts and to undermine its legitimacy.

South Korea's strategy of reunification boils down to building national power, with emphasis on economic power. The ultimate goal is to "prevail over communism." Unlike Syngman Rhee, Park Chung Hee eschewed any explicit threat of invading the North. Nonetheless, he failed to articulate clearly how North Korea, which has steadfastly rejected the UN formula of holding free elections in all parts of Korea based on the principles of one man, one vote and the secret ballot, would be induced to join hands with its archrival as what can only be a junior partner. What is patently clear, however, is that North Korea's own blueprint is totally unacceptable to South Korea. Park's successor, Chun Doo Hwan, has put forth a comprehensive proposal for reunification, beginning with the conclusion of a provisional agreement and the exchange of cabinet-level permanent envoys between Seoul and Pyongyang and proceeding to the drafting and ratification of a constitution for a unified Korea.

Operational decisions, by definition, are less stable than strategic ones. They encompass a number of tactical episodes and represent adaptations to changes in the operational environment that fall short of strategic transformation. The most striking change in the operational directions of the two Koreas was signaled by the initiation of dialogue in the early 1970s. Sparked by a dramatic change in the external setting of the Korean peninsula—the rapprochement of Washington and Beijing, the principal allies of the two Korean adversaries—the dialogue reflected the first joint efforts by the two Koreas to find solutions to their common problem of national partition. It never really got off the ground, not only because of the depth of mutual distrust but, more importantly, because of the incompatibility of their respective strategic aims.

Other noteworthy operational decisions have included North Korea's decision, first unveiled in 1974, to seek direct dialogue with the United States; its attempt to revive the North-South dialogue in early 1980 in the wake of Park Chung Hee's assassination; its proposal, unveiled in October 1980, for the establishment of the "Democratic Confederal Republic of Koryŏ"; South Korea's decision to normalize relations with Japan in 1965; its decision to send combat troops to Vietnam in the same year; its proclamation of an open door policy in 1973; and its massive diplomatic offensive in the area of reunification in 1982.

Numerous tactical episodes mark the checkered history of inter-Korean relations. Initiatives taken by one side have necessitated tactical responses by the other. President Park Chung Hee's proposal on June 23, 1973 for the simultaneous entry of North and South Korea into the United Nations as separate members was promptly countered by President Kim Il Sung's proposal for the entry of the two Koreas as a single member under the rubric of the "Confederal Republic of Koryŏ." When Park proposed in January 1979 a meeting of the "authorities of the South and the North" at a mutually convenient time and place, North Korea resorted to the tactic of symbolically downgrading Park by having a nongovernmental body, the Central Committee of the Democratic Front for the Reunification of the Fatherland make a counterproposal for the convening of a "great national conference" of representatives of political parties, social organizations, and patriotic individuals.

Pyongyang reacted in a similar fashion to the proposal made jointly by Presidents Carter and Park in July 1979 for tripartite talks among "senior official representatives" of North Korea, South Korea, and the United States. It rejected the proposal but suggested that it would not object to Seoul's participation as an observer in bilateral talks between Pyongyang and Washington. Finally, when President Chun Doo Hwan proposed in January 1981 that a summit meeting be held between the presidents of the two Korean states either in Pyongyang or in Seoul, North Korea countered with a vehement denunciation of Chun, calling him an "illegal president" who was totally unfit to participate in any negotiations with North Korea. Pyongyang specifically cited Chun's bloody suppression of the Kwangju Rebellion as a major disqualifying factor. Pyongyang's response to a barrage of proposals emanating from Seoul in 1982 was essentially in the same vein.

Seoul's successful bid to initiate Red Cross talks with Pyongyang in August 1971 was, strictly speaking, not an initiative but a tactical response to North Korea's unprecedented declaration four days earlier that it was willing to talk with any body in the South, including the ruling Democratic-Republican party. When North Korea made another unprecedented gesture in January 1980 by referring to its southern rival as the Republic of Korea in its bid to resume the dialogue, South Korea reciprocated the gesture and then proposed preliminary talks for the convening of a meeting of the prime ministers of the two Koreas. President Chun's overtures toward the North in 1981 and 1982 were obviously based on a number of tactical considerations, not the least of which was a desire to counter President Kim Il Sung's October 1980 proposal for the establishment of a Democratic Confederal Republic of Koryŏ.

The impact of the various foreign policy decisions has been mixed. If the occurrence or nonoccurrence of the consequences that are manifestly intended by the decision makers is used as the criterion of evaluation, many of the key decisions emerge as striking failures. Pyongyang's reunification strategy is a case in point. Not only has the intended outcome failed to materialize, notwithstanding more than two decades of tenacious efforts by North Korea, but the goal remains as elusive as ever. Nor has Pyongyang made any headway in attaining the twin intermediate goals of inducing the withdrawal of US troops from South Korea and installing a democratic regime in Seoul. Equally sterile have been Seoul's persistent efforts since the late 1970s to resuscitate the dialogue. Neither the late President Park's proposals for the resumption of talks at the official level nor President Chun Doo Hwan's ringing declaration that "I shall go to Pyongyang, if invited" have produced any tangible results.

It would be an error, however, to conclude that the impact of such policies and actions has been either negative or nil. For they typically entail symbolic payoffs or perform some latent functions. For example, both Pyongyang and Seoul have utilized their foreign policy pronouncements as tools of propaganda and diplomatic competition. Both have also used them for internal political purposes. In Pyongyang's case, reunification has become a national obsession in whose name a gargantuan effort at nation-building has thus far been justified. The continuing presence of US troops, instead of serving as a reminder of the failure of Pyongyang's policy, has provided its ruling elite with a ready-made object of intense political indoctrination, a tool for strengthening the unity of the people. Seoul, for its part, has held up Pyongyang's refusal to respond positively to its initiatives as proof of the latter's aggressive designs, which in turn have been used time and again as pretexts for curbing civil liberties and enhancing the powers of the incumbent regime.

There have also been some policies whose outcomes have been quite favorable. North Korea's policy toward its feuding Communist neighbors is a notable example of a skillful balancing act that has enabled Pyongyang simultaneously to champion independence and to receive substantial assistance from both Beijing and Moscow. Equally efficacious has been North Korean diplomacy in the Third World and beyond, which has paid off in its admission to the UN system, in the passage of a pro-Pyongyang resolution in the UN for the first time in its history, in its admission to the Nonalignment Movement, and in the adoption of a series of pro-Pyongyang statements in the conferences of the nonaligned countries.

South Korea, too, has enjoyed several notable successes. Although its campaign to influence policymakers that touched off the Koreagate scandal was a major blunder, it has successfully weathered the crisis, and managed not only to maintain but also to strengthen its security and economic ties with the United States. President Chun Doo Hwan's visit to the United States and his meeting with President Reagan in February 1981 represented a diplomatic coup of considerable proportions for Chun. Judging from its results, the late Park Chung Hee's decision to normalize relations with Japan appears to have been a profitable one for South Korea. That decision, together with his equally controversial decision to dispatch combat troops to Vietnam, helped to lay the groundwork for Seoul's spectacular economic growth. Finally, Chun Doo Hwan's tour of the countries of the ASEAN in mid 1981 appears to have produced sizable payoffs for his regime.

FOREIGN POLICY IN COMPARATIVE PERSPECTIVE

How, in broad terms, does the foreign policy of North Korea compare with that of South Korea? And how do both stack up against those of other nations? We have already noted that the two Koreas share three basic patterns in their conduct of external relations: (1) the pursuit of the triple strategic goals of legitimacy, security, and development; (2) the accent on self-reliance; and (3) the intermingling of rigidity and flexibility. One may justifiably question the validity or utility of such generalizations on the ground that the postulated similarities are more imaginary than real—that they are based not so much on the actual convergence of behaviors as on the generality of the concepts employed.

The problem is a real one, and may be linked to the notion of "patterns": by definition, patterns are abstractions from the universe of discrete behaviors and, as such, possess a high level of generality. An excessive amount of distortion, however, can be averted by highlighting some of the differences *within* each of the patterns and by shifting the focus of comparison to discrete behaviors.[1] As previously mentioned, the two Koreas differ not only with respect to the specific contents of the strategic goals they share at the conceptual level but also in terms of the relative primacy of the goals. Nor do they accentuate self-reliance to the same degree. As far as the frequency and vigor with which self-reliance is extolled and flaunted are concerned, North Korea clearly outperforms South Korea. While the gap narrows considerably in terms of actual practice, Seoul is more openly dependent upon its interactions, both commercial and other, with the outside world than Pyongyang is. Finally, to say that both Seoul and Pyongyang manifest a blending of rigidity and flexibility in their respective international behaviors is not the same as suggesting that they are comparable in terms of the degree of rigidity or flexibility displayed. To this observer, Pyongyang's foreign policy seems to contain a higher quotient of rigidity than Seoul's.

Take their responses to the Sino-American opening in the early 1970s. The most noteworthy response of both, as we have seen, was a temporary softening of their hostile posture toward each other, which led to the North-South dialogue. Our analysis of the conduct of the dialogue showed, however, that North Korea was more dogmatic than South Korea—for example, in the former's insistence that the easing of the state of military confrontation should precede cultural, economic, and other exchanges. Pyongyang's thus far unsuccessful attempt to have direct bilateral talks with Washington also presents a striking example of the absence of flexibility on the former's part. Not only has Pyongyang failed to provide any incentives to Washington for a positive response by, for example, suspending polemics for an extended period of time, but it has refused to accept the repeated message from Washington that no talks will be held without the participation of Seoul.

This leads us to another aspect of the differences between the foreign policies of the two Koreas—namely, the relative potency of the various input or explanatory variables. Ideology, for example, appears to be a more potent variable in North Korea's foreign policy than in South Korea's. The seeming rigidity of Pyongyang's posture toward Washington is related to the positive ideology of *chuch'e* and the negative ideology of antiimperialism. The former enthrones the virtue of national pride and self-respect, while the latter reinforces

---

1. On the importance of differentiating between "pattern behavior" and "discrete behavior," consult Maurice A. East, Stephen A. Salmore, and Charles F. Hermann (eds.), *Why Nations Act: Theoretical Perspectives for Comparative Foreign Policy Studies* (Beverly Hills, CA: Sage Publications, 1978), pp. 196–197.

Pyongyang's conviction that "US imperialism" is its mortal enemy. All this makes it exceedingly difficult for North Korea to extend an olive branch to Washington until and unless the latter softens its posture first. Hence the complete absence of any conciliatory language in its proposals for direct negotiations with the United States. "We have made our move," DPRK Vice-Premier Chong Jun Gi told a group of visiting US scholars in Pyongyang in July 1981, "and it is the United States' turn to act." Chong made it clear that North Korea would not even make any symbolic concessions with the aim of inducing change in Washington's attitude.[2] In the case of South Korea, ideology has frequently been eclipsed by pragmatic considerations. Notwithstanding its strong antipathy to communism, Seoul has formally embraced the policy of improving relations with any and all "nonhostile" Communist nations and has adjusted its rhetoric and actions accordingly.

Another variable that appears to have more explanatory power vis-à-vis North Korea than it does South Korea is political dynamics. To a striking degree, the rigidity of North Korean behavior is attributable to the exalted position of the supreme leader in its political system. As we have seen already, this hampers the operation of a rational decision-making process—in the sense of facilitating a reasonably comprehensive and dispassionate evaluation of policy options—and constrains the capability of the system, particularly the foreign policy apparatus, to collect and transmit information regarding the operational environment. The problem seems to be negligible in South Korea where the concentration of power in the hands of the top leader has not been carried to the same degree as in the North. Nor has it been accompanied by any concerted attempt at building a personality cult around him.

Let us now compare the foreign policy behaviors of the two Koreas with those of other nations. In order to make our task manageable, we shall make an impressionistic assessment of the extent to which selected propositions about foreign policy in general conform to or deviate from the Korean data examined in this study. Consider, first of all, the proposition that "there is a positive relationship between decision-makers' perceptions of hostility and the level of violence of their nation's foreign policy acts."[3] The preceding survey

2. I was a member of the delegation, which included five other American scholars of Korean origin; I asked the question about Pyongyang's policy toward the United States. As I noted in the preceding chapter, Chong denied, erroneously, that the North Korean press had attacked President Reagan personally. The interview was conducted on July 31, 1981 in Vice-Premier Chong's office in one of the buildings housing the DPRK Administration Council in Pyongyang.

3. Patrick J. McGowan and Howard B. Shapiro, *The Comparative Study of Foreign Policy: A Survey of Scientific Findings* (Beverly Hills, CA: Sage Publications, 1973), p. 56. The original quotation is in italics.

leaves little doubt that the top political leaders of the two Koreas have perceived each other as extremely hostile. The level of violence used against each other, however, does not appear to have been commensurate with the degree of perceived hostility. For the latter has remained more or less constant, while the former has fluctuated. In overall terms, both sides, with the notable exception of the Korean War period (1950–1953), have exercised restraint. On the other hand, the periodic crises triggered by North Korea's use of violence against the United States may be linked with the consistently high degree of perceived hostility on the part of Pyongyang.

Another proposition based on comparative data states that "the greater the degree of centralization in a government, the more likely that the nation will be involved in foreign conflict."[4] If conflict is defined to encompass "both diplomatic and violent foreign conflict,"[5] then both North and South Korea have experienced conflict on numerous occasions. Their conflict with each other has ranged the whole gamut, from a shooting war to mutual recriminations. North Korea has experienced conflict of sorts with both of its principal allies, the Soviet Union and the PRC, and diplomatic conflict with both Western and Third World nations, namely, Australia (1975), Argentina (1977), Mauritania (1977), and Iraq (1980). Finally, Pyongyang's three decades-long conflict with the United States, notwithstanding its attempts since 1974 to enter into direct negotiations with Washington, can only be described as monumental. South Korea, too, has periodically engaged in conflict of a mild variety with the United States and, more particularly, Japan. However, it lacks an object of perennial conflict that would rival Pyongyang's "American imperialism." Is one warranted in construing North Korea's greater involvement in foreign conflicts as a function of the slightly greater extent to which its government is centralized? I am inclined to believe that ideology and historical legacy have more to do with Pyongyang's track record than does the degree of centralization.

Still another conventional wisdom derived from the literature of comparative foreign policy alerts us to the phenomenon of covariation between economic development and diplomatic activity.[6] Although the Korean data do suggest that a steady increase in the level of economic development of both Seoul and Pyongyang has been paralleled by a growing vigor in their respective diplomatic activities, they also reveal that the relationship is by no means linear. The busiest period in South Korean diplomacy in terms of adding new diplomatic partners was the early 1960s, when it was embarking upon, but had not yet made any significant headway in, economic development.

4. Ibid., p. 70.   5. Ibid.   6. Ibid., p. 108.

The related proposition that "the greater a nation's trade, the more ties of other kinds it will have with other nations"[7] receives only a partial confirmation from the Korean experience: for both the trade-oriented South and the autarkically inclined North have forged a staggering number of diplomatic, cultural, and other ties with the rest of the world. Nor does the slight edge in the number of diplomatic partners Seoul enjoys over Pyongyang adequately reflect the fact that the former's trade volume is thirteen times that of the latter.

We have already alluded to the influence of ideology on the formulation of foreign policy. Does the Korean experience lend support to the finding that "ideology seems to be a more potent force in the formulation of policy than is national interest"?[8] Seoul's track record does not support this finding, but Pyongyang's probably does, although the evidence is not clear-cut. If, as noted above, the relative inflexibility of Pyongyang's policy toward the United States stems in large measure from its ideology, North Korea's oscillating posture toward the Sino-Soviet dispute may bespeak the primacy of national interest over ideology.

Another postulate in the field of comparative foreign policy is that cultural similarity of nations is inversely related to the level of violent behavior between them.[9] This postulate, however, is modified by the additional insight that "for nations already in violent conflict, cultural and racial similarity will not reduce (or increase) the *intensity* of the violence."[10] The relevance of these ideas for the two Koreas is not crystal clear. On the one hand, if one posits their cultural similarity, then the intensity of their conflict can be explained away by the fact that they were "already in violent conflict" when their mutual interactions began; the Korean War broke out within two years of the establishment of the two rival regimes. On the other hand, it can be argued that the cultures of the two Koreas are more dissimilar than similar, particularly if one focuses on their respective political cultures. Indeed, one of the strongest impressions I brought out of North Korea after a visit of two and a half weeks in 1981 was the enormity of the gap—political, ideological, cultural, and other—between North and South Korea. If that is the case, the proposition is supported by the Korean case.

Several studies using longitudinal data from a large number of nations have found that "external aggression expressed is highly related to amount of aggression received" and that "conflict sent" is directly related to "conflict received."[11] The records of the two Koreas

7. Ibid., p. 115.
8. Ibid., p. 126.
9. Ibid.
10. Ibid., p. 127.
11. Ibid., p. 149.

tend, by and large, to support these findings. The aggressive behavior of the two Koreas toward each other forms a vicious circle, although isolated incidents of violence cannot always be explained in terms of stimulus and response or provocation and retaliation. North Korea's resort to violence against the United States may also be viewed as conforming to the same basic pattern. In the more spectacular of the incidents—notably, the *Pueblo* incident, the EC-121 incident, and the Panmunjom ax-murder case—there were certainly provocations by the United States from the North Korean perspective, although the amount of violence used by North Korea was disproportionately large, especially from the American point of view. What Pyongyang's behavior underscores is the need to focus on the *perceptions* of the actor regarding the amount of aggression or conflict received.

It has also been shown that "the pattern of threats nations direct at each other and the subsequent level of fear affects the foreign policies of nations."[12] We have seen a number of cases in which such a syndrome was operative. The emergence of a military regime in 1961 for the first time in South Korea's history, coupled with the militantly anti-Communist posture it adopted, appeared to heighten the level of fear in Pyongyang, leading the latter to seek military alliances with Moscow and Beijing. The abortive commando raid on the presidential mansion in Seoul and the forcible seizure of the USS *Pueblo* in Wonsan Bay in January 1968 laid bare both the vulnerability of South Korea and the United States and the bellicosity of North Korea. They resulted in the upgrading of Seoul-Washington security cooperation and the beefing up of their combined arsenal in South Korea.

Studies investigating the linkage between foreign aid and political influence have yielded mixed findings. On the one hand, "economic assistance [by the United States and the Soviet Union] has proven to be a useful instrument for establishing political entree, maintaining a presence, and gaining access to decision-makers in less developed countries." On the other hand, the actual influence of the donor on the policies and behaviors of the recipient has been found to be "modest at best." "Even very specific attempts at influence—in the form of sanctions withholding aid—have been largely unsuccessful."[13] The Korean data seem to be congruent with these findings. With the notable exception of the formative stage of the two Korean states, when their respective patron states wielded major influence, the principal donors of aid to Seoul and Pyongyang have had but modest success in influencing the behaviors of their recipients. The United States, for example, was unable to abort the coup d'etat by Park Chung Hee in 1961; nor did its feeble attempts to check the sei-

12. Ibid., p. 151.   13. Ibid., pp. 155–156.

zure of power by Chun Doo Hwan in 1980 succeed. The most spectacular demonstration of the limits of American influence over South Korea was Syngman Rhee's defiant release of North Korean prisoners of war in 1953. North Korea's major benefactors—the Soviet Union and the PRC—have been equally unsuccessful in keeping their client state in line, but in this case the dynamics of their conflict have been a major factor blunting their political clout.

It is almost trite to stress that "variations in the external environment tend to be related to variations in foreign policy over time." Subsumed under this bland proposition, however, is the significant finding that cooperative behavior and conflictual behavior "are associated more with variations in international situation than with variations in domestic situation."[14] The Korean situation appears to lend some support to this finding. The first major breakthrough in inter-Korean relations, the initiation of dialogue, came in the wake of momentous change in Korea's international environment, and the first serious, albeit unsuccessful, attempt to revive the dialogue also materialized against the backdrop of significant developments in the international arena. This, I hasten to add, is not to suggest that internal factors have not played a major part in perpetuating the basically conflictual relationship between the two Koreas. Indeed, the probability of significant change in inter-Korean relations hinges equally on dramatic developments in internal and international situations.

That the top leaders of Seoul and Pyongyang alike have used foreign policy or international relations to enhance their own power at home is consistent with the findings of other studies, which show that foreign policy actions in various contexts "may serve to solidify the position of top leaders," "are effective in alleviating the tension on political leaders in a cross-pressure situation," and "have been used by leaders . . . to create internal political unity."[15]

Finally, how do the Korean data square with the proposition that "the failure of a foreign policy leads to radical, rather than incremental, shifts in that policy"?[16] The failure of North Korea's policy of forcible reunification in 1953 did indeed lead to a shift in its reunification policy, but whether the new policy, the strategy of building up triple revolutionary forces, represents a radical or an incremental shift is open to debate. What complicates our evaluation is the uncertainty regarding Pyongyang's true intentions. Has it really jettisoned any hope of invading the South again? The successive leaders of South Korea have said no, and their principal ally, the United States, apparently concurs in that view. My own position is that whatever the

14. Ibid., pp. 161–162.   15. Ibid., p. 202.   16. Ibid., p. 207.

hopes and aspirations of the North Korean leaders may be, the *probability* of renewed invasion is rather low.[17] This view has been reinforced by my firsthand observations of the fruits of North Korean investments in economic construction and of the pride with which the North Korean leaders show them off to foreign visitors, of whom there has been an interminable flow in the past several years. It struck me as highly improbable that North Korea would be willing to risk the destruction of what it has so laboriously built up over the past three decades.

On the other hand, the unmistakable failure of a number of Pyongyang's policies—the policy of seeking direct negotiations with the United States, for example, and the policy of building up pro-North Korean revolutionary forces in the South—has not led to any modification, let alone a "radical shift," in either their contents or in the tactics used to advance them. In the case of South Korea, while the failure of its policy toward Japan to produce any substantive payoffs led eventually to a radical shift—namely, the policy of diplomatic normalization at the price of substantial concessions—the principal factor in the equation was not the perception of the sterility of the erstwhile policy but a change in political leadership in Seoul. The adoption of the much-vaunted open door policy in 1973, although based on the failure of Seoul's previous policy (the so-called Hallstein doctrine) was in reality less a radical shift in that policy than a ratification of faits accomplis.

In sum, the behaviors of the two Koreas turn out to be neither neatly congruent with the dominant patterns in the world arena nor completely deviant cases. They conform to the established patterns in many respects, but there are also a fair number of unique circumstances that help make aspects of their respective foreign policies sui generis. Finally, the inconsistency between the Korean data and some of the propositions examined above does not necessarily invalidate the latter, given their predominantly probabilistic orientation.

POLICY IMPLICATIONS

Although this study has been concerned with the description and analysis of the foreign policies of the two Koreas, it cannot claim to have been wholly unencumbered by the author's value judgments. Intellectual honesty decrees, therefore, that I spell out in the open what

17. For an elaboration of this view, see B. C. Koh, "The Korean War as a Learning Experience for North Korea," *Korea & World Affairs* 3, 3 (Fall 1979): 366–384.

I see as the normative implications of my endeavor. If one should shy away from committing the logical fallacy of deducing what ought to be from what is, one need not be timid in articulating what can be.[18] The brief discussion that follows, however, assumes that the boundary line between the realms of what ought to be and what can be is far from clear-cut and that the two overlap to a significant degree.

The point of departure for our short excursion is a consideration of the principal values that need to be and can be maximized with respect to the two Koreas. First and foremost, peace in the peninsula needs to be preserved. Preserving peace and ensuring that it will not be disrupted will benefit not only the Korean people but their neighbors in northeast Asia and in the world at large. A related value is the well-being of the Korean people, which the prevention of war and the elimination of conflict will go a long way toward promoting. The values of individual dignity, liberty, and equality ought to be and can be pursued with more vigor in a peaceful environment. Finally, the abatement or disappearance of the danger of war will make it possible to devote the bulk of the finite resources available to the Korean people to construction rather than to destruction; they can get on with the task of creating happiness instead of squandering their efforts on deterrence.

What are the conditions that will facilitate attaining these values? The ultimate condition, needless to say, will be the peaceful reunification of the peninsula, leading to the establishment of a truly democratic government. Short of that, a substantial easing of tensions, the resumption of dialogue, and the initiation of multifaceted intercourse between the two Koreas will go a long way toward the approximation of some of the constructive values. The initiation of North-South intercourse, for example, implies the opening up of each society to the other, which in turn will provide an eye-opening experience for the inhabitants of North and South Korea alike; they will experience culture shock on discovering that the conditions in the other society are a far cry from what they had been led to believe—that neither the South nor the North is the kind of a living hell depicted by each other's propaganda and control apparatus and that both societies have notable strengths as well as weaknesses. Should such an opening indeed take place, it would surely necessitate radical changes in the policies of both sides, of which their respective citizenry—

18. In the words of Max Lerner: "Machiavelli sought to distinguish the realm of what ought to be and the realm of what is. He rejected the first for the second. But there is a third realm: the realm of what can be. It is in that realm that what one might call a humanist realism can lie. The measure of man is to extend this sphere of the socially possible." As quoted by Alvin W. Gouldner in *Patterns of Industrial Bureaucracy* (New York: Free Press, 1964), p. 28.

hence the Korean people as a whole—would become primary beneficiaries. Furthermore, the end of diplomatic competition between the two Koreas will signify the end to the waste of precious resources in undercutting each other—a counterproductive ritual in which there are no real winners and only losers, namely, the entire Korean people.

What, then, are some of the concrete steps that must be taken to realize these intermediate conditions? Each side must begin by showing its good will toward the other. There are both small, risk-free measures and relatively large, somewhat risky measures that can potentially reduce the level of animosity in the peninsula: not using the pejorative and inaccurate term "puppets" (*koeroe*); calling each other by their official names once in a while; stopping propaganda broadcasts aimed at each other; stopping all provocative military activities such as shooting across the DMZ, dispatching spies and infiltrators to the other side, conducting reconnaissance flights over the claimed territory of the other side, or conducting military exercises and war games. These steps need to be taken on a unilateral basis initially, and the other side should be given plenty of time to assess their implications. Implementing moves step by step, from small to large measures, and without any fanfare or publicity will probably enhance the chances of a favorable response from the other side. Even if they should turn out to be unsuccessful in eliciting reciprocal measures, the small and inexpensive steps need not necessarily be reversed. In fact, such a gesture will mean a symbolic victory for the party concerned.

The final push for the resumption of dialogue should be made covertly, not through the public forum. There are numerous places where behind-the-scenes contacts can be made between the representatives of the two Koreas, such as the United Nations, where both have permanent observer missions, or the scores of capitals in which diplomats of both countries are posted. The process that led to the publication of the North-South joint statement on July 4, 1972 should serve as a model and a precedent. It should also suggest some of the pitfalls to be avoided. The sincerity of both parties and ample discussion of the meanings and implications of the phraseology of any joint statement that may emanate from such encounters are absolutely essential.

Notwithstanding the commitment of both Seoul and Pyongyang to *chuch'e*, the four Pacific powers cannot be completely left out of the process described above. Their stakes are too great to be ignored, and their influence on the Korean question still remains considerable. The best course of action for all of them, however, will be to take a low-key approach. The less noise the great powers make, the greater the prospects of harmony, *provided the two Koreas have already made preliminary contacts.* At the same time, great power stakes and influence call for an expenditure of every effort in the direction of creating conditions conducive to the rapprochement of the two Korean states.

To consider briefly what the United States is potentially capable of contributing, I start with the proposition that US policy toward Korean reunification has been singularly sterile. The amount of attention and priority Washington has given to the problem has thus far been disproportionately small and peripheral. The contrast with America's Middle East policy is striking. Do not American stakes and interests in the Korean peninsula warrant a higher priority and a more imaginative policy than what we have witnessed thus far?

At the very least, Washington needs to pursue an independent policy and to take some calculated risks. It should differentiate between the interests of the Korean people as a whole and those of any particular regime. One possible way to break the current impasse in Korea is for the United States to respond positively to North Korean overtures. I must hasten to point out that agreeing to talk with North Korea initially on its own terms—that is, without the participation of Seoul—does not mean that the United States will help North Korea attain its goals. Getting the process started is important. Those of us who have had a chance to visit North Korea and talk with its officials and academics can testify that their level of ignorance of the United States is appalling and that the amount of misinformation in their heads is monumental. There are mirror images of villains and maniacs between Pyongyang on one hand and Washington and Seoul on the other. Dialogue is bound to ameliorate the situation, for the latter cannot deteriorate any further, short of a shooting war.

Should the United States decide to talk with North Korea, it should make the continuation of dialogue contingent upon the resumption of dialogue between Seoul and Pyongyang. The North Koreans, in my view, are so eager to improve relations with the United States that such a tactic is likely to work. Such a procedure would allow them to save face and jettison their counterproductive policy at the same time. Should this senario be implemented, three sets of dyads would come into being: (1) North Korea-US talks, (2) North Korea-South Korea talks, and (3) South Korea-US talks. This would be a functional equivalent of the trilateral talks proposed by Presidents Carter and Park in 1979. The eventual realization of direct three-way talks is highly probable in the context of this scenario.

How credible are the ideas outlined above? Do they really lie in the realm of what can be? My short-term prognosis is rather pessimistic. The known predispositions of the current leaders of the two Korean states and the United States make it unlikely that a breakthrough of any sort will occur in the near future. The kind of mutual exchanges envisaged above would entail destabilizing consequences for both of the incumbent Korean leaders, and they probably know it. Leaders, however, are mortal human beings, and the history of a nation and the destiny of a people need to be looked at from the perspective of generations and, perhaps, centuries. From such an intermediate-term or a long-term perspective, change is not only possible but inevitable. One major question is the nature of succession that is likely to occur in North Korea. Should Kim Il Sung's current plan to have his son, Jong Il, succeed him be implemented without a hitch, the prospects for significant change in inter-Korean relations will probably remain as clouded as ever. Even such an eventuality would merely postpone, not preclude, change. In a word, a Korea free from fear—fear of war, fear of hunger, and fear of oppression—is surely within the realm of what can be, if not for the current generation, then for the generations to come.

BIBLIOGRAPHY

ENGLISH SOURCES

Books, Monographs, and Pamphlets

Abramowitz, Morton. *Moving the Glacier: The Two Koreas and the Powers.* Adelphi Paper No. 80. London: International Institute for Strategic Studies, 1971.
A Handbook of Korea. Seoul: Korean Overseas Information Service, 1982.
A Handbook on (Inter-Korean) South-North Dialogue. Seoul: Research Center for Peace and Unification, 1979.
Allison, Graham T. *Essense of Decision: Explaining the Cuban Missile Crisis.* Boston: Little, Brown, 1971.
Asia 1977 Yearbook. Hong Kong: Far Eastern Economic Review, 1977.
Baldwin, Frank, ed. *Without Parallel: The American-Korean Relationship Since 1945.* New York: Pantheon Books, 1974.
Barnds, William J., ed. *The Two Koreas in East Asian Affairs.* New York: New York University Press, 1976.
Brecher, Michael. *The Foreign Policy System of Israel: Settings, Images, Process.* New Haven: Yale University Press, 1972.
Clough, Ralph N. *Deterrence and Defense in Korea: The Role of U.S. Forces.* Washington, D.C.: Brookings Institution, 1976.
Chung, Chin O. *P'yongyang Between Peking and Moscow: North Korea's Involvement in the Sino-Soviet Dispute, 1958–1976.* University, AL: University of Alabama Press, 1978.
Chung, Chong-Shik, ed. *Korean Unification: Source Materials With an Introduction.* Vol. 2. Seoul: Research Center for Peace and Unification, 1979.
Chung, Joseph S. *The North Korean Economy: Structure and Development.* Stanford: Hoover Institution Press, 1974.

Confrontation With Dialogue. Korea Policy Series, No. 5, July, 1972. Seoul: Korea Overseas Information Service, 1972.
Cumings, Bruce. *The Origins of the Korean War.* Princeton: Princeton University Press, 1981.
East, Maurice A., Stephen A. Salmore, and Charles F. Hermann eds. *Why Nations Act: Theoretical Perspectives for Comparative Foreign Policy Studies.* Beverly Hills: Sage Publications, 1978.
Easton, David. *A Framework for Political Analysis.* Englewood Cliffs: Prentice-Hall, 1965.
Forging a New Era: The Fifth Republic of Korea. Seoul: Korean Overseas Information Service, 1981.
Gouldner, Alvin W. *Patterns of Industrial Bureaucracy.* New York: Free Press, 1964.
Han, Sungjoo. *The Failure of Democracy in South Korea.* Berkeley: University of California Press, 1974.
Henderson, Gregory. *Korea: The Politics of the Vortex.* Cambridge: Harvard University Press, 1968.
———, Richard N. Lebow, and John G. Stoessinger, eds. *Divided Nations in a Divided World.* New York: McKay, 1974.
How the Political Talks Between the North and the South Have Proceeded. Pyongyang: Central Committee of Korean Journalists Union, September 25, 1973.
International Institute for Strategic Studies. *The Military Balance, 1981–1982.* London: IISS, 1981.
Khrushchev Remembers. With an introduction, commentary, and notes by Edward Crankshaw. Translated by Strobe Talbott. New York: Bantam Books, 1971.
Kim, C. I. Eugene, ed. *Korean Unification: Problems and Prospects.* Kalamazoo: Korea Research and Publications, 1973.
Kim, Hak-Joon. *The Unification Policy of South and North Korea.* Seoul: Seoul National University Press, 1977.
Kim, Han-Kyo, ed. *Reunification of Korea: 50 Basic Documents.* Washington: Institute for Asian Studies, 1972.
———. *Studies on Korea: A Scholar's Guide.* Honolulu: University Press of Hawaii, 1980.
Kim, Ilpyong. *Communist Politics in North Korea.* New York: Praeger, 1975.
Kim, Il Sung. *For the Independent Peaceful Reunification of Korea.* New York: International Publishers, 1975.
———. *For the Independent Peaceful Reunification of Korea.* Rev. ed. New York: Guardian Associates, 1976.
———. *Juche! The Speeches and Writings of Kim Il Sung.* Edited and introduced by Li Yuk-sa. New York: Grossman, 1972.
———. *Report to the Sixth Congress of the Workers' Party of Korea on the Work of the Central Committee.* Pyongyang: Foreign Languages Publishing House, 1980.
———. *Selected Works.* 7 vols. Pyongyang: Foreign Languages Publishing House, 1971–1979.
———. *Talks With Executive Managing Editor of Japanese Yomiuri Shimbun*

and His Party. Pyongyang: Foreign Languages Publishing House, 1977.
―――. *The Non-Alignment Movement Is a Mighty Anti-Imperialist Revolutionary Force of Our Times*. Pyongyang: Foreign Languages Publishing House, 1976.
Kim, Joungwon A. *Divided Korea: The Politics of Development, 1945–1972*. Cambridge: Harvard University, East Asia Research Center, 1975.
Kim, Kwan Bong. *The Korea-Japan Treaty Crisis and the Instability of the Korean Political System*. New York: Praeger, 1971.
Kim, Se-Jin, ed. *Korean Unification: Source Materials With an Introduction*. Seoul: Research Center for Peace and Unification, 1976.
――― and Chang-Hyun Cho. *Korea: A Divided Nation*. Silver Spring, MD: Research Institute on Korean Affairs, 1976.
Kim, Young C., ed. *Foreign Policies of Korea*. Washington: Institute for Asian Studies, 1973.
―――. *Major Powers and Korea*. Silver Spring, MD: Research Institute on Korean Affairs, 1973.
――― and Abraham M. Halpern, eds. *The Future of the Korean Peninsula*. New York: Praeger, 1977.
Koh, Byung Chul. *The Foreign Policy of North Korea*. New York: Praeger, 1969.
Kuznets, Paul W. *Economic Growth and Structure in the Republic of Korea*. New Haven: Yale University Press, 1977.
Lasswell, Harold D. *Power and Personality*. New York: Viking Press, 1962.
Lee, Chae-Jin and Hideo Sato. *U.S. Policy Toward Japan and Korea*. New York: Praeger, 1982.
Lee, Chong-Sik. *The Korean Workers' Party: A Short History*. Stanford: Hoover Institution Press, 1978.
Lee, Mun Woong. *Rural North Korea Under Communism: A Study of Sociocultural Change*. Rice University Studies, Vol. 62, No. 1. Houston: Rice University, 1976.
Major Speeches by Korea's Park Chung Hee. Seoul: Hollym Corp., 1970.
Major Speeches by President Park Chung Hee, Republic of Korea. Seoul: Samhwa Publishing Co., no date.
McGowan, Patrick J. and Howard B. Shapiro. *The Comparative Study of Foreign Policy: A Survey of Scientific Findings*. Beverly Hills: Sage Publications, 1973.
New Year Press Conference by President Park Chung Hee, January 1977. Seoul: Korean Overseas Information Service, 1977.
Oh, John Kie-chiang. *Korea: Democracy on Trial*. Ithaca: Cornell University Press, 1968.
Oliver, Robert T. *Syngman Rhee and American Involvement in Korea, 1942–1960*. Seoul: Panmun Book Co., 1978.
Our Effort Toward Peaceful Unification. Seoul: National Unification Board, 1978.
Paige, Glenn D. *The Korean Decision*. New York: Free Press, 1968.
Park, Chung Hee. *Our Nation's Path*. Seoul: Hollym Corp., 1962, 1970.
―――. *Korea Reborn: A Model For Development*. Englewood Cliffs, NJ: Prentice-Hall, 1979.
―――. *The Country, The Revolution, and I*. Seoul: Hollym Corp., 1963.

Report on the Investigation of Kim Dae-jung. Seoul: Korean Overseas Information Service, July 1980.
Republic of Korea, Economic Planning Board. *Major Statistics of the Korean Economy.* Seoul: EPB, 1979.
Rosenau, James N., ed. *Comparing Foreign Policies: Theories, Findings, and Methods.* Beverly Hills: Sage Publications, 1974.
Scalapino, Robert A. *Asia and the Road Ahead: Issues for the Major Powers.* Berkeley: University of California Press, 1975.
―――, ed. *North Korea Today.* New York: Praeger, 1963.
――― and Chong-Sik Lee. *Communism in Korea.* 2 vols. Berkeley: University of California Press, 1972.
Snyder, Richard C., H. W. Bruck, and B. Sapin. *Decision-Making as an Approach to the Study of International Politics.* Princeton: Princeton University, Organizational Behavior Section, 1954.
―――, eds. *Foreign Policy Decision-Making.* New York: Free Press, 1962.
South-North Dialogue in Korea. Nos. 5–28. Seoul: International Cultural Society of Korea, 1964–1982.
South and North Korea: Differing Approaches to Dialogue. Seoul: Research Center for Peace and Unification, no date.
Sprout, Harold and Margaret. *Man-Milieu Relationship Hypotheses in the Context of International Politics.* Princeton: Princeton University, Center of International Studies, 1956.
Suh, Dae-Sook. *Korean Communism, 1945–1980: A Reference Guide to the Political System.* Honolulu: University Press of Hawaii, 1981.
―――. *The Korean Communist Movement, 1918–1948.* Princeton: Princeton University Press, 1967.
――― and Chae-Jin Lee, eds. *Political Leadership in Korea.* Seattle: University of Washington Press, 1976.
Terrill, Ross. *800,000,000: The Real China.* New York: Delta Books, 1971.
The Building of an Independent National Economy in Korea. Pyongyang: Foreign Languages Publishing House, 1977.
The Republic of Korea's Basic Position on South-North Dialogue. Seoul: Research Center for Peace and Unification, 1979.
The Truth About the Attempted Insurrection by Kim Dae-jung and His Followers. Seoul: Korean Overseas Information Service, August 1980.
Toward Peaceful Unification: Selected Speeches by President Park Chung Hee. Seoul: Kwangmyong Publishing Co., 1976.
Tunnels of War. Seoul: Korean Overseas Information Service, 1978.
US Arms Control and Disarmament Agency. *World Military Expenditures and Arms Transfers, 1969–1978.* Washington, 1980.
US Central Intelligence Agency, National Foreign Assessment Center. *Korea: The Economic Race Between the North and the South.* Washington, January 1978.
US Congress, House of Representatives, Committee on Foreign Affairs. *The Korean Conundrum: A Conversation With Kim Il Sung.* Report of a study mission to South Korea, Japan, the People's Republic of China, and North Korea, July 12-21, 1980. 97th Congress, 1st session, August 1981.
US Congress, Senate Committee on Foreign Relations. *U.S. Troop Withdrawal*

from the Republic of Korea. A report by Senators Hubert H. Humphrey and John Glenn. 95th Congress, 2d session, January 9, 1978.
US Congress, Senate Select Committee on Ethics. *Korean Influence Inquiry*. 95th Congress, 2d session, October 10, 1978.
US Department of State. "President Carter: Soviet Invasion of Afghanistan." *Current Policy*, No. 123, January 4, 1980. Washington, 1980.
———. "President Ford's Pacific Doctrine." *News Release*, December 7, 1975. Honolulu, Hawaii. Washington, 1975.
———. *Report on Korea, 1977*. Special Report No. 40, January 1978. Washington, 1978.
———. *Report on Korea, 1980*. March 30, 1981. Washington, 1981.
———. "The Global Challenge and International Cooperation." Speech by Secretary Henry A. Kissinger before the Institute of World Affairs, University of Wisconsin, Milwaukee, Wisconsin, July 14, 1975. Washington, 1975.
———. *The Record on Korean Unification, 1943–1960: Narrative Summary with Principal Documents*, Department of State Publication No. 7083, Far Eastern Series No. 101. Washington, 1960.
———. "The U.S. Role in the United Nations." *Current Policy*, No. 11, March 1976. Washington, 1976.
———. "United States and Asia." Speech by Secretary Cyrus Vance before the Asia Society, June 29, 1977, New York. Washington, 1977.
Yang, Sung Chul. *Korea and Two Regimes: Kim Il Sung and Park Chung Hee*. Cambridge, MA: Schenkman Publishing Co., 1981.

Articles

"America's Role in Consolidating a Peaceful Balance and Promoting Economic Growth in Asia." Address by Secretary Vance. *Department of State Bulletin* 77, 1988 (August 1, 1977): 143.
Awanohara, Susumu. "Letter from Seoul." *Far Eastern Economic Review* (Nov. 12, 1976), 78.
———. "North Korea: Deeper in Debt." *Far Eastern Economic Review* (June 6, 1975) 52.
Cho, Soon Sung. "The Changing Pattern of Asian International Relations: Prospects for the Unification of Korea." *Journal of International Affairs* 27, 2 (1973): 213–231.
———. "The Politics of North Korea's Unification Policies, 1950–1965." *World Politics* 19, 1 (January 1967): 218–241.
Chung, Joseph S. "North Korea's Development Strategy and Economic Performance." In *Korea: A Divided Nation*, edited by Se-Jin Kim and Chang-Hyun Cho. Silver Spring, MD: Research Institute on Korean Affairs, 1976.
Clemens, Walter C., Jr. "GRIT at Panmunjom: Conflict and Cooperation in a Divided Korea." *Asian Survey* 13, 6 (June 1973): 531–559.
Cumings, Bruce G. "Kim's Korean Communism." *Problems of Communism* 23, 2 (March 1974): 27–40.

Galtung, Johan. "Divided Nations as Process: One Nation, Two States, and In-between: The Case of Korea." *Journal of Peace Research* 9 (1972): 345–360.

Grinter, Lawrence E. "South Korea, Military Aid and US Policy Options." In *The National Security Affairs Forum*. (Washington: National War College), Spring/Summer, 1975.

Hahn, Bae-ho. "Korea-Japan Relations in the 1970's," *Asian Survey* 20, 11 (November 1980): 1087–1097.

Han, Sungjoo. "South Korea and the United States: the Alliance Survives." *Asian Survey* 20, 11 (November 1980): 1075–1086.

———. "South Korea's Participation in the Vietnam Conflict: An Analysis of the U.S.-Korea Alliance." *Orbis* 21, 4 (Winter 1978): 893–912.

Harrison, Selig. "One Korea?" *Foreign Policy* 17 (Winter 1974–1975): 35–67.

Henderson, Gregory. "Korea: The Preposterous Division." *Journal of International Affairs* 27, 2 (1973): 204–212.

Jo, Yung-Hwan. "Japanese-Korean Relations and Asian Diplomacy." *Orbis* 11, 2 (Summer 1967): 582–593.

Kihl, Young Whan. "Comparative Study of the Political Systems of South and North Korea: A Research Note." *Korea & World Affairs* 5, 3 (Fall 1981): 383–402.

———. "Korea's Future: Seoul's Perspective." *Asian Survey* 17, 11 (November 1977): 1064–1076.

———. "North Korea: A Reevaluation." *Current History* 53, 474 (April 1982): 155–159, 180–182.

Kim, Chonghan. "Korea's Diplomacy toward Africa." *Orbis* 11, 3 (Fall 1967): 885–896.

Kim, Hong N. "Japanese-South Korean Relations in the Post-Vietnam Era." *Asian Survey* 16, 10 (October 1976): 981–995.

———. "South Korea's Relations with Japan." In *Foreign Policies of Korea*, edited by Young C. Kim. Washington: Institute for Asian Studies, 1973.

Kim, Samuel S. "Pyongyang, the Third World, and Global Politics." *Korea and World Affairs* 3, 4 (Winter 1979): 439–462.

———. "The Developmental Problems of Korean Nationalism." In *Korea: A Divided Nation*, edited by Se-Jin Kim and Chang-Hyon Cho. Silver Spring, MD: Research Institute on Korean Affairs, 1976.

Kim, Se-Jin. "South Korea's Involvement in Vietnam and Its Economic and Political Impact." *Asian Survey* 10, 6 (June 1970): 519–532.

Kim, Seung Hee. "Economic Development of South Korea." In *Korea: A Divided Nation*, edited by Se-Jin Kim and Chang-Hyun Cho. Silver Spring, MD: Research Institute on Korean Affairs, 1976.

Kim, Young C. "North Korea's Reunification Policy: A Magnificent Obsession." *Journal of Korean Affairs*, 3, 4 (January 1974): 15–24.

Ko, Seung K. "North Korea's Relations with Japan since Detente." *Pacific Affairs* 50, 1 (Spring 1977): 31–44.

Koh, B. C. "*Chuch'esong* in Korean Politics," *Studies in Comparative Communism* 7, 1 and 2 (Spring/Summer 1974): 83–97.

———. "Dilemmas of Korean Reunification." *Asian Survey* 19, 5 (May 1971): 475–495.

———. "Ideology and Political Control in North Korea." *Journal of Politics* 32, 3 (August 1970): 655–674.
———. "North Korea: A Breakthrough in the Quest for Unity." *Asian Survey* 13, 1 (January 1973): 83–93.
———. "North Korea and Its Quest for Autonomy." *Pacific Affairs* 38, 3 and 4 (Fall/Winter, 1965–1966): 294–306.
———. "North Korea and the Sino-Soviet Schism." *Western Political Quarterly* 22, 4 (December 1969): 940–962.
———. "North Korea in 1977: Year of 'Readjustment'." *Asian Survey* 18, 1 (January 1978): 36–44.
———. "North Korea 1976: Under Stress." *Asian Survey* 17, 1 (January 1977): 61–70.
———. "North Korea: Old Goals and New Realities." *Asian Survey* 14, 1 (January 1974): 36–42.
———. "Political Leadership in North Korea: Toward a Conceptual Understanding of Kim Il-sŏng's Leadership Behavior." *Korean Studies* (Honolulu) 2 (1978): 139–158.
———. "South Korea, North Korea, and Japan." *Pacific Community* (Tokyo) 6, 2 (January 1975): 205–219.
———. "The Battle Without Victors: The Korean Question in the 30th Session of the UN General Assembly." *Journal of Korean Affairs* 5, 4 (January 1976): 43–63.
———. "The Korean War as a Learning Experience for North Korea." *Korea & World Affairs* 3, 3 (Fall 1979): 366–384.
———. "The Korean Workers' Party and Detente." *Journal of International Affairs* 28, 2 (1974): 175–187.
———. "The *Pueblo* Incident in Perspective." *Asian Survey* 9, 4 (April 1969): 264–280.
———. "The Revolutionary Strategy of North Korea." *Pacific Community* (Tokyo) 2, 2 (January 1971): 354–364.
———. "The United Nations and the Politics of Korean Reunification." *Journal of Korean Affairs* 3, 4 (January 1974): 37–56.
Koo, Youngnok. "The Conduct of Foreign Affairs." In *Korean Politics in Transition*, edited by Edward R. Wright. Seattle: University of Washington Press, 1975.
Ledyard, Gari K. "The Historical Necessity of Korean Unification—Past History—Present Imperatives—Future Prospects." *Korean Journal of International Studies* 6, 2 (Spring 1975): 39–51.
Lee, Chae-Jin. "South Korea: The Politics of Domestic-Foreign Linkage." *Asian Survey* 13, 1 (January 1973): 94–101.
———. "The Direction of South Korea's Foreign Policy." *Korean Studies* (Honolulu) 2 (1978): 95–137.
Lee, Chong-Sik. "Korean Partition and Reunification." *Journal of International Affairs* 18, 2 (1964): 221–233.
Lee, Hong Yung. "Korea's Future: Peking's Perspective." *Asian Survey* 17, 11 (November 1977): 1088–1102.
Lee, Pong S. "An Estimate of North Korea's National Income." *Asian Survey* 12, 6 (June 1972): 518–526.

---. "Pattern of Economic Development: A Comparative Study of North and South Korea." Paper presented to the workshop on comparative study of North and South Korea, sponsored by the Joint Committee on Korean Studies, Social Science Research Council and American Council of Learned Societies, January 16–17, 1976, San Juan, Puerto Rico.
Lyman, Princeton N. "Korea's Involvement in Vietnam." *Orbis* 12, 2 (Summer 1968): 563–581.
Paige, Glenn D. "North Korea and the Emulation of Russian and Chinese Behavior." In *Communist Strategies in Asia*, edited by A. Doak Barnett. New York: Praeger, 1963.
Pak, Ki Hyuk. "A Comparative Study of the Agricultural Systems of North and South Korea." In *Agrarian Policies and Problems in Communist Countries*, edited by W. A. Douglas Jackson. Seattle: University of Washington Press, 1971.
Reischauer, Edwin O. and Gregory Henderson. "There's Danger in Korea Still." *New York Times Magazine*, May 20, 1973, pp. 42–56.
Richardson, Ron. "Breaking the Shell." *Far Eastern Economic Review*, June 26, 1981.
Scalapino, Robert A. "Current Dynamics of the Korean Peninsula." *Problems of Communism* 30, 6 (November–December 1981): 16–31.
Shaplen, Robert. "New Chapters in Korea, I and II." *New Yorker*, Nov. 25, 1972, pp. 116–147; Dec. 2, 1972, pp. 128–155.
Shim Jae Hoon. "The Answer is No." *Far Eastern Economic Review*, July 31, 1981, p. 22.
Shinn, Rinn-sup. "Foreign and Reunification Policies." *Problems of Communism* 22, 1 (January–February 1973): 55–71.
---. "North Korea in 1981: First Year for De Facto Successor Kim Jong Il." *Asian Survey* 22, 1 (January 1982): 99–106.
"South Korea's Growing Role as a Military Supplier." *Business Week*, June 29, 1981, p. 72.
Sprout, Harold and Margaret. "Environmental Factors in the Study of International Politics." *Journal of Conflict Resolution* 1, 4 (December 1957): 309–328.
Suh, Dae-Sook. "A Preconceived Formula for Sovietization: The Communist Takeover of North Korea." In *The Anatomy of Communist Takeovers*, edited by Thomas T. Hammond. New Haven: Yale University Press, 1975.
---. "South Korea in 1981: The First Year of the Fifth Republic." *Asian Survey* 22, 1 (January 1982): 107–115.
Suhrke, Astri. "Gratuity or Tyranny: The Korean Alliances." *World Politics* 25, 4 (July 1973): 508–538.
Triska, Jan F. "A Model for Study of Soviet Foreign Policy." *American Political Science Review* 52, 1 (March 1958): 64–83.
Winn, Gregory F. T. "Korean Foreign Policy Decision Making: Process and Structure." *Colloquium Paper*, No. 4, Center for Korean Studies, University of Hawaii, Honolulu, 1976.

KOREAN SOURCES

Ahn Byung-Joon. "Wolnamjŏn ihu Han'guk-kwa Miguk ŭi oegyo chŏngch'aek kyŏlchŏng kwajŏng pigyo" [A Comparison of the Foreign Policy Making Processes in South Korea and the U.S. in the Post-Vietnam War period]. Paper presented to the third joint conference of the Korean Political Science Association and the Association of Korean Political Scientists in North America, June 18–20, 1979, Seoul, Korea.

Chŏng Kwang-mo. *Ch'ŏngwadae* [Blue House]. Seoul: Ŏmun'gak, 1967.

Chosŏn chung'ang yŏn'gam [Korean Central Yearbook], 1960–1980. Pyongyang: Chosŏn Chung'ang T'ongsin-sa, 1961–1980.

Han Ch'ang-wan. *Pak Chŏng-hŭi taet'ongnyŏng, Kim Chong-p'il paksa* [President Park Chung Hee, Dr. Kim Jong Pil]. Seoul: Chŏnggyŏng Podo-sa, 1967.

Kim Chong-sin. *Pak Chŏng-hui taet'ongnyŏng* [President Park Chung Hee]. Seoul: Hallim Ch'ulp'an-sa, 1970.

Kim Il-sŏng chŏjak sŏnjip [Selected Works of Kim Il Sung]. 7 vols. Pyongyang: Chosŏn Nodong-dang Ch'ulp'an-sa, 1967–1979.

Kim Il Sung. *Choguk ŭi chajujŏk p'yŏnghwa t'ong'irŭl irukhaja* [Let Us Achieve the Independent and Peaceful Reunification of the Fatherland]. Pyongyang: Chosŏn Nodong-dang Ch'ul-p'an-sa, 1980.

———. *Chosŏn Nodong-dang che 6-ch'a taehoe esŏ han chung'ang wiwonhoe saŏp ch'onghwa pogo* [Report to the Sixth Congress of the Workers' Party of Korea on the Work of the Central Committee]. Pyongyang: Samhak-sa, 1980.

———. *Sinnyŏn-sa* [New Year Address], 1981. Pyongyang: Samhak-sa, 1981.

———. *Uri hyŏngmyŏng esŏui chuch'e e taehayŏ* [On Chuch'e in Our Revolution]. Pyongyang: Chosŏn Nodong-dang Ch'ul-p'an-sa, 1970.

Kim Yŏng-t'ae. *Memarŭn choguge tanbinŭn naeryŏtta: Pak taet'ongnyŏng ŭi palchach'wi* [Rain Falls on the Barren Fatherland: The Footsteps of President Park]. 2 vols. Ch'unch'ŏn, Kangwon-do: Youngjin Ch'ulp'an-sa, 1969.

Koh Byung Chul, Kim Se-Jin, Park Jae Kyu, Lee Young Ho, and Choi Chang Yoon. *Pukhan oegyo-ron* [On North Korean Diplomacy]. Seoul: Kyŏngnam Taehak Kŭktong Munje Yŏn'gu-so, 1977.

Minju Konghwa-dang sanyŏn-sa [Four-Year History of the Democratic-Republican Party]. Seoul: Minju Konghwa-dang Kihoek Josa-bu, 1967.

Pukhan chŏngch'i-ron [On North Korean Politics]. Seoul: Kŭktong Munje Yŏn'gu-so, 1976.

Pukhan chŏnsŏ [North Korea Handbook], *1945–1980*. Seoul: Kŭktong Munje Yŏn'gu-so, 1980.

Republic of Korea, Ministry of Foreign Affairs. *Han'guk oegyo ŭi isimnyŏn* [Twenty Years of South Korean Diplomacy]. Seoul: Oemu-bu, Oegyo Yŏn'gu-won, 1967.

———. *Han'guk oegyo samsimnyŏn* [Thirty Years of South Korean Diplomacy], *1948–1978*. Seoul: Oemubu, Oegyo Yŏn'gu-won, 1979.

———. *Hyŏnhwang* [Current Situation]. Report submitted to the Committee on Foreign Affairs of the National Assembly, Republic of Korea, 101st extraordinary session, March, 1979.

Republic of Korea, Prime Minister's Office. *1979 nyŏndo chung'ang sanghwang-p'an (an)* [Central Status Charts for 1979 (draft)]. Seoul, 1979.

T'ong'il Hyŏngmyŏng-dang chuyo munsŏ-jip [Principal Documents of the Revolutionary Party for Reunification]. No publisher listed, 1979. 3 vols.

Yun Pok-jin. *Kim Il-sŏng wonsunim ŭi ŏrin sijŏl iyagi* [Tales of Marshall Kim Il Sung's Childhood]. Tokyo: Minch'ŏng Ch'ulpan-sa, 1963.

JAPANESE SOURCES

"Dokyumento: Kim Tae-jung shi rachi jiken" [Document: the Kim Dae Jung Kidnapping Incident]. *Sekai* (November 1973), 137–173.

Gaimu Shō. *Waga gaikō no kinkyō* [Recent Trends in Our Diplomacy], 1980. Tokyo: Ōkura Shō, Insatsu Kyoku, 1980.

Gendai Chōsen Kenkyū-kai. *Chōsen yoran* [Korea Handbook], 1973. Tokyo: Jiji Tsūshin-sha, 1973.

Jinmin Chūgoku [People's China] (Beijing), October 1975.

Kim Il Sung. "Chōsen no tōitsu to kokusai jōsei" [Korean Reunification and the International Situation]. *Sekai* (January 1979), 146–157.

———. "Kakumei to kensetsu no dōtei" [Paths of Revolution and Construction]. *Sekai* (February 1976).

Kita Chōsen kenkyū [North Korean Studies] (Tokyo), 1974–1981.

Ko Chun-sŏk. *Sengo Chōnichi kankei-sha* [History of Postwar Korean-Japanese Relations]. Tokyo: Tahada Shoten, 1974.

Oda Makoto. *"Kita Chōsen" no hitobito* [The People of "North Korea"]. Tokyo: Ushio Shuppan-sha, 1978.

———. *Watashi to Chōsen* [Korea and I]. Tokyo: Tsukuma Shobō, 1977.

Shūkan Asahi [Weekly Asahi] (Tokyo). October 15, 1976, pp. 24–26.

Sumiya Mikio. *Kankoku no keizai* [The South Korean Economy]. Tokyo: Iwanami Shoten, 1976.

Suzuki Kenji. "Kita Chōsen mita mama" [North Korea Observed]. *Kokusai kankei shiryō*, No. 4 (October 25, 1975). Tokyo: Kokusai Kankei Kyōdō Kenkyū-sho.

Tamaki Motoi. *Kin Nichi-sei no shisō to kōdō* [The Thought and Behavior of Kim Il Sung]. Tokyo: Korea Hyōron-sha, 1969.

Toyota Aritsune. *Kankoku no chōsen* [The South Korean Challenge]. Tokyo: Shōden-sha, 1978.

Yamaguchi Kyūta. *Chiyonrima no kuni Chōsen* [The Country of Ch'ollima: Korea]. Tokyo: Tōkai Daigaku Shuppankai, 1972.

NEWSPAPERS AND PERIODICALS

Asahi shimbun (Tokyo)
FBIS (Foreign Broadcast Information Service) *Daily Report*, Vol. 4: Asia & Pacific (Arlington, VA)
Han'guk ilbo (Seoul)
Hapdong News Agency (Seoul), absorbed by *Yonhap New Agency* in January 1981
Korea Herald (Seoul)
Korea Times (Seoul)
Korea Central News Agency (Pyongyang)
Korea Newsreview (Seoul)
Kŭlloja (Pyongyang)
Kyōdō News Agency (Tokyo)
Mainichi shimbun (Tokyo)
New York Times
Nodong sinmun (Pyongyang)
North Korean News (Seoul)
Press Release of the Democratic People's Republic of Korea Permanent Observer Mission to the United Nations (New York)
Pyongyang Radio
Pyongyang Times
Tong'a ilbo (Seoul)
Vantage Point (Seoul)
Yomiuri shimbun (Tokyo)

INDEX

Afghanistan: as issue in the nonalignment movement, 222; North Korean reaction to Soviet invasion of, 209; Soviet invasion of, 24, 25, 142
Africa, 148, 155, 156, 225
Agency for National Security Planning: KCIA renamed as, 115; role of, in foreign policy, 119
Algeria, 149
"Alignment of the nonaligned," 22–24
Allison, Graham T., 111
American aid to South Korea, 210–211
American military presence in Korea, 169, 220; as a deterrent to North Korean invasion, 10, 56, 88; Chun Doo Hwan's views of, 106
America's Middle East policy: contrasted with US policy toward Korean reunification, 251
Anti-American sentiment in South Korea: Kim Il Sung's views on, 92; North Korean elite's views on, 93
Anticommunism: as South Korea's dominant ideology, 78
April 19, 1960 student uprising: effects of, on Kim Il Sung's strategic thinking, 126
Arab oil embargo, 26; effects of, on North Korea, 42

Argentina, 244
Arms industry: comparison of, in North and South Korea, 57–58
Association of Southeast Asian Nations (ASEAN), 241; Chun Doo Hwan's tour of, 189, 226–228; economic ties between, and Seoul, 227; Seoul's arms exports to, 227–228
Australia, 156, 244
Ax killing, of American army officers by North Korean soldiers, 169. *See also* Panmunjom incident

Beijing: North Korea's economic relations with, 43–44; North Korea's perceptions of, 91; North Korea's relations with, 12, 13; South Korea's relations with, 30. *See also* People's Republic of China
Belgrade, Yugoslavia, 221
Benin, 225
Blue House, 115, 117. *See also* Presidential Secretariat
Bongo, El Hadi Omar, 171
Brecher, Michael, 4

Cambodia: as an issue in the nonalignment movement, 222
Cameroon, 225, 226

265

Carter, Jimmy: human rights policy of, 25, 68, 212, 234; joint proposal by, and Park Chung Hee for tripartite talks, 182, 204; Kim Il Sung's reaction to, 169–170; lifts the ban on travel to North Korea by US citizens, 31; North Korea's denunciation of state visit of, to South Korea, 184–185; plan by, to withdraw American ground troops from South Korea, 29, 170, 213; response of, to the Soviet invasion of Afghanistan, 25; state visit of, to South Korea, 29, 183
Central People's Committee, 109
Chad, 225
Chaju (independence), 72
Ch'amgo sinmun (Reference News), 113*n*
Chang Myon: policy performance of, 15
Chang Yong Ja, 67
Charip (self-reliance), 72; Park Chung Hee's version of, 84
Chawi (self-defense), 72
Chedo ŭi t'ong'il (unification of systems), 147
Chinese People's Volunteers, 195
Chinese assistance to North Korea, 208
Choi Kyu Hah: as an interim successor to Park Chung Hee, 62; foreign policy pursued by, 16; reaction of, to North Korean overtures, 143, 186; replacement of, as President, 64
Choi Kwang Soo, 226
Choi Yong Gon: visit of, to the PRC, 207
Ch'ŏllima movement: as an emulation of the Great Leap Forward, 16, 205
Chong Jun Gi: on North Korean policy toward the United States, 202, 243
Ch'ongnyŏn, 175; alleged role of, in the attempted assassination of Park Chung Hee and the murder of Mrs. Park, 178, 216, 217; leaders of, included in the North Korean delegation to a proposed conference of North and South Korea, 192
Chuch'e (self-reliance), 232, 234, 242, 250; goal of, in all domains of North Korean society, 91; as North Korea's national ideology, 14, 231; as a factor in North Korea's tactical decisions, 185; in North Korean economic construction, 45; in North Korean society, as perceived by a visitor, 74; South Korean version of, as expounded by Park Chung Hee, 74–76, 84
Chuch'e sasang (the ideology of *chuch'e*): as expounded by Kim Il Sung, 71–74; propagation of, abroad, 233
Chun Doo Hwan: announces plan to produce F-5M fighter-bombers, 57; attitude toward *chuch'e*, 76; changes made by, in the foreign policy apparatus, 115; criticism of Park Chung Hee, 104; decision of, to commute Kim Dae Jung's death sentence, 235; first year in office reviewed by the press, 66–67; images of the Soviet Union and the PRC, 106–107; measures by, to improve South Korea's political climate, 66; on political parties in South Korea, 105–106; on the role of American troops in South Korea, 106; overtures toward North Korea, 162–164, 187, 204, 226; overtures toward North Korea, rejected by Pyongyang, 188–189; overtures toward North Korea, symbolic significance of, 188; pledge by, to transfer power peacefully in 1987, 65, 66, 105; proclaims an expanded emergency martial law, 62–63; role of, in foreign policy, 114; seizure of power on December 12, 1979, 16, 62, 144; steps in the consolidation of power, 62–65; suppresses the Kwangju uprising, 93; visit of, to the United States, 187, 189, 213; North Korean reaction to Chun's US visit, 202
Chun Doo Hwan, Mrs., 67
Chung, Joseph S., 40
Chung Seung Hwa: arrest of, by Chun Do Hwan, 62
Clough, Ralph N., 54, 56
Colombo, Sri Lanka, 169, 225
Commando raid: on the South Korean presidential mansion by North Korean agents, 133–134, 167
Committee for Cultural Relations With Foreign Countries, 109–110
Committee for the Peaceful Reunification of the Fatherland, 141; proposes a joint conference of politicians in

North and South Korea, 191–192
Committee for the Reunification of the Fatherland, 111
Confederal Republic of Koryŏ, 204; proposal for, by Kim Il Sung, 167
"Confederation," 238
"Consultative Conference for National Reunification": proposal for, by Chun Doo Hwan, 162–163
"Cross recognition": North Korea's rejection of, 185
Cuban missile crisis: North Korean reaction to, 206
Cult of personality surrounding Kim Il Sung, 16–17, 17n; as an issue in North Korea's relations with Moscow and Beijing, 205; as the cornerstone of North Korean foreign policy, 234; dimensions of, 67–68, 68n, 233; effects of, on *chuch'e*, 73; effects of, on foreign policy, 113, 114, 167, 168, 243; sources of, 80–81, 236
Cultural Revolution in China: and North Korea, 206, 207
"Curb loan scandal," 67
Czechoslovak Communist party, 167

December 12, 1979, coup, 64, 114, 115n, 142. *See also* Chun Doo Hwan
Demilitarized Zone (DMZ), 164, 170, 181; discovery of underground tunnels in, 136–137; incidents along, 133; proximity of, to Seoul, 54, 56, 103, 104
"Democratic Confederal Republic of Koryŏ," 240; endorsement of, by South Korean dissidents, 192; Kim Il Sung's proposal for, 144–146; probable North Korean aims, 146–148; Pyongyang's efforts to generate support for, 222, 223
Democratic Front for the Reunification of the Fatherland, 166, 182; response of, to Park Chung Hee's overtures, 180–182; statement of, on Chun Doo Hwan's proposal for a summit meeting, 191
Democratic Justice party, 65, 105–106
Democratic Korea party, 66
Democratic-Republican party, 135, 142, 240
Democratic Socialist party, 105

Deng Xiaoping: visit of, to North Korea, 207; visit of, to the United States, 19, 180
Denmark, 45, 149, 161
De-Stalinization: Pyongyang's response to, 205
Détente, 21, 24, 78
Dialogue: between Seoul and Pyongyang, 18
Dietmen's League for Promotion of Japan–[North] Korea Friendship, 218
Diplomatic relations: effects of, on UN votes, 196–198; establishment of, 195
"Dominationism," 143, 143n; as a substitute for "hegemonism," 209
DPRK (Democratic People's Republic of Korea). *See also* North Korea
—Academy of Social Sciences, 111
—Constitution of 1972, 109
—Ministry of Foreign Affairs: memorandum of, issued on June 26, 1978, 88–89; role of, 109; statement of, on February 14, 1982, 90; statement of, on the joint proposal by Carter and Park, 184; structure of, 110

Eastern European Communist parties: congresses of, 206
EC-121 incident, 2, 58, 167, 246
Economic development: as a foreign policy goal, 12–13
"Economic diplomacy," 230, 233
"Eight-point program for reunification," 135, 139
Eisenhower, Dwight D., 211
"Equidistance" policy: Japan's, toward the two Koreas, 218; North Korea's, toward Moscow and Beijing, 207
Ethiopia, 225
Europe, 156
"Everready" (Washington's covert plan to topple Syngman Rhee), 211
Exclusive legitimacy, 152, 230

FBIS (Foreign Broadcast Information Service) Daily Report: North Korean counterpart to, 113–114, 113n
Finland, 45, 149, 161
"Five-point proposal on reunification," 168
Ford, Gerald R., 27
Foreign policy system: definition of, 4–6

"Formalism" in foreign policy, 114–115, 118
"Four nature-remaking tasks," 53
"Friendship price": of crude oil charged by Beijing to Pyongyang, 43–44

Gabon, 171
Gambia, 226
Geng Biao: visit of, to North Korea, 207, 208
Guam Doctrine, 212

Hahm Pyong-choon, 117
Haig, Alexander M., 25
Hallstein Doctrine, 226, 248
Hamani, Diori, 225
Han Sungjoo, 155, 210
Han'guk ilbo (Seoul): reviews Chun Doo Hwan's first year in office, 66, 67
Havana, Cuba, 224, 225
"Hegemonism": as an issue in Sino-North Korean relations, 208, 209
Helicopter incident of July 1977, 170
Hereditary succession in North Korea: China's attitude toward, 208. See also Kim Jong Il
Ho Dam, 110; attends the New Delhi conference of nonaligned nations, 222; enunciates an eight-point program for reunification, 135; visits New York, 170, 171
Ho Jong Suk: condemns "Team Spirit '82," 90
Hu Yaobang: visit of, to North Korea, 207
Hua Guofeng: visit of, to North Korea, 207, 209
Husak, Gustav: visit of, to North Korea, 167
Hyon Jun Guk, 110, 218
Hyŏngmyŏng chŏnsŏn (Revolutionary Front), 133
Hyŏngmyŏng yŏngnyang (revolutionary forces), 123

Iceland, 149
Income distribution: in South Korea, 37–38
Indochina: Communist takeover in, 102; conflict in, 1
Indonesia, 227, 228
Information: role of, in foreign policy making, 113–114

Institutional Investor (New York): interviews Chun Doo Hwan, 105–106
International Friendship Exhibition Hall, 234
International Institute of Strategic Studies (London), 54
"Invitational diplomacy," 233
Iran, 244
Iran-Iraq war, 22
Ivory Coast, 225
Izvestia (Moscow): criticizes China for trading with South Korea, 208

Japan, 85; economic cooperation with South Korea, 152–153; economic cooperation with South Korea, Park Chung Hee's views on, 99; North Korea's policy toward, 94; North Korea's relations with, 31–32; Seoul's quest for a $6 billion loan from, 99–100, 218–219; significance of, for Korea, 214–215; textbook controversy, 219; trade between, and North Korea, 217–218
"Japanese militarism": Kim Il Sung's perceptions of, 93–94
Jonathan, Leabua, 225

Kaplan, Gilbert E., 105
Kardelj, Edvard, 171
Karmal, Babrak: Kim Il Sung's message to, 209–210
Kennedy, John F.: policy of, toward the Park Chung Hee regime, 211–212
Khrushchev, Nikita: cancels a planned trip to North Korea, 205
Kim Chi Ha, 192
Kim Dae Jung: abduction of, 85, 137, 168, 235; arrest of, by Chun Doo Hwan, 63; death sentence of, commuted by Chun Doo Hwan, 187; effects of abduction on Seoul-Tokyo relations, 216; name of, included in the North Korean proposal for a conference, 192
Kim Il, 141, 142, 186; visit of, to Moscow, 206
Kim Il-sŏng chuŭi (the ideology of Kim Il Sung), 18
Kim Il Sung: articulates reunification strategy, 123–126; characterizes North Korea as a paradise on earth, 97; criticism of, by Chinese Red

Guards, 206; criticizes Beijing and Moscow, 131; credibility of, in South Korea, 80; commitment of, to Korean reunification, 2; denunciation of, by South Korea, 156, 193–194; early background of, 81; emphasis on independence, 14; hosts a banquet for delegates to an international conference, 223–224; images of South Korea, 124–125; indicates a willingness to negotiate with South Korea, 139, 194; meets with Lee Hu Rak, 158; on *chuch'e*, 71–74; on Chun Doo Hwan, 148; on Marxism-Leninism, 71, 77–78; on the Nonalignment Movement, 220; on how to develop the revolutionary capability of the South Korean people, 125–126; on Sino-American rapprochement, 87–88; on South Korea as a US colony, 91–92; political thought of, compared to Mao Zedong thought, 81; proposal for "confederation" by, 132; a psychological interpretation of, 235–236; re-elected to Presidency in 1977 and 1982, 61–62; rejects the proposal for a simultaneous entry of the two Koreas into the United Nations, 168; role of, in foreign policy making, 113; social distance between, and his subordinates, 117; title changes from premier to president, 167; visits the PRC, 205, 207

Kim Jae Kyu, 62

Kim Jong Il: campaign to legitimize the designation of, as his father's successor, 68n; mentioned by Chinese leader Geng Biao, 208; name of, omitted in North Korean proposal for a conference, 192; praised by delegates to an international conference, 224; succession of, to Kim Il Sung, 252. *See also* Hereditary succession in North Korea

Kim Jong Pil: arrest of, by Chun Doo Hwan, 63; role of, in the settlement of the dispute with Japan over Kim Dae Jung, 216

Kim Kyung Won, 117

Kim Sin-jo, 134

Kim Sŏng-jin, 182

Kim, Stephen Cardinal, 142

Kim Yong Ju: announces the suspension of NSCC (North-South Coordinating Committee) talks, 140; meets with Lee Hu Rak, 158

Kim Yong Nam, 110

Kim Young Sam: retires from politics, 64

Kimura Toshio, 217

Kissinger, Henry A., 23, 26

"Koreagate" scandal, 29, 212, 241. *See also* Park Tong Sun

Korean Central Intelligence Agency (KCIA), 67, 212; director of, makes a secret visit to North Korea, 140; North Korea's condemnation of, 137; role of, in the abduction of Kim Dae Jung, 85, 137, 216; role of, in the assassination of Park Chung Hee, 62; role of, in foreign policy, 115

Korean minority in Japan, 151, 215; effects of, on Seoul-Pyongyang rivalry, 32

Korean nationalism, 70–71, 235

Korean People's Army (KPA), 124

Korean War, 151, 244, 245; Chinese intervention in, 79, 205; effects of, on ideology, 235; effects of, on the North Korean economy, 40; effects of, on Park Chung Hee's strategic thinking, 129; effects of, on the South Korean people's attitudes, 79–80; Kim Il Sung's appraisal of, 127; Moscow's failure to provide an all-out support to North Korea in, 79

"Koreanized democracy," 75

Kosygin, Alexi: visit of, to North Korea, 205, 206

Kuno Chūji, 218

Kwangju Rebellion, 64, 66, 213; aftermath of, 93; foreign eyewitness accounts of, 63n–64n; Pyongyang's reaction to the suppression of, 148, 191, 239; sparks for, 63; suppression of, 63–64, 144

Kye Ung Tae, 228

Lasswell, Harold D., 80, 235

Latin America, 155, 156

Lee Bum Suk, 117

Lee Chol Hi, 67

Lee Hu Rak: mentions the need for structural change, 160; views of, on North-South joint statement, 159; visit of, to North Korea, 140, 158

Lee, John M., 88
Le Figaro (Paris): interviews Park Chung Hee, 101–102, 103
Legitimacy: as a factor in foreign policy, 9, 195
Lenin, Nikolai, 77; theory of imperialism, 77, 93, 127
Lesotho, 225
Lho Shin-yong, 226
Li Jong Ok, 141, 186, 221, 223; visit of, to the PRC, 207

Madagascar, 226
Malaysia, 227, 228
Mao Zedong, 77, 81
Martial law: Chun Doo Hwan's lifting of, 187
Martial Law Command, 63
Marx, Karl, 77
Marxism-Leninism: eclipse of, by *chuch'e*, 74; effects of, on Kim Il Sung's perceptions, 93; Kim Il Sung's views on, 71, 72, 77–78
Marxist-Leninist party, 125, 238; North Korea's attempt to create, in South Korea, 132–133
Marxist-Leninist *weltanschauung*, 125
Mauritania, 244
May 16, 1961 coup, 34, 128; use of *chuch'e* as a justification for, 76
Middle and Near East, 155, 156
Middle East, 148, 225
Military balance: in the Korean peninsula, 54–57
Military expenditures: comparison of, in North and South Korea, 58–61
Minjokchŏk t'ong'il (national unification), 147
Minju Chosŏn (Pyongyang): rejects Chun Doo Hwan's proposal for a summit meeting, 190
Mobŏmsaeng (model student) syndrome: of Park Chung Hee, 82–85
Moscow: North Korea's perceptions of, 91; North Korea's relations with, 12, 13; South Korea's relations with, 30. *See also* Soviet Union
Multipolarity, 28
Mun Se Kwang, 216
Mutual defense treaty: between North Korea and the PRC, 2, 205; between North Korea and the Soviet Union, 2, 205; between South Korea and the United States, 2, 15
Mutual nonaggression agreement: proposal for, by Park Chung Hee, 179
Myohyang-san (mountain in North Korea), 234

National Assembly, 65, 67, 132; role of, in foreign policy, 115, 120
National Council for Unification, 62, 76
National Press Club: Chun Doo Hwan's speech to, 104, 105, 106
National security: as a foreign policy goal, 10
National Security Council: role of, in foreign policy making, 115, 115*n*
National Unification Board: role of, in foreign policy making, 120
New Delhi, 221–222
New Democratic party, 142, 159
New York Times: Interviews Kim Il Sung, 88, 139; reviews Chun Doo Hwan's first year in office, 67, 165
New Zealand, 156
Netherlands, the, 149
Neutral Nations Supervisory Commission, 141
Newsweek: interviews Park Chung Hee, 103
Niger, 225
1988 Olympic Games, 164, 228
Nixon, Richard M., 212; visit of, to the PRC, 87, 135
No Tae Woo, 115*n*, 164
Nodong sinmun (Pyongyang): as the mouthpiece for Kim Il Sung, 87; comments on the arson incident in Pusan, 93; criticizes Chinese ideographs, 206; denounces Carter, 171; denounces Park Chung Hee, 172; praises independence and *chuch'e-sŏng*, 206–207; reacts to Park Chung Hee's assassination, 95–96; rejects Chun Doo Hwan's overtures toward North Korea, 189, 191
Nonaligned countries: conference of heads of state or government of, 169
Nonalignment Movement: North Korea's admission to, 219
Normalization of diplomatic relations: between South Korea and Japan, 15, 29, 134, 151–153, 215; between the

PRC and Japan, 25–26; between the US and the PRC, 19, 24, 180
North Korea. *See also* DPRK
—as a potential aggressor, 10, 12
—diplomats: expulsion of, from Scandinavian countries, 44–45
—economy: *chuch'e-hwa* (*chuch'e-*orientation) of, 49, 50, 74; *hyŏndae-hwa* (modernization) of, 49, 50, 74; *kwahak-hwa* (science-orientation) of, 49, 50, 74; problem areas in, as analyzed by Kim Il Sung, 48–49, 50, 96–98
—invasion of South Korea, 166
—threat to South Korea: as perceived by Chun Doo Hwan, 104
—foreign debt, 42, 45; Kim Il Sung's explanation of, 44
—foreign trade: Kim Il Sung's emphasis on, 46, 46n, 49–50; principal partners in, 46–47
—international position: change in, 148–149
—per capita income: as estimated by South Korea, 50n; as reported by Kim Il Sung, 50
—sense of insecurity, 88–91
North-South Coordinating Committee (NSCC), 158, 182; Pyongyang's demand for a reshuffle of, 137. *See also* NSCC talks
North-South dialogue: emergence of, 157; pace of, 101; Park Chung Hee's use of, to justify the extension of his power, 159
North-South joint statement, 131, 182; background of, 173–174; Chun Doo Hwan's invocation of, 188; conflicting interpretations of, by Seoul and Pyongyang, 137–138, 159; endorsement of, by a conference of the nonaligned nations, 221; publication of, on July 4, 1972, 101, 158; Pyongyang's invocation of, in Red Cross talks, 176; Seoul's covert aims, 159–160; Seoul's failure to reach an understanding with Pyongyang, 203
Norway, 45, 149, 161
NSCC talks: breakup of, 168; problems and hurdles encountered during, 177–178. *See also* North-South Coordinating Committee

Oceania, 156
"October Revitalizing Reforms": ideological justifications for, 17; Park Chung Hee's imposition of, 65; Park Chung Hee's justification for, 103; use of dialogue as a justification for, 138. *See also* *Siwol Yusin*
Operational direction: definition of, 130

Pacific powers, 250; Korea's interaction with, 79; stakes of, in Korea, 2–3
Pak Sung Chol: discloses the background on secret North-South talks, 157; news conference by, on the North-South joint statement, 138; views of, on the North-South joint statement, 159; visit of, to South Korea, 158
Panmunjom incident, 3, 246; American response to, 56n. *See also* Ax killing
Park Chung Hee: articulates reunification strategy, 128; as a practitioner of *chuch'e*, 74–76; assassination of, 61, 62, 142; assassination of, North Korean reaction to, 95–96; assessment by, of the Communist takeover in Indochina, 102; attempted assassination of, 133–134, 167, 178, 216; calculations of, in North-South dialogue, 174; denunciation of, by North Korea, 157, 193–194; early background of, 82–84; effects of his Japanese background on foreign policy, 153; efforts of, to secure US support for his military regime, 211; extension of power by, 62; infringement of human rights by, 231; joint proposal by, and Jimmy Carter for tripartite talks, 182; "model student syndrome" of, 236; overtures of, toward North Korea, 156, 204; policy of, toward Japan, 215; proclaims an "emergency decree" (*wisuryŏng*), 157–158; proposes an unconditional resumption of dialogue, 187; publishes a special statement regarding foreign policy for peace and unification, 137, 160–161; reaction of, to Sino-American rapprochement, 98; reaction of, to the UN's adoption of two conflicting resolutions on Korea, 196; repressive measures of, 234; role of, in

Park Chung Hee (*continued*)
  foreign policy making, 114; seizure of power by, 225; social distance between, and his subordinates, 117; sources of his strategic thinking, 129; August 15, 1970 speech of, 193–194; stress by, on economic development, 34; use of anticommunism as a political tool, 79; use of *chuch'e* as a justification for the "October Revitalizing Reforms," 17; use of North Korean threat to perpetuate his rule, 80; use of North-South dialogue to perpetuate his rule, 138
Park Chung Hee, Mrs.: murder of, 178, 216
Park Tong Sun, 29, 212. *See also* "Koreagate" scandal
Pattern behavior: as contrasted with discrete behavior, 241–242
Peace treaty: proposal for, between North and South Korea, 179
People's Liberation Army, 195
People's Republic of China (PRC), 179, 244; images of, in South Korea, 80, 100–101; Pyongyang's ties with, 204–205
Philippines, the, 227
Political repression: Park Chung Hee's denial of, in South Korea, 103
"Political type," 80, 235
Pŏnyŏng (prosperity), 84
President (*chusŏk*): foreign policy powers of, in North Korea, 110
Presidential dominance in foreign policy making, 114
Presidential Secretariat: role of, in foreign policy making, 115. *See also* Blue House
"Protest diplomacy," 218
Pueblo incident, 2, 58, 167, 246

Reagan, Ronald: denunciation of, by North Korea, 201–202; hardline policy of, toward North Korea, 31; on the United States as a Pacific power, 27; policy of, toward the Soviet Union, 25; summit meeting between, and Chun Doo Hwan, 16, 29, 213, 235
Red Cross talks: Seoul's proposals for, 136, 139, 157; South Korean aims in, 172–173
Relative legitimacy, 230

Renmin Ribao (Beijing): publishes details regarding Chinese aid to North Korea, 208; rebuts charges by Moscow, 208–209
Republican National Convention, 169
"Revolutionary forces," 237
Revolutionary Party for Reunification, 140, 175, 181, 192; efficacy of, 136; origins of, 133
Revolutionary potential of the South Korean masses: Kim Il Sung's views on, 94–95
"Rhee line," the, 152
Rhee, Syngman: exclusion of, by North Korea from the scope of potential negotiating partners, 167; failure of, to pursue economic development, 13–14; overthrown in the April 1960 student uprising, 126; policy of, toward Japan, 215; policy of, toward the United States, 211; release of anti-Communist North Korean prisoners, 15, 211, 231, 247; role of, in foreign policy making, 114; social distance between, and his subordinates, 117; use of anticommunism as a political tool, 79
ROK (Republic of Korea), *See also* South Korea
—Army, 129
—Constitution of 1972: foreign policy powers of the President specified in, 118–119
—Constitution of 1980: foreign policy powers of the President specified in, 110
—Ministry of Foreign Affairs: role of, 115; structure and powers of, 119–120
—Treaty of Normalization between, and Japan, 94, 152
Russo-Japanese War: and Korea, 1
Rwanda, 226

Sadae chuŭi (sycophancy), 79
Saemaŭl (New Village) Movement: effects of, on income distribution in South Korea, 37
Salisbury, Harrison E., 88
Seikei bunri (separation of politics from economics), 217, 218
Sekai (Tokyo): Kim Il Sung's interview with, 91, 172
Selassie I, Haile, 225

Senegal, 226
Shiina Etsusaburō: visit of, to South Korea, 217
Shin Hyon Hwack, 143, 186. *See also* Sin Hyŏn-hwak
"Siege mentality," 91
Sierra Leone, 226
Sin Hyŏn-hwak, 141. *See also* Shin Hyon Hwack
Singapore, 227
Sino-American rapprochement, 238; effects of, on Korea, 18, 157; effects of, on North Korea, 135–136; North Korean reaction to, 78, 87–88; significance of, 24
Sino-Indian border clash of October 1962: North Korean reaction to, 206
Sino-Japanese War: and Korea, 1
Sino-Soviet dispute: as a factor in the improvement of Sino-American and Sino-Japanese relations, 28; as an exception to the general trend, 24; effects of, on North Korea, 14, 231
Sino-Soviet rivalry in North Korea, 30–31, 208
Siwol Yusin (October Revitalizing Reforms): compared to the Meiji Restoration and Taiwan's political system, 17; justifications for, 98; Park Chung Hee's use of *chuch'e* as a justification for, 75–76
Sixth Congress of the Workers' Party of Korea: Kim Il Sung's report to, pertaining to *chuch'e*, 73–74; Kim Il Sung's report to, pertaining to the economy, 51–52; Kim Il Sung's report to, pertaining to reunification, 144, 146
Son Chae-sik, 164
South Korea. *See also* ROK
—economy: factors contributing to the growth of, 35; problem areas in, 35–38; prospects for the growth of, 39–40
—foreign debt, 37
Southeast Asia, 155, 225
Soviet Union: aid to North Korea, 208; images of, in South Korea, 80; Pyongyang's ties with, 204; role of, in the birth of the DPRK, 9; visit to, by the South Korean citizens, 162
"Special statement regarding foreign policy for peace and unification," 203; North Korean reaction to, 167–168
SR-71 incident, 3
Stalin, Josef, 77, 113*n*
Standard Operating Procedures (SOP) in foreign policy, 118
State Administration Council, 109
Status of the United States Armed Forces Agreement between the Republic of Korea and the United States, 154–155
Stokes, Henry Scott, 165
"Strategy of triple revolutions," 123
Sŭng'gong t'ong'il (unification by a victory over communism), 128
Supreme People's Assembly, 62, 132; joint session of, and the WPK Central Committee, 111; role of, in foreign policy making, 110, 115
Sweden, 45, 149, 161
Systemic constraints on foreign policy making, 237; in North Korea, 114; in South Korea, 117; North and South Korea compared, 117

Tanaka, Kakuei: letter of, to Park Chung Hee, 217
Tangbo (Party News), 113*n*
TANJUG (Yugoslav news agency), 171
"Team Spirit '82," 89; North Korean reaction to, 90
"Team Spirit" exercises: North Korean reaction to, 88–90
"Team Spirit '78," 88
"Team Spirit '79," 182
Thailand, 227
Third World, 85, 155, 219, 223, 224, 225, 232; growing influence of, 22–23; North Korea's diplomatic campaigns in, 9–10; North Korea's relations with, 148
Three principles of reunification, 137–138, 158; Seoul's covert aims in agreeing to, 174
"Three revolutionary lines," 73
Tito, Josip Broz, 171, 221; death of, 224
Tokto (or *Takeshima*) Island, 152
Tonghak Rebellion, 1
T'ong'il Chuch'e Kungmin Hoeŭi (National Council for Unification), 76
Trilateral talks: functional equivalent to, 251
Tripartite talks, 182, 183, 184, 239

Triska, Jan F., 130
Two-Koreas policy: South Korea's de facto espousal of, 19

Uganda, 226
Underground tunnels, 136–137
United Front: in Kim Il Sung's strategy of reunification, 125
United Nations: as a possible site for contacts between Seoul and Pyongyang, 250; diplomatic competition in, by Seoul and Pyongyang, 195–196; effects of the Nonalignment Movement on, 23; Pyongyang's criticism of Seoul's proposal for a simultaneous admission of the two Korean states to, 185; role of, in the birth of the Republic of Korea, 9; role of, in the Korean War, 2; Seoul's proposal for a simultaneous admission of the two Korean states to, 161, 196, 203, 227
United Nations Command: dissolution of, 179; dissolution of, demanded by a conference of nonaligned nations, 221
United Nations Food and Agriculture Organization, 223
United Nations formula for Korean reunification, 15, 128–129, 238
United Nations General Assembly: deliberations of, on the Korean question, 9, 161; effects of deliberations on the Korean question on South Korean diplomacy, 156; North Korean participation in deliberations of, on the Korean question, 149, 150; passage by, of a pro-North Korean resolution, 150, 180; resolutions of, on the Korean question, 225; Resolution 195 (III) of, 9, 152; Thirtieth Session of, 10
United Nations Security Council, 162
United Nations system: North Korea's entry into, 161, 200, 241
United States, 85; as a Pacific power, 2, 27; North Korea's quest for dialogue with, 31, 92–93, 150–151, 169, 184, 195, 200; role of, in the birth of the Republic of Korea, 9
United States Central Intelligence Agency: alleged role of, in South Korea, 92; comparison by, of North and South Korean economic capabilities, 48; estimates by, of North Korean trade, 45n–46n
United States intelligence community: reassessment by, of North Korea's military capability, 213
Upper Volta, 226

Vance, Cyrus, 27
Vernay, Alain, 101
Vicious circle, 230; of repression and opposition in South Korea, 95
Vietnam War: American intervention in, Kim Il Sung's reaction to, 131; effects of, on Kim Il Sung's strategic thinking, 126; South Korean participation in, 134, 154–155, 212; North Korea's advocacy of a socialist united front in, 207
Voice of the Revolutionary Party for Reunification, 190
War: danger of, in Korea, 2
Western Europe: North Korea's relations with, 149
Wickham, John A., Jr., 93
Workers' Party of Korea (WPK), 181; Central Committee of, 141; Political Bureau of the Central Committee of, 77, 109, 222; in North Korea, 109; in North Korean reunification strategy, 124
World Health Organization (WHO): North Korea's admission to, 149, 161, 203
World War II: aftermath of, 1; and Korea, 2

Xinhua News Agency (Beijing), 146

Yi Chong-sang, 192
Yi Hŭi-song, 142
Yomiuri shimbun (Tokyo): Kim Il Sung's interview with, 139, 169–170
Yu Chi Song: comments on the Chun Doo Hwan regime, 65–66
Yugoslavia, 171; North Korea's relations with, 220; visit to, by South Korean citizens, 162
Yun Po Sun, 142

Zaire, 226
Zero-sum game, 230
Zhao Ziyang: visit of, to North Korea, 207, 209
Zhou Enlai: visit of, to North Korea, 205, 207

Designer:	Sandy Drooker
Compositor:	G & S Typesetters, Inc.
Text:	10/12 Aster
Display:	Helvetica Black Caps
Printer:	Braun-Brumfield, Inc.
Binder:	Braun-Brumfield, Inc.